TOTAL PRAISE
THE AUTOBIOGRAPHY

Richard Smallwood

GODZCHILD PUBLICATIONS

Copyright © 2019 Richard Smallwood

Published by Godzchild Publications
a division of Godzchild, Inc.
22 Halleck St., Newark, NJ 07104
www.godzchildproductions.net

Printed in the United States of America 2019 - 1st Edition

Library of Congress Cataloging-in-Publications Data
Total Praise: The Autobiography/Richard Smallwood

ISBN-13 978-1942705970

1. Richard 2. Smallwood

Cover Photo by Derek Blanks (Derek Blanks Photography, Atlanta GA)

2019

This book is lovingly dedicated to the memory of my mother,
Mabel Ruth Locklear Smallwood

TABLE OF
Contents

"Read the book and know the man. Richard Smallwood offers a sensitive, honest, joyful – and sometimes heartbreaking – account of his growth and development through family and music and faith while also revealing, through the lense of personal experience, an informative and moving depiction of the history of gospel music and its icons."

Phylicia Rashad

ACKNOWLEDGEMENTS

Special thanks to Rosa Clements, Robert Clements, Michael Clements and all of my family.

To Rev. C. L. Smallwood

Thank you to all my extended family and friends who loved, encouraged and prayed me through this process.

Thank you to Carolyn Francis who helped guide me through this process with her amazing ministry of therapy.

To Sandra Ellen Fagans
To Wesley Arnold Boyd
To Roger and Betty Holmes
To Kelvin Leach
To Robert McKenzie
To Gentry McCreary
To Billy Ray Hearn
To Tara Griggs-McGee
To James "Jazzy" Jordan

Thank you to those teachers, professors and mentors who are so much a part of the reason for who I am today.

Mrs. Fannie Borden
Mrs. Lottie Robinson
Mr. Bernard Barbour
Miss Roberta Flack
Mrs. Joyce Liebowitz
Mrs. Beatrice Gilkes
Mrs. Anne Burwell
Dr. Thomas Kerr Jr.
Mrs. Georgia Jessup
Mrs. Regina Jervay
Dr. Pearl Williams Jones
Rev. Cleavant Derricks
Gwendolyn Hines Jennifer
Donny Hathaway

To Phylicia Rashad

To those musical friends who inspired me the most
Edwin R. Hawkins
Andráe Crouch
Aretha Franklin

To those gospel groups who help establish my foundation and love for gospel music:
The Famous Davis Sisters of Philadelphia Pa.
Ruth Davis
Audrey Davis
Alfreda Davis

Thelma Davis Blassingame
Jackie Verdell
Imogene Greene
Curtis Dublin

The Famous Ward Singers
Clara Ward
Marion Williams
Kitty Parham
Henrietta Waddy
Frances Steadman
Esther Ford
Willa Ward-Royster
Gertrude Ward
Thelma Jackson

The Roberta Martin Singers of Chicago Il.
Roberta Martin
Lucy Smith Collier
Gloria Griffin
Norsalus McKissick
Archie Dennis
Eugene Smith
DeLois Barrett Campbell
Romance Watson
Louise McCord

To the Edwin Hawkins Singers
To the Smallwood Singers
To my Vision family
To Steven Ford

To the gospel pianists who were my inspiration:
Herbert "PeeWee" Pickard
Lucy Smith Collier

To the classical composers who shaped my writing:
Johann Sebastian Bach
Sergei Rachmaninoff

To the Broadway composers who shaped my writing:
Rodgers and Hammerstein
Lerner and Loewe

To the Motown writers who helped to shape my writing:
Holland, Dozier, Holland, Ashford & Simpson, and every early
Motown artist who came through that amazing company.

To Jared L. Sawyers
To Rosslyn "Cookie" Rowe

To my church family Metropolitan Baptist Church
To my Pastor Emeritus Dr. H. Beecher Hicks Jr
To my Pastor Maurice Watson

PROLOGUE

"YOU ARE MY SUNSHINE"

The words jumped out at me from the little, painted sign on the Internet art site. I immediately thought of Mom. From the time I was a toddler until I got to early elementary school, she would randomly sing it to me.

You are my sunshine
My only sunshine
You make me happy
When skies are grey
You'll never know, dear,
How much I love you
Please don't take my sunshine away

As Mom began to age, and I would walk into a room, her whole countenance would light up and she would exclaim, "There's my Sunshine!!!" As time progressed even further, it would almost become her nickname for me. She'd just refer to me as "Sunshine."

"I've got to have this little sign," I thought. I wanted to place it on my bedroom wall facing the foot of my bed so it would be the first thing I'd see when I awakened every morning. It would be a constant reminder of the bond we'd always have. The picture on the Internet was so small, and its quality was so poor, that I could barely see the colors. I tried to find another picture that was larger or another sign with the same phrase. I saw a few, but nothing that I particularly liked. My color-coordinated senses kicked in and I wondered, "If I did order the picture without being sure of its color, would it be blaring color that wouldn't match with the rest of my room?" I kept coming back to that little photo of that memorable phrase, and finally, just pressed the "order" button, hoping for the best. Imagine my surprise when it arrived at my house in perfect condition and coordination! The border around the words was the exact gold color as my wall trimming. It was as if the artist had painted it for my wall. It made me smile each time my eyes fell upon it. It watched over me at night, and it was the first thing I saw when I opened my eyes.

Mom called me her sunshine and she certainly was mine. What others didn't know, however, was that behind her radiant smile, with which everyone fell in love, hid a terrible, dark secret. It was one that, I imagine, was never far from her thoughts. It was one that, I imagine, at times, kept her awake at night. It was one that she never told anyone about until the latter years of her life. No one, including me, ever saw a hint of it because all we saw was that loving, upbeat personality and that smile. I didn't know it at the time, but her secret was one that would, one day, tear at the very core of my being.

CHAPTER 1
WHERE IT ALL BEGAN

My mother, Mabel Ruth Locklear, was born in Durham, North Carolina, on January 12, 1915, to Richard and Nellie Weaver Locklear. I am my grandfather's namesake, and he was named for his mother's older brother. Richard's father, about whom I've never known much, was a Lumbee Indian, the present-day descendants of the Cheraw tribe, which have existed in Robeson County, North Carolina, since the eighteenth century. His mother, Clara Williams Holloman, was African-American. (Granddad/Grandpa) Richard worked as a tobacco stemmer, and later, a janitor at Liggett and Myers Tobacco Company in Durham. He also had one brother, Arthur Holloman, whom I never met. No one ever talked about Grandma Nellie's father, who was White and was said to have had Irish roots. Her father, Dr. James Frederick Cain, or "Old Doc Cain," as he was called by those whom he enslaved, was a Confederate soldier and surgeon during the Civil War. Before and after the war, he ran a private medical practice in his Hillsborough community in Orange County, North Carolina. Nellie's mother, Annie Weaver, was African-American and was enslaved on Doc Cain's plantation. Grandma Nellie had a half-sister, Viola Weaver, with whom she shared the same mother. Grandma Nellie was a "domestic," which means she did "day work," like cooking and cleaning, for White families in Durham. By all accounts, she was a wonderful woman. Aunt Viola, on the other hand, was a colorful character. She carried a switchblade and, from what I hear, she didn't have a problem using it on a man or a woman. On the weekends, she'd go out and get drunk, fight, and cut. Many times, my grandfather, Richard, would have to bail her out of some brawl she had gotten herself into. She had an extensively creative and colorful vocabulary and could conjure up some cuss words at the drop of a hat that you had never been called before in your life.

Mom was an only child for most of her life, but she ~~tells~~ told the story of a beautiful baby sister named Annie being born into the family when she was only three years old. Mom adored her little sister, but little Annie died from gastro-enteritis at only five months old, and Mom was inconsolable. After a neighbor told her that babies came from the cabbage patch, my grandmother found my mother looking diligently under the cabbage leaves in the garden for another baby sister. Eventually, Mom explained to my grandmother what she was looking for and what the neighbor told her, and Grandma Nellie, who was a wonderful person but was known to have a bit of a temper, marched over to the neighbor's house and laid her soul to rest.

My grandfather, Richard, was an avid hunter and fisherman. Although my mom and my grandmother were very close, Mom was a bit of a daddy's girl as well as a tomboy. Sometimes, she would accompany him on his hunting trips and fishing adventures. My childhood was full of stories she would tell me about, like hanging with her dad on his excursions, the adventures they would have together, and encountering snakes all the time, which always terrified her. Also, from what I can gather from stories Mom told me, my grandfather most likely suffered from depression. Before he married, he would hop trains and travel all over the south, never settling down or living in one place. That seemed to be when he was happiest. He would tell Mom about his many excursions while traveling, one of which included terrifying ghost stories, which, of course, left Mom up at night because she was afraid to go to sleep! After he and my grandmother married, and after my mom was born, Mom would experience my granddad's bouts with melancholy from time to time throughout his life. Sometimes he would just disappear for days or weeks at a time. Mom would have to go looking for him, and a couple of times, she found him in another town by himself, living in a tin shack by the river where he could fish. She'd find him sitting in a sort of daze, looking very sad and lonely, staring into space.

"Daddy," Mom would say, "It's time to go home."

Quietly, he'd respond, "OK," then he'd follow her like a little kid as she took him home. They never talked about it after it occurred. It was almost as if these episodes had never happened. They grew up quite poor, but Mom was, nonetheless, happy because my grandparents adored her and lavished her with love and good, down-home cooking. Most of her relatives lived nearby. Down the street, lived my grandmother's other half-sister, Lula Cain. No one ever talked about the fact that they were half-sisters, and actually, most knew nothing about it. Both of them shared the same White father, "Old Doc Cain," but they didn't mention it to anyone because Nellie and Lula considered it shameful to have a White father. Even when Lula passed at the age of 97, there was no mention of her father on her death certificate or in her obituary. Lula's mother was Winnie Weaver, an African-American. Winnie, and Nellie's mom, Annie, were sisters. Although slavery had ended in 1865, as late as 1880, they were all still living on Old Doc Cain's plantation called Pleasant Grove, which was later renamed Hardscrabble. Perhaps they were sharecropping, but at any rate, the whole Weaver/Cain family was still housed under one roof at Hardscrabble. Cain is a name that goes back many years in my family. In fact, my great-great-great-great-grandfather was Jack Cain, a Black man born around 1768. He was born in slavery, more than likely owned by the Cain family, and died not long after Emancipation. He is found still alive at the age of 102 on the 1870 census, the first census on which formerly enslaved people would appear. In his final days, he lived with his daughter and my great-great-great-grandmother, Darcus Cain, and her family. He very well may be the first person in my family born in America. Grandma Nellie's half-sister, Lula Cain, later married Maurice "Mann" Banks, and together, they had a boy and a girl, Rivers and Bessie. Mann had a number of different jobs that were normal in the South for African-Americans during that time. He was a porter, a butler, even a coachman, and finally, a tobacco factory laborer, as many were in Durham. Mom grew up not knowing that Lula was her aunt. For all she knew, Lula was a 7th or 8th cousin, very distant, if even related. Whatever the relation, everyone loved Lula. She was the matriarch of the family, and the whole community affectionately called her "Cousin Lula" or "Momma Lula."

It was many years later, not long before Lula's death, when Mom found out what Lula's real relationship was to her. However, they were always very close. My Mom remembered Lula cooking baskets of food for her and sending it down to her parents' home. Lula's daughter, Bessie, grew up and married

Robert Clements. They had two children – Robert, whom everyone called "Brother," and Olivia. Bessie's brother, Rivers, never married.

Mom and her parents were members of the Mt. Vernon Baptist Church in Durham where they sang in the choir. My grandfather, I understand, had a great bass voice and was very artistic. He was a talented wood carver who could perfectly carve anything that he viewed. Mom inherited my grandfather's creative talents, as she was a talented artist who could draw and paint exquisitely. When I was a teenager, I would try to convince Mom to become a commercial artist, but she never would. She even played the piano a little bit, but never took any kind of lessons or pursued it. She loved music and had an incredible musical ear though. Although I always felt, in terms of range, that she was probably a soprano, Mom sang alto her entire life, and could sing any alto part that you threw at her, no matter how difficult. Mom kept a "thankful" journal of her life in her latter years. She would write this in her journal about her parents:

Our family was poor financially, but rich in love and fellowship. My mother, Nellie, was a beautiful woman, uneducated but born to be a lady. She had high moral standards and a deep faith in God. She loved me unconditionally, but never failed to correct me when I was wrong. She taught me how to be a lady. She taught me that cleanliness is next to Godliness, and that love makes the world go 'round. I am what I am today because of my mother. My father, Richard, was a quiet man, also uneducated but somehow, he had inherited a storehouse of knowledge from his Indian father. He loved the outdoors, knew the name of every tree, the plants that were good for the healing of the body, and berries and nuts that were good to eat in the woods. He could cut hair, mend shoes, draw pictures, carve figures, fish, and hunt - and he was an excellent cook. We had so much fun together fishing in the rivers, out from Durham, N.C. At home the three of us sang trios: Mama soprano, Papa bass, and I sang alto. We worked jigsaw puzzles and listened to ghost stories told by my father. Prayer was heard often in the house. Mama was always calling on God for our protection and needs, followed with much thanksgiving. Many people had the pleasure of eating papa's sweet potato pudding, his peach cobbler and macaroni & cheese. I'm grateful for all these memories and many more that come from day to day.

When I read about the kind of prayer warrior that my grandmother was, I recalled a story that Mom told me about a tornado that hit Durham when she was a small child. She and my grandmother watched as the twister touched down a couple of blocks from where they lived, destroying houses in its path as it slowly moved in the direction of their home. Mom said she was terrified. Her mother grabbed her and ran into the house. They had no cellar, or basement. She said her Mom put her on her lap, sat in her rocking chair, held her tightly and began to pray like my Mother had never heard her before, her voice resounding and calling on God above the roar of the approaching twister. Mom says she remembered vividly that when the twister got to the intersection before their block, it turned and went behind the houses on their block and took out all the outhouses in the back including theirs, but didn't touch a home on their street. Grand-mom knew the power of prayer. As a result of that memory though, my mother was terrified of any kind of high winds all of her life.

Unfortunately, there seems to have always been some sort of prejudice in the black community about differences in complexion. During that era, colorism was much more prevalent than it seems today. Aunt Viola and my Grand-mom Nellie shared the same mother, Annie Weaver, but had different fathers. Because Nellie's father was white, and Viola's father was black, their complexions were very different, Viola being dark and Nellie being light. Viola had a complex about being darker than her light-skinned sister and although she loved Nellie to life, when she got drunk many times it would come out. Mom tells the story of going back to Durham years later to visit Grand-mom Nellie after she had gotten very ill. Viola was at the table and she was as drunk as a sailor. Viola was rambling on and on and for some reason she started on the whole dark/light issue. She then proceeded to tell Nellie that she thought she was better than she was because she was light and called her a yellow "bitch." Everyone tried to ignore her and blame it on the liquor, but she went on and on and wouldn't shut up about it. All of a sudden, Mom got fed up with Viola's verbal attack on Grand-mom Nellie, so she grabbed a butcher knife from the table and went straight for Aunt Viola's head. Mom thought if she could just cut her throat, it would stop the hateful words coming out of Viola's mouth. When Viola saw mom coming at her with a knife in her hand she sobered up quickly, screaming "Get her Richard, get her Richard!" My Grandfather Richard grabbed my mother and wrestled the knife out of her hand and calmed things down. I think that was the last time she ever went on a drunken verbal attack against my grandmother. Ironically, as a kid I used to visit Viola all the time. After she got older, she was the sweetest, quietest, and kindest person. There was never even a hint of the old Viola from "back in the day."

I've always hated that prejudice is sometimes found in our own culture. We have enough problems outside of our race with racism. I remember Mom telling me when she was young how she had the biggest crush on a dark-skinned brother who lived down the street. She was so smitten, she would have married him in a heartbeat. But her mom discouraged her from the attraction because he was too "dark." I never could understand the perception of the color of someone's skin making them any less of a person or better than another. It has always sickened me. I remember being a freshman at Howard. The newly elected homecoming queen, Robin Gregory, was darker than most of the previous homecoming queens (who were light-skinned and had long flowing hair). She was a beautiful caramel complexion and had a short afro, a hairstyle that had just started to become popular in 1967. As a freshman, I could never understand the controversy over her complexion, her hair and those who had issues with her being elected homecoming queen.

Although Mom didn't know that he was her cousin, she was especially close to Lula's son, Rivers. Most of Mom's cousins were grown or much younger, but Rivers was a little over two months older than Mom. So, when they were kids, he would come down to the house and play hide-and-seek, tag, and all the fun games that kids played back then. For years, I didn't know his actual name because I had never seen it written down. I thought my family was saying *Revis* or *Rivis*. It wasn't until years later when I saw his name written out that I realized that Cousin Lula had named him Rivers Banks!

Somewhere around Mom's teen years, a minister by the name of Chester Lee Smallwood began to travel to Durham quite frequently to preach and run revivals. He was a native of Waynesboro in Burke County, Georgia. Grand-mom Nellie and Mom would go to hear him frequently. When Chester Lee Smallwood first laid his eyes on Mom in the congregation, he turned to the host pastor and announced, "That's going to be my wife."

"Do you know her?" the host pastor asked.

"Not yet," Rev. Smallwood replied, "but I plan to meet her because that is definitely my future wife." Most of Durham was not privy to the fact that Rev. Smallwood had been married three times before. His first marriage was to Lottie Lee Pope in 1920. She was from his hometown. That marriage lasted nine months and he was married again in 1920 to Mabel Harvey of Waterbury, Connecticut. A daughter, Dorothy, was born from that union in 1925, and then, ironically, Rev. Smallwood married another Mabel in 1927 who was an actress! She was his third wife, from New York. This marriage was so short it was allegedly annulled amid the accusation by his third wife that Smallwood had not been divorced from the first two wives! My mother knew nothing of this and said that Rev. Smallwood began to "court" her, but she wanted nothing to do with him. She said she had no attraction to him. But still, he would come to the house and would take her out on little dates. Later, she would tell me that she never loved him. She did say that she cared for him, for his wellbeing, but that's basically where it ended. At the age of 19, Mom "ran away" with him to get married. I asked her, "If you didn't love him, why in the world did you run away with him?" Her answer was simple: it was a way to get out of Durham. In my mom's mind, there was no future for her there. You either had to do domestic work or work in the tobacco factory, and she wanted to do neither. When she told me that, I chalked it up to the times she lived in. Many people didn't marry for love; they married for other reasons. Still I wondered, as much as she adored her parents, why would she leave Durham and marry someone to whom she wasn't even attracted? Every time she recounted the story to me, she'd always use the term, "ran away." But what was she running away *from*?

Mom and Rev. Smallwood were married in Washington D.C. in 1934. Mom was 19 and Smallwood was 36. Mom was very attractive, stylish and one of the warmest and most outgoing people you'd ever want to meet. I believe she became a trophy wife to him. She was the perfect minister's wife or first lady; extroverted, a people-person who had a heart for being a blessing to others, a great public speaker, and certainly an asset to any minister who would have married her. After they married, they moved extensively all over the country with Smallwood founding churches as they moved. Times were hard as Smallwood did odd jobs because most of the churches were small and certainly could not afford to give him a substantial salary. So, sometimes their living conditions were not the best. Mom was so unhappy, but she stuck it out like many women did during that era.

My grandfather Richard was very upset that Mom "ran off" to marry this preacher. In fact, the first Christmas they were married, my grandfather showed up in D.C. at their door. Smallwood went to the door, looked out and saw my grandfather standing there with a long-wrapped package in his hand. So he ran back to Mom terrified without opening the door, thinking that my grandfather had brought his shotgun with him and was planning to blow his brains out for running off with his princess. Mom went to the door, opened it and found out that her father had come for a visit, bringing a Christmas gift and basically to give his blessings.

On March 6, 1939, sometime after my Grand-mom Nellie had been diagnosed with terminal colon cancer, my grandfather Richard committed suicide in Durham. He went under the back porch with his shotgun—supposedly to shoot rats (a problem that had gotten out of hand)—when suddenly, my grandmother and others who were in the house heard a loud bang. I imagine at first they didn't think much of it as my grandfather's mission was to go outside and shoot a few worrisome rodents. But one of the neighbors who had been sitting with my Grandmother went out back to check on Richard after he had not returned for a while and found him dead. My Grandfather used a strong long-forked branch, placed the muzzle of the shotgun to his chest, placed the branch on the trigger, pushed and literally blew his heart out. The branch was later found lying next to the shotgun. When my Mom got the call she thought my grandmother who was gravely ill had passed. Imagine her horror and shock when she found out that it was her father instead. She was a daddy's girl. That was her heart. She said one of the hardest things she ever had to bear was to walk down that aisle at Mt. Vernon Baptist Church in Durham, pushing her Mom in a wheelchair behind the casket of her father. I don't believe she ever got over that. My grandfather didn't leave a note to explain why he took his life. In fact, the newspaper initially reported that they weren't sure if it was a suicide or an accident, but it was eventually ruled a suicide. I always felt that it had so much to do with the undiagnosed depression that we believe he suffered from, intensified by his wife's imminent death. He was a very quiet man, who kept to himself. He never talked about his feelings. I'm not sure what other issues he may have been dealing with. All my life I've had such a profound feeling of missing this man—my namesake—a man I never met. I've always had this strange feeling that he was watching over me and very near.

Mom moved my grandmother to D.C. after the funeral so that she and Rev. Smallwood could care for her. Soon after, they moved to Harrisburg, Pennsylvania where Rev. Smallwood began pastoring the Zion Baptist Church. On

October 4, 1940, 17 months after my Granddad passed, my Grandmother Nellie Locklear passed at only 50 years old. Never having known either of them has always been one of the biggest regrets of my life.

CHAPTER 2
BEGINNINGS OF ME

In September of 1948, Rev. Smallwood was called to pastor the New Springfield Baptist Church in Atlanta, Georgia, located at 182 Linden Ave, NE. On November 30th of that same year, 14 years after Mom married Rev. Smallwood, I was born in Fulton County. I was a C-section baby. Mom tells the story that my head was so big, when I started to make my turn my head got caught and I got stuck sideways. So, when they got me out, my head was mashed in on one side and she was so afraid that it was going to stay that way. The doctor explained that my head was still soft and, every day, Mom would mold it with her hands until it was back to normal. However, it didn't help with the size of it, which certainly took some time to grow into. She said whenever she'd go to the store to buy me a snowsuit with the matching cap, she'd always have to go up a larger size to find a hat that could fit my head. And while no one was looking, she would switch caps to find one that would fit me. Mom was my complete heart and we were incredibly close. You could definitely call me a Momma's boy. Being an only child, I probably was a bit spoiled. Although I grew up relatively poor, I never felt that way. The love I received was more than enough to make up for whatever material things I lacked. However, some kind of way, Mom always seemed to come up with a way to get me whatever I needed. I was never hungry, and I always had clothing. I remember I'd get a suit once a year, and a new pair of shoes for Easter. I'd wear that suit or maybe the one from the previous Easter, until the next Easter came around. Then, it was time to get another one. Even on Christmas, which was her favorite time of year, whatever toy I wanted, it always seemed to make its way under the tree. Although I can remember a couple of times living in some deplorable situations, most of the time our living conditions were not bad at all. Mom had many different kinds of jobs. I remember her working at a factory where they made garden hoses. From time to time she would bring home pieces of the plastic for me to play with. She was also a school crossing guard when I was in elementary school. In 1960, she went from house to house taking Census for the government. In the 60's she also worked at a factory that made transistors for transistor radios. But most of the time, she did the same thing Grand-mom Nellie had done. She did the very same thing that she told me she left Durham to keep from doing: she was a domestic. Years later when I saw the movie "The Help," I identified with it in so many ways, because in the summer my Mother (who I could not stand being separated from for any length of time) took me to work with her. I became friends with the kids from some of "those white families" and they were my playmates.

Rev. Smallwood always did odd jobs: sometimes a night watchman and sometimes janitorial work. At other times he was out on the road, traveling and evangelizing. It had to be a struggle for them financially, but with the help of God we made it. One thing that I disliked was that we moved from state to state and city to city constantly. The excuse was that my father was ready to found (establish) a new church in a new city. But moving frequently was a habit with my mother and father long before I was born. He founded and pastored churches all over the country, many of which are still thriving. Even after my birth in Atlanta, we didn't stay there long. We were on the road again before I was even walking or talking. I'm sure there were many places that I can't recall, but I do remember living in Grand Rapids, Michigan with my Godparents, Rev. and Mrs. Toliver, when I was very young. I was a precocious kid and quite a nosey one at that. While we were living in Grand Rapids, Mom found out that my godfather was having an affair. His wife, Mrs. Elizabeth Toliver, was distraught and was discussing it with Mom one day as I played with my toys on the floor. I had just started talking, but not very well. Now, the young lady with whom he was having the affair had given him a very expensive pen and pencil set as a gift. My godmother was very upset about the whole issue. Mom was lending an understanding ear for her to vent. But little did they know; my ear was just as attuned to what was being said. So, when Rev. Toliver came home, the first thing I did was jump up on his lap, point at the pen in his suit jacket pocket, and loudly ask, "God-daddy, is that the pen the lady gave you??" Fortunately, my talking still left a bit to be desired and he didn't quite understand it. But before he could decipher what I was asking, Mom, who had immediately understood what I was trying to ask, scooped me up from his lap and said, "God-daddy is tired, don't bother him right now" and whisked me out of the room. From then on, anything they didn't want repeated, they made sure they said it when I was out of the room.

My nickname is Buddy and I was very seldom called Richard as a child, unless I was in trouble. I can hear Mom's voice now, piercing the atmosphere coming from another room in the house shouting, "RICHARD SMALLWOOD" when I had done something that I had no business doing. I knew I was in trouble then. In fact, some of my family, college and childhood friends still call me Buddy. Buddy was my uncle's nickname also. John, which was his actual name, was the oldest brother of the Smallwood clan and was killed in battle during World War I. I guess my nickname was sort of a memorial to him. Before we ended up in D.C. when I was ten years old, I can remember living in New York, Paterson, N.J., Elmwood, P.A., Philadelphia, P.A. on two different occasions, and of course part of my summers and some Christmases were spent in Durham visiting my Mom's family. I was told that all these wonderful people whom I visited in Durham were my cousins. However, I was always told that they were very distant cousins, and hardly cousins at all. For the life of me, even as a kid, I could not understand if we were so distant, then why in the world did all of us look so much alike? Mom could never seem to explain to me how these cousins were actually related to me, other than saying it was "complicated." My cousins themselves never talked about it. All I knew was that we were related in some way. When I was very small I'd always stay with my cousin Cleveland Cameron, also called "Uncle Clee," when I'd visit Durham. As a very small child, I think somewhere inside I wished that Uncle Clee could be my father. Uncle Clee was my cousin but later I found out the exact relation. He was my great-great aunt's son. He was always so nice to me. He was married to the nicest woman whom I affectionately called Aunt Sue. I especially remember spending Christmases there. Aunt Sue would bake the best Christmas pastries and the house would smell incredible. As I got older, me and Mom would sometimes stay with Miss Fanny, who had been a neighbor of my Grandparents and my Mom as she was growing up. I remember the most fragrant huge bushes that grew on either side of her front door that filled the air around her house with the most wonderful smell. However, as I got older, I'd usually stay with Cousin Lula who would spoil me rotten. By then, Cousin Lula was staying with her daughter Bessie and her husband, Willis. Bessie had been married twice, first to the father of her children, Robert Clements, and then to her second husband, Willis Allison. Lula would cook anything I wanted and let me do anything I wanted. As a kid, I had a really finicky appetite, but Lula could get me to eat things that I would have never thought of eating at home - like grits and scrambled eggs, which were normally sworn enemies of mine. She'd also cook anything that I requested. After hearing what Lula cooked for me and what she let me get away with, Mom used to shake her head and say, "that Lula spoils you." But Mom couldn't talk much. I was an only child and she'd spoil me too. Most of my relatives were grown and there weren't any cousins around my age except for Denise who was Olivia's daughter and Lula's granddaughter. We were a few years apart and, while growing up, we'd always play together during my visits. Sometimes I would visit my Grandfather Richard's mother, Clara. She was quite old as I recall and died when I was in junior high school. Another cousin who I remember vaguely was Bessie's brother, Rivers. He didn't come around that often, at least I don't recall him doing so. But every now and then I'd see him. I absolutely loved whenever I got the opportunity to go to Durham. It was a feeling of comfort, of belonging and acceptance that I felt whenever I was there.

Cousin Lula's brother's name was Octavius but he was called Ockie Cain. He shared the same parents as Lula, Dr. James Cain and Winnie Cain. Cousin Ockie owned a sort of convenience store located next to his large, beautiful home in Durham. He'd always give me candy. I remember thinking as a kid that anyone who owned a store had to be rich. My family said he was also the first black man who owned his own taxi company in Durham. I found out later after I was grown that he had been one of the biggest bootleggers in the state. So I'm sure that he wasn't poverty-stricken. All I know is that he treated me like royalty and I always loved going to his store. Next to his store was a beautiful pond. I've always had a fascination with water and loved to sit and watch that pond for hours. The pond had goldfish in it, and I remember it being pretty deep, because you couldn't see the bottom of it. Arranged around the pond were these beautiful, white stone ducks. I remember thinking how much fun it would be to see those ducks floating on the water. I just figured that if it's a duck, it should be able to float regardless of what it was made of. One time I got up enough nerve to put one of the ducks in the water and watch it float. It was heavy, so I took my foot and began to push it closer and closer to the water. Imagine my horror as the stone duck hit the water and I watched it immediately sink out of sight to the bottom of the pond. I began to cry knowing that my Mom was going to KILL me. I told Mom through my tears that I had "accidently" knocked the duck over. I'm not sure if she believed that it was an accident or not. But Cousin Ockie heard me crying and immediately comforted me and told me not to worry about it. He'd get the duck out and all would be well. I remember thinking, "How in the world is he going to get that duck out of that deep pond?" It was many years later that I found out that the bottom of the pond was where he would hide his illegal liquor from the authorities (some of whom were his customers). I'm sure access to the bottom was not a problem!

****

I always felt that my relationship with my father Rev. Smallwood was strained. As a child, I always wanted to please him, and I always wanted to get his approval. But there was never a bond between us. I used to look at the relationship bond between my Mom and me and wonder why there wasn't a similar relationship between my father and me. I was very uncomfortable if I was alone with him, even as an adult. I never knew what to say or what to do. I can't say he didn't love me in his own way, but at the same time there were too many other issues that got in the way of him really showing it. I'm not even sure if he knew how to show it. I did love him, but it was not the kind of love that I experienced with my Mom. I always felt guilty because there were times that I actually disliked him. Being taught to honor my mother and my father as far back as I can remember created confusion and guilt in my mind when my feelings for him were negative. When I look back, I understand that I also feared him. I'm not sure when the beatings from my father started. As far back as I can remember, he was beating me. I was never a bad child. I was shy and never had enough nerve to get into any serious trouble. I did have a stubborn streak (probably do until this day), and I'm not saying that I didn't deserve a whack every now and then. From time to time, Mom would spank me. She loved me but didn't play when it came to discipline. That was the way most black families disciplined their children during that time. But his spankings were different. They were brutal and severe. I couldn't figure out exactly why he would beat me so much. There were times when it seemed that there was no reason. He just did it. He would usually beat me with the belt, but sometimes with his hand. I can remember a particular beating when I was very small. I looked up into his eyes while I was crying, and his eyes were blood red. It was a frightening look. I couldn't identify what it was then, but looking back, it was a look of intense rage, fury and resentment.

Many times, during my childhood I would feel this resentment and something that bordered on dislike from him. After a while, I think I got used to it and just chalked it up to him being the way he was. These beatings continued from early childhood to junior high school. At some point when I was very small these beatings began to birth a sort of defiance in me, against him. At the same time, there were times when he seemed proud and encouraging and I couldn't sense those negative feelings. Although Rev. Smallwood's father was born about five years after the end of slavery, it seems that he still witnessed some of the horrors that were part of it. As a kid, my grandfather still saw black males, hands tied to a tree, stripped and beaten with a whip by white males. When my father was a kid, his father would beat him and his siblings the same way. Their hands would be tied to a tree out back and their shirts removed if they had any on. He would then proceed to beat them the way he had witnessed as a child. My father never tied me to a tree, but the beatings were so intense and for seemingly no reason other than him seeming to have something against me. They lasted for many years.

The majority of my father's family lived in New York after migrating from Waynesboro in Burke County, GA. Originally, he had eleven brothers and sisters. However, by the time I was born there were only two brothers, Marion and Joe, and four sisters, Ossie, Sophia, Anna and Netha. When I was very small my father's parents were still living: Leventas his father, who died when I was one, and Vianna his mother, who died around the time that I was in high school. I don't remember his father and I was never close to his Mom, nor did I know her that well other than seeing her when we would visit New York. They were both very elderly and quite feeble by the time I came along. They were born in the 1870s, about six years after the end of slavery. I imagine that their parents were slaves. They were affectionately called Mom and Pop Smallwood.

I loved all of my aunts and uncles and they loved me as well. I was the only boy as all my father's brothers and sisters had girls. I guess I was viewed as sort of the golden child. So they definitely catered to me. I especially loved my Uncle Joe who was known as a ladies' man and a confirmed bachelor all of his life. He was a butcher by trade and was someone else I wished had been my father. My Aunt Anna had a granddaughter around my age named Michelle. So, whenever I would go to New York she would be my playmate. All my other cousins were much older. Ossie and Netha were Baptists and Anna and Sophia were Apostolic. Sophia was married to an Apostolic bishop and lived in a big house on Long Island that had an organ. I remember being fascinated as I had never really seen one before and I would stand and stare at it, longing to touch it, but afraid I would break it somehow. I was very young, but I also remember her telling my father that he, my Mom and I were all going to hell because we were Baptists. I didn't understand denominations or doctrine back then. I was a small child at the time, but I remember how much her words hurt. If she loved me, how could she say such a thing? As time went on, and as she got older, she mellowed quite a bit. I remember as an adult catching a train to New York to see her in the hospital right before she passed. I really loved my aunts and uncles. Ossie, or Aunt Sister as she was lovingly called, always seemed the sweetest one out of everyone. Netha was the socialite and lived in DC. She always seemed like a lot of fun, but she had a temper on her. They all loved my Mom and welcomed her into their family with open arms and affectionately called her "Aunt Honey."

When I was six, we lived in Brooklyn, NY for a summer. My father got a job as a night watchman at a laundromat. Sometimes I would go with him to work at night. The laundry had one of those old-fashioned elevators with the lever that caused it to go from floor to floor. I would play on the elevator all night long going up and down from floor to floor. That is the only time that I can remember having fun with my father and really enjoying his company.

We lived in a beautiful, old brownstone in one of the first-floor apartments. I slept in the living room on a couch that let out into a bed while my parents slept in the back room. I remember one night hearing someone trying to get into the door. I could hear them fiddling with the lock. I laid there terrified, seeing the shadow of the person under the door by the light reflected in the hallway. I was too afraid to call for Mom, so I just laid there paralyzed, expecting the door to fly open at any moment. I just knew some robber was about to break in. However, after what seemed like hours of them trying to unlock the door to no avail, they finally left. I don't think I slept a wink until daylight, terrified and waiting for them to come back and try again. Thank God they didn't.

There were three beautiful young ladies who lived in the apartment behind us. They were a singing group and had moved to New York to try to make it in the music business. I remember they had the most beautiful voices and their harmony was so tight. I was fascinated by them and spent many hours at their apartment listening to them sing. Harmony was something that fascinated me, and the more harmonic possibilities I could hear, the better. I often wondered what happened to them and whether they ever become successful. I can't recall their names. Soon after that we moved to Philly.

CHAPTER 3

THE LOVE OF MUSIC

I was born loving music. I can't remember a time that it wasn't an integral part of my existence. Mom said when I was very young, before I began to talk, while still in the crib, I would hum melodies that I'd heard, especially songs that I'd hear at church. She was astonished by it because clearly, they were recognizable. Mom informed my father of what she had heard me do and he didn't believe it. He told her it was impossible for a baby who had not even begun to talk yet to hum melodies. However, he was shocked when one day he walked into my room and heard me doing one of my concerts from the crib. They began to become aware that I had some kind of musical gift. Although I was already humming, I began talking late. When I finally did start the first thing I learned how to say was "milk," or the way I pronounced it, "mulk." It was my favorite thing in the world. Somehow Mom taught me how to spell it, so I'd say "M-I-L-K, MULK!" For quite a while, other than "mommy," that's all I could say. At the age of two they bought me a toy version of a blue baby grand piano. I wasn't quite able to pick out melodies on it just yet, but I would bang out rhythms and hum my favorite melodies as loud as I could to my mother and father's delight. I'm sure Dad knew he had a budding church musician.

Music was always playing in my house, and although my parents frowned upon me listening to secular music in the house, Mom listened to it on the radio all the time when I was younger. There weren't any all-gospel radio stations then, and you usually heard gospel music only on Sundays. But Mom enjoyed listening to the pop/jazz artists of that day such as Nat King Cole, Sarah Vaughn, Ella Fitzgerald, Harry Belafonte, Rosemary Clooney, Johnny Mathis, Patti Page and others. She'd also listen to classical music stations sometimes. Somewhere in my mind those great melodies of those pop standards started to take root. Subconsciously, I began to embrace the importance of good, solid melodies. I remember something that happened when I was very young that has always been a defining moment in my life. Rev. Smallwood was out of town and I was sleeping with my Mom in a big, king-sized bed. I was awakened by the most wonderful music one morning. To my left my Mom was standing at the ironing board, ironing. To my right, there were these beautiful long windows with the sunlight streaming through. I could even see little specks of dust dancing in the sunlight. On the radio was the amazingly warm voice of a female vocalist singing, "Moonlight in Vermont." There was my Mom, the person that I loved more than anything, along with the most beautiful sunlight I ever remember seeing and an amazing song and haunting melody with lush orchestrations, all happening at the same time. It was like I knew at that moment that my love affair with music would be a lifetime relationship, and that God could not have picked a better Mother for me.

In that instant I had been awakened to something very magical and special. It was such an overwhelming feeling that all was right with the world and, in some kind of abstract way, it spoke to the importance of music and my Mom in my life. It always stands out as such an overwhelming memory. Although I don't recall the announcer stating the name of the artist who was singing, after much research I believe it might have been the Jo Stafford version of that song. It sounds just like what I remember coming out of that radio. My love for music grew and grew. Rev. Smallwood played and sang as well. But I remember as a kid feeling that he played "old timey" music, because he had a bluesy, barrel house style of playing gospel music; almost like the clubs of the early days. But he always encouraged me to pursue my passion for music and to develop my own style.

By the time I was three years old, I had begun climbing up on his upright piano and picking out melodies with my right hand. By five I was adding bass with the left hand and simple two-part harmonies with the right. During that time, Mom bought me a record player for one of the Christmases that we spent in Durham. Actually, it was a toy more than a record player in that it was made of plastic. I remember that the speaker was in the arm of the player and it ran on batteries. But it played music and that was the most important thing to me. Mom began by buying me children's records, nursery rhymes, stories and even hymns. I remember one day listening to a hymn called "Jesus Tender Shepherd Lead Us." I began to sing along with it and suddenly realized that I was harmonizing and actually singing alto. I ran for Mom and told her to come listen. Mom was the consummate alto and sang in the choir all my life. She had an incredible ear for harmony. She listened to it and said, "BOY, You REALLY ARE singing ALTO!!!!" I think she was shocked that, at such a young age, I had learned how to harmonize. From then I harmonized every melody I heard and relished the fact that I could do so. It was also around this time that my father began to take me with him on some of his preaching dates. Before he would preach, he would stand me up in a chair or on a table where people could see me. He would sit at the piano to play and I would do the "sermonic" solo. My two solos were "Real, Jesus is Real to Me" and "I Thank You Jesus, I Thank You Lord." Although very shy, when I heard the music and I began to sing, the fear seemed to dissipate. Music had an almost magical effect on me. In the first or second grade, I remember being a part of the glee club, which I was ecstatic about. But the one thing I most remember was the lady who played piano for us. I can't remember her name, but I remember staring at her thinking "what an amazing pianist." I remember us learning Fred Waring's "The Night Before Christmas," which I loved. But I think I was more interested in what was going on in the accompanying piano than the vocals. I remember banging out what I remembered her playing when I got home.

My little toy record player didn't last very long. I played it all day, every day, and it finally wore out. Mom immediately got me a little portable electric one that I still have to this day. I learned to play the piano by emulating the recordings that I heard on this record player. I learned how to sing, and certainly how to harmonize just about anything I heard. It was also around this time that Mom began to buy me gospel recordings. Certainly I had heard them on the radio, but to own them myself was heaven. The very first gospel recording that she bought me was a 78 on the Gotham label by The Famous Davis Sisters called, "Get Right With God." I must have played it until the grooves were worn completely smooth. The "B" side was called "Tired, My Soul Needs Resting."

By this time we had moved to Philadelphia, the home of the Davis Sisters, and Mom began to take me to see them when they were in concert. I was in love with gospel music.

To sit there and see Ruth, Alfreda, Thelma, Audrey Davis and Jackie Verdell "wreck a church" was the most incredible thing I had ever experienced. I knew each voice, who sang what, and who led what. I attended their concerts so much that I knew the order of songs in their set and what was coming up next. If they varied in the order, when Curtis Dublin on the piano would play two or three chords of the intro, I knew immediately what song they were getting ready to sing. It was undoubtedly one of the most amazing sounds that I'd ever heard. The only accompaniment was a piano. There were only two microphones and the background vocals gathered around one mic while the lead singer took the other mic. The harmonies, the blend, the power of their voices; it was all indescribable. It was known throughout the gospel community that if the Davis Sisters were on a musical, you automatically put them last. Ruth Davis, affectionately called Baby Sis, was the "power house" of the group. She had a huge, powerful voice with an incredible vocal quality and could have easily been a blues singer. When she would squall, it was like the very walls would shake. Folk would fall out left and right from the power and anointing in her voice. When she and the sisters finished singing there was nothing left to do but say the benediction and go home. Any group that dared to venture forth after them was committing sheer suicide. They never left anything standing when they finished. They sang to packed out houses, and they were always late getting to the venue. I remember watching the door waiting for Alfreda to lead them in, checking in my mind to see if everyone was present and accounted for. They were probably my very first gospel influence; from Curtis' incredible precision on the piano, to the tight harmonies of their vocals. I began to think as a very small child…this is what I want to do.

While the Davis Sisters were more of a "down home" southern-styled group, soon after I was introduced to the recordings and the concerts of the second group that would also have a profound effect on my life. They were the Famous Ward Singers, also a native Philly group and probably the premiere group of their time. They wore elaborate gowns covered with "bling," and elaborate hair styles, usually extravagant wigs, and were always dressed "to the nines." I remember one outfit they had which was a black velvet robe covered in tiny little sequins. Around the neck and sleeves was red velvet. It was around this time that I decided that I wanted a robe. I was going to be a gospel singer and that was it! Somehow Mom scraped some money together and had someone make me a long, black choir robe. I remember taking the red netting from an old Christmas stocking and putting it around the sleeves, trying to make a Ward Singers robe. Clara was an accomplished pianist and songwriter and her singers were like none other. The harmonies were beautiful and unique. Use of diminished chords and diminished vocal harmonies, which were quite daring for gospel music during that era, songs in ¾ meter as opposed to the normal "gospel" 2/4 and 4/4 and sopranos with incredible ranges and the tightest harmonies that were sung in the stratosphere were the order of the day when it came to the Famous Ward Singers.

They were the first vocal gospel group I had heard to sing four- and five-part harmonies using sevenths and, sometimes, female bass parts. Henrietta Waddy and Frances Steadman brought up the bottom to the harmonies. These ladies literally could sing bass. Henrietta was the "show woman" and Frances had one of the richest deepest contralto voices in gospel music of that day. The quality of her voice was so soothing and "laid back." Clara did alto, but was known to do whatever part was needed and took the role of lead in many of their hits. Kitty Parham held the middle, strong and clear, and the top was one of the most extraordinary voices ever, in the person of Marion Williams. Her range extended from low tenor growls to whooping first soprano. She could demolish a church with her Baptist preacher squalls, singing "Surely God is Able." When it was released in 1949 it was reported to be the first gospel record to sell one million copies and was the Wards' biggest hit. Her other signature song was "Packing Up Getting Ready To Go." I used to watch her when she got to the vamp of "Packing Up." She would pick up flag poles and pocket books from ladies in the audience, putting them on her arm, her shoulder and whatever else she could, proceeding down the middle aisle "on her way to glory" with her "luggage."

Thelma Jackson was also one of the Ward singers during that era. She was a fiery singer with a rich vibrato and an incredible soprano range. Willa Ward was Clara's sister and she also sang soprano on many of the recordings, but I very seldom saw her in person when Mom would take me to hear them. I found out later that Willa was married and busy raising her family as well as focusing on her own music career. While many say that Willa was the originator of the high soprano "woooo" in the early days of the Ward singers, it was Marion who "trademarked" it. The Beatles, Little Richard and of course every soprano in every gospel choir or gospel group adapted it in some way or the other. Gertrude Ward, Clara and Willa's Mother, was the spokesperson, manager and a shrewd businesswoman. They sang some of the most incredible songs composed by not only Clara, but also the major composers of that day such as Rev. Herbert Brewster whose theological and scripturally-based lyrics were like no other. The Davis Sisters and the Ward singers were "superstars" in their own right. Deaths, funerals, breakups, marriages or any significant happenings of any of the members were always featured in the black newspapers in Philly. Clara even did advertisements and endorsements that were featured in the paper for hair and health products. If Clara used it, sales would skyrocket.

During that era, gospel singers were huge in popularity. In the black community, they were just as famous as any movie star. Their fans were die-hard supporters, who knew all about them, including every song they had recorded, and kept up with everything that they did. Some of them even had fan clubs. I also listened to the Caravans, Robert Anderson, The Angelic Singers, The Original Gospel Harmonettes with Dorothy Love Coates, and later The Roberta Martin Singers and The Imperial Gospel Singers as well as others. One of the early recordings my Mom bought for me was the organ solo "Amazing Grace" by Rev. Maceo Woods. I marveled at his technical skill on the Hammond organ and longed to one day be able to play one. Also, my father bought me a sermon recording by Rev. C.L. Franklin called, "The Eagle Stirreth Her Nest." I was a little too young to understand the theological implications of the sermon, but when I heard Rev. Franklin preach, it was like my hair would stand on end and my eyes would fill with tears. It made we want to cry, run and holler, but I wasn't sure exactly why. All I knew is that I was hearing something powerful.

But the Davis Sisters and The Clara Ward Singers were my mainstays during my early childhood; especially since I could experience them both live almost any weekend. The pianistic artistry of The Davis Sisters' pianist, Curtis Dublin, and Clara Ward began to have a profound effect on my development as a pianist. Watching the singers "work" a microphone, singing creative harmonies, blending their voices as one, and their incredible stage presence began to have an impact on me as well. I would stand in front of the mirror practicing and pretending that I was a part of these groups, depending on what recording was on the phonograph. I would imagine that I was singing in front of thousands of people and would create additional harmonies to the background vocals already recorded. I would emulate every song on the piano and try to play exactly in the style of both pianists. When they would do something musically different in their live concerts than what was included on the recordings, I would incorporate that on the piano as well when I got home.

I remember on the Wards' recorded version of "Packing Up," the chord progressions on the end "vamp" went from I to IV. I immediately noticed that when they sang it live though, Clara on the piano as well as the background harmonies went from I to VI. I had no idea during that time what musical theory was, nor the technical names of chords. I just knew that she played it differently live than the recorded version. So when I would play it on the piano at home, I'd play her "live" interpretation of the chord changes. I couldn't have been more than seven years old, but very seldom did a note or a chord escape my ear. I listened to these recordings day after day and my pianistic ability and my ear for picking up whatever I heard began to grow even more.

CHAPTER 4
MY FIRST SONG

My first attempt at writing a song was disastrous at best, as I recall. I was probably five or six years old. I worked on it feverishly and in my five-year-old mind, I thought I had completed a masterpiece. I don't think I understood the importance of lyrics at that time, which my Mom explained to me when I proudly sang and played it for her. It was called "Shout For the Weary Alone," which made no sense whatsoever. The melody and arrangement were fairly nice though. It was very much a 1950's traditional gospel song. I started off with a rubato, free tempo solo singing "Shout for the weary alone, Shout for the weary alone, Shout for the weary, He'll take you to the end, Shout for the weary alone." Then it sped up to a fast tempo chorus, "Let us shout, shout, shout! Let us shout, shout, shout! Shout for the weary alone." I remember Mom's expression well as I proudly performed it for her. It was a "how do I encourage this child, without hurting his feelings" kind of look. She said, "The music sounds good baby, but the words make no sense at all. You have to make sure that your words are clear in terms of their meaning." My little feelings were a little hurt, but as I look back in laughter I guess we all have to start somewhere.

One evening when I was probably about 7 years old, after hearing an awesome concert by my idols The Ward Singers, some of the members of the group were greeting people in front of the church where they had just performed. Mom took me up to meet them. It had to be one of the most awesome moments of my life. After Mom introduced us, I remember Marion Williams, my favorite, looked at me and exclaimed, "Isn't he precious?" All the while she gave me the biggest hug, smothering me in her ample bosom. I was in heaven! Mom went on to explain what a big fan I was, that I had all their recordings and that I played the piano. I remember Clara exclaimed, "That's wonderful! Play something for us!" My shyness kicked in big time and panic consumed every fiber of my being! I grabbed on to Mom and managed to get out a weak, "no, that's alright." I still kick myself even today for passing up the opportunity to play in front of the very people who inspired me. However, the extreme shyness and having to perform in front of someone I admired, was paralyzing. It is something that took a long time for me to overcome.

My love and desire to do gospel music began to grow even more. Not only would I stand in the mirror for hours singing along with the recordings pretending I was the lone male singer in the Davis Sisters or the Ward Singers, but I would abduct the Christmas tree angels from Mom's Christmas decorations. I had just the right number of angels for them to be either the Davis Sisters or The Ward Singers, depending on what mood I was in. My mom took a box of matches and made a toy piano. She took used wooden matches and wrapped aluminum foil around the top, put a cardboard platform on the end for a stand and made microphones. She made the stage out of a box that had once contained Whitman's chocolates. Mom was always very artistic, and it worked well with my huge imagination. I would put on the recordings and my angels would become one of those groups that I idolized so much. I'd have concerts all day with the decorations. I was definitely an odd child. I'd rather do that or play the piano than go outside and play. My music became my escape and my refuge from the growing fear and the uncomfortable feelings I had toward my father. Sometimes after the beatings, I would retreat to my room and turn the music on as loud as I could and lose myself in the music until it was bedtime. I read a quote from the great Maya Angelou which described it so perfectly. She said, "Music was my refuge. I could crawl into the space between the notes and curl my back to the loneliness." In my case, I could curl my back to the pain.

At the same time, I remember how excited I was when my father would take Mom and I out driving. We'd leave early in the morning and just ride out and view the countryside. Invariably, we'd stop at one of the many roadside diners we'd pass, and I'd be treated to pancakes and a tall, cold glass of milk. That was heaven to me. Sometimes we'd find pony rides and I could live out my fantasy of being a cowboy while riding the ponies. Other times we'd find a carnival and they would wait while I would get on every ride I was big enough to ride. We'd usually end the excursion by eating hot dogs and cotton candy. Those times hold warm memories for me. Around the age of five, Mom tried to find a piano teacher to teach me. By then I had started to duplicate what I would hear on the radio or on recordings pretty well. My hands were very small, and I was still working with two fingers of the right hand and one on the left. Soon I would go to three-part harmony in my right hand. The attitude of most piano teachers during that time was that I was too young, and a five-year-old's attention span wasn't long enough. They had no idea how much I loved the piano and that I would play it all day if I was allowed. So, some music teacher had the bright idea of putting me in a rhythm band. Mom thought, *well it's a music class so this might help point him in the right direction.* It turned out to be a class full of kids playing the kazoo! It was simply taking this plastic, blue little instrument and singing through it, which would produce this strange, ugly little nasal duck sound. I hated it. I didn't last very long. I told Mom that I wanted to take piano lessons, and this wasn't it! Mom took me out of the class, but still no one would take me on as a student because they thought I was too young, so I began to teach myself as my ear became stronger.

Probably somewhere around this time we were living with a lady by the name of Mrs. Coe who was also an usher at Rev. Smallwood's church. She had some children who were older than I with whom I played, especially one girl by the name of Delphine who became my good friend and playmate. What I remember most is that Mrs. Coe had a TV, which I watched religiously. I remember my favorite TV shows around that time were Ramar of the Jungle, Romper Room, Ding Dong School with Miss Francis, and of course Superman. When Miss Nancy of Romper Room would look in her magic mirror and name all the children she could see in television land, I waited for her to call my name every day. However, I don't recall her ever "seeing Richard," at least not while I was watching. The one thing I remember about Mrs. Coe is that she shouted in church a lot. In fact, one particular Sunday she accidently hit a lady while she was shouting and knocked her out. I made it a point never to sit close to Mrs. Coe.

By the time I turned seven, my mother finally found a teacher for me. Her name was Fannie Borden. Ms. Borden certainly had her work cut out for her. My ear was "dangerous" and anything I heard I could duplicate note for note. I'm not sure if Miss Borden was aware of my playing by ear, but her desire was to teach me how to read music. Somewhere in my mind, I decided that I didn't need to learn how to read. Why read when I could just hear it and play back what I had just heard? So I began a long journey of deception with my piano teachers. Of course, she explained the concept of the lines and the spaces, time signature, accidentals and rhythm. All of what she was saying seemed too time consuming to me. So, when I was assigned a piece to learn from my Eckstein Beginners music book, I'd ask Miss Borden to play it. She was always too happy to do so and as she played it through, I had my recorder in my brain in full operation. Once I got it in my head, the rest was history. I could play it back to her exactly as I heard it. The following week with my eyes on the page as if I was reading, I'd play back to her exactly what she had played the week before. She'd give me a gold star on my page and we would continue to the next assignment for the following week.

I got away with this for a long time until many years later, when I was in junior high school. While Miss Borden was my teacher, I broke my right arm. I was at school one day and at recess we decided to play cowboys. Of course, during the 50's the most exciting thing you could pretend to be as a kid was a cowboy or Superman - at least in my mind. Cowboys ruled the TV, from the Lone Ranger, Gene Autry and Roy Rogers to Hopalong Cassidy. Mom was against me owning any kind of toy guns, but I had my bows and arrows with the suction cup tips. Of course, I didn't have my toy ammunition at school, however it was decided that I would be the bad guy. I think that I was the cowboy who had robbed a bank or something. I was always a klutz and as my mom would say, I was forever "falling over my feet." At any rate, the cowboy sheriff had captured me and was taking me to jail. I decided before he got me to the area that we had designated as the jail, that I would make a run for it. I got loose from the "sheriff's" grip and took off running as fast as I could. During the run, I tripped. Before I knew it, I was flying through the air. When I came down, I put my right hand out to brace myself from the fall, but my hand bent under towards my arm and I came down on the concrete on the back of my hand and wrist. I heard a loud snap as I hit the ground and felt a sharp pain in my arm. I stared at my right arm as the tears began to well up in my eyes, and I realized that something was horribly wrong. My arm had changed shape. Instead of it being straight it looked like a stick that someone had snapped in the middle.

I remember taking a deep breath and letting out a yell that was probably heard several blocks away. The teacher got me to the nurse, who immediately called Mom. It upset Mom so much that she ran out of the house without her house keys and later had to climb back in through the window when we got back. I had no idea that they would have to "set" the arm at the hospital, or even what that really was. After x-raying it and seeing that it was broken in half right in the middle, the doctor called for another doctor. I was instructed to lay my arm on the table. One doctor grabbed my wrist and hand while another one grabbed my elbow. The one at my hand yelled "pull" while he yanked my hand and did sort of a karate chop with the palm of his hand where the break was. At the same time the one at the elbow pulled in the opposite direction. The bone immediately snapped back in place. However, the yell I gave when I first broke it held no comparison to this one. As Mom used to say, I could have awakened the dead. Mom tried to calm me down, with tears in her eyes. When they finally got me subdued, they wrapped it with bandages which hardened into a solid cast. I thought the cast was really cool. It went from mid-hand to past my elbow. I don't think it hit me until I was on the way home: *how in the world would I play the piano?*

I remember the cast had to stay on for two or three months. I couldn't go without playing the piano for one day. Although I couldn't take piano lessons during that time, I decided I would still come up with a way to play while I was at home. Certainly there was nothing wrong with my left hand, so I could play the bass part to any song that I chose. I had two fingers sticking out of the cast on my right hand: my index finger and my middle finger. Although my thumb was out, I couldn't position the cast just right to use it. So, I positioned my shoulder so that my two fingers would touch the keyboard and play two-part harmony while I played the accompanying bass with my left. My arm was out of commission for two or three months, but I never stopped playing or practicing. Of course, it was neat to get all the attention as well as getting my friends to sign my cast. The only issue was when it was time to take the cast off and the doctor pulled out a circular saw. I almost passed out as he began to saw away at the cast, thinking that he was going to cut my arm off. Mom said I turned white as a sheet, screaming bloody murder, as the blood drained from my face in expectation of my newly healed arm being cut off.

******

My shyness began to grow more severe. I've dealt with social anxiety most of my life and the fear of being in public. I really think it started in school. It seemed the larger the school the worse it got. I've learned how to work around it, but it is still an issue that I face from time to time. I hated school starting around the sixth grade and the early part of junior high school. Getting called on in class and talking in public were terrifying. I developed an impediment of speech. I didn't necessarily stutter but would stumble over my words and my brain just seemed to freeze up. Kids can be so cruel at times, and there were times when they would laugh, snicker or whisper, and I was mortified. When I got home, I would retreat to my room and my music.

Mom used to say that I was an odd child. I just never liked to do the things other kids liked to do. It was all about music. She said even as a baby and a toddler I was always so serious. I never smiled much, especially in public. When people would ask to hold me in church, and they began to talk "baby talk" to me, Mom said I would glare at them until they got uncomfortable and handed me back to her. Honestly, I've never really felt like I "fit in." Even though I had friends, as a kid many times I felt alone and isolated. It almost feels like I'm some kind of alien from another planet, in a world where no one really "gets me." Even as I became an adult, the anxiety before I would sing or play was sometimes unbearable. If there was a public gathering I had to attend, especially if I was by myself, I would "go through changes," knowing that I had to walk into a room full of people many of which I didn't know. It's something I've struggled with all of my life. But once I sit down at the piano and begin to play, the anxiety leaves, all feelings of fear usually disappear, and I feel as much at home as if I were sitting in my living room by myself. One thing it taught me was how to be a good actor, not letting anyone know that I was uncomfortable. This escalated and later in life I would have to get professional help.

When I was pretty small I can remember being a junior usher. I vividly remember sitting on the back row of the church with all the other junior ushers, playing and talking and seeing Mom eyeing me from the choir stand. All I needed was that look from Mom and I knew to shut up. I knew what was waiting for me when we got home. Even worse was Rev. Smallwood stopping his sermon and telling me to stop playing from the pulpit. I'd always hope they'd forget by the time we got home. Unfortunately, they never did. When I was about seven years old my father told me, "It's time for you to play for church." Of course, being as shy as I was, the idea of playing in front of people as opposed to just around the house terrified me. I told him I couldn't play in front of people. His response was that if he had to put a curtain around the piano and me so that I couldn't see the congregation, I was going to play. So, at the age of eight I was playing for his church, teaching and directing the choir but without the curtain. Of course, after a while it became second nature to me. However, the shyness never completely went away. On stage, all shyness disappears as ministry kicks in and God takes over. Off the stage is a different thing. My parents instilled in me at a very young age a knowledge and love for God. Being a PK (preacher's kid) I was in church all the time. Being the pianist for the church I was in the church even MORE than all the time. But it was the foundation of my relationship with God and was the training ground for later ministry.

Mom was a great teacher and taught me to read at an early age. She would buy me books and I would read everything in sight before I even started school. My ability to read made me even more inquisitive about life, about who God was and about things that I didn't understand. In 1956, we moved from Philadelphia, PA to Paterson, NJ. I accepted Christ and was baptized by my father not long after, when I was seven years old. We didn't have a TV when I was growing up. I'm not sure if we just couldn't afford one, or if it was that my father was against TV. He was old school Baptist and didn't believe that one should go to the movies. Also, he believed that girls or ladies shouldn't wear pants, one couldn't read comic books on Sunday, one didn't iron or wash on Sunday, one couldn't listen to any music other than Christian or classical, or dance, and certainly one couldn't go to parties. And the list went on. It was all sin in his eyes. However, Mom went against him when it came to a number of things, especially the movies. She and I became full-time moviegoers from a small child. I was a Walt Disney fanatic and I think Mom took me to every animated feature he ever did. Because I didn't have television my time at home was spent reading, listening to music, playing the piano or just generally playing, like all kids. I did love toys.

CHAPTER 5
THE HOUSE IN PATERSON

My family always seemed to be very sensitive of things "supernatural." My grandfather Richard had a lot of supernatural experiences. Mom did as well. I remember her telling me about how they moved to a house in Washington, D.C. on Q St. N.W. when they got married. Mom played the piano a little bit. I remember her favorite song to play was "I'd Rather Have Jesus," in the key of *C*. In fact, when I was a little boy I used to stand at the piano, listen to her play, and sing it. It's the only song I ever remember her playing. After settling into this house, she noticed that whenever she sat at the piano in the living room she had the most unsettling feeling that someone was standing behind her. When this would happen, she would suddenly feel a cold chill in the air and her hair would stand up on the back of her neck. As time went on, when she was seated at the piano the floorboards would creak behind her as if someone was standing there. She stopped sitting at the piano soon after. Another time she and a friend were sitting in the living room talking when all of a sudden they heard the distinct sound of someone with high heels coming down the hallway toward the door near them. Mom wasn't sure if someone had broken in or what, but she began to feel that eerie sensation she got when seated at the piano. Before anyone could say anything, they both went over the back of the couch and hid from the supposed intruder. The footsteps slowly got nearer the door. The doorway was still visible as they looked under the couch. As they viewed the door, the footsteps came right to it and stopped. There was no one standing there. Mom's friend went into hysterics and started laughing uncontrollably. She had to slap her before she finally quieted down. They were terrified. Later when my father came home, he saw what looked like the figure of a woman standing in the shadows behind the door. He immediately thought it was my mother who was known to hide behind objects and jump out to scare him for fun. So, laughing, he hollered "I see you!!!" He then ran back to the kitchen where he encountered my mother cooking. "How did you get back here so fast?" he asked, out of breath. After Mom explained that she had been cooking the entire time, he realized that he had seen something else behind that door.

Maybe that kind of sensitivity to things in the spirit realm is genetically based. I'm not sure but I've definitely had my share of similar experiences, good and bad. In Paterson, we lived at 112 Godwin Street. Down the street was the Thankful Baptist Church, which my father founded. Instead of names during that time, the schools in Paterson were numbered. I attended Number Six Elementary School. We lived in a golden yellow, wood-framed house trimmed in brown. We lived on the first floor, which had been turned into a two-bedroom apartment. The owner, Mrs. Hammond, occupied the second level of the house. She was a nice senior citizen for whom I used to run errands from time to time. Both of my parents worked while we were in Paterson and I was a "latchkey kid." When I got home from school I'd be there by myself until my parents got home from work. I would entertain myself by either playing the piano, reading, or listening to records, especially the Davis Sisters. I've always liked my music loud and I would turn up the volume as loud as my little record player would allow. The little speaker in my record player was very small, so I could only raise the volume a certain amount without distortion. Little by little, I began to notice that sometimes when the music was playing I could distinctly hear someone calling my name, "Buddy." It wasn't a loud voice. Just someone at average volume speaking it: "Buddy." I would turn the music off and listen intently and would hear nothing. I'd turn the music back on and sometimes it would go on playing normally, but other times I'd hear that soft voice again calling, "Buddy."

At times when this happened, I would go to the steps that led upstairs to Mrs. Hammond's part of the house and call up asking if she had called me, thinking that she may need me to go to the store for her. But her answer would invariably be, "no Buddy, I didn't call you." So I'd go back into the apartment and turn the music on again. For some reason, I was never afraid, at least not at that point. I didn't tell Mom about it until years later because I didn't pay it too much mind. I think I was too young to feel that there may have been something strange about the house. I remember Mom telling me that, before I could talk, sometimes I would see things and point at them, seemingly in fear. Mom said it would scare the life out of her, because she had no idea what I was looking at. She saw nothing. But she said I was adamant about something in front of me, and I'd point, making nonsensical sounds, trying to get her to understand what I saw. This would just drive her crazy and frighten her even more.

*****

I've always believed that before we are born, we are with God in the spiritual realm. It's where we initially come from, and it's where we will return. Sometimes I think children are more attuned to the spiritual realm because it hasn't been that long since they were there. At any rate, the calling of my name at the house on Godwin Street continued off and on until one night, I had an extremely frightening dream. I thought I was in the house by myself. The house looked the same however it seemed to be very long in length. I just remember standing in one of the rooms, and I heard the voice begin to call my name. This time, it was different. It called me in sort of a "sing songy," elongated way. "Buhhhh-deeee" The voice was chilling and there was something somewhat evil about it. All I know is that it frightened me out of my wits. It kept calling in the same way and seemed like it was getting closer to me. I woke up screaming. My parents' room was right next to mine and I could hear them running towards my room. I grabbed Mom and held on for dear life as I tried to explain to her, "Someone was calling my name!" Mom comforted me as only mothers can, until I stopped crying. Then she said, "Baby, you just had a bad dream." She sat there with me until I went back to sleep. But to me it seemed like more than a bad dream. There was something about it that I just couldn't put my finger on, something that was different than a regular dream.

The bad dreams continued sporadically until one night I awakened and saw what appeared to be a figure sitting at the bottom of my bed. This was not a dream. It was a woman dressed in the kind of clothing that women probably wore in the 1800's. The dress was purple and long and high at the neck, with a cameo at the center of the collar. Her hair was completely white and was in kind of an upsweep with a bun on the top. She said nothing, but sat there in sort of a mocking way staring at me with a blank look in her eyes. I was terrified. Mom said she was awakened by me screaming "Get off my bed. GET OFF MY BED!" Again, she and Dad came running. The figure disappeared as they ran into my room. My experiences were getting more frightening. My father had prophesied that I was going to preach when I grew up so he got me a Bible around that time. We are not talking a children's bible, your New Testament or hand-sized Bible, but the size Bible that would be on the podium of a pulpit in a church. I was tiny and it was huge. It had great pictures in it that were very colorful and I loved looking at it. Although I read very well, trying to understand what the King James Version meant at seven years old was impossible. So I took pleasure in just dragging it around the house and looking at the pictures, admiring what a beautiful looking book it was. My Mom and Dad suggested I take the Bible to bed with me at night. Maybe that would alleviate what was going on. I think by then they were becoming quite worried and were aware that something strange was going on. Dad gave me a Bible but Mom gave me a teddy bear when I was about three. That bear was my constant companion. Many times, when I would get the unexplained beatings from my father, I would run to my room, shut the door and tell "Teddy" what had been done to me. I can remember dragging the Bible in one hand and Teddy in the other, putting them in the bed first and then climbing into the middle. The minute I started going to sleep with the Bible next to me, the dreams and the other experiences stopped. I experienced weeks and weeks of peaceful sleep so I thought the dreams had run their course, so eventually, I proceeded to bed without the bible. But the moment I stopped sleeping with the Bible, the dreams and the "sightings," if you will, returned. It started to become a terrifying period in my life. I was afraid to go to sleep at night because I had no idea what the night held for me.

As I remember the layout of the house, when you came into the front door you were immediately in the living room. You then walked through the living room and entered the kitchen. To the right of the kitchen there was a front bedroom and a back bedroom. The smaller, front bedroom was mine and the larger, back bedroom was Mom and Dad's. You could sit in either bedroom and look out the door and see what Mom was doing in the kitchen. One particular night, I went to sleep without my constant bible companion. Suddenly, and I'm still not sure why, I was awakened. Everything was quiet but I could see what looked to be a small circular dim light, a kind of orb moving around in the kitchen. I remember thinking that someone had broken into the house and what I was seeing was the beam from a flashlight in the kitchen. My heart began to race, because they would definitely get to my room first if they were searching around the house. My eyes became transfixed on the moving light. It wasn't a bright light, more of a dim light with an almost bluish tinge to it. All of a sudden, the light started moving toward my doorway. There was nowhere to run, unless I ran past it, and I certainly didn't have that much nerve. I rose up in the bed and watched it slowly move toward the entrance of my room. When the light reached my doorway, it stopped and then began to change. Although it had the same pale, bluish tinge to it, it began to look like smoke or some kind of mist. The smoke began rising from the floor where the light had been, higher and higher, filling the doorway. I remember so clearly holding my mouth open, astonished by what was happening. My heart was pounding in my head. I can't ever remember being that afraid, before that moment or since that moment.

I got a feeling in the pit of my stomach that there was something horribly wrong with what I was seeing. The smoke began to take shape. I watched it as it shifted, changed, swirled, and little by little I saw the form of a man taking shape. By this time, the smoke was a little higher than the top of the entrance of the doorway. Suddenly, there stood the figure of a man. He was Caucasian and looked very young, maybe early 20s or late teens. He wasn't completely solid. I could see through him just a little, like he was translucent. It was almost like looking at a figure on an old black-and-white TV. There was no color to his clothing or his complexion. It was all just the same pale, bluish color that the light had been. At this point he stepped into the doorway inside my room. I remember him being so tall that he bent over, as not to hit his head on the top of the doorway of the room. He didn't say anything to me. He just stared at me. I must say, his eyes were "pure evil." They were absolutely horrifying, and they looked like they were staring straight through to my very soul. I wasn't sure if he was coming closer to the bed and if he was going to touch me. All I know is that I began to scream as loudly as I could for my Mom.

I heard Mom and Dad's feet as they hit the floor and began running toward my room. Mom told me later that they ran into each other trying to get to my room. The moment I heard their footsteps, the figure began to change slowly. The shape began to change back to a wispy, kind of grey, smoky mist. It went back to the doorway and began rapidly shrinking. By the time Mom and Dad reached my doorway, it had completely dissipated. I was hysterically screaming, "There was a man in here! There was a man in here!" My father was convinced that someone had broken into the house. While Mom was trying to calm me down, he looked in closets, under the bed, and in the kitchen and living room for the intruder. Of course, there was no one anywhere to be found. I don't remember if I ever went to sleep that night.

It's a terrifying memory that will always be present in my mind. Even today, I can't sleep with a bedroom door open. All doors have to be closed and the TV has to be on before I can relax.

Years later, after we moved from that house and I grew older, my Mom relayed a story to me. At some point the owner of the house, Mrs. Hammond, took her down in the basement. Some of the first things my mother saw were old books on witchcraft and black magic. There were skulls, candles and other demonic paraphernalia. Mom was horrified. She immediately questioned Mrs. Hammond as to what it was and, more importantly, why it was down there. Mrs. Hammond told her that it belonged to her husband who used to practice some kind of black magic. I'm not sure if he was deceased or if they were divorced. But he had left all of this behind, and she had stored it down in the basement. Mom then told me, "All of the paraphernalia that I saw was stored directly below where your bedroom was." I was sleeping directly over it. As I got older I used to ask Mom why all of these frightening things seemed to follow me. She answered that God had a calling on my life and work for me to do. She said the enemy and negative forces didn't want to see that happen and wanted to frighten and discourage me.

One positive thing about staying in Paterson is that I began my lifelong love affair with animals. Mom always loved animals as well and had pets throughout her childhood and early adult life. My first pet was a turtle named Tommy. I loved that turtle, and a while later, it became ill. I think Mom was afraid that it was going to die, and she didn't want me to see that. I didn't even realize it was ill, although I remember it had started to turn a strange white color around its mouth. She told me that Tommy would be happier out in the wild with all the other turtles and convinced me that, in order for him to be happy, he needed to be turned loose. So, we found a beautiful pond in a park and I put Tommy in the water and watched him swim across the pond. Poor Tommy probably starved because I had fed him for most of his life. I felt satisfied that I had done a good deed, although I hated to see him go.

Another day I was looking out the window and saw these older boys with a little black kitten. There was a 2x4 on the ground with a huge spike sticking out of it. They were trying to throw the kitten onto the spike and impale it. I ran outside immediately and snatched the kitten from them. I then ran back into the house wondering how in the world I was going to explain a kitten in the house to my parents. My father hated all kinds of animals and believed they should never be inside a house. But Mom, from whom I got my love for animals, persuaded him that we should keep the cat after hearing my story. I named him Smokey and he was a part of our family for a number of years. My father even came to love him.

While we lived in Paterson, I remember Mom telling me that Thelma Davis of the Davis Sisters had passed. She was only 26 years old and had died from post-partum complications after the birth of her child. I was devastated. It was like someone in my family had passed. I was so fascinated by these groups and the music they made; probably borderline obsessed. I had become such an avid follower that it was like I knew them personally. They had become so much a part of me and of my life. These were the people I looked up to, even though I didn't know them personally. I think I actually went through a little grieving period. I just felt so close to all of them. I'm embarrassed to say I even had my own little funeral for her, with one of the little Christmas tree angels. I was the strangest little kid. I remember someone interviewing my Mom once. They asked her what kind of child I was. She answered, "He was a wonderful child; very quiet, very imaginative and very odd." She was definitely right.

I also remember a young man, probably in his early twenties, who was my piano teacher. I can't recall his name, but it seems like he may have been a college student. I remember him trying his best to get me to read fluently. He gave me a manuscript book and each week he would fill it with different notes on the lines and spaces of both clefs. I had to write the correct letters under the notes. Of course, I could do that very easily if I could count the lines or spaces and figure out the note. But that didn't help me if he put a piece of music in front of me to read at sight. I just had this mental block about reading notes. As far as I was concerned, my ear was good enough to get me through. I was so glad when we left Paterson. Even out of the good memories that happened there, the most prevailing ones are of that terrifying house.

CHAPTER 6

MY LOVE OF CLASSICAL MUSIC

W̲e moved back to Philadelphia again and into a three-bedroom home at 4932 Westminster Ave in West Philly. We stayed there for several years. During this time, my father founded another church. I attended the James Rhodes Elementary School and returned to attending concerts of the gospel greats of that era. Our next-door neighbors were a couple I fondly called Miss Rosa and Mr. Bill. They had a huge television set in their living room, and I would climb over the bannister that joined our front porches and go watch TV almost every day after school. Many evenings, my entire family would go over there and we'd all watch it together. I remember wanting a television of my own so badly.

My next piano teacher was Lottie Robinson, a beautiful African-American elderly lady with mixed gray hair worn in an upsweep. Although she didn't realize I couldn't read at all, I think she did realize that my reading wasn't up to par. She would drill me on the lines and spaces and sometimes would rap my knuckles with a pencil to no avail. In my mind, I was still resolved not to learn to read. Of course, I continued to pretend that I was reading. She also would play whatever new musical piece she assigned me. I'd hear it, record it in my mind, and that's all I needed. She did realize that she could push me to do more difficult music than what was in the beginning music books, and that's exactly what she did. I remember her pulling out the Chopin Waltz in C# Minor Op 64 #2. I remember thinking it was the hardest thing that I had ever heard or seen, but after listening to it for a while, I realized that even though I had no clue how many sharps C# Minor contained, my ear could hear it. It was just a matter of getting my fingers acclimated to the feel of the key and getting it up to tempo. It wasn't long before I did it.

I began to love this genre of music. She also gave me a beautiful arrangement of the hymn "Sweet Hour of Prayer" with four or five variations. It was a showstopper. When I performed both pieces in Mrs. Robinson's student recital, I got a mention in the local newspaper with a picture and all. It was the first press that I ever received. My Mom and Dad were so proud and I'm not sure how many copies of that newspaper they bought and distributed! At around the age of eight or so, I wrote my real first song. I remember fiddling around at the piano and all of a sudden, this simple little melody popped into my mind. It was in ¾ time and I put a waltz motif in the left hand to accompany the melody. I remember thinking that for some reason it sounded like a lullaby, so I called it "Richard's Lullaby." The lyrics just seemed to pop into my head, lyrics that made sense this time. Before I knew it I had completed a song. The strange thing is that, as immersed as I was in gospel music, one would think I would have written a gospel song. But it wasn't. The style was more classical and very melodic.

Sleep my baby sleep
Night is drawing nigh

Sleep my baby sleep
Hush and don't you cry
Stars are standing by
To lead you through the night
Sleep my baby sleep
Till the morning light

Looking back on it, I guess it was really poetic for an eight-year-old kid. Where in the world did I learn the word "nigh?" Somehow my teachers at school got wind of my song and I was asked to play it for assembly in front of the student body. I think I also performed one of the pieces that I had done in Mrs. Robinson's recital. I still have a note from one of my teachers, Mr. Johnson, that reads, "Richard, I enjoyed your playing this morning in assembly. I especially enjoyed 'Richard's Lullaby.'"

****

Mom continued to buy me recordings of the Ward Singers, The Davis Sisters and others. It was during this time that she brought me a recording that was new and different. It was classical music, a recording of Rachmaninoff's Piano Concerto #2 in C minor. She told me to listen to it and, if I liked what I heard, she would take me to some classical concerts. I was familiar with classical music slightly from my piano lessons, and sometimes hearing it on the radio, but had never experienced it on this level. The minute the recording began to play, and the melody began to soar, I fell in love. Rachmaninoff had a way of crafting some of the most amazing melodies that no other composer could duplicate. It was music that reached inward and touched a place that had never been touched before. I heard chords, harmonic progressions, and a level of orchestration that I had never experienced; and it was awesome. When I expressed my love for this kind of music, Mom began to buy me more of the same, along with my gospel recordings. Soon after, she began to take me to hear Eugene Ormandy and the Philadelphia Orchestra in concert. It was incredible! I guess the stage had been set and God had begun to lay the foundation for the musician and the composer that I was to become.

We would go hear the Ward Singers on Friday, and on Saturday we'd go to the Philadelphia Academy of Music for a classical concert. Wanamaker's Department Store in downtown Philly had a huge pipe organ and concerts were given every day at a certain time. Mom would take me down there and I would be mesmerized by the music I heard at those concerts. I began to pick up, by ear, many of the various classical pieces that I heard from different sources, and would sit down and emulate them on the piano. This began to widen my chord vocabulary and I began to play around with voicings and harmonies not necessarily found in gospel music progressions. It was a time of musical discovery and I couldn't get enough of it. I remember Mom taking me to see the animated film, Walt Disney's *Sleeping Beauty*, and realizing that the songs and background music for the film were from Tchaikovsky's "Sleeping Beauty Ballet." My knowledge of classical music and its composers began to increase at an early age.

I was always a child who lived in a fantasy world. I loved anything that had to do with make-believe. Fantasy was more comfortable to me than reality. In my mind, and depending on what day it was, I was a superhero, a famous gospel singer, a cowboy, a child star like Beaver on "Leave it To Beaver" with my own TV sitcom, or I lived in some mythical land with magical powers. I would sometimes imagine my life as a sitcom. I even created a theme song for my "imaginary show" that I would sing when I got up in the morning. I think creative people tend to have huge imaginations. It was also an escape for me.

When I look back over my childhood, Mom always exposed me to all things musical. I told her, years later when she was near death, that God could not have picked a better mother for me: to nurture me, to teach me about God and how to love him, to love me unconditionally, and to help lay the foundation of whom I was to become. I know that I was given to her, and placed in her care for a specific reason and purpose. I know that God was using her and giving her ideas about how to inspire me musically throughout my childhood. When I was six years old, she took me to see my first opera. There was a movie released in 1954, based on the opera "Hansel and Gretel" by 19th century composer Engelbert Humperdinck, written especially for children. The movie used puppets to portray the characters and used stop motion animation, which was very cutting edge for that time. I had no idea what an opera was, but she took me to see it and exposed me to it. The excitement of the animation captivated me, but the music of the opera transported me into that world of fantasy that I knew so well as I sat and watched. The melodies and the sound of orchestration washed over me like waves from an ocean as they took me on a journey that I'll never forget. I was so inspired by what I saw and heard as a six-year-old. I remember dreaming about the movie later, dreaming that I was actually in it, meeting the characters and hearing the music over and over in my head. Ironically, several years later when I began to take piano lessons, the prayer from Hansel and Gretel would be one of the pieces that Mrs. Robinson would assign me. The harmonic progressions of that piece still captivate me. Music, and what it did to my mind and spirit, was the most exciting thing I had ever known.

****

While living in Philly, I remember my sister Dorothy Jean coming to visit us. Dorothy was my father's daughter from his first marriage. Although Dorothy was my sister, we didn't grow up together and we didn't live in the same house, so I always considered myself an only child. But I was fascinated with Dorothy, although I didn't know her well. I had always wanted a sibling, and used to worry mom at times about having a baby brother. To me, Dorothy was one of the most beautiful women I had ever seen. She was much older than me. In fact, there are a number of photos of her holding me when I was a baby. There was a picture of her on our mantle and it stayed on display wherever we moved. I remember staring at it at times thinking, "Wow, that's my sister. She's so beautiful that she could be a movie star!" I remember Mom telling me, at some point, that Dorothy had a serious drinking problem. When Dorothy arrived, I remember being shocked at the way she looked. It was not at all the young girl in the picture, not even the one in the pictures with me as a baby. The alcohol had begun to take its toll. Her face and lips were bloated to the point that she didn't look like the same person in the pictures. But she was so sweet. I remember her looking at me, smiling, and saying, "Look at my brother and how he's growing," then giving me the biggest hug. That was all I needed. I was in heaven because my sister was there. I remember her going out one evening, staying out very late and coming home inebriated. I don't think Mom and Dad were too happy about that. But Dorothy was a grown woman, married - and I believe, divorced - by that time. Still, even as a child I remember being concerned about what was clearly a major alcohol addiction problem.

One weekend, Mom took me to hear another gospel group that I was not as familiar with as the Davises and the Wards. I had some early recordings by them, one in particular called "I Have a Home For You." But the Wards' and Davises' recordings were my mainstays. Because they were from Chicago, I had never had the opportunity to hear this particular group in person. However, this night they made an appearance at a local church in Philly. Mom told me that Romance Watson, one of the singers, married the daughter of this prominent pastor in Philly at whose church they were appearing. That was the night I heard the Roberta Martin Singers in person for the first time. I remember a beautiful, portly young lady step to the mic to sing a song called, "Teach Me Lord." Her voice was mesmerizing, a cross between an opera diva and a down-home gospel singer. Her name was Delois Barrett Campbell. I was fascinated by her beautiful and clear soprano tones. She could slip fluidly from her head to her chest voice, which was big and full. Her voice was powerful. When she sang, she smiled. Her smile was gorgeous and I was transfixed. On the piano was a young lady by the name of Little Lucy Smith, the goddaughter of Roberta Martin. Her playing, with its classical overtones, arpeggios, jazz inflections and traditional gospel sound, changed my very life. I wanted to play like she did. Most of my experience with gospel music was all-female groups. The only mixed groups I had heard were choirs. I was never that much into quartets, although later I really began to appreciate groups like The Dixie Hummingbirds, Sam Cooke and the Soul Stirrers, The Golden Gate Quartet and others. However, female voices had always been my preference. But here was a small group with male and female voices. Along with Delois Barrett Campbell, Eugene Smith was the narrator and one of the lead singers, and could "set up" a song like no other. Norsalus McKissick was the house wrecker, with his powerful, husky baritone, and would jump off stages twice his height. Romance Watson, cool as he wanted to be, had an amazing voice that could slip from falsetto to natural at the drop of a hat. And Gloria Griffin, a powerful vocalist who would walk the aisles singing "God Specializes," until there was no one left standing in the place, were all a part of this one dynamic group. These folks could sing! I think by that time, Roberta wasn't traveling with the group any longer because I never remember seeing her in person. However, the Martin Singers began to take a major place in my heart in terms of the gospel groups that I loved. Their style would also have a profound impact on the groups that I would form and participate in throughout my adult years. Little did I know, as an adult I would have one of the biggest honors of my life: playing for this incredible group of singers.

They had a way of what I call "milking" a phrase or a word by use of dynamics, going from decrescendo to crescendo and swelling their voices on certain musical phrases. This kind of vocal dynamics I had never heard before in gospel music. The harmony was rich and full, girded by the rich male voices on the bottom, which supported the incredible female voices in the middle and on the top. When they stepped to the mic at the opening of that concert, after a mesmerizing piano solo by Little Lucy which served as the introduction, and opened their mouths and sang "Only a Look at Jesus," I was never the same.

****

During that era so many black composers published their own music starting with the father of gospel music, Thomas A. Dorsey. Roberta Martin, his protégé, followed suit and did the same. I remember Mom buying me the sheet music to "Teach Me Lord" that night, and another house wrecker, "God is So Good To Me." I could barely read music, but I remembered exactly what Lucy played in my head, as well as the vocal harmonies. I went home that night and headed straight for the piano, put the sheet music in front of me - for lyrics more than anything else - and played and sang at full voice what I had heard earlier at the concert.

Something happened during this time. I'm not sure exactly what happened, but one day Mom basically told me that my father lost the church that he founded. He then began traveling again. During this period, I missed him so much. Somewhere around this time in 1959, I started keeping a journal and as I look through it now, I kept reiterating how much I missed my father. I kept writing that I couldn't wait until he came home so he could spend time with me. On October 4, 1959 I wrote,

"Well, it is a lovely day. I am overjoyed because today, my father is coming as I mentioned yesterday. I will have a lot of new things to show him such as a new can opener for the wall, a toy bluebird, a truck, an old time jalopy, a sweater and many other things. I'll be glad when he comes. Yes I shall be very, very glad to see him. He has been sending me money with his letters and I have two pictures of myself that I'm going to give him. I just can't wait to see my daddy. If he stays tomorrow, I will play a game of catch with him. Next month I will be 11 years old on the 30th."

I entered this later on that evening:

"Well my Daddy finally came. Oh boy am I so glad. I couldn't be any happier."

I do remember that he came home for a short period of time, and played catch with me in the backyard. He may as well have given me a million dollars. I couldn't have been happier. The next day I wrote,

"We played ball today. We are not sure but we think my father is going to be called to a church in Baltimore or Tarboro NC. He brought me a record today. He is going back to Baltimore tomorrow. Boy! Will I be sad! It is horrible for me, to have him leave again."

Within a matter of weeks, we were moving to Washington, DC. That kind of time spent with him was very short-lived. He was off again in several days, evangelizing somewhere in the country. He never really spent much time with me actually, unless he was asking me to play something on the piano, going over hymns with me or giving me a beating for which I couldn't figure out the reason. When I read my journals from that time period, I am amazed by how I used to think about my father. Even though the beatings were frequent and the relationship was strained, I really loved him and wanted that connection with him so badly.

He was a stickler for hymns and he is the reason why I'm so well-versed in them today. He would open the Baptist Hymnal and call out the page numbers, and I would dutifully find the hymn and play it, while he sang standing behind me. Sometimes he would make me transpose them and play them in different keys. I used to hate it! But now I'm so thankful, because if it had not been for his insistence, I would not be as well-versed in hymnody as I am, or really know how to transpose. Even though

I did not look forward to these hymn sessions, they were a way to connect with my father and communicate on some level. However, the bond that I was searching for between him and myself would never happen. I only found acceptance from him through music. I believe that he was proud, as he bragged on me constantly in terms of my musical accomplishments. But I wanted him to love me because I was his son, not because of anything musical. Honestly, music was the only connection that we had. It was the only thing we had in common. As I got older, I became numb to the resentment that I sometimes felt, and accepted it as part of my life. To me, this was normal, so I stopped trying to fix it.

Even after he passed away, I was still trying to make him proud. I remember getting my first recording contract with Benson Records, and driving out to the cemetery to "tell" him about it. I remember my first car, and other important happenings in my life, when I would run out to the cemetery immediately, stand over his grave and tell him what was going on in my life, as if he were standing there listening. For years, I would have a regular "show and tell" session at his gravesite. As I really think about it, I may have "talked" to him more in death than when he was alive.

From time to time, I still had those strange experiences where I would "see" things. However, it was never as bad as what I experienced in Paterson. There were times though when I would wake up and stare into the dark, and I would see that familiar blue-grey smoke. I knew that in a minute it would form into some being, so I'd dive under the covers. When I got the nerve, I'd look out again and it would be gone. One night, when my father was traveling and I was missing him so much, I was sleeping with my Mom which I usually did when he was on the road. I awakened in the middle of the night and the bedroom door was halfway open. Behind the door I saw the smoke swirling and forming into something. But I couldn't look away. Slowly it started to take shape until I recognized immediately who it was. It was my father. I never quite understood what it was I saw, and why I saw it. I know without a doubt, however, that it was him. He wasn't looking at me, but looking away to the other side of the room. In fact, he was standing sideways so I basically saw his profile. I thought he had come home during the night to surprise us and hadn't told us. I immediately began to shake Mom who was in a deep sleep. "Mom," I shouted, "Daddy's home."

Mom sort of grunted "Huh?" arising from her comatose state. "Mom, WAKE UP!!!! Daddy's home!!!" I said again, this time shaking her violently. She woke up, sat up in the bed to see what I was shouting about, and immediately the figure began to fade, turned into the smoky substance and disappeared. I shouted excitedly, "Mom he was here, he was just here!" She sort of looked at me and said, "Buddy, you were dreaming," and turned back over. I know I wasn't dreaming. I was wide awake as I watched it happen. Then I began to fear that something had happened to my father. However, we heard from him the next day and he was fine. I don't know why I saw what I saw, but I do know one thing: it wasn't a dream. As I got older those kinds of experiences seemed to phase out, or morphed into something else. However, I think what it did was make me very sensitive to the essence of people. I grew into being able to sense if someone had something spiritually positive or negative about them. It's as if I became sensitive to their aura or who they really were. Sometimes I ignore the warning signs, which has always been detrimental.

****

In 1958, The Ward Singers—the group I idolized, the ones that I went to see almost weekly sometimes, the ones of whom I owned more recordings than any other group—broke up. The news spread like wildfire through Philadelphia. The Wards were not only icons in the gospel world, but Philly was extra proud because they were Philly born and bred. I remember standing in awe, seeing their custom-made limo driving through the streets of Philly, which served as transportation for the singers. For me, it was like seeing a glimpse of the Queen of England or the President of the United States. They were my rock stars and movie stars. I was heartbroken. I felt the same way I did when I got the news that Thelma Davis had passed. Although Clara had become a gospel icon and was incredibly gifted, the individual members had become iconic themselves. When they made appearances, fans couldn't wait to hear their favorite individual singers. Those singers together had created a vocal sound that could not be duplicated.

The breakup was over the group working so hard and not being fairly compensated. Clara's mother Gertrude was known to be shrewd in her dealings and tight with money. Many times, Gertrude would personally count the ticket sales for their concerts, although she was not the promoter. A portion of the group lived in an apartment building that she owned and they had to pay monthly rent to her out of whatever salaries they made from singing with the group. They had recently done a TV show for which the network issued individual payment checks in each member's name. The members were not informed of this. However, one of the singers supposedly witnessed the individual checks being deposited into a general account. She reported it back to the rest of the group and it was the final straw that broke the camel's back. I guess years of allegedly being treated unfairly finally took a toll.

Marion Williams had recently announced to Mrs. Ward that she would be leaving. The entire group, who ironically was scheduled to go on tour with Clara in the next couple of days, made a mass exit. Clara had to find singers in just a couple of days to do the tour. In fact, Gertrude reached out to the Imperial Gospel Singers, a group of Philly singers with whom I would become familiar much later, and they served as singers for the tour. Although Clara found some permanent Ward Singers to replace those that left and continued singing all over the world for many years to come, the sound was never the same to me. I never followed the Wards after that. Soon after the breakup, Marion Williams formed a new group made up mostly of the original Wards. They were named the Stars of Faith. I began to follow them as faithfully as I did when they were the Ward Singers.

CHAPTER 7

WASHINGTON, DC

In 1959, when I was 10 years old, we moved to Washington, DC. By this time, I was so tired of moving from place to place. Because I was shy, it was difficult to make new friends and then constantly have to go to new schools. By the time I would acclimate to my new environment, make friends and get comfortable in my surroundings, it was time to move again. I remember several years after moving to D.C., my father announced that he was ready to move again. Mom put her foot down and told him, "If you want to move, then YOU move. I'm not going to be dragging my child around from state to state anymore." That was that and he never brought it up again.

The explanation that I received for moving to D.C. was that my father would be starting up yet another new church. Initially after moving to D.C. we stayed with my father's sister, Netha, and her husband Tom Taylor at 1915 Alabama Ave, SE in Anacostia. Aunt Netha was a beautician by trade and owned a successful beauty shop called Marinetta on Florida Ave, NW. I was in the sixth grade when we arrived and began attending Stanton Elementary School. I entered in the middle of the fall semester. The D.C. public school system had only been integrated for about five years when I arrived, and Anacostia which had one time been an all-white neighborhood, had become racially mixed as well. So it was the first time I ever attended a racially mixed school. I had never experienced any kind of racism as a small child, and because I had always been brought up in black communities and schools I didn't know much about it.

I do remember, probably in the mid-50's, traveling to Durham with my Mom on the train. On the way the train stopped at various cities letting people on and off. I can't recall exactly where it was, but it stopped at a particular station and I looked out the window and noticed a bathroom on the platform with a sign on it that read "Coloreds." I started reading very well at a young age, but I didn't understand the meaning and asked my mother exactly what it meant. I don't think she was ready to explain racism or segregation to me at such a young age, and she just said, "Oh baby, that's the way things used to be a long time ago." Years later, after thinking about the fact that this happened in the early to mid-fifties, I'm sure it was the way things still were. As a child, I don't think I really understood what racism was. As far as I can remember I never experienced it firsthand. At least I wasn't aware of it. I don't think it ever really hit me until several years later when those four precious little girls were killed in the 16th Street Baptist Church bombing in Birmingham. I remember how hard that hit me. These were kids around my age, killed doing something I did every Sunday all of my life (attend church). I remember thinking "how could someone do that?" I didn't understand it.

Being at a racially mixed school for the first time was a pleasant experience in terms of my fellow students, although I wasn't that fond of my teacher Mrs. Magnusen. Mrs. Magnusen was the first Caucasian teacher I had in elementary school. All of us kids used to call her "Maggie," (behind her back of course).

She certainly was not the friendliest teacher that I had ever experienced, and she was very stern and angry looking all the time. In truth, she was downright mean! The school system in Philadelphia was not on the same level as DC's. DC students had already begun to study algebra and I didn't have a clue what it was. Also, coming in the middle of the semester meant that I had missed a lot of the fundamental concepts. They had started preliminary studies of algebra in the fifth grade, but it seemed like Greek to me.

Math has always been my worst subject. It never made sense to me. I didn't understand it, nor did I want to understand it. When we finished fractions in elementary school I was done and never learned much in math after that. I could go no further. So, coming to DC, seeing that my new classmates were working on algebraic equations, was quite a shock to me. I was embarrassed of not understanding any of the fundamental concepts while everyone else did. So I suffered in silence. Mrs. Magnusen had no mercy on me, despite the fact that I was from another city and had never experienced that form of math. She seemed not to care as I struggled. She would call me to the board to work an equation and glare at me as I made a fool of myself. This made me dislike her even more. As I look back I think I may have been dealing with ADD unknowingly. In fact, years later as an adult, I was all but diagnosed with it. I remember when someone would try to explain something to me that I didn't understand, I could hear their voice but it was so difficult for me to comprehend what they were saying. It was like the words were hitting me in my face and falling to the ground, as opposed to entering my ears and being processed by my brain. I could hear the words and see the person, but it was like my brain would just tune out. I had no control over it. However, the minute that the subject changed to music or something else that I had great interest in, it's like my brain would click back into motion. I still deal with that from time to time even today. Of course, back then no one knew what ADD or ADHD was. I have no idea how I even passed the sixth grade, other than by the grace and mercy of God. I had always gotten good grades in school and was a B-plus student, but when I got to DC my grades began to fall to average and below average. I'm sure we must have taken some kind of music class in sixth grade, but I don't have much memory of it. I vaguely remember learning a song for graduation. That's about it. All I wanted to do was get out of that school and out of Mrs. Magnusen's class.

All of that, combined with beatings from my father (which had become quite commonplace), began the initiation of my anxiety. Moving to a new place where the schoolwork was so advanced, I started to become anxious whenever I had to go to school. Sometimes I'd get sick at the stomach in the mornings or have excruciating stomach aches, knowing I had to go. Mom took me to the doctor but they couldn't find anything wrong. I began to dread school. Whereas I was an A and B student all my life, my grades began to drop which was embarrassing to me. I felt dumb, less than the other students, and out of place. This anxiety started a pattern that would last through much of my public schooling and continue into adulthood.

One of the things that excited me about staying at my Aunt Netha's house was that they had a TV. I had never had one, but loved watching it at friends' and neighbors' houses all of my life. Here, once I got home from school, I could go down in the basement and watch all of the shows that I loved. I think my favorite had to be Superman. I even dressed like him for Halloween when I went trick-or-treating. I wanted to be him.

I longed for his powers! I've jumped off many a bed, cape flying in the wind, hoping some way I would take off through the air. So, for a time my family and I had a wonderful time watching TV together in the basement of my Aunt's home. Uncle Tom, her husband, was a really nice guy, very quiet and mild mannered and didn't have much to say. Aunt Netha on the other hand was the opposite: outgoing, loved a good time, sweet, but could turn on you at the drop of a hat.

One day I came home from school and went down to the basement to turn on the TV. The sound came on but there was no picture. It was working perfectly the night before as we all had watched it before bedtime. When my Aunt Netha came home and found it wasn't working, she was furious. She said nothing to Mom or me about it, but lit into my father. She said this TV was her husband Tom's "hobby" as the basement was his sanctuary, and insinuated without actually saying it that either my Mom or I had broken it. Clearly, looking back, the picture tube had simply blown and no one had anything to do with that. But that caused an uncomfortable interaction between her and my parents, so they immediately sped up the search for a place of our own. To add insult to injury, my beloved cat Smokey ran away. I always thought he was trying to get back to Philly where he was familiar and felt at home. We never found him and I was heartbroken. We ended up moving, soon after, to NE Washington: 705 10th Street to be exact. It was a one-bedroom, upstairs apartment in a row house.

The Christmas of '59 was one of the poorest Christmases we had ever had until that point. I remember we couldn't afford a Christmas tree. So mom, not to be outdone, took Christmas cards and arranged them in the shape of a Christmas tree and taped them to the wall. Earlier in a hardware store around the corner on H St NE, I had seen a magic show and a toy truck that transported cars. That's what I wanted for Christmas. I have no idea how Mom did it, but on Christmas morning under the Christmas card tree, there were the toys I had asked for. Christmas was one of Mom's favorite times of the year and she always made sure it was festive and great, at least as much as she could. As a kid, I thought Santa Claus was the most exciting person in the world. Mom went on letting me believe that someone with a red suit and beard was bringing me the toys. I could never understand how he got in the house, because we never had a chimney. Mom assured me that she left the door unlocked for him. At the same time, I was an avid lover of comic books, with super heroes like Superman and Batman being my favorite. I loved other ones like Dennis the Menace also. In any case, I remember being in the 2nd or 3rd grade and reading a Dennis the Menace comic book in which Dennis' father dressed up as Santa Claus in order to fool his son into thinking there really was one. Panic hit me! Were they insinuating that there was no such thing? I remember running to Mom and asking, "Mom!!! Is there REALLY a Santa Claus??" She paused, looked at me, smiled and said, "It's time for you to know. No, there isn't." I was crushed! My little fantasy and dreams shattered. However, Mom still always managed to make Christmas the best time of my life, even after I found out the truth. She loved Christmas!

Soon my father found another place a couple of blocks up the street at 1201 I Street NE. There was a storefront on the first floor and over it was a two-bedroom apartment. We moved in soon after and he started a church on the first floor. It was called White Stone Baptist Church. During this period, I met some of the closest friends of my life, some of whom are still very close to my heart. It was a great community with many kids my age living all around me. Mom and Dad would go from house to house in the neighborhood and talk to the parents about letting their kids come to Sunday school. They figured if they could get the kids interested in church, then the kids in turn would eventually convince their parents to come. Mom had such a rapport with kids and they followed her like the pied piper. The genuine love that she showed them, the kindness, and the way that she cared was second to none. To many she became like a second mother. To some she became the mother that they never had.

Being an only child, sometimes it was a little difficult for me because I was fiercely protective of Mom and felt that she belonged to me only! But I soon realized I had a Mom that I had to share with many. It was a part of who she was, and it was a part of what she was called to do. She later told me that when she was a little girl Jesus appeared to her in a vision and told her that she would "spread sunshine" to many people during her lifetime. It was exactly what she did. I remember I used to think that everyone's mother had an outgoing and loving personality, because that's what moms do. But after meeting some of my friends' moms, I soon realized that I had someone really unique and really special for a Mother.

The church filled up with kids, most of whom were around my age. The great part is that they all lived in the community and became my playmates and closest friends. It seemed like there were so many big families around me. There was the Givens family on the corner across the street. There was the Brown family and the Jones family around the corner, who both had huge families. Then there were smaller families like Sandy and Tarbara, the Irving sisters down the street who lost their Mom when they were quite young and were being raised by their aunts. My Mom became like a surrogate mother to them. There were the Days who lived around the corner, Barbara and Calvin. Calvin was one of my hanging buddies. He was killed years later in the Vietnam War. The Wrights lived down the street and around the corner on H Street. Valerie and John, or "Butch" as we called him, were brother and sister and used to fight like cats and dogs. Mom played the role of referee and peacemaker between those two for many years. I think that sometimes Mom was the only reason they didn't kill each other, although they loved each other to life. Val and John's cousins, the Samplers, lived several blocks down on 10th St. Not far from us was a little section called Trinidad. Up there lived families like Brenda and her brother Ventress, the Jenkinses, and yet another set of Browns who were their cousins. We all became like a big family.

Many of them I ended up going to school with and all of them ended up attending White Stone Baptist Church. Most of the ones around my age ended up in the choir I formed which sang for Sunday Morning Service. I was 11 years old and had put together a first-rate kids' choir. Those kids could really sing! I delighted in putting together harmonies and instructing them on what to sing. I remember that we did a lot of Roberta Martin and a lot of Clara Ward, as well as other standard gospel songs that I would rearrange to fit their voices. However, my Dad was insistent that along with the gospel songs, we had to do one or two hymns per Sunday. I am thankful for him instilling those great songs of the church in me. It shaped so much of my musical development.

My father had a big, ancient-looking limousine that he bought from a funeral home. He would pile all of us kids into the car and carry us around with him on his preaching engagements. We'd invariably get treated to ice cream after many of those engagements. In fact, many times he would take whatever little "love offering" he would get from preaching and feed all of us.

The unexplainable beatings by my father continued. The resentment inside me started to grow. It was a very strange feeling: love on one hand, but on the other hand resentment and fear of him. I remember once he and I were in the kitchen looking at the family photo album. He was sitting and I was standing, leaning on him. There was a particular photo of me as an infant, sitting on a blanket in the yard, crying. My face was "torn up" and it was clear that I was displeased about something. My dad looked at the photo and said to me, "I don't like that picture." Surprised I asked, "Why not Daddy?" His reply was, "I don't like the face you're making." Still not understanding his disdain for the picture, I asked again. "Why daddy? I was only crying and I was just looking like this" I said, and then began to emulate the face in the picture. I remember he looked at me with intense anger, and suddenly he slapped me across the room. I remember feeling so confused through the tears, wondering, "What in the world could I have done to warrant him hitting me?" I hadn't done anything. More and more I began to sense that on some level, at times he didn't like me. Mom used to hammer that bible verse into my head as a child, "Honor thy mother and father that thy days may be longer upon the land which the Lord thy God giveth thee." I used to think that I wouldn't live past 16 or so. How could I honor someone who treated me like that?

Another time, Mom wasn't feeling well. She was our chaperone and usually oversaw my choir rehearsals. My father instructed me to call the entire choir and tell them that rehearsal had been canceled. I was sitting at the desk going through the list calling everyone. He was standing over me listening to the conversation. He instructed me to tell the kids that rehearsal was canceled because Mom wasn't feeling well—I'm not sure if I got tired of going into detail with every choir member, because

I have always been strong willed—However, I inadvertently didn't mention that Mom was ill to one of the members and the minute that I hung up, he slapped me so hard that I fell out of the chair and onto the floor. He grabbed his belt and grabbed me and just started to beat me. I didn't think he was going to stop. I remember crawling on the floor trying to get away, trying to get up, but he just kept beating. The blows became more and more severe. At some point I was able to get up and run to the bathroom. I slammed the door and locked it as he continued to rant outside the door. Moments later he left the house. I still didn't come out of the bathroom. I was crying and furious that he would beat me like that, and still unsure of what I had done that merited that kind of beating. Sometimes, I would think maybe I deserved it on some level, and must have been missing the point as to exactly why.

A half hour later, he came back, but I was still locked in the bathroom. I remember him knocking on the door telling me that he had bought me some ice cream, and asking if I wanted any. I remember telling him no and wondering why he was now trying to be nice to me after just beating me only a half hour earlier. It was like he realized he was wrong, and in some way was trying to make it up to me. Honestly, sometimes the love and hate emotions inside me for him would confuse me so much. I began to want to rebel. Whatever he told me to do, I wanted to do the opposite. I also felt guilty and condemned for not liking him. After all, he was my father. At the same time, there were still the feelings of wanting his approval and wanting his love. At times my feelings were so confused and conflicted that I didn't know how I felt about him.

CHAPTER 8

THE ROUGH DAYS AND THE GREAT MEMORIES

In March of 1960 I wrote in my journal, "Sometimes our family doesn't have money to buy bread." Throughout my lifetime, we went through some very poor times. There were times that I probably didn't realize just how poor we were. I can't remember what city it was. However, I remember my father moving us into a dilapidated store on the first floor that, of course, he planned to fix up and turn into another church. There was a two-room apartment on the second floor. It was basically a kitchen, a bedroom and a bathroom. I remember the kitchen being infested with roaches. Newspapers covered the windows because we had no blinds or shades. I remember having an aversion to pork and beans because it reminded me of the roach eggs I would see all over the kitchen. We had no furniture of our own, but the top floor was already furnished. In addition to a queen-sized bed, the bedroom had a couch that let out into a bed, which I slept on. After a couple of nights sleeping there, I awoke to find myself covered with bumps. My mother was horrified not knowing what caused it. The next night, she got up in the middle of the night and came over to my bed with a flashlight. I think she must have had an idea of what was happening. When she turned on the flashlight, to her horror, she found that my body was covered with bed bugs. We moved out soon after, but that is still a horrific memory.

Although where we were living then was clean and nice, we hardly had any money. There were times when we had to scrape money together and eat at the Chinese restaurant because our gas was cut off and Mom couldn't cook. However, as long as I had my Mom and my music, nothing else really mattered. I didn't realize what being poor actually was, because I didn't know much of anything else. We were always struggling to make ends meet. I remember bill collectors calling and I would answer the phone and they would tell me that they were going to put my parents in jail, or come and take all of our possessions, including all of mine. That was frightening, because as a child I believed that was something they could do. One thing I can say for my parents is that, very often, they did without so I could have. There has never been a time in my life when I was hungry or went without a meal, no matter how poor we were. I'm sure there were times when they didn't eat so that I could. However, I was never aware. Mom had done domestic work in Philadelphia and she continued it in DC and began working for a lady by the name of Mrs. Clothier.

In 1960, in addition to doing domestic work, my mom got a new job taking the 1960 Census. She was assigned a neighborhood and she went from door to door recording how many people lived in each house or apartment, what their names were and how they were related. During this time, she ran across a family giving away puppies. Imagine my surprise when she brought home a brand-new puppy one day after work. My cat had run away when we first moved to DC, and it had been hard to recover from the loss. But here was a brand-new puppy. Both my Mom and I tried to come up with a plan to explain it to my father who, although he had embraced Smoky the cat, was still not a lover of animals. He certainly was not going to accept a dog. Mom and I came up with a plan that we would tell him a "white lie," that Mrs. Clothier gave it to her as a present and she couldn't return it because that would hurt her boss's feelings. Surely, he wouldn't throw the puppy out if she told him that. I immediately named the puppy Skippy and when my dad came home, before mom and I could explain, the puppy ran under the table and began to bark furiously at my father like he had just broken into the house. "Where did THAT come from?" he exclaimed. Mom began to explain frantically our made-up story about her boss who had given her a puppy and how he wouldn't be a bother. His response to her was, "that thing gotta get outta here!! It's gotta GO!" He wasn't having it. I turned on the waterworks, started crying at the top of my lungs and grabbed the puppy and ran into my room. I'm not sure what Mom told him, but he didn't say anything else about it for the rest of the evening. The next day when my father came home, Skippy greeted him like he was a long lost friend. He seemed to sense that Daddy didn't like him. So it was like he set out to change his mind. Unlike the day before, he jumped, wagged his tail, and had a fit as if Daddy was the greatest thing since sliced bread. My father's eyes grew wider than they already were and he said, "Look at that little thing! He LIKES me!" Daddy began to giggle like he was six years old over the attention he was getting from Skippy. That was it. Skippy was home free. He knew he had a friend for life.

My dad adored him and Skippy became my constant companion until I was well out of college. He was like the little brother I never had. I could always depend on him to give me unconditional love. He never realized that he was a dog. He was about as human as any dog I've ever seen. When he'd hear the ice cream truck he'd beat me to the door, knowing that whatever I bought was going to be partly his. It's funny how recently I found out that chocolate is poisonous to dogs. I never knew that as a kid! When Skippy would follow me to the store, whether I was getting brownies or a chocolate bar, he ate half of whatever chocolate I got, and he never got sick.

He was a great watchdog as well, and no one came within three feet of the house without us knowing it. He was fiercely protective of all of us, but at the same time he loved everyone he met. In the summer especially, I carried him everywhere I went. Many summer mornings we'd all go fishing down at Haines Point. That's when the water was clean and safe. Mom would make bait out of cornmeal and cheese. I'm sure her dad must have taught her to make it when she was a child. I'm not sure why, but the fish would tear it up. I'd usually end up catching more fish than everyone else. Skippy would make friends with everyone in the vicinity, and by the time we were ready to go home he knew everyone and everyone knew him. For many years, he was an integral part of my life and the life of my family.

In 1957, about four years before we moved to DC, my cousin Robert Clements (Bessie's son and Cousin Lula's grandson) moved from Durham to D.C. and married a beautiful 19-year-old from Rocky Mount, NC named Rosa Stanley. She and my Mom both had hair down their backs. I remember the first time I saw her, thinking how beautiful she was. About five years after they were married, Robert and Rosa had two sons, 18 months apart. The oldest was Michael and the second was Robert, named after his dad. When they were small, Michael began to call his little brother "DeDe" because he couldn't pronounce Robert, and that nickname stuck with him until today. Robert and his family would visit the churches and our homes. Sometimes Mom would go and see Rosa and the kids. I don't ever remember Dad visiting with us, but the visits were frequent.

Somewhere around the end of the sixth grade and the beginning of the seventh, I decided to start a gospel group. I longed to sing in musicals around town and emulate my favorite gospel singers. I knew that in the White Stone choir I had the talent to realize this dream. So I approached Mom and my father about it. They approved, so I picked ten kids from the choir. Since most of my gospel music idols were named after a family or the leader of the group, I decided on the Richard Smallwood Singers. I approached brother and sister John and Val Wright, along with their cousin Veronica Sampler, the Irving sisters Sandy and Tarbara, Minnie Givens and Brenda Jenkins, along with her cousin Shirley Brown and Barbara Day and Lelar Jones.

They were as excited as I was and we immediately began rehearsals. We were all between the ages of 10 and 14. We had a big debut at the church one Sunday afternoon, and before you knew it, word began to spread and we began to sing all over town! If we weren't piled into the limo with the choir going from church to church with my father, we were piled in with the Smallwood Singers, going from musical to musical. There was another kids' group called the Spiritualettes with whom we sang on programs quite a bit. They were the kids and relatives of Rev. Edgar Williams, who was a friend of my father's. We were somewhat of a novelty, because a little kid my age playing the piano and directing a kid's ensemble was quite unheard of. People seemed to love to hear us sing. One of the top religious radio announcers in the D.C. area, Madame Lucille Banks Robinson, who was quite the celebrity in the area, heard us and began to invite us to her many musicals. She would have a huge birthday musical every year and she would invite local, popular gospel artists as well as national artists. We were always on the bill. She would call Mom and say, "Mrs. Smallwood, I want Richard and the children on my musical." When Madame Robinson called, you answered, and we were only too happy to oblige. During that time she ruled the airways. I think that was the beginning of my exposure in the D.C. area, because we traveled around the city so much. We'd also sing for Colonel Ed Brown, another very popular gospel religious announcer in the D.C. area. Somewhere around this time, I thought I'd try my hand at writing again. I hadn't really written anything since "Richard's Lullaby," when I was in Philly. I wrote a song called "Sinner, Confess your Sins," my second serious attempt at songwriting. It became a little hit and we began to sing it everywhere we went. I wanted to write more songs, but for some reason there seemed to be something missing. As hard as I would try, the songs just didn't sound right to me when I tried to write again.

***

In June of 1960, I graduated from Stanton Elementary School. After moving from my aunt's home to NE Washington, I had to catch a trolley car over to SE Anacostia every morning. We never told them that I had moved, so I got to attend the same school even though it was out of my zone. Now, moving to Jr. High school, I would be attending a school that was close, which was a relief to me. In the fall I entered Browne Jr. High. As time went on, my grades continued to fall. It was hard to concentrate and some of the major courses were hard to understand. Although

I began to make friends, and although I had my White Stone family members who attended with me, my anxiety about school got worse. The stomachaches, headaches and being sick on school mornings continued. Just the thought of having to go, made the pain even more intense and terrified me. Mom began to keep me home more and more, due to sickness. However, the moment I knew I didn't have to go to school, the pain would go away. At the end of my seventh grade year I had to go to summer school for a Math Lab. Math continued to be my worst subject. I feel like I never caught up after moving to DC from Philly.

Mr. Stinson was the principal of Browne Jr. High and no one liked him much. He tried to run the school like a prison, it seemed. One day during the winter of my eighth grade year, I was leaving my locker soon after getting to school. I had so many books and other junk in my locker that when I closed it, the top and the middle lock caught, but the bottom one didn't. I didn't realize it and went on to my homeroom class. Mr. Stinson discovered that it wasn't completely closed and called me down to his office. He berated me about not closing the locker completely, and as punishment he took my locker away for a period of time. This meant that in the middle of winter I had to carry my coat, all six or more books, and my book bag with my notebook and whatever else I had, to all of my classes. Then I had to carry them all home, whether I had homework or not. Somehow, during that time, I lost my French book. By this time, I didn't care. My grades weren't good. I never wanted to go. I couldn't understand some of the subjects, especially Math, and I felt overwhelmed and beaten down. The anxiety became almost unbearable. I think this is when depression started to manifest. But who knew what depression or anxiety was? I certainly didn't. I'd never heard of it.

The only shining light at Browne Jr. High was music. Mrs. Smith was my seventh grade music teacher. She was an older lady, but I loved being in her class and learning the songs that she taught. In eighth grade, we got a young, exciting, fun-loving music teacher by the name of Roberta Flack. Roberta had recently graduated from Howard University and Browne was one of her early teaching assignments before she ventured into the music business. I loved her. I loved to hear her sing and I loved to hear her play. She was young and she was "hip." She taught us exciting songs to which we could relate. Her playing was upbeat and she used exciting new chords that I hadn't heard before. I would go home and play everything exactly as I heard her play it. By then I had become quite an accomplished pianist for a kid. Ms. Flack's class was undoubtedly my favorite. Of course, years later, jazz pianist Les McCann would discover Roberta playing at Mr. Henry's, a restaurant/club on Capitol Hill. That would lead to a record contract with Atlantic Records and the rest is history.

I also had a huge crush on my homeroom teacher Miss Hunter, but she eventually married a fellow Browne teacher and became Mrs. Ailier, which I wasn't happy about. When report cards came out at the end of my eighth grade year, I was devastated. Not only did my grades fall even more, but I was also informed that I would have to repeat the entire eighth grade. I felt dumb, defeated and worthless. How would I tell my mother? She would KILL me. What would my classmates say who had all been promoted to the next grade? What would my friends say? I was embarrassed, and most of all, I felt like a failure. That final day of school, the walk home seemed like the longest ever, knowing I had to face my Mom. Mom was a loving person, but she didn't take any mess when it came to discipline. Plus, I felt

I had disappointed her. When I finally got home and gave the report card to Mom, and between my tears explained what had happened, her response was surprisingly different than I thought it would be. She told me that I would have to work harder than I'd ever worked before, and that she believed in me and knew that I could do it. To keep from having to go back to Browne and deal with the embarrassment of facing my fellow students, she said she would look into the possibility of transferring me to another school while I was out for the summer. I don't remember what my father said about it. I don't think he said much of anything. By this time, the rift between my Aunt Netha and my parents had cleared up, and she began to come over for dinner as if nothing had happened. In fact, Aunt Netha became one of my biggest allies throughout the rest of her life. I remember later, during one of the poor Christmases we had, her gift to me was my very first reel-to-reel tape recorder. You couldn't tell me I wasn't a recording artist, as I would tape song after song, me singing and playing the latest gospel songs.

Summer was the greatest time in that NE community. If the White Stone crew was not at my house, then we were out skating, playing or going somewhere together. The Atlas Theater was right around the corner on H Street. For fifty cents on Saturday you could see a cartoon, a double feature, and watch them over and over all day until the theater closed. By the end of the day, we'd know all the dialogue to the movies, and the theme songs. I loved when horror movies came to the Atlas and I delighted in scaring the girls who were already traumatized by watching the horror features. I remember seeing *Imitation of Life* there, a movie that was so sad that the ushers passed out tissues to everyone in the theater. By the time Mahalia Jackson began singing, "Soon I Will Be Done," there was mass weeping, wailing and gnashing of teeth all throughout the theater. There wasn't a dry eye in the place.

There were our favorite eating places, like the convenience store around the corner on H Street, where you could get penny candy, your favorite candy bar, Utz Potato Chips and Ne-Hi or Rock Creek Sodas, which had every flavor imaginable. In the opposite direction on H Street was the little family-owned bakery which had the best brownies on the planet. I'd go around and get a whole dozen and eat every one. Sometimes they'd throw some extra in and give me a baker's dozen since I was a regular customer. Further down the street was Miles Long who had the best cheesesteaks anywhere, along with piping hot crinkle fries covered with salt pepper and catsup. High's Ice Cream was down on the corner where you could get a hand-dipped, single scoop, double scoop or triple scoop cone of butter brickle ice cream, or any flavor that you desired. Of course, two of my favorite things was going to Circle Music a couple of blocks down and spending hours going through the record bins for the latest gospel record. Woolworth's five and ten cent store had just as large a collection of records and I would spend hours browsing and listening to Sam Cooke, Otis Redding and all the R&B artists blasting over the loud speakers and all the music that I wasn't allowed to listen to at home. H Street was the place! Every summer there was a carnival that would come to Benning Road at a vacant lot which was right across from Spingarn High School. We'd walk down H Street to Benning Road and would ride the carnival rides all day, go through the scary house screaming at the top of our lungs and eat cotton candy and hot dogs and check out the freak shows like the Snake Woman and the 500 pound woman. It didn't take much to entertain us. Sometimes we'd walk down to the Union Station, get in the picture booths and take crazy pictures for twenty-five cents. They also had recording booths, which cost 50 cents. You could stand in the booth and sing, talk or whatever you wanted to do. The booth would record what you did and once you finished, a record would come out of the slot that you could take home and play. I did a couple of those, one with my friend Brenda Jenkins and one by myself. It's funny to hear how I sounded before my voice changed. I sometimes hated my voice being so high and as I got older, I was embarrassed by it. I didn't think it would ever change. I was pretty small in stature. I was bullied occasionally, but this one particular guy much larger than I started pushing me around once, making fun of my high voice. My friend John, or "Butch" as we called him, who was a part of the Smallwood Singers was older, bigger and much taller than I. Butch was known to fight, and when he got wind that I had been picked on because of my voice, Butch went looking for the perpetrator. Once he found him, he threatened to wipe up the entire playground with him and began to prepare to do so. The bully made a hasty exit and he never picked on me again. Actually, later we ended up becoming friends. The White Stone crew did have one odd pastime that we still can't explain. Some Sunday afternoons, if we didn't have anywhere to sing, we'd walk to Mt Olivet Cemetery after dinner, which was up the street. We'd play there until it looked like it may get dark soon and we'd race out the gate before the darkness caught us. I'm not sure what that was about. I always had a fear of dead people. Maybe it was a way to try to conquer my fear. I'm not sure. But we'd play tag, read the tombstones and the dates. There was one tombstone with the name Foy Tucker inscribed on it. For some reason to 11- and 12-year-olds, the name Foy seemed the funniest thing in the world. We began to make fun of the name, mocking it and running around the cemetery. Minutes later after laughing at the name we looked back towards the tombstone and there was a man dressed in all black standing there looking at us. Someone screamed "OH MY GOD! IT'S FOY TUCKER"!! And we all ran screaming out the entrance and down the street towards where we lived, swearing that Foy had come back from the grave to get us for laughing at his name.

Another time, we found a small building with an unlocked door. Someone dared someone else to open the door and of course we did and found a closed casket on the inside. We pushed Brenda through the door where the casket was sitting, closed the door and all piled on the door holding it shut so she couldn't get out. I'm not sure where Brenda got the strength from, but she came barreling out of that door knocking all of us asunder hollering to the top of her lungs as we all were bent over laughing hysterically at her. If we weren't doing any of those things, we were playing church. Butch would usually be the preacher and I of course on the piano although sometimes I would be the guest speaker. The rest of the kids were either singing or shouting. We were some weird and crazy kids. As I look back on that part of my childhood, those had to be some of the most fun times of my life. We had no cares, no worries and it was all about playing and having fun with each other. It was a wonderful period.

Around this time, The Roberta Martin Singers would come and run "revivals" at the Bible Way Church pastored by Bishop Smallwood E. Williams. All my life people thought that he and I were related in some way. But Bishop's first name was Smallwood, not his last. The Martin Singers would come into D.C. on Sunday mornings and appear on Bible Way's broadcast as a way of advertising that they were in town. Starting on Monday nights, going through Friday, they would do free concerts every night. Only a free will offering was required. The lines would go down the street and around the corner to get into the church. Mom would take me every year and sometimes some of the White Stone crew would go as well. By this time Archie Dennis, a fiery incredible baritone with a great range, had replaced Romance Watson. Still in place were Gloria, Norsalus, Eugene and Lucy at the piano. This was the configuration that would come every year. I would always try to sit on the piano side or as close to it as I could so I could watch Lucy. She was my idol. She had a style that no one could duplicate. Little by little, I began to notice that my approach to gospel piano took on more and more of Lucy's pianistic characteristics. After a while, I noticed that I didn't even have to think about it much, but so many aspects of her piano stylings automatically began to merge into mine. When they were in town I would go almost every night. I couldn't get enough of the sound of the Martin Singers. I bought up every picture that they had on sale and got autographs. Every recording and every songbook that was available, I took home with me. I began to try to teach the Smallwood Singers the Martin approach to phrasing and dynamics. Still loving the Davis Sisters and The Stars of Faith who were the former Ward Singers, The Martin Singers took their rightful place and became the third of the three influential singing groups in my life during that time.

CHAPTER 9

THE ELEPHANT IN THE ROOM

One day, my mother approached me and said she needed to talk to me about something very important. I remember sitting on the living room couch. She said that she needed to talk to me about something "adult." As I look back, this was a big deal. We very seldom talked about "deep stuff" in my family. Many things were just left unsaid. Sometimes the proverbial elephant was in the room, and although everyone may have seen it, no one acknowledged it. I would understand some of the reason for that much later in life. Mom continued by telling me that my father had sexually molested one of my little female friends, a member of our church. Most of our information about sexual matters at that age was very limited. Most of our parents never talked to us about it and a lot of the things that we learned were from rumors, myths, whatever we could learn in the street and information that was passed around by our friends and classmates. There were no videos, no cable channels or sexually explicit recordings, so it was a very mysterious subject and we were naïve about a lot of things. However, I knew that this was bad and that it was very wrong. I remember feeling shocked and bad for my friend. I also remember feeling fear as to what would come from this. Mom continued that she would have to go and talk to my friend's guardian and wasn't sure how this was going to turn out. That's the last I heard about it. My friend didn't leave the church and she and I never mentioned it. Mom didn't mention it again. I didn't understand at the time that clearly my father was a very sick man and this was usually not a "one time" thing, but a horrible illness and addiction.

Years later, after we were all grown, we had a reunion of most of the original "baby" Smallwood Singers. As we sat eating dinner, I began to explain the vision that I had for writing my autobiography. Everyone was so excited and encouraging. Before our reunion was done, I got up the nerve to talk about my father and his "problem." I asked if he had ever sexually molested any of them when we were children. Two people raised their hands. Tears welled up in my eyes. I was shocked. I was embarrassed. I was furious with him. I started apologizing. I felt responsible in some kind of way. They assured me that it wasn't my fault, which realistically I knew it wasn't. However, there was still something inside me that made me feel guilty about his actions, even though I had done nothing wrong. At the same time, even with this discovery, even with the physical abuse, there was a part of me that loved him. There were so many conflicting emotions continuing inside me. How could I love someone that did these terrible things? Did that make me a bad person? Later I would find out about more molestations that happened around the same time during the White Stone era. The more I heard, the more it sickened and embarrassed me, and the more upset I became. I also kept feeling responsible.

Thinking back on the many poor and lean times we had, we were blessed that we were never homeless. Even when we had to leave where we were living at the time, we immediately moved to another place. I'm sure our credit must have been horrendous and how we were able to continue to get into the next home or apartment I have no idea, other than the grace of God. I just know that even in all that was going on, God still had His hand on us, and definitely had His hand on me. I didn't know it then, but He had a calling on my life, an assignment that had been predestined before the world was formed. I knew as a kid what I wanted to do and I never wanted to do anything else. I wanted to be a gospel artist. But never in a billion years did I ever think that I would realize such a dream. It seemed too far-fetched and a goal too unrealistic to even think about reaching.

During this time, my piano lessons were sporadic. I don't think we could find someone that suited me for what I needed, and probably couldn't afford it. For a short time, I took piano from a really nice lady named Mary Lacy Moore. Basically, she taught me gospel songs and hymns. I had been playing those since I was six or seven years old, so it wasn't a challenge to me and I found myself bored. I remember she had a house full of kids and whenever I went for my lessons there were kids all over the place. It wasn't too long before I stopped my lessons and for a time I continued on my own.

I'm not entirely sure what happened with White Stone Baptist Church. I think my father fell behind on the rent for the church, as well as our home, and ended up losing it. Our congregation was pretty small, but it was like family. At the same time, kids can't financially support a church. We did have some adult members, but not a lot of them as I recall. I just remember that we had to move again. That was basically the end of White Stone Baptist Church. For a short time after we moved out of that building, we congregated in a basement at The Stoddard Baptist Home on Maryland Ave. N. E. For a short while, my dad was called to pastor Christ Memorial Baptist Church. It wasn't that far from Bible Way. Some of the Whitestone Crew began attending there but we didn't stay there very long. Later he started the Montello Ave. Baptist Church but by then I was playing elsewhere. He later gave it up for some reason to a Rev. Eugene Wright who assumed the role as pastor. Some of the members stayed there while some merged with our sister church, the Solid Rock Baptist Church down the street from old White Stone, pastored by Rev. Nehemiah Rhinehart. Others went elsewhere. We however moved to 419 14th Street NE on the corner of 14th and Duncan Streets. It was a three bedroom, two level house, and the first full sized house we had lived in, since we had moved from Philly.

Even though it was a little walk from my old community, I was heartbroken that I wasn't as close in proximity to my old family. However, many of them would come over to see Mom who was like a second Mom to many. I made some new friends in that community but it was never the same as the old White Stone crew. In the fall, I entered a new school and started the eighth grade all over again at Eliot Junior High School. Eliot was the complete opposite of Browne. For me, it was a much more pleasant atmosphere. The principal Mrs. Dotson (who we called turkey legs behind her back) was a really nice person. Mrs. Georgia Mills Jessup was my homeroom teacher. Mrs. Jessup was an art teacher and a professional artist as well. Years later, she would become a very important figure and make important contributions to African American art. I loved her. She was pretty and she recognized my creative side and always encouraged me. My Spanish teacher was Mrs. Regina Jervay. Unlike French, I loved Spanish and it seemed to come so easy to me. Mrs. Jervay was a fascinating and loving teacher whom I adored. Of course, the teacher probably who had the most influence on me had to be Mrs. Joyce Leibowitz, my new 8th grade music teacher. She was the first Caucasian teacher I had since Mrs. Magnusen in the 6th grade. But unlike her, Mrs. Leibowitz was one of the most loving, caring teachers I had met. She immediately put me to work when she discovered my talent, playing for the choirs and playing for her classes. She also had a knack for getting me out of classes to come spend the period in her room to help her, which I loved. Math was still not my friend and I hated gym because I was such a klutz and would fall over my own feet. I had no coordination unless it was playing the piano. I don't think I had an athletic bone in my body although I always wanted to. Mrs. Lee as we fondly called her, would get me out of those classes many times and I would end up playing for her classes while she taught the class different songs. Mrs. Lee would put on these amazing spring festivals and Christmas programs where the choirs would sing and I would play. I learned so many pop standards by composers like Cole Porter and tunes from Broadway Musicals by Rogers and Hammerstein. Sometimes she would let me do piano solos as well. The most important thing is that she really encouraged me in music. However, at times she would pull me aside and say, "Richard you have to give optimum effort in the subjects that may not be easy to you as well." My grades began to climb across the board, although I don't think my Math ever got above a C. My Mom even got one of my friends to tutor me who was quite the genius in Math, to no avail. It just absolutely made no sense to me and I hated it. I remember a Math teacher, who could not understand my confusion when it came to anything mathematic, saying to me, "You excel in music and music is one of the highest forms of math." I remember thinking, well maybe if you sing it or play it, I'll get it. Another thing about Eliot is that I found students who were just as interested in music as I was. They even loved classical music too! We all became close and soon formed a "music club" that would take turns hosting meetings on the weekends at our different homes. Two of my best friends at Eliot, Rufus Wright and Michael Evans, played clarinet and flute respectively. I loved to accompany them on the piano on their different instrumental concertos, and we would rehearse and rehearse at my house for the next assembly at school. It was during this time that I also discovered something about myself that I wasn't completely aware of. My best friend Michael Evans would have me turn my back to the piano and he would play a note or sometimes a chord and I could identify each note he was playing. I had something called "absolute pitch" or "perfect pitch." It simply meant that I could identify every note that was being played without looking. I vaguely remembered in Philly that I could always tell what notes Mrs. Robinson was playing without looking at her fingers. I would also remember seeing colors when she would play a note on her piano, with G being a bright orange. I just thought it was something everyone could do and didn't give it much thought. I guess that was the reason why I had been able to pick up music that I heard so quickly and accurately all of my life. I also began to take piano lessons again. My Mom found a teacher who was very popular in our community by the name of Bernard Barbour. Mr. Barbour was a wonderful person who challenged me in continuing with formal lessons. He gave many recitals in which I participated. I remember times when my parents didn't have the money to send me to my lesson. They would call Mr. Barbour telling him I wouldn't be able to come because they were short on money that week. His response would always be, "Don't you dare keep Richard home because of that! Send him right on to lessons. I'll be waiting." He was such an encouragement to me, and one of my biggest cheerleaders. However, like all of my previous teachers, I continued to fool him into thinking that I could read. I had gotten really good at that! My ear began to get stronger and stronger, and there was hardly any song that I couldn't duplicate on the piano if I heard it once.

Around this time, Mom began to do domestic work for a new lady named Mrs. Hardy. Mrs. Hardy was a widow and had three or four children. As I recall, her girls were older than I, but she had a son that was right around my age. So during the summer when I was out of school, Mom would take me to work with her. I loved going to Mrs. Hardy's home. It was located in Chevy Chase, MD, and it was unlike any home I'd ever been in. Her son and I became friends very quickly. We'd play all day while Mom would clean. It was a bit strange though, now that I look back on it, that everyone including the children called Mom "Mabel." I was always taught that one should address adults by "Mr. or Mrs.," followed by their last name. But it was a different time in the 60's. However, the Hardy family treated Mom like she was a part of their family. Many times, the kids would confide in Mom about their problems and their issues. Wherever Mom was, and whomever she met, she would always become that confidant, or that person you could talk to. Mrs. Hardy's husband had been an exec at Columbia Records. Columbia at that time was one of the major labels that recorded and released sound tracks from Broadway shows and movies. So, the Hardy family owned a huge library of this genre. While Mom was working, Mrs. Hardy would give me free reign to explore and listen to her extensive collection of Broadway Music. I was listening to "The Sound of Music," "Carousel," "Camelot," "My Fair Lady" and soundtracks from other Broadway musicals. I fell in love with that kind of music. Rogers and Hammerstein's songs had incredible melodies, great harmonic progressions, and incredible lyrics and once again, as other genres had done, this new type of music began to take hold of my mind and my ear. I began to love this genre so much that I joined the Columbia Record Club and every month I would get either a new Broadway recording, a movie score or a Classical album. My love for music and different styles began to grow even more. God was still laying the foundation for the kind of music I would write. I really learned how to write with the melody being the most important thing. Harmony was the second most important, and lastly the beat. Of course, good solid lyrics were always of prime importance. Now a lot of composers write from beats, and the beat dictates what the song sounds like. Because a good solid melody was so important in pop, classical and show tunes then, it became of prime importance to me when I started to create my own music.

My ear was also leaning toward new music that I wasn't allowed to listen to in the house. That was Motown. Owner Berry Gordy had a roster of young artists on his label that I loved. Artists like the Temptations, The Marvelettes, Mary Wells, Martha and the Vandellas, Little Stevie Wonder, The Miracles, The Four Tops and The Supremes were blowing up on the radio. Their popularity was spreading all over the country and abroad. I seemed to sense a kind of sophistication about their music that other secular music didn't have. Three young men - Holland, Dozier and Holland - quickly became my favorite composers from the Motown family. The harmonic progressions they came up with fascinated me because they were different. Modulations or borrowed chords would appear in their songs in unlikely places and it all worked so wonderfully together. That driving Motown beat was infectious and I loved it. However, C.L. Smallwood was not having it in his house. So, for a time I had to listen to it at friends' houses and outside the home. But I felt myself falling in love with this music. Another group around that time that took the world by storm was the Beatles. Although I was never into their performances per se, I began to recognize at some point that they were some incredible writers. "Yesterday," "Hey Jude," "Eleanor Rigby," "The Long and Winding Road" and so many more songs caught my attention. Really good, strong songs with great structure and melody seemed to always catch my ear even as a kid.

Around this time a friend of my Mom and Dad moved to Washington DC. When Dad married Mom and moved her to D.C. in 1934, he was already pastoring The New Hope Baptist Church, which he founded in 1933. Years later it would be renamed the Greater New Hope Baptist Church. His minister of music at that time was Cleavant Derricks Sr., a multi-talented conductor and composer. Years later he would become a well-known writer and pen one of the most famous gospel songs, "Just a Little Talk With Jesus," as well as many other gospel standards. Many years later, Cleavant Derricks was called to the ministry, ordained and began pastoring. Now he was returning to D.C. with his family to pastor the Pleasant Grove Baptist Church in D.C. He was married to an incredible pianist, Carrie Derricks. They had three children, Cleavant Jr and Clinton (identical twins about a year younger than me), and a younger daughter named Lovie Gwendolyn whom everyone called "Tootie." The twins would grow up to become actors. Clinton Derricks-Carroll who was part of the original cast of Vinette Carroll's, "Your Arms Are Too Short To Box With God," and Cleavant who appeared in movies like "Moscow on the Hudson" with Robin Williams as well as starring in the original cast of "Dreamgirls" for which he won a Tony award. Both went on to achieve many accomplishments in the business. I had not been playing for any churches since the end of White Stone, and Rev. Derricks approached my parents and asked could I play for his church, Pleasant Grove. Since his wife Carrie played the piano, he wanted to know if I could play the Hammond B3 Organ. I had never played one in my life. The only organ that I was familiar with was the little "off brand" one that we once had at White Stone. However, I figured if it had keys I could do it. It was just a matter of trying to master the pedals and figure out the registrations. The most exciting thing was that they were going to put me on salary. It would be my first real job. I started playing at Rev. Derricks' church when I was fourteen. What an honor it was. Here was a world-famous composer with whom I would have the pleasure of working. His sons Cleavant and Clinton, whose nicknames were June and Jitterbug, and I became great friends. They shared my love for gospel music and sang as well. Many times we would form a trio and perform for the services at church. At one point, we even wrote a song together called "Jesus Will Make A Way." Already I was hearing progressions that were a little different for that time. I remember Rev. Derricks critiquing the song because, harmonic progression-wise, it started different than most gospel songs. But I would always hear things differently and many times would be misunderstood because of it. It wasn't long before I joined Pleasant Grove Baptist Church. As time began to pass, I started to become more comfortable on the Hammond B3. The choirs were great there and the music was diverse. Although Rev. Derricks was a gospel music composer, he was classically trained, loved anthems and knew them well. Sunday morning worship had to include hymns and anthems as well as gospel. I began to learn some of the standard anthems of the church, such as "Let Mount Zion Rejoice," "Lift Up Your Heads O Ye

Gates," Mozart's "Gloria," Schubert's "The Omnipotence" and Rossini's "Inflamattus." Mrs. Derricks was an inspiration to me, and I marveled at how she could switch from the classic anthems to the latest gospel song without missing a beat on the piano. I would listen to her playing style closely and would emulate some of the things that I would hear her do. She influenced me greatly. I think since the days of Little Lucy Smith, I was always fascinated with women who could really play. One thing I had to do was go home and really practice those anthems. I still didn't read music well, but if I went over them with a fine-tooth comb and practiced hard, as well as depended on my ear, which still picked up everything I heard, I could pull it off. I was not going to be embarrassed when I had to play those songs along with Mrs. Derricks or in front of Rev. Derricks. Rev. Derricks also became the director for the D.C. Chapter of the National Baptist Convention Choir. Mom sang alto in the choir and they gave concerts frequently in the area. I began to play for them as well. Everything musical that Rev. Derricks was involved in, he would take me with him. I grew musically by leaps and bounds. He encouraged me, he challenged me and he pushed me. I remember him telling my Mom one time, referring to me, "That boy can play the horns off a goat!"

By this point, I had become really versed in playing in most of the keys. Of course, the flat keys were always the "gospel keys." However, there was one flat key that terrified me and that was the key of Db. Five flats were just too much for me, and my fingers could not acclimate to the feel of that key. Of course, playing the Hammond organ along with someone else who was playing the piano had its perks. If you weren't sure of a chord or a passage, you could do a "riff," hold a note or a myriad of other things to cover your lack of knowledge. Then you would pick back up with the chords when the part with which you were familiar came back. So whatever song the choir would sing in Db, there was a lot of "riffing" and holding of notes on my part until the song got back to the tonic or the "home chord." One particular night, the Baptist Convention choir was having rehearsal. Unfortunately, Mrs. Derricks was out sick so I was on the piano. Rev. Derricks called for one of those "Db songs" that the choir sang. I can't recall the name. I began to sweat profusely, and my heart began pounding in my head. I was going to be exposed for all to see. I did get through the introduction, but as the song progressed my playing became worse and I stumbled playing wrong chords and accidentals until it fell completely apart. It became obvious to Rev. Derricks and the entire choir that I hadn't a clue what I was doing or what key I was playing in. Rev. Derricks, always the diplomat, stopped the song in the middle and said, "I think we'll go over this one next week," and called out the next song. I was mortified. I'm sure there was a puddle of sweat on and under the piano bench. I went home that night and began to practice in the key of Db. This would NEVER happen to me again. Mrs. Derricks returned at the next rehearsal, but I came back knowing how to play in that key fluently, and it ended up being my favorite key. I was never going to be embarrassed like that again or caught in public not being able to play in Db. How ironic that the key that once terrified me ended up being the key in which I would write "Total Praise," years later.

Somewhere around this time "Peace Be Still" by Rev. James Cleveland and the Angelic Choir of the First Baptist Church of Nutley NJ was released. It swept the nation like a tidal wave. Every choir including ours was singing it. I could emulate note for note what John Hason played on Peace Be Still on the piano. In fact, I became a great admirer of his playing and for a while it influenced my approach to gospel piano playing. Both of the twins could emulate Rev. Cleveland and sound exactly like him, ad-libs and all. Jitterbug would lead it, and it became a hit at the church. Of course I ran out to get the album and my life was changed. I became a James Cleveland fan. I began to collect every album I could find by him. One of the albums that I got by Rev. Cleveland was "The Love of God" with the Voices of Tabernacle of Detroit, Michigan. The song we did at church was on it, the old standard "I Know It Was the Blood." However, unlike the up-tempo traditional version I knew that we sang during Communion, Rev. Cleveland's version had a blues feel to it. Before I heard the actual recording, I marveled at the way Mrs. Derricks would play it on the piano and the jazzy blues riffs she would do on the piano. However, when I heard the actual original recording of it on Rev. Cleveland's album, I realized from where she got it. Whoever was playing the piano on this album was incredible. They had an incredible touch, incredible technique and their approach to playing the piano was unlike anything else I had ever heard in gospel music. Not since Lucy Smith had I heard someone whose playing had such a profound effect on me. I scanned the back of the album looking for the credits. I soon found the name: Pianist, Herbert "Pee Wee" Pickard. I was mesmerized by his playing and frustrated that I couldn't emulate some of the amazing things that he would do on the piano. I soon found out that the album "Peace Be Still" was number three in a series of volumes released by Rev. Cleveland and the Angelic choir. I went back and collected the first two. As time went on, other volumes were released. As I began to listen to some of the later volumes, I realized that the sound of the piano wasn't John Hason any longer, but still sounded very familiar. It was Herbert Pickard. I would play those recordings where he was featured on the piano over and over. I would sit down and practice until I was exhausted. There was one passage on "I Find No Fault," on one of the James Cleveland and the Angelic Choir volumes, where he did a descending chromatic scale in harmony. That was NOT easy. I remember thinking, how did he finger that? How did he come up with those awesome nuances? I remember trying to duplicate every riff, every chord and every run that "Pee Wee" would do on the piano. It's funny how after a while, your influences begin to creep into your playing without your knowledge. They become a part of who you are without you even trying. Eventually it melts into your own individual style and becomes a part of who you are. Somewhere between your influences and the style that you bring to the table, your own unique sound begins to form. I began to become majorly influenced by this great musician.

CHAPTER 10
THE THINGS A LITTLE MONEY CAN BUY

I loved being at Pleasant Grove. I met great friends and I loved the music. I loved how, before the choir would march in every Sunday, the deacons would sing common meter hymns and old devotional songs (some that I'd never heard before). The way the congregation would join in with incredible harmony was wonderful. This style could be traced all the way back to Africa, with the call and response between leader and congregation. There were no accompanying instruments with these songs, just the sound of feet on the wooden floors and handclaps. The Spirit would get so high from these songs that sometimes the choir couldn't get down the aisle to march in because the congregation was in the aisles shouting! Most of the members and their families were originally from the south and they brought these songs with them after moving "up north." It was a glorious thing to hear and behold. Deacon Dawkins, one of the elder deacons in the church, used to sing an old devotional song called "There's a Handwriting on the Wall." The lyrics went on to say, "Come and read it, see what it says." It was taken from the biblical story of the prophet Daniel and King Belshazzar.

Deacon Dawkins would tear up that song every time he sang it. The way the congregation would join in harmony was amazing to me. Everyone just seemed to know how to harmonize in the congregation and how to fit it all together. I had never heard anything like it. I remember how the devotion leaders would "line out" the hymns. In other words, they would sing a couple of the lines of the hymn and then the congregation would fall in with the most amazing harmony in response. I think it might have been one of the first times that I heard the old hymn, "I Love The Lord He Heard My Cry," lined out in that way. Hearing that hymn as much as I did proved very useful to me later on in life.

Another thing that was exciting is that I was getting "paid!" It certainly wasn't a huge salary, but it was the first one I had ever gotten in my life and it was enough to help with my school clothes and buy little things that I wanted or needed. I had always been fashion-conscious, whether I could afford it or not. You weren't allowed to wear jeans when I was in school. Guys had to wear dress pants or khakis and girls had to wear skirts or dresses. Guys in high school were not considered well-dressed unless you had an array of colorful Ban-Lon shirts, several pairs of gabardine pleated pants or "gabs" as we called them and several Kangol caps. Foot joy shoes were the order of the day, or Chuck Taylors when it came to tennis shoes. Cavaliers, on 7th Street NW, near Howard University, was the men's shop to go to when obtaining those latest fashions. With my salary and additional help from Mom, I could buy some of these things.

As a member of the Columbia Record club, there were many times that they would have special offers. One day I noticed they had a ten-inch black and white television for sale if you were a member of the club. You could pay in installments and now that

I had somewhat of an income, I felt that I could swing it. We had never owned one and I had wanted one as far back as I could remember. I approached my Mom about it and she thought it was a great idea, but assured me I would have to be diligent in paying the installments. Within several weeks, my brand new TV came. I can still smell the "new smell" that it had. I think the only thing that ever excited me more at that point, was music. I set it in the living room as opposed to my bedroom so Mom could view it as well. Of course, when baseball season occurred, we couldn't get my father from in front of it. However, I'd take it up to my bedroom after ten and started the habit of falling asleep with it on. Today I still have to have the TV on wherever I am, but now I use the timer to cut if off after I've fallen asleep. As a kid, I watched Bonanza, The Man from U.N.C.L.E., I Dream of Jeannie, Bewitched, Dick Van Dyke, Carol Burnett, Ed Sullivan, Hollywood Palace and of course the Superman repeats. Looney Tunes, from Bugs Bunny to Daffy Duck, were Saturday mornings. Chiller, Thriller and Alfred Hitchcock were my faves. Shindig and Hullabaloo were my favorite music shows where I could see all my favorite artists performing from Motown. Mom and I fell in love with the incredible voice of a young girl named Barbra Streisand and watched every TV special that she had. Mom used to say "I believe that gal got some black in her. She has soul in her voice." But my favorite show of all time was "I Love Lucy." Although I've seen every episode probably thousands of times, and know all the lines, I never tire of watching who I consider to be one of the greatest comediennes of all time. One of my favorite episodes is when Lucy, Ricky, Fred and Ethel get on each other's nerves with their annoying habits. Ricky incessantly taps on the table, Lucy stirs her coffee cup loudly, Ethel eats loudly and Fred jingles his keys in his pocket.

My dad had Fred's habit. He would stand in the living room door while Mom and I were watching TV, not watching what was on the screen, but staring into space jingling his keys in his pocket. It drove me and Mom crazy. Sometimes it would be accompanied by a whistle. So, we'd have to turn up the volume to drown out the noise. Sometimes you weren't aware he was near until you heard the jingling and there he was. During the early 60's the famous dance show, "American Bandstand" was segregated and blacks were not allowed to dance on the show. DC's answer to segregation was to start their own local dance TV show called "Teenarama Dance Party," where black teens could go on TV and dance to the latest R&B music. It was created by DC's WOOK radio owner Richard Eaton, DC Teenager Cal Hackett and radio personality, Al Jefferson. Not only did it predate "Soul Train" but WOOK TV was the first black-owned TV station predating BET. Hosted by DJ Bob King and sponsored by WOOK radio and Miles Long Sandwich Shops (the best subs anywhere), all my friends would flock to get on the TV show. It aired live and came on six nights a week. Black artists such as Jerry Butler, Chubby Checker and many others who would come to perform at DC's Howard Theater would stop by Teenarama to perform. How I longed to go on the show. Of course, because of Smallwood's stance on secular music, which he considered the "devil's music," as well as any kind of dancing other than a "holy one," I was not allowed. However, "Teenarama" came on when he usually was not at home and I blasted the house with it, while I watched and learned all the latest dances such as hand-dancing of course, the jerk, the twist, the shotgun, the Madison, the mashed potato and the list went on. I would watch almost every day to see if I would recognize one of my friends or classmates. Another one of my good friends, Patricia Wigglesworth, taught me all the latest dances when I went over her house. Her mom would cook and we'd dance all afternoon. On one particular day, my best friend from Jr. High, Michael Evans was at my house and "Teenarama" was on. I turned the volume up as far as that little black and white ten-inch TV would go and we both jumped up in the living room and started to dance our hearts out. That went on probably for at least twenty minutes. I never heard the front door open, but all of a sudden above the den of the latest Motown song blaring from the TV, I heard it. *Jingle, jingle, jingle.* I froze and my heart dropped not knowing what would happen next. Mike's eyes were closed and he was dancing up a storm. I slowly turned around to see Smallwood standing in the door observing the gyrations, jingling his keys. He headed straight to the TV and turned it off. Mike stopped dancing, looking confused as to what happened. He turned slowly to Mike and said, "Son I don't know what you do at your house, but we don't listen to that mess here and we don't dance in this house." Then, he looked at me as he walked out the room and said, "And Richard… YOU know better." It had to be one of the most embarrassing moments of my life. When you're that age, your parents can just embarrass you at the drop of a hat by saying normal "parent things" in front of your friends. However, to tell your best friend that "we don't dance here and turn off that junk" was mortifying to me. Michael respectfully said "yes sir" and looked at me with a half-smile and a "poor Richard" look of pity. I just loved music and all kinds. However, by the time I got to high school, I went to every dance that my school would give and danced myself into a sweat. I'm not sure if Smallwood knew, but Mom didn't care. Whenever I wasn't sure where Smallwood was in the house, all I had to do was follow the jingle.

I used to get so frustrated because although I could watch R&B on television, my father would not allow me to listen to it at home. I'd go over Rev. Derrick's house and hang out with his kids and they could listen to any kind of R&B they wanted. I just loved music! It didn't matter what genre. If it was great structure, good lyrics, and interesting harmonies, I loved it. I remember Mom, myself, the Derricks and the Baptist Convention Choir going to Detroit to perform at the National Baptist Convention. While we were there, June, Jitterbug and I found a record store. It was like heaven. Of course, it had every latest thing from Motown. They were buying all kinds of R&B records. I made up my mind then and there, I'm gonna buy me some secular records. I never will forget, I bought an album by Smokey Robinson and the Miracles, a compilation of their greatest hits called "From the Beginning," and two 45's: "Dancing in the Street" by Martha and the Vandellas and "A Quiet Place" by soul singer Garnet Mimms. I remember seeing Mom in the hotel lobby when we got back. She saw I had a bunch of records, and she looked at me and said, "I see you got some records, who has something new out?" I knew she expected me to say the Roberta Martin Singers or some Tchaikovsky Concerto. I answered, "Oh, it's R&B." She looked stunned and said, "Hmmmm OK, you better watch it." I wasn't sure if she was saying that because of her disapproval of secular music or if she was trying to warn me of what my father would say. How would he react to that? I came up with a plan. Most of the times during my listening sessions at home, I'd mix the genres up. I'd listen to gospel for about an hour and then I might change to Classical or something else. So, I thought "Why don't I just insert the R&B records into my "listening list" as if it were the most normal thing in the world?" That's what I began to do. Of course, when I first started playing the R&B records, I'd bring the volume down very low and when I'd go to another genre, I'd blast the volume.

As time went on, little by little, I'd bring up the volume for the R&B in increments at a time. As time went on, the volume for my R&B music ended up being just as loud as everything else. My father never said a word. I was shocked! As fast as I could, I began to buy up all the Motown and other R&B records my finances would allow. Finally, the possibilities were limitless in terms of the music I could listen to in my house. Of course, the R&B of today is very different than it was then. If the profanity of today had been in that R&B I bought back then, there is no way I could have brought it into the house. I long for the days of wonderful, poetic lyrics. It was just good, innocent and fun music about love.

***

I completed the 8th grade and the 9th grade without a hitch. Although I was in the school zone to go to Eastern High School, McKinley Technical High School on the other side of town had a music major program, an art major program, a laboratory techniques program and an architecture program. These programs were designed to prepare students for areas that they wanted to pursue in college, with the lab techniques program preparing those who wanted to continue into medicine. The Music Major program seemed perfect for me. I auditioned, passed and entered McKinley Technical High School in the fall of '64. Mrs. Beatrice Gilkes was the head of the music major program. She was a graduate of Howard University as well as Oberlin and was a gifted teacher and pianist. It was a great program. Of course, you took your regular subjects that were required, but you also took Music History, Music Appreciation and theory, and of course choir. Thank God my voice had finally started to change. My

10th grade year, I actually was more of an alto but I would sing tenor. I was just grateful I was no longer a soprano. By the time I was in the 11th grade, I was a true tenor and my voice started settling into what it would become. However, it was a struggle trying to figure out what keys I sang in now. I used to have this really crazy head voice that I could play with, but after my voice changed that was gone. At the same time, it was a bit of a shock trying to figure things out vocally. Like Eliot, McKinley had many students who shared the same kind of love for music as I did. I had some of the most gifted classmates, especially the vocal majors. Our choir was second to none. Every morning at 8:15, we were assembled for rehearsal under the direction of Mrs. Gilkes. We'd get asked to sing for all the major events around town. At one point, we ended up being the choir for the concert version of Porgy and Bess featuring the original Porgy, Todd Duncan, with The National Symphony Orchestra. Rumor around town and in the music circles had it that Mrs. Gilkes had added some voices from Howard University to the choir because there was no way that a high school choir could sound that good. However that wasn't true. It was just McKinley High School's choir with no additions, singing with all of our might and all of those amazing gifts. I also remember us doing Howard Hanson's "Song of Democracy" with the National Symphony at Constitution Hall. Mrs. Gilkes began to trust me with some of the accompaniment for the choir. One of the songs that I remember playing for the choir was Brahms' "How Lovely Is Thy Dwelling Place." By now even though I couldn't read it at sight, with practice I could fluently read all the notes and get it under my fingers. Still my ear helped me tremendously and if I could hear a recording of it, or someone else play it, it would help me even more. I loved Mrs. Gilkes' classes. She was an amazing teacher, an accomplished pianist, choral director and musician of the highest caliber. It was the first time that I was taught about the theory of classical music, and how it was all put together. I already loved Tchaikovsky from his Swan Lake and Sleeping Beauty ballets, but found a new love and respect for him as I studied his beautiful Romeo and Juliet suite. I discovered many new classical pieces as well as studied many of the standards I had been listening to for most of my life. Mrs. Gilkes was a taskmaster though, and we were tested thoroughly on all that we learned.

My Grandmother Vianna Smallwood passed while I was in High School. My family traveled to New York to the funeral. I never knew her well, but the thing I recall the most is seeing my sister, Dorothy. I hadn't seen her since I was probably nine years old. By now the alcohol had consumed her body and her face, I barely recognized her. I can see her in my mind hugging me and smiling at me saying, "that's my brother, Buddy." I remember wondering in my mind, what happened to make her do this to herself. I remembered the picture of the beautiful young girl on the mantle at home. There was no hint of that girl in the person standing in front of me. I remember being so upset by what I saw. I never knew Dorothy well, but that was my only sister and I loved her.

While I was in High School, my mother got very sick. She had kidney disease and one of them had to be removed. The remaining kidney was only working at about 70 percent of what it should have been. The doctors said she wouldn't live to see me graduate from high school. The kidney was removed and the doctors could not have been more wrong. Mom not only lived to be 90, but she never even went on dialysis. God's preordained plan for our lives will always supersede man's speculation.

Sometime before I graduated from junior high school, someone informed me about a program at Howard called the Junior Preparatory Department. It was for elementary, junior high and high school students who excelled in music. If one passed the audition, you could take piano lessons and music theory from the Howard professors. My teacher, Mr. Barbour, told Mom that he thought he had taken me about as far as he could and that it was time for someone to take me to the next level. I remember being quite nervous as I went for my audition to get into the Junior Department. The head of the department was Mrs. Anne R. Burwell. She greeted me in her studio on the third floor of Howard's Fine Arts Building with a warm smile. Mrs. Burwell had a motherly spirit about her and I immediately felt at home. However, when I sat down at the piano, things began to change. She first asked me to play something. I played some of the pieces I had learned from Mr. Barbour. She then asked for scales. My scales were a bit raggedy I think, because it was something I hated practicing. Although I had to do scales with Mr. Barbour, he focused more on the performance pieces. She then pulled out a piece that I had never seen before, put it in front of me and instructed me to sight read it. That old familiar, head pounding heartbeat surfaced as I began to sweat. How would I get around this? I tried to use my old tactic that I had used all my life and asked her to play it for me. She refused my request. I explained to her that I just wanted to get the "feel" of the piece in terms of how she wanted me to play it, my ear being poised and ready to record! She again refused and said she didn't care about the feel. All she wanted me to do was play what I saw in front of me. I took a deep breath and plunged into the piece. It was a catastrophe. Mrs. Burwell didn't stop me though. For about three minutes, which seemed to me like an eternity, I stumbled, played wrong notes, wrong rhythms, and wrong accidentals. The fact that she let me continue and didn't comment for a while made the whole process more embarrassing and more excruciating. After there was no more left to fall apart, she finally tapped her pencil lightly on the piano and said, "That's enough." She paused, and then said to me "Richard, you can't read." Someone had finally called me out. I protested that if I had time to look over it, I could do better. She explained that she didn't need me to look it over, but to play it by sight. She then said to me that she recognized a tremendous gift in me, but my weakness was most definitely my lack of reading skills. She said, however, she was going to accept me in the program, and her job was going to be to teach me how to read so that when I entered college I would be prepared. She basically said that if it killed her and me, I was going to be a fluent reader by the time I graduated High School.

My first instructor in the Junior Department was Lloyd Schupp. I remember the first lesson he pulled out a book of Bach pieces and assigned one to me. After working on the piece, I came back and announced to Mr. Schupp that I hated Bach. His music made no sense to me. It was just a bunch of hard notes that kept moving. I was used to music from the Romantic period with lush, big chords and harmonies. I never will forget how Mr. Schupp looked at me and said, "Richard, Bach is going to become your favorite composer." I remember saying to myself "no way." Little did I know, as I began to understand this genius of a composer, and how the musical pictures he painted all fit together, it started making sense: Mr. Schupp had to be some kind of a prophet. Bach soon took a hold of me, like an original Clara Ward singer and I began to find every kind of recording I could that featured his music. The master of counterpoint and thematic improvisation became and still is my absolute favorite composer. If you listen hard to some of my more classical oriented pieces you can definitely hear his influence even today.

Soon after, Mrs. Burwell began to teach me. When I would go in for my lessons, the first thing I would do was play my scales. Then she would pull out some dusty manuscript in front of me and instruct me to sight read it. It was a long journey and a long process. I had relied on my ear for so long that relying on my sight was not an easy task. I would plunge into whatever piece she would put in front of me. Sometimes, I may get five measures into it without falling apart, but the moment I would make a mistake, Mrs. Burwell would instruct me to go back to the beginning. I just knew that God had placed her in my life to pay me back for something horrible I must have done. But little by little it became easier, and I would recognize the notes in front of me immediately and the flow to my playing became smoother and smoother. By the time I graduated from high school and from the Jr. Department, I had become a fluid sight-reader. Mrs. Burwell became like my second mother. She would fuss at me when I wasn't up to par in not only my music, but also my studies. But she was such a nurturing, loving person. I did a recital during my final year in the Jr. Department (which was required by all students their senior high school year). During my preparation for my recital, I met Professor Thomas Kerr, Jr., the head of the Piano Department at Howard. He mentored me through some of the harder pieces for my recital. Little did I know, he and Mrs. Burwell would have a profound impact on my life during my Howard college years. My sight singing instructor in the Jr. Department was Gwendolyn Eichelberger, a very gifted and warm teacher who enhanced my sight singing ability. Howard's Jr. Department really prepared young students well who were looking to continue with music once they enrolled in college. There were some amazingly gifted young people in that program.

Another gospel group started coming to DC around that time from Philadelphia called the Imperial Gospel Singers. Mom and I loved to go hear them sing. Although they had been around since the late fifties, I discovered them in the middle sixties. The members were Anna Smallwood who was the founder, Louise Smoke, Connie Antrom Noble, Rosie Wallace and Rudeen Collier. These ladies had some incredibly tight harmony. They were known for some great songs such as "If You Wait" and "Fountain of Blood," many of which I taught whatever my current group was at the time. Louise Smoke was known to be the house wrecker with "In My Father's House." They definitely influenced me as well. It seems to me that they never got the national recognition they deserved, especially considering how good they were.

For a short time during high school, I got three of my old White Stone crew and former Smallwood Singers together to form a group. The Smallwood Singers had not sung in quite a few years. So I called Val, Brenda and Sue. I added a neighbor, Mary Ponton, who was a bit older than we were and we began to sing around town again. For some reason, I wanted to be more anonymous and didn't want to call them the Smallwood singers, so I named them the Gospel Stars. Most of our songs were by The Imperial Gospel Singers, The Stars of Faith, The Roberta Martin Singers and the original Wards. We had robes and Mom made some fancy stoles on them to snazz them up a little bit. However, I was a part of so many other activities, we didn't stay together that long.

The Derricks twins and I decided to start a secular group as well. Male groups like the Temptations, the Miracles, the

Contours, Frankie Valli and the Four Seasons were the order of the day. So we decided to follow suit and form our own. While I was a student at McKinley Tech, the Derricks twins were students at Cardozo High School. There was a big dance at Cardozo and we were the special guests. One of the twins' classmates and friends was added to the group as well and so there were four of us. We named ourselves the Mark 4 (I guess after the car of the same name). We were the hit of the dance and the girls screamed and swooned. Our "killer" song was "The Whole World Is A Stage" by the Fantastic Four. My father did not know about THAT performance. We danced, had steps and everything! One performance that he did know about is that I did a solo performance at McKinley's spring talent show of "Unchained Melody" by the Righteous Brothers. Years later, that song would be made popular in the movie *Ghost*, starring Whoopi Goldberg and Patrick Swayze. Mom and Dad came to the talent show as they came to everything that I did, and seemed to be as proud as they could be about my performance. During my high school years, I also was accompanist for several of my classmate vocalists during many of the talent shows. I was always somewhere learning the latest accompaniment for a Dionne Warwick or a Nancy Wilson song, which were the mainstays for the female vocalists during that time. I loved the music of Burt Bacharach who wrote most of Dionne's songs, because the harmonic progressions were so contemporary for that time. They also were a challenge to learn because they weren't the norm. I loved a challenge. Although I hadn't started writing seriously at that time, Bacharach had his influence on me as well.

I remember the beginning of my senior year in High School, Mrs. Gilkes approached me about helping to get me a scholarship to Howard after graduating. She said, "We need to get you some money. I'm going to take you up there and talk to the Dean about it." Never a truer statement had been said. My parents in no way had the money to pay for my college education. She took me along with several other fellow students to meet Warner Lawson, who was the Dean of the School of Music. I was so nervous! Although I was a student in the Junior Department, and had seen him several times from a distance, I hadn't personally met him before. After all, this was the head of the School on the college level. She took me in her car to Howard. Dean Lawson was very nice and cordial. I'm not sure of all that Mrs. Gilkes had told him out of my presence, but I remember her singing my praises and expressing to him the need for financial help and the asset I would be to the school. I think with the combination of me being a Junior Department student and her recommendation, I was promised a full scholastic scholarship to the School of Music upon entering Howard as a freshman. Of course, keeping it was contingent upon my maintaining a B average or above in my studies. I'll never forget Mrs. Gilkes for making that happen for me. God was placing people in my life to bring me to my destination. As I was continuing to prepare for my Junior Department Recital and preparing to graduate from High School, I remember practicing hard to get the pieces I had been assigned right. One particular day, while getting ready to leave the school after practicing, one of my friends Julius James who went to high school with me ran up to me and said, "Guess what? I'm so excited! I really want to go over to Andrew Rankin Chapel this evening. Donny Hathaway is giving a concert over there." Rankin Chapel was the name of the chapel at Howard University. It was directly across campus from the School of Music. My response was, "who is Donny Hathaway?" Julius, whose older sister was already a student at

Howard's School of Music, explained that Donny was a student at Howard who was incredibly gifted. I remember making a mental note of wanting to hear him one day. It wouldn't be long before that desire was fulfilled.

I was nervous about performing at my last recital for the Jr. Department. I always became so nervous whenever I had to play classical music before an audience. In some way, it seemed so structured, and not free and improvisatory like gospel music. At the same time, I loved it more than I could articulate. In May of 1967 the recital went very well and my teachers were pleased. Mom and Dad beamed, stood and cheered as I took my final bow and I finished my time in the Jr. Preparatory Department of Howard.

***

Spring of 1967 was senior prom time. I wondered if I would even be allowed to go. I had attended a number of school dances during my time at McKinley, so I prayed that I would be able to. I don't think I ever really asked if I could go. I just proceeded as if I was going. Dad had an old, beat up car, but it got us around. I was allowed to attend my prom, but I didn't want to be seen driving a hoopty. Thankfully, Aunt Netha stepped in and rented me a brand new car. After renting my outfit from the tuxedo shop, which was a dark blue double-breasted, two-button tuxedo jacket with black formal pants, I was as clean as the board of health and ready to step out in style. I was a bit shocked that my father even allowed me to go! My date Bonita Battle and I double dated with a good friend from high school, Robert Jenkins, and his girlfriend, Alicia Adams. My father even let me stay out all night! We did the after parties, and after breakfast and had a ball. It was hard to believe that the sun was coming up when I drove up in front of my house. I had never seen that sight, unless I saw it from my bedroom window.

I graduated from McKinley High School in June of 1967. Robert Jenkins was tragically killed in a motorcycle accident in the fall of that same year when we were both freshmen at Howard. That was the first death of someone my age I had ever experienced and I remember it not being easy for me to deal with. During that summer of '67, Rev. Derricks gathered several people from his choir at church, a couple of people from the National Baptist Convention Choir, Pearl Williams and Queen Esther Young, the twins, his daughter, wife and myself and did a tour. We went everywhere by car and a van. It was a great experience. We performed in school auditoriums, churches and in places where he had pastored and had connections. We sang a number of songs he had written plus some of the popular gospel songs of that day and even a few anthems. It was my first time having a taste of "the road," but that experience laid a foundation for something that would be a great part of my life later. Before I left to go on the tour, Mom informed me that we would be moving to a new house and by the time I returned the move would be complete. Sure enough, when I got back we had moved to 4635 Deane Ave. N. E. It was a first floor apartment in a very nice house. An elderly doctor who was the owner of the home lived next door where his practice was located.

CHAPTER 11
HOWARD UNIVERSITY

In the fall of 1967, I entered Howard University's School of Music as a freshman. When I started taking classes in college, I stopped playing for Pleasant Grove Baptist Church so that I could concentrate solely on my studies and keep that "B" average I needed to maintain my scholarship. Registration was a nightmare. This was before the days of computers and pre-registration. To register, we would stand in line in the gym forever trying to sign up for our classes. I went in that morning and didn't come out until that evening. I was so confused. After standing in one line for hours I was told that the class I wanted was closed. Then I had to go stand in another line. However, I always say that if life were a DVR and you could rewind it to the part of your life that you'd want to live over again, I would choose my years at Howard. Despite registration, it was the best four years of my life. I made friends who became lifelong relationships and I learned about life and music. It was a time of figuring out who I wanted to be and what I wanted to be in life, and it marked the beginning of who I was to become. As a child, I never felt that I fit in. In school and outside of my close friend relationships, I always felt like a fish out of water. I was this musical, shy kid that didn't share a lot of the same interests as other kids my age. That's hard for a child to deal with. Children want to be accepted; they want to be a part of something. Because of the music program at McKinley, I began to experience an environment where I felt more comfortable. However, at Howard for the first time, I felt like I was completely surrounded by people who had the same interests as me. Many of us had the same story in terms of not being accepted like many creative people. But this was the first time that I felt like I was at home. I felt like I belonged, like a jigsaw puzzle finally fitting into the big picture.

I entered Howard as a Piano Major and a Voice Minor. I think my professors from my Jr. Department years wanted me to become a classical concert pianist, but I wasn't sure. I knew that I loved classical music, but I didn't know if that was really what I wanted to do. Either way, everyone knew that whatever path I chose, it would definitely have something to do with music. My freshman classes consisted of Music History, Sight Singing & Ear Training, Music Theory, Voice and of course, Piano. My piano instructor was the Chairman of the Piano Department who had mentored me for my Jr. Department Final Recital, Professor Thomas H. Kerr Jr. Mr. Kerr, a native of Baltimore, Md., was an incredible pianist as well as a classical composer. He was an instructor second to none. He undoubtedly was the best piano instructor I've ever had. I cannot stress enough the influence that he had on my growth as a pianist. He literally changed my approach to playing the piano and the way I approached the instrument forever. Not knowing that he could play other genres of music (I found that out later), Mr. Kerr had also played in clubs to pay his way through college. Once he played the pop standard "Smoke Gets in Your Eyes" for me during a lesson. The chord progressions he played blew me away! I had never heard these chords before! Of course, I ran down to the practice area and tried to emulate everything he did that day.

The Fine Arts Building, also known as Lula Vere Childers Hall, was a four-level building. On the third floor was the School of Music, which housed the studios of the music professors, a small recital hall and classrooms. On the second floor was the Art Department where incredible professional artists like the late Lois Mailou Jones (who painted and influenced others during the Harlem Renaissance) and Sam Gilliam (one of America's foremost Color Field painters) taught. Ironically, Mr. Gilliam had taught art at McKinley in the Art Major program that was offered there as well. The first floor housed the fine arts library, the art gallery, the Dean's office, the student lounge and the Drama Department. The Drama Department also led into Ira Aldridge Theater, a small venue with a stage on which the Drama department could mount productions. Next to Ira Aldridge was Cramton Auditorium, Howard's main venue where all major concerts and assemblies took place. The basement of the Fine Arts Building was divided into two sections, one that included the offices and studios of the instrumental instructors, the band room and the other "practice areas" which were a series of rooms filled with pianos where students could practice. The practice area had an organ room which contained a pipe organ for students and instructors. Walking into that practice area for the first time, had to be one of the most intimidating experiences of my life. In 1967, it seemed that every gifted African-American migrated to Howard University. It was like the Mecca of black universities. Opera diva, Jessye Norman, had just graduated the year before I entered. I would see her around school when I was in the Jr. Department. Debbie Allen entered Howard as a freshman with me and was enrolled in the drama department, and her sister,

Phylicia Allen (who would later become Phylicia Rashad) was an upperclassman in that same department. Also in drama were Linda Gravatt, Charles (Charlie) Brown, and Clyde Barrett. Each of them were talented artists in their own right who would go on to do plays, TV and film.

In the music department, you had Alphonso Mizell of the Mizell Brothers team. He and his brother Larry would later become major producers and writers for Motown, the Jackson 5, A Tribe Called Quest and the list goes on. Also, there was Donny Hathaway, one of the most incredible gifts ever, whom I had yet to meet at that point. Donny's roommate was Leroy Hutson, who would later work extensively with the late great Curtis Mayfield. Leroy became a solo R&B artist in his own right and took Curtis's place as lead singer in the famous R&B group The Impressions when Curtis left to go solo. When I think back on that time, there were as many students who were just as gifted as the recognizable names in all the departments who never made it to the "big time." I had never seen that much talent in one place in my life, especially talent of that degree. That's not even mentioning the names of incredible classical vocalists such as Cynthia Clary, the late Charlae Olaker, and Jessye Norman and the list goes on. As I walked down the hall in the practice area, I heard the most incredible voices, the most incredible piano technique, strings, horns, woodwinds, and organ all entering my ear and stirring my musical sensibilities at the same time. I honestly began to doubt whatever gifts I had, and wondered would I even be able to keep up with all of the talent that I was hearing around me. The pressure made me work even harder.

There was a friendly competition in the School of Music. You didn't want to be outdone, or caught lagging behind. That made you consciously work to do your best. I think I was somewhat encouraged in my abilities as well as a bit nervous when Mr. Kerr informed me that he wanted me to repeat my Jr. Department recital for the entire School of Music. I think it was one of the few times, if not the first time, that a freshman had given a complete recital upon entering the University. I didn't mind playing for the other first-year students, but playing for the upper classmen and the faculty was terrifying. Mr. Kerr started to refresh my memory and my fingers on the recital I had given that previous May. Andrew Rankin Chapel was where most of the major recitals were given at that time. The recital went well, Mr. Kerr was very pleased and I was pretty proud of myself as well.

College was different. There were no teachers who stayed on top of you to make sure you did what you were supposed to do. You were basically on your own. You were given your assignment and expected to complete it. Every professor piled on the work as if their class was the only one that you were taking, and many times it didn't seem like there was enough time to get everything done. No excuse other than death or near death was accepted. But still the music department had a feeling of family and the instructors were definitely concerned about your wellbeing. Dr. Doris McGinty was my Music History professor. She was brilliant. She was the first woman, and just as importantly, the first African American to graduate from Oxford University in England with a Doctorate in Musicology. She even wrote one of the textbooks for our class. We always had a running joke that Dr. McGinty knew what time each day that Bach went to the bathroom. She knew dates, times, eras, what was composed, when and how with such accuracy that it was amazing. Of course, she expected us to know it as well. I was always known to procrastinate and wait until the last minute to study. I remember there were times when I would study all night the night before an exam and would fall asleep and wake up only to find out that I hadn't finished studying. One particular time, after not studying thoroughly, I made up my mind to just go to class, put my name on the test, and pass it in and accept my "F" with grace. I was so exhausted. I discussed it with one of my good friends, Charlae Olaker, who said she wasn't prepared either and was going to do the same thing. So we sat next to each other and prepared to write our name on our exams and give them back to "Doc" as we called her. Of course, that particular day "Doc" announced that she was giving an oral exam instead and we would each be asked one question in front of the whole class and it would be "A" or "F." Immediately I began to sweat, because I knew NOTHING. When "Doc" got to Charlae who had sworn she knew nothing as well, and asked her the question, she gave the perfect answer and received an "A." Of course, when "Doc" got to me, the question she asked me may as well have been in Greek. I hadn't a clue as to what the answer was. I just looked down and said, "sorry Dr. McGinty, I don't know." "Alright, Mr. Smallwood" she replied, "that will be an 'F'" and she pressed on to the next student. I wanted to strangle Charlae who I thought would have at least gotten an "F" with me so I wouldn't be alone in my ignorance. Another time I remember falling asleep sitting on the back row in class. I was half asleep and half awake when I heard Dr. McGinty bellow, "Mr. Smallwood, is that you in the back with your eyes at half-mast??" I was so embarrassed. Everyone put their head down and laughed. However, I loved "Doc." She was a great person, and most of the time my work was on point. My first semester, I received an "A" and was quite happy. It was not an easy class, but "Doc" made it a fascinating one. Many years later after I graduated, I would accompany "Doc" on her many lectures around the city. As she would talk about African American music and the different aspects of it, I would demonstrate on the piano the examples that she would discuss. I remember feeling so proud that she would even request me to help her out. I admired her so.

My theory professor was Yvonne Hobson who knew the theory of harmony backwards and forward. I remember finally learning the correct names of the chords I had played for so many years and theoretically how they were constructed. Mrs. Hobson also was an extraordinary pianist whom I loved to watch play. I still had a fascination for women who could master the piano. I remember her playing one particular contemporary piece where the performer was required not only to play the keys, but to pluck the strings on the inside of the piano. I was fascinated. She was brilliant. Years later, one of the great moments of my life would be looking out from the stage of Constitution Hall while performing as she sat on the front row in the audience, beaming proudly.

My voice teacher was Louise Burge. Miss Burge one time had been a premiere classical vocalist. At one point, she was being groomed to be the next Marian Anderson. I'm not sure what happened exactly, but rumor had it that she acquired a new vocal coach who was trying out a new vocal technique on her and literally destroyed her voice. She woke up one morning to find her voice completely gone. To hear Miss Burge sing you would have never known that she once was a great singer, because little of it was left. However, she could teach you the techniques of singing without even thinking about it. She was comical without even trying. Her speaking voice was between tenor and baritone and she talked very fast and sometimes she'd launch into these nonsensical syllables and no one was quite sure what she was saying. I got so tickled in her class just hearing her talk to me. Her speech pattern always reminded me of Aunt Clara from the

TV show, "Bewitched". She usually spoke in third person. So, if I were running late for her class, when I'd enter the door she'd say something that I wasn't quite sure of and then "LAWD, He's late. No telling where he's been". She was a very tall stately looking woman. You could tell in her youth she must have been quite beautiful. She was beautiful and "big boned" as my mother would say. She was not fat or obese by any means, but tall, large and solid. Her hands were larger than mine and when she hit your diaphragm to tell you to support the tone, it was like getting the wind knocked out of you. In fact, when I first started taking voice, and couldn't readily understand the concept of supporting the vocal tone from the diaphragm, she instructed me to lie on the couch in her studio. She instructed me to start vocalizing slowly climbing up the scale. When it started getting a little high, my voice started giving out. She let out a "support that tone from here!!" and proceeded to sit on my stomach. With that extra push of her body weight on my diaphragm, I sang notes that day that I never knew I had in my range! I think she especially loved me because I used to play for her voice classes to help her out, which I loved to do. I certainly didn't have the kind of classical voice that she probably was trying to pull out of me. But I was determined to learn how to sing correctly so that I could preserve my voice to sing whatever kind of music I would end up doing. I loved Miss Burge!

One night, Miss Burge took some of us to an incredible concert at Peabody Conservatory in Baltimore. Baltimore is just a forty-five minute drive from DC and Miss Burge took her car, had one of the students drive and we all piled in. Unknown to us, an ice storm happened while we were in the concert and when we came out, everything was iced over. Miss Burge was sure that we could make it back to DC if we drove slowly. As tall as she was, I'm not sure why she was in the back seat. However, she was with several other students while I was in the front with the driver and another student sitting in the middle. We stopped for a stoplight and a couple of us noticed in the rear and side view mirrors that there was a bus behind us that was sliding on the ice. It was a bit of a distance behind, however it was definitely sliding in our direction and inching closer and closer to us. It clearly had trouble stopping. Someone suggested hurriedly that we better get out of the car immediately just in case the bus ended up on top of us. The doors swung open immediately so that we could make our exit. However, it was a two door, so those in the back would have to wait until those in the front exited the door. I guess we were moving too slowly for Miss Burge with the bus still sliding in our direction. The next thing I remember was Miss Burge's longer than average leg climbing over my shoulder from the back before I could get out, and that booming low voice uttering something fast and unrecognizable. I didn't know it was possible for her to move that fast! She beat the front seat occupants getting out of that car. We all did get out though. Fortunately, the bus never hit us and it finally stopped sliding. She somehow got us a room at the dorm at Peabody because it was just too dangerous to drive back to D.C. We spent the night sleeping on the floor and laughing all night at Miss Burge and how fast she could REALLY move.

My Ear Training and Sight Singing teacher was Evelyn Davidson White. Mrs. White evoked the fear of God in most of her students. She was the daughter of a minister and would make you feel three inches tall if you failed to do your best in her class. In her words, she was disappointed and God was too! She was an incredible conductor and assisted Dean Warner Lawson in conducting the University Choir and later started The

Collegiate Chorale and the Evelyn Davidson White Chorale. Having perfect pitch, sight singing class was never hard for me, although at times I would have problems reading the rhythms if they were unusually complex. Of course, Anne Burwell taught me how to sight-read piano scores in the Jr. Department. But reading and singing a single vocal line at sight had never been much of a problem for me. Mrs. White was a sweetheart outside the class, but once she entered those doors, she became a Gestapo taskmaster and she did not play around. I remember this red dress she would wear at times, with black patent leather high heels. Everyone said whenever she wore that dress, a surprise test was imminent. Nine times out of ten, it was pretty accurate. When she wore it, word would spread around on the third floor, "Mrs. White has on the red dress!" Everyone would scurry down to the practice area to put in some extra study hours because more than likely there was a surprise test on the horizon. Sitting in her classroom, you could hear her coming down that hall with those high heels clicking and we would tremble in terror. I also remember one particular classmate questioning her authority and, needless to say, by the time she finished chastising him, nothing was left to be said. She rose slowly from behind the black baby grand piano at which she was sitting and bellowed, "Mr. Jones, LEAVE MY CLASS, AND NEVER BOTHER TO DARKEN MY DOORSTEP AGAIN!" Even though she was a hard taskmaster, everyone loved Mrs. White dearly and respected her to the highest. I don't think the poor brother ever graduated. After one of those encounters she would usually turn back to the class and give the hardest test she could come up with. You were never late for Mrs. White's class. If you were one minute late, you couldn't come in. If you got an "A" in her class, you'd best believe you deserved it and had worked like a slave for it. She didn't give "gifts." However, if you did your work, when you left that course you knew how to sight-sing with no problem. She loved her students and wanted everyone to do their absolute best, but she made you work. At the same time, Mrs. White had this motherly, loving way about her. So you feared her, but at the same time you wanted to please her. She was the consummate musician and to earn her respect meant the world.

I remember many years after I graduated, my phone rang. I picked up the phone and said "hello." The voice on the other end said, "Richard? This is Evelyn Davidson White." For a minute my heart began to pound and I reverted to a frightened student wondering, "Oh God, what did I do?" She went on to say how proud she was of me and that although she hadn't talked to me in years, she had been following me. She said "Richard, I was watching TV not long ago and you came on with an ensemble. You sat down at the piano and began to play and those lovely singers opened their mouths. It was wonderful! You all weren't performing…you BECAME the music." That compliment will live with me forever. For someone whom I respected so much, looked up to (yet feared), it meant so much for her to not only approve of what I did, but also respect what I did.

CHAPTER 12

A LITTLE GOSPEL GROUP
CALLED THE CELESTIALS

After performing my recital at the beginning of my freshman year, word began to spread about the little skinny freshman, a new piano major in town. Not only that, word got out that I also played gospel. Of course, gospel at that time was something you dared not play in the Fine Arts Building. In fact, you were not allowed to play gospel, jazz or pop. You could not even play it in the practice area and if you got caught you would be reprimanded or threatened with suspension. Of course, we played it nonetheless and sometimes would have a lookout to make sure neither the Dean nor the security guard, Mr. Coleman, was patrolling the halls. Mr. Coleman would report you to the Dean if he heard you playing anything other than classical music. Many times during my time at Howard, especially the first couple of years, I learned how to go from James Cleveland to Chopin in the twinkling of an eye when someone shouted, "Here comes the Dean!!" Cheryl Hilton Rucker, a graduate of the School of Music from that era, reminded me of that time when Donny Hathaway was at the piano in one of the practice rooms playing gospel music, and the room was filled with students clapping, singing and having a good time. Someone even put up a makeshift sign on the door that said "Lula Vere Childers Memorial Baptist Church," but when they spotted the Dean coming, the room went dark. Someone turned off the light. Someone else yanked the sign off the door, and everyone held their breath until the Dean exited the practice area. Yet everyone still played it and sang it. We just had to be on the lookout. Of course, once classes were over and the Dean and faculty had gone home, it was pretty much free reign. Mr. Coleman would fuss at us if we weren't working on lessons, but we didn't pay him much mind. At any rate, I was practicing for my piano lesson one day. The door opened and in walked an upper classman. He was tall, thin and smelled like he had taken a bath in Aramis cologne. He had an air of confidence, but nonetheless was very friendly.

"Hi," he said.

"I hear you're supposed to be able to play well and you're a piano major. Not only that, but I hear you play gospel."

I wasn't sure how to respond and weakly said "Uh hi, yes I play gospel."

He paused and then said, "Well play something." I've always hated when someone says "play something." From a child, whenever I was told to play something, every song I had ever known would immediately escape from my head and memory. I'd sit there like I had never played in my life trying to think of something to play. This time was no different. I can't remember what I played, but I ended up finally thinking of something and playing a little bit of it.

"That's good," he said. "My name is Wesley Boyd. I'm a junior and a piano major. Can you sing?"

"A little bit," I replied.

"Sing something," he commanded.

Here we go again.

I sat there for a minute until one of the Martin Singers songs popped into my head. I began to sing, "God Specializes." By this time, I was sweating big time. Here was an upper classman (and a piano major at that) taking me through the third degree. I finished a verse and stopped and there was a moment of silence. Then Wesley said to me, "Good! I have a gospel group called The Celestials. It's three of us guys and we need another singer and a pianist to help us out. Are you busy later on this evening?"

"No," I said, "Not after my last class."

"Good" he replied. "We have rehearsal tonight. Meet us in the practice area around seven. Just follow the sound of the singing until you find what room we are in."

With that he left. I sat there, stunned. First of all, he didn't ask if I was interested, he didn't ask if I had the time or if I wanted to be a part of a group. It was more of a command than anything else. I felt like I had been summoned to some kind of audience in front of royalty. One part of me was flattered. The other part was terrified. I had no idea what to expect, but I knew that I was going to go to the rehearsal. As I entered the practice area that evening, there weren't many people practicing, but in the distance, I could hear the unmistakable sound of gospel music. I followed the sound until I found the room and opened the door. I had never heard such a massive sound coming from three individuals. It was big, choral like, with massive vibrato. It filled the little room they were singing in and spilled over into the hallway. Wesley had the biggest, clearest voice I'd ever heard. He was sitting at the piano accompanying. I recognized the face of one of the other singers, Daniel Hodge from seeing him around the Fine Arts building. He was also a part of the University Choir. His voice was big with a classical feel to it, but nonetheless gospel. The other face I didn't recognize. He was leaning on the piano with his eyes closed, head tilted to the side, leading the song. What was coming out of his mouth was mind blowing. Understand that in 1967, other than Shirley Caesar and Aretha, there weren't a lot of singers who did what we now call "runs." The technical term for it is "melisma" which is defined as the singing of a single syllable of text while moving between several different notes in succession. This brother was singing these "runs" so quickly, and with incredible precision, that I couldn't keep up. I had never really heard that before and I was thinking, "How does he do that with his voice?" Not only that but he had one of the most soulful voices I'd ever heard with a hint of sadness to it. When they finished, the sound of their last note was still ringing in my head. Wesley turned to me and then said to the other two, "this is Richard, the guy I was telling you about." He introduced me to Danny and then he introduced me to his cousin, Edward Sully, who had just sang the stew out of the song that I had walked in on. Sully, as we called him, was a Liberal Arts student majoring in Foreign Languages. We all exchanged pleasantries, and then Wesley asked me to sing and play "God Specializes." Everyone seemed to be pleased with my performance, or at least they were being nice to me because I was visibly nervous. Then he asked me to sing something with the group. I can't remember what it was, but it was something that I was familiar with. Their voices were so massive that I could only tell I was singing because I could feel the vibration of my voice in my chest. After we finished, everyone seemed satisfied with the blend and how we sounded together, although I was out of breath trying to keep up with the sheer power of their voices. Danny wryly said, "He has a nice voice. It's one of those peculiar kinds of little voices that you can't really hear that well when singing in a group setting, but if he's not singing then you miss the part." No one really commented, but there was an awkward silence as I felt like I was five inches tall. To be completely honest, I was a little bit annoyed by his statement. But, Danny was right. I couldn't sing as loud as those guys. I didn't understand the power of singing from the diaphragm, but I would learn in time. In time, Wesley and Sully would become two of my best friends and would end up singing with me for years. Wesley then told me when and where the next engagement was. He didn't ask if I could be there, or if I was interested in becoming a part, or what did I think of the group. Just like that, I was a member of the Celestials which I would find out later was the first gospel group on Howard's campus. Both Wesley and Sully were from North Carolina and cousins. Wesley being from Reidsville and Sully being from a little place called White Town. When Wesley and Sully moved to DC in 1964 to attend Howard, Wesley decided to start a gospel group to continue the tradition to which they were both accustomed in North Carolina. That's how the Celestials came to be. There were certainly no outlets like that at the time on campus. Wesley was an incredible classical pianist, but his roots, like mine, were gospel. As much as we loved classical music, those of us who came from that tradition missed that part of our culture, our heritage and our faith. One of our first engagements as I recall was in Hartford, Connecticut where some of Wesley's relatives lived. I remember we caught a Trailway bus to Connecticut and it was only Wesley, Sully and myself. I still have the audio tape from that night and listen to it fondly. I was scared to death. Wesley, who was the student assistant to Carolyn Grant, the head of the voice department at Howard, was an incredible vocal coach as well and had worked with us on blending and projection. So, I was feeling much better about being able to keep up with those big voices. At that time, Wesley and I would take turns playing for the group. However, I felt more comfortable at the piano. I didn't like standing up while people looked me over. Wesley who was not one for speaking in public and definitely was not the narrator type, assumed that position that evening at our concert. Maybe he did it because it was his family's church. However, Sully and I were probably worse. Neither of us could speak in public well and probably were several steps lower than Wesley. Out of the three of us, he was the best suited if someone just had to do it. The church was not the liveliest church; in fact they were pretty quiet, but showed their appreciation by their smiles and with their applause at the end of each song. I think Wesley got a little frustrated with their silence so he proceeded to tell them, "Now I want everybody to take a good look at us now. We CAME to praise the Lord! So when we start singing…I don't want nobody peeping around, ok? Ok!"

There were hundreds of blank stares including me and Sully's. No one was quite sure what he had just said. There is a tradition in the Black Church for a preacher or a singer to tell the audience (especially if the audience isn't familiar with them) to do all the "checking out" of what their attire might be or how they look when they first get up, so that when they start singing or preaching as the case might be, the congregation can get with them and have a good time together. In other words, get the unfamiliarity over with so we can become unified and praise the Lord. I think that's what Wesley was trying to say. After the concert was over, I think we laughed all the way back to Washington, D. C. We were a hit in Connecticut and everyone seemed to enjoy the concert. It seemed like we were always singing in conservative, non-responsive churches. They seemed to enjoy us though, and kept calling for us to come back. One particular night, we were singing in a church where no one in the audience moved except to applaud when we finished each song. We were singing the Caravan's hit, "Comfort Me." Sully was tearing up the lead and I was at the piano. I guess Wesley must have sang himself happy because all of a sudden, in the middle of the song, he started hollering to the top of his lungs, "COMFORT ME JESUS, COMFORT ME LORD, COMFORT ME JESUUUSSS!!" It startled Sully and I because it came from out of nowhere, with no warning. None of us had ever seen Wesley shout and other than shedding tears (which he would do in a minute), I don't think I ever saw him do it again. We had to stop the song and Sully had to sit him in one of the chairs in the pulpit and fan him as the audience politely and sympathetically applauded. I'm not sure if they had ever seen anyone shout before either. Of course, we never let Wesley forget it and we would embarrass him with the "comfort me" shout at the most inappropriate of times.

Not long after this occasion, I remember trying to find a free room in the practice area. I passed a room with Wesley, Sully and another young man seated at the piano whom I didn't recognize. I walked in the room while he was singing. The voice was incredible: big, rich, beautiful and silky, all at one time. His pianistic abilities were mind-boggling. He stopped, turned around and looked at me with the friendliest smile. Wesley said, "Richard, this is Donny. Donny this is Richard." It was my first time meeting Donny Hathaway face-to-face. Donny greeted me with a warm handshake. Before I came on the scene, Donny would sometimes play and sing with the Celestials. By now, although still a student, he had started performing, traveling and making a name for himself. However, this particular day he was working on an arrangement of "Calvary." He immediately started teaching us the background part. It started off like the slow, original Calvary, but the chorus sped up to an up-tempo beat.

Well, they crucified my Lord
But He never said a mum'bling word
(No, no, no, no, not a word!)

The whole room was rocking. I was in awe of his gift. Wesley had a mini reel-to-reel tape recorder. After Donny taught us the background parts, he suggested that we "put the song down." Donny started off on the solo singing, blues-like, slow, wailing and soaring.

Calvary, Calvary, Calvary, Calvary
Calvary, Calvary, Surely he died on
Calvary.

It made goose bumps rise on your arms. Then all of a sudden without warning, the tempo changed and we came in with the background while Donny ad-libbed. MAN! What a feeling it was in that room! I knew that I was in the presence of something great and someone special. I don't know whatever became of that tape, but how I wish we had kept up with it. After that, Donny would arbitrarily stop by my room if he saw me playing and would listen. Sometimes he would sit down and show me chords and different songs. We shared the same piano professor, Dr. Thomas Kerr Jr. But also, we shared the same love for gospel music. Donny was so creative and full of innovative, new musical ideas. He was a musical genius. He would use jazz chords in gospel music, which was unheard of then, but yet those standard gospel progressions were still present. He would also use other harmonic progressions that were just foreign to the basic gospel music formula. He knew how to weave in and out of them in such a profound manner and make it all work. When I look back, he really taught me to be bold in my musical ideas and to step out, experiment and not be confined to the norm. He taught me not to be afraid of being unique. In other words, step outside the box. He and another good friend, Gwendolyn Hines, were two of my biggest influences my freshman year. Gwen could really play! She was a killer vocalist as well. Her writing and arranging were awesome. She and Donny would show me their latest compositions and the latest harmonic progressions they had come up with, and I was in heaven. Little by little I was getting the urge to write, but I wasn't quite there yet. However, I had begun to do new arrangements of already existing songs. Donny and Gwen taught me two arrangements of hymns that were awesome. I can't recall who arranged which, or maybe they collaborated on them. I'm not sure. One was "Nothing But The Blood," a very jazzy arrangement of the old hymn but in waltz tempo. The other was the hymn, "Heavenly Sunlight" whose melody, modulations and weaving in and out of keys literally blew my mind. Little by little while keeping the traditional style of gospel that I knew so well, I started getting ideas on how to incorporate new sounds that were not the norm. I wanted to write badly, but I wanted to create something new, something that no one had ever thought about doing before. I just wasn't sure how to do it.

By this time, Donny was gaining popularity all over the local area. I remember we went to hear him at Ed Murphy's Supper Club, a local black owned establishment, and we sat in amazement at the talent of this gifted brother. I was always so in awe of him.

Donny had a great heart and had no problems accompanying fellow students in the Howard talent shows. He always had a genuine smile and a kind word for everyone. Although it was his senior year, he didn't graduate. He left school my second semester as doors began to open up for him. I remember excitedly buying his first album, "Everything is Everything," and listening in fascination as the days of the practice area started to come back to my memory. I saw Donny one more time after he became nationally known. I was at Greater New Hope Baptist Church, ironically one of the churches that my father had founded before I was born. He had come to attend a musical there. Dr. Joan Hillsman, a mutual friend, musician and ethnomusicologist, came in with him and sat on our row. I was still awe-struck by his gift! And although I had known him since my first semester, my shyness kicked in. I figured he would never remember me. By now, he was immensely popular and had accomplished so many great things. I remember him leaning over and looking down at me with that big smile and waving like I had just seen him the day before. He was not only a great talent, but also a humble person and a huge influence on me musically. I don't know why so many creative geniuses have issues with various forms of mental illness. At some point those who knew him at Howard began to hear of strange and bizarre behaviors in Donny's concerts as well as in general. This was unthinkable to hear about the jovial and loving Donny that we knew. None of us knew at the time that he was battling with paranoid schizophrenia. I never saw a hint of anything like that when we were in school. At the news of his death, I was stunned. It took me a while to process the whole concept of losing such an awesome gift to the music world, as well as such a great person.

CHAPTER 13

THE BELOVED DR. KERR, DR. KING AND DOROTHY JEAN

The greatest lesson Mr. Kerr taught me was how to approach playing different genres of music. Unlike other faculty instructors, he had no problem with me playing whatever kind of music I chose to play, but he said, "Know how to approach whatever genre you are playing. You can't play Chopin like you play James Cleveland." I remember when I began lessons with him, everything was loud and percussive. He taught me about arm weight and how to use that as opposed to playing from the wrists or the hand. He also taught me the technique of how to bring out a melody so that it sings over the accompanying chords. He taught me the importance of touch and dynamics. I remember learning the Liszt Leibestraum, a gorgeous piece with soaring melodies and arpeggios. The climax of the piece requires a series of broken thirds between right and left hand in contrary motion, descending in half steps at break neck speed. After studying the piece one day during my lesson, Mr. Kerr turned to me and said, "There is no reason that you can't use that broken thirds passage in some of your gospel piano performances." Little-by-little the techniques that Mr. Kerr was constantly showing me as I increased my classical repertoire were beginning to show up in my playing outside the classical music realm, without me realizing it. My entire approach, in terms of technique and touch, began to change overall. He was one of my biggest supporters. I remember when the Celestials went to Reidsville N. C. to do a concert for Wesley's father. We got a telegram once we got there that said, "Knock 'em dead, children" signed Poppa Kerr.

The Celestials continued to sing throughout the DC area with appearances in Reidsville, NC, Pittsburgh, PA and other cities. Upperclassman Beverly Alexander, a soprano, who was another School of Music student, was added to replace Danny Hodge when he graduated. Not long after that, another music student in my class was added, alto Rosalind Thompkins. Rosalind and I could have been described as the "laughing twins." You seldom saw one of us without the other and we laughed at everything, constantly. We used to get in trouble all the time! She still is a dear friend of mine. By this point, I began to take more of a "hands on" role with the Celestials. I began to arrange songs to fit our voices, and sometimes I created additional choruses, verses or vamps. I knew Beverly's voice, Wesley's voice, Sully's voice and Rosalind's voice like the back of my hand. I took delight in trying to see how I could stretch their vocal gifts even further. With Wesley's vocal coaching and my arrangement of the vocals, a sound began to develop; something that was different. Wesley had the dominant voice in the group in terms of sheer vocal power, and he set the bar. Everyone else had to come up to that level in terms of tone and power. My technique approach was inspired by the Martin Singers, that sound and mix of male and female voices of which I had become enamored so many years before. When all of that combined, a certain unique sound slowly began to emerge.

One of the first recordings I got when I was around five years old was of a group by the name of the Caravans. The song was "Tell Him What You Want," and on the B Side, "Wait for Me." I didn't follow them like I did the Wards, the Davises and the Martins. But, through Wesley and Sully I was re-introduced to this incredible group of singers: Albertina Walker, Shirley Caesar, Cassietta George, Josephine Howard, Delores Washington and Inez Andrews. These phenomenal voices made up the Caravans, as I knew them in the '60's. They were a powerhouse of female vocalists, with every singer being a soloist in their own right. Albertina Walker, the leader and founder of the group, would later become known as the "star maker" as so many of those vocalists went on to have successful solo careers of their own. James Cleveland was even one of the early pianists for this group. I was so fascinated by this group that I went back and collected every album they had made so as to have a complete library of their work. In the '60s, they became one of my favorites.

During this time, the military draft was in effect. Everyone was required to serve in the military. Only health issues and certain occupations were reasons for exemption. When a boy turned 18, he would have to register with the Selective Service system. During my senior year in High School, I registered. Around my junior year at Howard, the selective service system sent me a letter requiring me to take my physical examination to be drafted as soon as I graduated from college. The Vietnam War was in full swing and I had friends who had already been killed in the line of duty. I was terrified. Being in the military was not something I ever wanted to do. I salute and admire those who protect our country, but I knew it wasn't for me. But, I had no choice in the matter. I didn't realize at the time that males who had no siblings were exempt, but they were. This law had been implemented because a mother had lost all five of her sons to a previous war. I'm sure Mom didn't know about this either, or I know she would have spoken up about it. So I was put on a bus and taken to a military facility in Virginia to go through my examination. They were waiting for the very second that I received my degree so they could snatch me. The doctors took me through all kinds of rigorous exams. However, at the end of my exam I was pronounced "underweight" for the military. I was painfully skinny in high school and in college. I was a pencil with an afro. In High School, mom had taken me to the doctor to see what he could do to help me to gain weight because I was so thin. I had become very self-conscious about it. He had me drinking a milk shake a day, which was right down my alley. A good thick milk shake is my favorite drink of all time. I would walk down to the drug store, or McDonald's for lunch and get a chocolate milkshake every day. I did not gain an ounce. How I wish the same were true today! The draft called me once again for another examination during my senior year at Howard. Again, I was found to be "underweight." I hadn't gained an ounce since the previous year. I know now that God was protecting me. I always had a strange feeling that if I had gone into the service I wouldn't have come back. Little did I know, His plan for me was more than I could have ever imagined then. Later the lottery system was implemented. Everyone's name was put in a lottery. Your number determined your military status. So if you were 1-A, then more than likely you would be drafted immediately. My number came back 1-Y, which meant that unless there was some kind of world war, I could not be drafted. I was being groomed, protected and prepared even then to somehow realize my destiny. I believe that before the foundations of the world existed, God had a plan for our lives. In fact, that's what the

Word of God says. We are all here for a purpose. My calling goes back further than I could ever trace in my family ancestry.

The second semester of my freshman year, I joined Howard's marching band. I played the glockenspiel, a sort of portable xylophone with a bell-like sound. We had one of the largest glockenspiel sections ever that year, due to the fact that many piano majors and minors joined the band that year. Since the glockenspiel was laid out like a piano keyboard, it was easy for anyone who had any knowledge of the piano to play. We had a ball, traveling to places like Morehouse College in Atlanta and playing and marching at half time for all of Howard's football games. I remember proudly marching down Georgia Avenue during the Homecoming parade. The band arrangements for glockenspiel were pretty boring though. Usually they were little unison lines so I would make up new arrangements. Since we had so many players I'd assign parts to everyone and we'd end up playing all kinds of great harmonies to the delight of our band director, Mr. William Penn. I was only in the band for a semester, but it was one of the highlights of my tenure at Howard.

The late 60's were a time for unrest and demonstrations in many universities across the nation. The Black Power movement was in full swing with leaders like H. Rap Brown, Huey Newton of the Black Panthers and Howard University graduate Stokely Carmichael taking active roles. Some of them began to come and speak at rallies at Howard. Stokely Carmichael was a frequent speaker at many of the rallies. Malcolm X also spoke out against the ills of racism, segregation and the importance of taking a stand. Students were encouraged to take active roles in changing our society, whether it was governmental or administrative. In the south, the civil rights movement was in full motion led by Dr. Martin Luther King. Through those movements, students became more vocal about their grievances. In March of 1968, 38 students disrupted the annual Charter Day ceremonies at Howard's Cramton Auditorium protesting policies of the administration and the President of Howard University, Dr. James Nabrit. They were only protesting what so many at the University at that time were feeling. They were reprimanded and told that they would be expelled. On March 19, 1968, in protest of the proposed expulsion of the students, several people demanded the removal of President Nabrit. They also requested that a Department of Afro-American History and Culture be established as well. Twelve hundred students walked into the Administration Building, sat down and refused to leave until their demands were met. The number of students grew as the days went on. I remember going over to the "A" building and taking part in the sit-in along with other friends. For four days, the students sat in. University activities and classes came to a standstill and on March 20 the University officially closed. When the students finally exited the "A" building on the fourth day, the majority of their demands had been met. The original thirty-eight students were pardoned and not expelled, although President Nabrit was not removed and stayed another two years. Howard became the first university where student activism actually closed down the entire university. Columbia University's anti-war demonstrations followed suit soon after and made headlines all over the globe.

Around this same time, tension arose in the School of Music at Howard. Students complained because there were no Black Studies classes offered in the Music department. There was no Jazz department, for example, and the only time you'd hear or study Black music would be Black classical composers such as Nathaniel Dett and others. Of course, the Howard University

Choir was famous for their unparalleled performances of Negro Spirituals, under the capable direction of Warner Lawson. But we were forced to study only the great composers of Europe. As musicians, we also wanted to study the contributions of great composers and genres within and among our culture. Our music was just as important and worthy of recognition as classical. But Dean Lawson was old school. He was not hearing it. For so many, jazz, gospel, and blues became something that they were ashamed of. I think it reminded them of poverty or it conjured up memories that they would rather forget. Some even embraced the erroneous concept that European music *was* authentic music, while the music that our people birthed was somehow low class and unworthy of acceptance.

At any rate, we as students were not given the opportunity to experience our own culture on a scholastic level. I think we were inspired by the recent takeover of the "A" building, and now a plan was conceived to take over the fine arts building. We decided to stage a sit in, organize a demonstration and basically shut the music department down. We weren't going to stop until Dean Lawson heard our demands. All we wanted was a black studies program in the Music curriculum and the implementation of a Jazz studies program in our department.

It was more about the music department than any of the other departments in Fine Arts so the demonstration was to directly affect us. Ironically, the drama department and the art department were very Afro-centric, so they studied the contributions of Black artists diligently. In fact, many times the drama department would call on me to bring gospel music to some of their productions. A piano was put on the elevator and brought up from the practice area in the basement and pulled out to the front of the fine arts building. I remember playing gospel music on that piano from sun up to sun down until there were blisters on my fingers. While I played students sang, clapped and embraced their culture unashamedly. The music we were forbidden to play in this building was performed unashamedly on the Fine Arts building's steps. This went on for a number of days. It almost became a non-stop concert, as students from other parts of the campus would gather in crowds to listen, clap, and sing along. Student leaders would speak periodically to make sure that the crowds of people who gathered in front of the Fine Arts steps were aware of what we were doing and why. Music students were encouraged not to attend classes so that the boycott would be effective. Some of us would spend the night in the Fine Arts lounge and start our demonstration again, first thing in the morning. Of course, there were those students who didn't understand. Of course, there were some who were not interested in the "black studies issue," so they went to class anyway. But, the majority of the Music students followed suit and the School of Music basically shut down. After about a week of singing, playing, rallying and sitting in, Dean Lawson granted our request to meet with him. The entire student body from the School of Music met in Ira Aldridge Theater and a list of our requests was given to him. I always thought Dean Lawson was a nice person, although he came across very stern, but he was from another era. He had been the dean of the School of Music since 1942. Change was not something he embraced. I think he was what some would call a "purist." So this new Afro-centric school that included Jazz and other musical art forms was something he didn't believe in. It had been the way it was for many years. However, because of our demonstrations, courses like African American Music Appreciation, The Business of Music and other courses began showing up in the curriculum. In 1970, the Jazz

Studies program was implemented, which included a jazz band and a Chair for the new Jazz Department, Dr. Donald Byrd. Our demonstration really brought about a change in the School of Music, much to our excitement. Dean Lawson retired soon after the sit-in and Mark Fax, who had been the assistant to the dean, took over. I always loved Mr. Fax. His sense of humor, his quiet demeanor, and his liberal views were refreshing. He was another incredible musician and composer, but he also understood contemporary ideas and concepts. One day some of us were in the practice room playing and singing gospel music to the top of our lungs. All of a sudden, before we knew it, Mr. Fax was standing at the door observing us through the window. We stopped in shock and in fear. He put his head in the door, smiled and said, "Carry on children." No doubt, things were changing! Dean Lawson passed away in 1971, three years after the takeover, and the same year that I graduated from Howard.

On April 4, 1968, news that Martin Luther King Jr. had been killed shook Washington, DC like an earthquake. I remember standing on my steps at 4635 Deane Avenue and seeing the smoke and the reflection of the fires in the sky as my beloved H Street, the area where I grew up, went up in flames as the riots began to spread throughout Washington, DC. All of the streets around Howard, such as 7th Street, Florida Ave and U Street were all basically destroyed. The aftermath looked like a war zone. It would be many years before many of those areas affected by the riots recovered. Some businesses never recovered. The world would never be the same after Dr. King's death. The African American community grieved and was inflamed in ways I had never before seen or experienced.

Around this time Mom informed me that my sister Dorothy was very ill and she was going to New York to see her. When

Mom returned, she told me just how ill she was and that it didn't look good. From what I recall, Dorothy had cirrhosis of the liver. Mom said she had become just a shadow of her former self. When I think of it, Mom was only ten years older than Dorothy. When she and Dad were first married, Dorothy would come and stay with them frequently. As I look back at some of those pictures, I believe that Mom was like an older sister to Dorothy. I believe that through the years she saw her slowly destroying herself, but was helpless to do anything. Not long after that, Dorothy Jean passed. She was only in her forties.

CHAPTER 14
OH HAPPY DAY!

O ne day, Wesley randomly approached me and asked, "Does Mrs. White know you have absolute pitch?" Of course she didn't. If she ever found that out, I knew she was going to work me even harder than she already was! In my mind, I could do without that. Wesley's idea was that it was unfair that she didn't know, because I was getting by with work that was really easy for me while other students were being challenged by it. But that was fine by me. I had come up with a plan. When Mrs. White gave us sight singing drills, I would always make sure that I made at least one mistake so she wouldn't catch on, but I could still get an "A" on the test.

I certainly didn't want her to catch on. But unbeknownst to me, Wesley went behind my back and informed Mrs. White of my absolute pitch. I found out later that she thanked him and told him she had a suspicion because my ear was awfully good. Soon after, we were sitting in class and Mrs. White passed out a test on intervals. The page consisted of a list of about twenty intervals. We had to start at the top of the list and sing them in whatever tempo Mrs. White set, while conducting at the same time. The only way you could get an "A" on this particular test was to do the whole page perfectly. It was a bit difficult and many were having issues trying to do so. I said to myself, I really want an "A" on this test, so I'm going to do all of them right and not make my customary one or two mistakes. When I finished the test with no errors the class began to applaud. Mrs. White stood up from the piano and said, "Class please do not applaud. I've had students in my class with absolute pitch before. That simply means Mr. Smallwood is going to have to work harder." Everything got deathly quiet and my life seemed to flash in front of my eyes. She then continued to the next person. I couldn't believe she knew, and called me out in front of the class like that. I did get my "A," but I paid for it. From then on, Mrs. White would always give me a different assignment than everyone else in the class. If we were studying Chapter 3 from our sight-singing book, for example, she'd give me Chapter 7. At one point, we had to sight sing the vocals to Bach's B Minor Mass. She gave me the violin part to sight-sing. I protested that I didn't have the range of a violin. Her instruction to me was that when it got too high, drop down an octave and continue on. She worked me, but good! What it did in the long run was challenge me. Although pitches were never a problem, my problem was sight-reading rhythms. She would find the hardest rhythm in our textbook and give it to me. I had to work. Music always came easily for me. So, I could just look at it while going over it in my head and basically do it. But I had to go down in the practice area and study, work and stretch myself. I thank God for instructors like her that didn't let me take the easy way out, just because it was easy for me. I wanted to strangle Wesley Boyd though.

At the end of each year, students had to perform scales, technical exercises and an assortment of pieces in front of the entire faculty. In our program, we called these exams juries. Juries were for applied majors in voice, piano and other instruments.

Faculty members could request whatever they wanted from their students, so you were never sure what you had to do. Piano majors had to play diatonic scales, both major and minor, in all three forms, in thirds, sixths and tenths with both hands. I was petrified every year. I hated them with all my heart. I also had to do a voice jury because I was a vocal minor. I could never remember English lyrics, much less foreign ones. Voice majors and minors had to sing in Italian, French and German. The only way I could remember was to write the lyrics on the palm of my hand. I remember singing an Italian song for my jury with my hands cupped dramatically in front of me as if I were in vocal concert, with the words written in them. However, I got through it!

In 1969, a song hit the radio and took the world by storm by the name of "Oh Happy Day." It was performed by the Northern California Community Choir and directed by Edwin R. Hawkins. I remember hearing it played on secular stations as well as gospel radio programs. I thought it very odd, because that was something you never heard—a gospel song being played on a secular program. In fact, it was the first time a track by a gospel choir had done anything of the sort. The song had an infectious Latin feel to it and was really nice. But up until that point, I hadn't heard anything else from the album. Wesley, who was known to hear everything, found out that the choir was coming to the Temple Church of God in Christ in D.C., where Bishop Samuel Kelsey was the pastor. I was very familiar with the church because a lot of us went there for Sunday Night Broadcast. There were a number of churches in DC, such as Refreshing Springs Church of God in Christ (Myrna Summers was one of the choir directors there), Way of the Cross Church, Star of Bethlehem Church of God in Christ (where Howard student and choir director extraordinaire Harvey Lewis Jr. was the minister of music), and Temple Church of God in Christ. Every Sunday, we would make our weekly pilgrimage to Temple's nightly broadcast, and it was always an amazing experience.

These churches had some of the best music and choirs in the city and we as students loved to hear what they had to offer. They were always having musicals as well. The Celestials had started to appear around town at some of these churches, especially Star of Bethlehem. I really wasn't that familiar with the Northern California Choir, other than "Oh Happy Day," and I remember asking, what else do they sing? Wesley didn't know but thought we should go and check them out. So the "three musketeers"— Wesley, Sully and myself—journeyed up to 14th and Park Road NW to check out this new choir. There were about forty young people in the Northern California Choir. I remember sitting there at Temple not knowing what to expect. When they opened their mouths and began to sing, "I Was Glad When They Said Unto Me," my life literally changed. First of all, I had never heard a sound like that coming from a choir. The sopranos had the clearest natural sound I had ever heard in gospel, almost bell-like. It sounded as if someone had put up surround speakers in the church and the sound was coming from everywhere. I had never heard harmonies like that in gospel music either. There was four-part harmony throughout the song, and in some instances, five-part harmony. Some harmonies were more jazz-like than gospel; some rhythms, Brazilian almost in nature. The only thing I could compare them to was some of the harmonic progressions I had heard Donny and Gwen play in the practice area. But a choir with an incredible sound was singing these progressions. Each lead vocalist who stepped to the mic was superb. The style of the vocalists was different though. It wasn't "hard" gospel, but gospel with almost a pop style to it. I didn't know anyone's name at the time, other than Edwin Hawkins who was on the piano. But I knew I would never be the same. Something in me changed that day. When I really think about it, hearing Edwin's music inspired me to finally take writing seriously. His arrangements changed my life. No one in the church was doing anything like that with those kinds of harmonies, chords and rhythms. Before, when I would try to write, it always seemed to be something missing to me, something not quite there. It seemed like I was limited musically in terms of where I could go. But here was a way to write using chords and progressions that were never before heard in the church. I loved it. It was fresh, unique and different. I wanted to write *that* kind of music!

Later that same year, Wesley told me that Harold Bell (the head of the Methodist Student Association) approached him about an idea that he and the Pentecostal Association had been talking about. They wanted to do a "back home revival night" in the chapel. They wanted down home preaching and gospel singing. After all of the unrest on campus, the idea was to take students back to basics: our faith, our beliefs and our spirituality. The Celestials were contacted to sing, but they also wanted to form a choir made up of students from all over the campus to be the official choir for that night. Wesley agreed to help put the choir together and asked me if I was interested. I thought it was an awesome concept, something that certainly hadn't been done before in the history of Howard. So we began to spread the word about the first rehearsal to all of our friends. Flyers were put up all over campus and info spread by word-of-mouth. Wallace Williams, son of Bishop Smallwood Williams of the Bible Way Church, was contacted to direct the choir. Wesley and I were the musicians. Wesley was more comfortable with the piano, so he played the piano and I played the Hammond B3. A few people came to the first rehearsal, but each subsequent rehearsal the numbers began to grow until we had to move the rehearsal to the chapel.

Dean Evans Crawford, the Dean of the Chapel, was more than welcoming. He let us rehearse there and supported our new undertaking fully. Students started coming from everywhere to be a part of the choir, from every background, from every religious belief, denomination, and from every school and major from Medicine to Music. The excitement began to build and spread about this new choir. It was something that just hadn't been done before. The chapel services at Howard on Sunday morning were nothing like what some had experienced growing up. Many times the sermons weren't much more than lectures. The hymns of the church were definitely sung, so were the beautiful anthems, but never a gospel song. Students who came from a more liberal tradition longed for that kind of freedom of worship. They wanted to be free to praise God in their own way. After all of the unrest, anger and tension on campus, healing was needed. A release was needed. At the same time, after coming to Howard, some students had strayed away from their spirituality and there needed to be a way to go back to our spiritual roots. Certainly, there were students who had come from a more conservative way of worship as well. However, it seemed everyone wanted to experience the spontaneity of worshipping in a setting where they could clap their hands, say "Amen," and if they felt like it, shout, dance, and run! All of this was a radical move during a radical time, and the "traditional powers that be," were not going to have any control of what we sang or how we chose to worship.

Someone contacted Willie F Wilson, a student in the School of Religion—a brilliant speaker, full of fire and conviction—to speak for the service. Willie was a good singer as well and sang a mean "Precious Lord, Take My Hand." I think "Oh Happy Day" was the first song we taught the choir during those rehearsals. By now, it had become the biggest gospel song in the country. The other song we taught was "Climbing Up The Mountain," by Mattie Moss Clark and the Southwest Michigan State Choir of the Church of God in Christ. Dr. Mattie Moss Clark was probably the first well-known, recording female gospel choir director in the country. I collected every one of her recordings. Not only was she the consummate choir director and trainer, but was also a great writer and arranger. Her writing influenced me greatly. She also was the mother of one of the most incredible gospel groups of all time, which would be known many years later as The Clark Sisters. In April of 1969, that historical service took place. Andrew Rankin Chapel was filled to the brim. An electric excitement filled the air! As the service began, almost two hundred students took the choir stand. Some had to stand on the floor, but as the choir began to sing Edwin Hawkins's "Oh Happy Day," hands began to raise in the congregation as the Spirit began to spread throughout the building. By the time the choir got to the bridge, "He taught me how to watch, fight and pray," there was no one left sitting in the building. Everyone was standing, singing along in corporate worship with the choir. Willie Wilson preached a dynamic sermon that evening and the power of the Holy Spirit fell (probably for the very first time in Andrew Rankin Chapel). Everyone was plugged into the same source. A feeling of unity and love covered that whole service!

At some point, the Celestials took the stage. We had already had a pretty big following on campus and the service began to climb higher and higher. By the time the choir got to "Climbing Up The Mountain," people were shouting in the aisles and in the choir. Some just fell out, some just cried, and the Spirit moved in that place. There were people who had never felt the presence of the Lord before in that way, who didn't know what else to do but cry. After the service ended, people were still shouting! One friend shouted so much that he just passed out! He literally had to be carried out of the chapel, across campus, over to the Fine Arts Building, with folk fanning him all the way. For those who were not there that night, word began to spread of what had transpired. People wanted to experience it again. The choir was so excited about the fellowship of singing together and the power they felt when doing so, that the idea began to form of making this choir an ongoing thing. Invitations began to pour in for the choir to perform in local churches. Word began to spread to the School of Music and some of the instructors were upset about the choir. Some vocal majors were part of the choir and they were instructed by their professors to get out of the choir or fail. The thought was that they'd "ruin" their voices singing that gospel music. Some did get out while others continued to sneak around and perform with the choir behind the instructors' backs. The choir began to rehearse weekly, preparing itself for the upcoming engagements. At that point, we called ourselves the Howard University Gospel Choir. We soon heard from the University itself saying we could not call ourselves that because we were not under the auspices of the University. The University did not want it thought that they were sanctioning this renegade choir by any means. We then changed our name to the Howard Gospel Choir, dropping the University from the name. The more that those in authority protested the choir, the more we sang. I still played the organ, but a few weeks after our initial performance a new musician came on the scene, pianist extraordinaire Henry M. Davis, who had also entered the School of Music as a student. Wesley preferred to sing, so Henry became the new pianist for the choir. Henry was not only an incredible pianist, but a great writer as well. He and other students such as fellow classmates, Leon Roberts and Harvey Lewis Jr., whose father Bishop Harvey Lewis Sr. was the pastor of Star of Bethlehem, began to write for the choir. Henry had his own group, "The Calvary Crusaders," which was made up of some of his family members. He was also a part of the late Robert Fryson's group, "The Voices Supreme," who had gained national prominence in the gospel music industry. Leon had his own group, "The Roberts Revival," and Harvey Lewis was the director of the Star of Bethlehem Youth Choir. All of us sang together on programs all over the area. It was a wonderful time of fellowship, learning and inspiration. It was around this time that I decided to write a song for the choir. It was an arrangement of "The Lord's Prayer." Some people had never heard "The Lord's Prayer" done as an up-tempo jam. But that is what I heard. So I did it! The arrangement had an anthem-like style, but with a beat. It became the official opening song for each Howard Gospel Choir concert. It was definitely influenced by the classical music genre as well as the progressions that I heard from Edwin Hawkins and Donny Hathaway. Although I had toyed around with writing as a kid, I look at this as my first official song, using all of the influences that had inspired me while at Howard. The popularity of the choir began to grow and grow. We could hardly keep up with the engagements as they began to spread outside the DC area, into other states. We would have annual anniversaries and pack out Cramton Auditorium. Each year we would wear new outfits and come up with innovative ways to march in. I remember one year, instead of doing an elaborate march down the aisle, we decided to come in via the orchestra pit onto the stage. The pit could automatically raise and lower itself. The idea was that we'd already be on the risers when the pit was lowered and we would start singing from there. As the song began to build, the pit would rise, and all of a sudden, you would see us coming up from the stage. We thought it would be a great and unexpected entrance as opposed to just marching down the aisle as we usually did. Well, the choir was rocking and singing as the pit was rising, but at some point, we rocked the pit off its track! It definitely was an unexpected entrance because for the entirety of the song, you saw the choir go up and down, up and down as the pit went out of control rising and lowering.

That choir would shout at the drop of a hat. It was very seldom that we could get through a concert without a number of our members falling out, or going forth in a dance. We were at one concert and one of the members got happy and in doing so, she lost her wig. Someone had the bright idea to pick it up and throw it over on top of the organ for safekeeping. The next thing I remembered was a quite large Afro wig landing on the top of the organ in front of me! I don't think I played another note as I was in stitches laughing for the rest of the night.

CHAPTER 15

THE JOYS OF THE HOWARD GOSPEL CHOIR

The Howard Gospel Choir began to increase in popularity, so we had to travel more extensively. We not only went to perform at churches, but other universities as well. Fisk had the Jubilee Singers, which made the Negro Spiritual popular all over the world, but Howard had the first on-campus Gospel Choir. Soon other universities began following suit. It then spread to high schools as well. We traveled to Bishop College in Dallas, Texas. We traveled to Grambling State University in Grambling, Louisiana. Man, oh man! Grambling was a nightmare. We were not treated well at all. We stayed in some of their unoccupied dorms during our stay, but while we were at the concert, our rooms were broken into! Clothes and personal items were stolen from choir members. Even as some choir members slept, they awoke to find Grambling students in their rooms. Of course, coming from Howard (the mecca of demonstrations and sit-ins), we decided to take our bus to the President of Grambling's house and sit out in front of it until he came out and heard our complaints. We sat for a good length of time. I'm not sure if he wasn't home or if he was afraid to come out.

After all, Howard was known not to play, but he never appeared. Eventually, we got back on the road to travel to our next stop, but no one forgot that nightmare. We also had an interesting incident when we went to perform in Dallas. Henry Davis, our pianist, went to a store across from the hotel one evening. As he was running back towards the hotel, the security guard from the hotel pulled his gun on him. I guess in Texas, at that time, seeing a black man running meant that they were guilty of something. We reported it to management, who basically ignored it and didn't even apologize. Again, our demonstration "sit-in" roots took over and we staged a sit-in in the hallway of the hotel all night. I've got Polaroid pictures of half of the choir sitting in the hallway in their pajamas and nightgowns. If you were at Howard during that time, you would start a demonstration in a minute! When I look back, we were definitely radical! We were not about to take any kind of injustice lying down.

Not long thereafter, the Gospel Choir did their first recording as a live concert in Cramton Auditorium. Henry wrote a song for the choir called "I Found God" and asked me to do the lead on it. It was a beautiful ballad. I was accustomed to sitting down and singing from the piano, other than those few times when Wesley still played for the Celestials. But now, I was the main pianist and Wesley always stood up and sang with the group. Well, someone suggested that I stand in front of the microphone. I was petrified. My shyness kicked in big time. The night of the recording came, and I remember I was literally shaking. But the Spirit of God came into Cramton, and I forgot all about my nervousness. The recording was released on a 45 and became very popular; it was one of the songs that the choir became known for. Later, another 45 was released that was written by music student and Howard Choir member, Leon Roberts. It was called "Keep

Your Hand in God's Hand" and was led by Celestial member, Rosalind Thompkins. I never will forget when Miss Burge, my voice teacher, told me she had heard the 45 of me doing the lead on "I Found God." She immediately demanded me to get out of that choir. She said, "all of that singing gospel is going to ruin your voice!" I had always respected Miss Burge and I loved her dearly, but now she was stepping on sacred ground. I remember telling her that gospel music was my heritage, a part of my culture and more importantly, a part of my faith, and I was not going to stop singing it. Miss Burge muttered some unintelligible phrases in her deep voice, and then she shook her head and said, "These kids, these kids!" But, she never mentioned it again. I think it really helped a lot that I was playing for her classes, and accompanying her students on recitals. So, I think as not to jeopardize that, she let the subject go. She did give me a "B" instead of an "A," but I didn't care. Gospel music was more important to me than anyone had realized at the time.

During my second semester of my sophomore year, I basically did nothing in terms of my studies. I didn't study and I didn't practice; I partied. Remember, I came from a very strict religious home and when I got to Howard, I figured it was time to do the things I had always wanted to do. Although I was still living at home (because dorm fees were too expensive), I didn't miss a party. Many times, I would get in trouble with my parents for coming home at three or four in the morning. I got the lecture, "As long as you're in this house, and under this roof, you will abide by my rules." When I look back, I think I was rebelling against my father and dealing with the residuals of abuse. When you turn eighteen or nineteen years old, you think you are grown. You think that you know everything and no one can tell you anything! Although I was still respectful to my parents, my mindset was that I was going to do what I wanted to do. I think some of it was my quest to "fit in." There was a world outside of music and I had no previous knowledge of it.

My instructors began to notice a change and Dr. McGinty called me into her office concerned that something was wrong. She said my grades had begun to plummet and that was so unlike me. I had always gotten good grades. She wanted to know if there were problems at home contributing to my performance. I was a bit embarrassed and told her no. Everything at home was fine. She instructed me to do better because I was headed for trouble in terms of my grades and my scholarship. Mrs. Burwell, who had guided me through the Junior Department, sat me down, I don't know how many times, and not only threatened my very life, but expressed her disappointment in me. Professor Kerr was exasperated with me. I think I learned one piece the whole semester which was the Toccata Op. 72 No. 5 by composer Camille Saint-Saëns and didn't learn it well enough to even perform it at the student recital. There were times when I was plowing away at some piece I had never practiced, thinking that I could fool him into thinking that I had, when he would hit the keyboard on his piano, get up and leave the room while I sat there. Usually he would never come back, so I'd just finish destroying whatever piece I was playing and then leave my lesson. One time he hollered at me saying that my playing reminded him of a "constipated scrub-woman." I'm not sure what that meant, but it wasn't good. Mr. Kerr had never been this way with me. But then on the other hand, I had never had this kind of poor performance in my work. Piano was my major and this was not a good sign. I was busy having too much fun with my friends and felt like eventually it would work itself out. God really took care of me during this period. I began to drink, trying to keep up with some of my friends. Honestly, sometimes I would be so drunk that when I left a party I couldn't remember how I got home. I would always drive to school because my father bought me a small Corvair so that I could get back and forth. It was about a twenty-five minute drive. I would go across the Benning Road Bridge every day. I'm surprised that I never ran into it, or worse, ran off of it. But through all of those late night trips home, some of which I can't even recall, I never had an accident.

One night, Wesley and I both left a party that had been at my play sister Ollie Milligan's apartment. Both of us were pretty messed up. I remember thinking, *I'm a bit too messed up to make it home.* So I came up with the idea of Wesley driving us to his house and, by the time he got there, I figured I would be sober enough to drive home. Wesley took over the wheel and I was slumped over in the passenger's seat. Near his house, I heard a slight bumping noise and Wesley stopped the car. I rose up to see what had happened only to see that Wesley had run into another car. It wasn't a bad accident by any means. I doubt if there was a scratch, but it was a slight bump into the other car. The driver got out of the car and was much older and bigger than we were. He instructed Wesley to get out of the car. He knew we were drunken crazy teenagers, but I think he wanted to take advantage of that. He instructed Wesley to give him all of his money to pay for the nonexistent damage to his car. Of course, as students we probably had a dollar in change between the two of us. Wesley started explaining, "Man we are students, I don't have any money." By this time I started to get scared. We certainly were too inebriated to fight, much less run. He had Wesley pull his pockets inside out to reveal the four or five dimes or nickels that were there. He demanded that Wesley give him every coin of change that was in his pocket. Wesley gave him every penny he had. The man got more upset and told Wesley "This ain't gonna help pay for nothing! Since you don't have any more than this, just let me hit you in your chest one time." Wesley's eyes got big and start pleading, "OH MAN, please don't hit me." The dude still insisted. "Let me hit you one time, man. I know that will make me feel better after you done hit my car." By this time, I had sat up fully and Wesley began pleading. Before I could blink, the man hit Wesley so fast that I never saw the blow. It had been snowing that week and the streets and sidewalks still had ice on them. The last thing I remember was seeing Wesley slide down the ice on his back after the man hit him. Wesley was certainly a little bit bigger than me. If that man had hit me I would have broken in two. I sobered up real fast and got behind the wheel and took off down the street leaving Wesley sliding. When I thought the man was gone, I came back. Wesley had gotten up and gone in the house by then. I rang the doorbell and Wesley came to the door clutching his chest hollering, "OH LAWD. I THINK HE BROKE MY RIBS." Of course, no such thing had happened and finally after I figured there was nothing wrong other than a sore chest, I got in the car and drove home. We laughed about that for years. There is an old adage that says, "God takes care of fools and babies." I certainly was in the former category. Of course, not coming from a drinking background, I'd just drink until I got sick. I remember coming home one night and throwing up all over the place. Mom was home and heard me and got up to see what in the world was wrong. I told her that I had gone to a party and ate some bad tuna fish. Of course, the whole house smelled like liquor and it was quite obvious what the problem was. She talked to me the next morning after cleaning up my mess. My father was a night watchman at the time so he hadn't been home. Mom had to open all the windows before he got home so he wouldn't know that I had been drinking. She also begged me not to drive if I was in that condition. The disappointment in her eyes hurt me more than anything else. I even tried weed. I think God really stepped in at that point. Each time I would try it, I would get the worst migraine I had ever experienced. I never got high, just had a migraine. God was intervening. I could have become an alcoholic or a drug addict. I had friends who unfortunately did. But God wouldn't let that happen. He had a work for me to do. I'm sure my protecting angels were working overtime, bruised wings and all. When the end of that semester came, Professor Kerr called me into his office. He informed me that first of all I had failed his class, and that he did not instruct the caliber of student that I had become; I could no longer be a piano major and needed to find another major. It felt like a building had fallen on me. My first thought was, "What in the world am I going to tell my parents?" I started pleading for my life, for my major, and for a second chance. I promised that I would change and become the student that I used to be. Mr. Kerr's response was, "You should have thought of that when you came in here this entire semester and wasted my time and yours." I was near tears by now. I had disappointed my instructors who had so much hope for me, I had disappointed myself, and now I was getting ready to disappoint the person who meant more to me than anyone on this planet, my Mother. I thought of the year that I failed the eighth grade. I felt like a failure. I guess Mr. Kerr saw the desperate look on my face. He said to me, "Richard, this is all I can do. I'll give you an incomplete 'F' on your transcript for this semester. If you can come to summer school, learn a complete recital by memory, pulling from all four periods, the Baroque, Classical, Romantic and Contemporary, and perform it at the beginning of the fall semester, then I'll erase the incomplete 'F' and replace it with an 'A.' If you fail to do it, then the incomplete 'F' turns into a permanent one and you'll have to find another major." Thank God for grace and mercy! I was determined to play the best recital known to mankind. I only had about six weeks of summer school to pull an entire recital together by memory. That summer found me at the School of Music working harder than I had in at least a year. When the fall semester of my junior year arrived, I gave my recital and thank God it was a success. Mr. Kerr was ecstatic about my performance and the incomplete "F" was erased and turned into an "A." If you had a scholastic scholarship, they would give you only one semester to mess up. If you messed up twice in a row, then your scholarship would be taken from you. I knew this year I had to work and bring my grades back up to that "B" average or higher that I so desperately needed. My mom and dad didn't have the money to send me to school. I needed that help in order to get my education. I worked like never before, bringing all my grades up that semester and reclaiming my "B-plus" average. I made a complete about face my junior year in all areas and never looked back. I just thank God for his protection during my insanity period.

In 1970, I got the most exciting news ever! Word had spread all over the country about this new Howard Gospel Choir and none other than Rev. James Cleveland invited us to California. The LA Chapter of the Howard University Alumni Association helped to sponsor it. Rev. Cleveland had set up a series of nightly concerts all over the Los Angeles area for the choir. I had never been to the West Coast and had never flown in my life. All of my traveling had either been by car, bus or train. However, once the flight started my nerves calmed down and we began to have fun like we always did when we traveled. LA was beautiful. I had never seen anything like it. As a kid, I had always wanted to go to Disneyland. But we certainly couldn't afford anything like that. However, I realized my dreams and got a chance to go. While there, I found out that I have motion sickness. We went on the teacups and I got as sick as a dog. I also found out that I could never ride anything that went in a circle other than the merry-go-round. Rev. Cleveland was a great host and I was in awe. He hosted gatherings at his home for the gospel choir and really made us feel welcome. Here was someone whom I had idolized as a child and I was not only meeting him, but I had an opportunity to see his home. I probably didn't say more than a couple of sentences to him along with some one-word answers. My shyness kicked in big time. To me, he was bigger than life and someone whom I really admired. I was in awe of Rev. Cleveland's choir, The Southern California Community Choir. I had their albums and was a huge fan. Howard's gospel choir was welcomed with open arms. The concerts were packed out each night. There were other artists from LA who sang each night, including Rev. Cleveland and we were the featured guests. Henry's "I Found God", the song that I led, was a big hit there that week, as well as my arrangement of "The Lord's Prayer" which we sang to open up each night. I was so excited about the great reception that "The Lord's Prayer" received each night from the different audiences. After all, it was the first song I had written since I was a kid and I was so proud of it. However, I was about to learn a life lesson about the music business. I believe that everything in life happens for a purpose and a reason. Life is like school. We are constantly learning and getting tested on what we learn. Sometimes we pass and other times we fail. It's all about getting back up during our failures, learning what we can from them and getting back on track. God was still preparing me for what was to come. That week in LA was a great success and it catapulted the choir's name to yet another level. People all over the country, including the West Coast, were talking about these singing college kids from Howard.

CHAPTER 16

LESSONS I LEARNED
THE HARD WAY

few months after we returned from Los Angeles, I was
listening to the radio. All of a sudden, I heard a familiar
introduction. Then I heard a choir begin to sing the
first couple of bars of my arrangement of "The Lord's Prayer."
It was the strangest feeling because I knew we certainly hadn't
recorded it, so it wasn't us. As I continued to listen I realized it
was my song; chord for chord, note for note. I didn't know what
to think. When the song ended, Cal Hackett, one of the most
popular DJ's in the area, announced whom the song was "by." I
was stunned. It was an artist from LA who had performed on
the very program that Rev. Cleveland had set up for us. I couldn't
believe it. Although they were new on the gospel scene, I had
admired them and had previously attended one of their concerts
when they came to DC. How could someone who called himself
a gospel artist steal from someone else and blatantly record it?
Understand that I knew nothing about copyrighting my music.
No one had ever told me. I didn't even know what it was. I was
just excited to write music the way I felt it. Because I dealt with
shyness and social anxiety all of my life, writing was an outlet for

me. Writing allowed me to express my heart through a vehicle that I was completely comfortable with.

I called the radio station. I asked to speak to the DJ, Cal Hackett. Cal knew me from the Celestials, and of course, as a student at Howard. He was lovingly called "the sunshine spreader" because of his sunny disposition on the air. He would later become a major radio personality who supported me in the beginning of my career. I told him how it was my song and we had performed it in LA and this person had stolen it. Cal, being the kind person that he was, told me that he only had one copy of it and he would not be playing it again. In fact, he told me to come down to the station as soon as I could and he would give me the copy and I could figure out what I wanted to do legally. I never will forget how much it meant to me that he believed me. I remember going to the radio station, WUST, and picking up the 45. I remember it being a yellow label and under the name "The Lord's Prayer" it read that the arrangement and music was by this LA artist. I was so hurt. I know the person probably didn't know that I wrote it specifically, in fact we didn't even know each other personally, but clearly he heard it every night that we sang it. He certainly knew that HE didn't write it. How could someone do that? I didn't know exactly what to do. I was a student and didn't have any money. Someone told me about a free legal office not too far from Howard. I found it and sat down with the recording in my hand to talk to the legal representative. After hearing my plight, the first thing he asked me was, "Son, where is your copyright form?" I remember asking, "What is that?"

He explained to me that copyrighting was a claim that I should have filed with the Library of Congress on completion of writing the song. This claim would establish me as composer and arranger of the song. He then went on to tell me that there was nothing I could do if I hadn't copyrighted it. It was my word against the artist's word. This particular artist would achieve some success later in the gospel field and later on go on to more major success in the secular field in the mid to late 70's. He became quite a name in the R&B field, and many of his allegedly self-written songs were well known. After what had happened to me, I would wonder sometimes, did he really write them? I left the office feeling devastated. It was my first hard lesson in this business called music. Just because it's gospel doesn't mean that there aren't people who will take advantage of you. Songwriters, COPYRIGHT your music!

The fall after our California trip, the King of Gospel, Rev. James Cleveland, consented to be our special guest for homecoming. He brought the Cleveland Singers with him and even did Henry's song, "I Found God," along with the choir. I shared the vocals with one of Rev. Cleveland's singers. We both shared a mic. I remember there was one little part in the song, where I did a little riff. As I got to that section and opened my mouth to sing it, the vocalist snatched the mic out of my hand and did a high note. I remember feeling some kind of way. Between my song being stolen and those little onstage antics, I was finding out that the gospel community wasn't always loving and affirming. As I look back, it's amusing. I was learning the ropes. But at the time, my little feelings were hurt.

Wallace "Hoppy" Williams remained the animated director of the gospel choir my entire time at Howard. His sister, Pearl Williams Jones, was a graduate of Howard and an incredible musician and gospel music historian. She became a mentor of mine and took me under her wing. She was a constant encourager to me and caused a number of doors to open later in life. In

1984, she created the first gospel music degree in the country for
the University of the District of Columbia. It was her concept
and she headed that department for many years. Because of her
vision, many students have graduated from that university with
a bachelor's degree in music with an emphasis in gospel. I did
an arrangement of "Jesus Lover Of My Soul" on the Smallwood
Singers' "Testimony" CD. The merging of that hymn and Bach's
"Jesu Joy Of Man's Desiring," was Pearl's idea and creation. She
was known all over the world for doing it as a vocal solo along
with her incredible mastery of the piano. When she passed,
I arranged it for the Smallwood Singers with harmonies and
recorded it in her honor.

By now, Edwin Hawkins had changed the name of the
Northern California Community Choir to the Edwin Hawkins
Singers. They began to come to DC frequently. They started
doing concerts at Cramton Auditorium as well. He had also
cut the number of singers down to make it more affordable for
travel. Most students at Howard (including myself) would never
miss the Hawkins Singers when they came to town. Eventually,
we began to befriend them. So much so, that they would call
ahead and let us know when they were coming. Our parents
would sometimes cook dinner for them. Wesley, who was an
amazing cook, would cook for them himself. I remember one
week they came and sang every night at a different church in
DC. Wesley, Sully, Ollie and I didn't miss a night. We started
to become good friends, and this friendship would last for all
of our lives. One night, we went to hear them at the Carter
Barron, an outdoor amphitheater in Washington, DC. A light
skinned, sort of stocky brother, with a big Afro stepped to the
microphone and began to sing a song called "All You Need."
I hadn't heard this voice before. The voice was incredible. At

some point in the song, the voice just began to climb higher and higher, not in falsetto but naturally, until it had gone from first tenor to alto range. It was clear as a bell, anointed, powerful and mesmerizing. Who was this singing like this? It was the first time I had heard this particular soloist in the Hawkins Singers. Very soon I would find out that it was Edwin's baby brother, Walter. By this time, the Hawkins Singers were undoubtedly my favorite gospel group. As far as I was concerned, there was no comparison. I could not wait until the next album was released or the next appearance in the area. It got to the point that we would get in my father's hoopty and drive to Pittsburgh or wherever they were. There was Tramaine Davis, whom Walt would eventually marry, a soprano's soprano, and soulful with an unbelievable range. When she sang in the background her voice cut through like crystal or diamonds breaking into an almost stereophonic sound. There was Ruth Ann Lyons, whose soprano was big, lush, beautiful and as clear as a bell. Ruth had so much power in her voice, that she was a soprano section unto herself. There was Norma Jean King, Edwin and Walters's cousin: another soprano whose range was incredible. It was light and ethereal but made up that wonderful soprano section quality that I heard that first day at Temple Church of God in Christ. Shirley Miller was another cousin and Norma Jean's sister. She was the lead singer on "Oh Happy Day," after replacing the original lead Dorothy Morrison. She was an alto, rich in quality and timbre that reached down to tenor. There was Barbara Gill, another strong alto who helped hold the alto section together. Then there was Elaine Kelly, a phenomenal voice that could destroy a church at the drop of a hat. Something about her vocal quality was similar to Walter's, and sometimes if they were ad-libbing together it was hard to distinguish who was who. Her voice didn't stop at alto range, which is what she sang, but would approach soprano with ease. In addition, Elaine had so much charisma, personality, stage presence and a killer smile. When she sang, she'd skip down the aisle and literally tear the place up. House wreckers like "Praise Him" and "Come and Go With Me to my Father's House" were the songs that everyone would wait for at a Hawkins Singers concert. Edwin's writing inspired me to take my writing seriously. I would sit down to write for the Celestials, and I would think on Edwin's style. We must have sang every song that the Edwin Hawkins Singers put out. The first song I ever wrote for the Celestials was an arrangement on the old hymn, "Must Jesus Bear the Cross Alone?"

By this time we had added a new member, Mary Lewis. Mary was a strong soprano with a great range. She was also a freshman in Liberal Arts from Buffalo, New York. Rosalind Thompkins was the alto with the crazy range that would wreck the house. Mary, or "Lou Lou" as Wesley renamed her, was the one that could sing the pretty high, clear soprano melodies. Sully was just Sully. That boy could sing anything. He would close his eyes and get into a zone and literally tear the place a part. His unique vocal quality and soulful sadness would pull at your heart. He also had a heart of gold. He sang from that heart, pure and true with no agendas other than his love for the Lord. Wesley was the glue that held the voices together. His voice was a powerful, clear sound that could carry the entire tenor section in itself.

Sometimes I had to put Wesley in a choir setting as the only tenor. But Wesley could balance that tenor section no matter how many were in the other sections. The Celestials were my first guinea pigs and I delighted in rehearsing with them over and over, hour after hour. I enjoyed experimenting on them vocally to see what I could make them do. Thank God they went right along with me. The Celestials' sound became tighter and stronger the more we rehearsed and the more I challenged them. I challenged their ears to hear unique intervals and harmonic progressions. Edwin Hawkins inspired four- and five-part harmonies in certain sections of the songs that I began to compose. Although we still sang songs from other groups and composers, I began to write more and more. The quality of sound that would later be known as the Smallwood sound had started to take form. By now we had decided that this just might be something that we wanted to pursue as a career. I was still a bit unsure of my writing ability, but Wesley and the group kept pushing me to do it. When I listened to other music on the radio or other local groups around, mine seemed so odd, so different than other things I would hear. It made sense to me, but I didn't know if it would make sense to anyone else.

Eventually, we decided to make a demo tape. I wrote four songs, "Peaceful Place," "He'll Make it Alright," "Give me Strength," and "Jesus is All You Need." We went to Mr. Ralph Dines who was the audio engineer and manager for Cramton auditorium. Mr. Dines would record all the senior recitals for the music majors. He allowed us to come to Cramton and record our demo, free of charge. After our demo was done, Wesley and I traveled to New York to shop it around. Of course neither one of us had much money, but I imagine we got some money from our parents, hopped a Trailway Bus and arrived in N.Y.

We stayed at the YMCA in Manhattan. At that time, it was about seven or eight dollars per night. It was clean and nice. So the YMCA became our home for several days. We got a phone book, and looked up all the record labels within walking distance. Neither of us had money for cab fare, nor do I think we were sure of how to get around on the subway.

The next morning, armed with our list of addresses for the largest record labels, we set out with our tape under our arm. I guess we never thought that we might have to make an appointment to see record execs. Surprisingly, we showed up unannounced and hardly had any trouble seeing anyone. We approached the receptionist in each office by saying, "We are students from Howard University. We want to know if you are interested in signing any gospel artists. We sing gospel music and we have a demo tape that we'd like someone to hear." Many people let us in to see the execs. Most of the comments were the same. Everyone was polite but basically said they weren't looking for gospel artists. Gospel music hadn't crossed over to secular labels yet. Edwin Hawkins was probably the only one at that time. Of course, it happened because of the huge success of "Oh Happy Day," and they were soon after signed to the secular company, Buddha Records. But certainly Edwin's success was not the norm for gospel artists.

I guess we never approached gospel labels because none of them were doing anything remotely like the music we were doing. I knew we'd get a flat out "NO" from any of them because everything was basically traditional in gospel music. Plus, since Edwin was my biggest inspiration at the time, I wanted to be on a secular label like he was. So Wesley and I went to Blue Note Records, the number one jazz label at the time and a subsidiary of Columbia Records. Dr. George Butler was the head of the label, and a graduate of Howard University. I'm sure hearing the name of his Alma Mater and seeing we were young students helped gain us an audience with him. Thankfully, he welcomed us with open arms. We sat in his big plush office as we told him about ourselves and what we were studying at Howard, and more importantly, what we were trying to do. I think we must have piqued his interest and he asked to hear our demo tape. As he listened to the tape, I saw his head bop and I saw a half-smile on his face as he listened to each song. After the last song, he looked at me. I just knew he was going to say that he wanted to sign us.

"Richard," he began. "You're ten years ahead of your time." I wasn't sure what that meant. I guess my face showed my confusion, because he began to explain: "This music is great and I'm loving what I'm hearing," he continued. "But it's so far ahead of what people are doing right now, that no one is going to get it. I wouldn't have a clue how to market it because it is so different."

I was heartbroken. I still didn't understand what he was saying. He told me, "Keep doing what you're doing. Don't get discouraged, and don't stop. You're going to have to wait for everyone else to catch up to you."

What was so different about what I did and why didn't anyone get it? I couldn't figure it out. It was what I felt. It was what I heard. I knew it was what I was being given by God. Why would God give me something that no one really understood? Was this all some kind of cosmic joke? Dr. Butler gave us his information and asked us to stay in touch. I was disheartened and I think Wesley saw it. He told me as we walked out the door, "Rich, you have an awesome gift. We are going to make this happen. The world needs to hear it." "Yeah," I thought. "But the world doesn't get it, and probably couldn't care less about it."

We were fans of the R&B group the Chi-Lites. "Have You Seen Her" and "Oh Girl" were huge all across the country. The label that they recorded for was Brunswick Records, which was also in walking distance of the YMCA where we were staying. We arrived at the front door and found it locked. We rang the bell and waited. Not long after that, a gentleman answered the door with a very pleasant smile. He had on an open collar white shirt and dark pants with a cap on his head.

"May I help you?" he asked.

Wesley, as usual, explained who we were. I was never a talker, and still was incredibly shy. So most of my comments would be yes or no, especially if I didn't know you. So whoever talked better than I, was always the spokesperson. After hearing about us, he invited us in. The Brunswick offices were beautiful. He showed us around. He took us to the actual recording studios and showed us a number of rooms. Lastly, we ended up in the boardroom, which contained a beautiful huge and long mahogany table with plush chairs around it. At the end of the table was a huge reel-to-reel tape recorder that was mounted on the wall. He invited us to sit down and tell him more information about us. After telling him we had some music for him to hear, he asked to hear the demo tape. He put it on and put the volume all the way up so that the sound literally bounced off the walls of the boardroom. He immediately began to get up and dance around when the mid- to up-tempo tunes came on. "Man, this is BAD!" he shouted, dancing around the room. Well that's a good sign, I thought. "Who wrote these tunes?" he asked. "I did," I said softly.

"Maaan, you BAD!" He exclaimed and continued to dance. After the tape had finished, he started from the beginning and played it again. This time he was a little more reflective and he said, "We just need to change the feel on a couple of the tunes, and make it more driving." I was thinking to myself, sir, if you sign us you can change whatever feel you want.

He continued, "Man with the right band and orchestration, man this would be BAD!" He then got up and began to dance again. We were delighted because he was delighted and smiled and nodded his head to the beat as he danced. After the tape had finished the second time around, he exclaimed, "Man, we need to sign you guys!" I couldn't believe he was saying this after all the people who had turned us down. He continued, "Man this is an off day, the building is basically closed and I just came in for a little while. My secretary is not even here. Just tell me this. Are you interested in a contract?"

"YES SIR," Wesley and I both shouted at the same time, trying to hold our composure.

He said, "First of the week, my secretary will be drawing it up and we are going to send it to you." I can't remember if he gave us a card, or just jotted his number down. I remember his name was Alonzo Tucker. At any rate, he gave Wesley his name and number and asked for the address to which he could send the contract. Wesley, who had managed the Celestials from its inception, gave him his address. I couldn't wait to get outside the building to yell, holler, and jump or something. When we closed the door behind us, Wesley and I looked at each other and began to run around the street like we had lost our minds.

"WE GOT A CONTRACT," we shouted. We were elated. There was no need to stay in N.Y. any longer. Of course, this was before cell phones so we tore down the street trying to find a pay phone. The minute we found one, I called Mom and gave her the news. She was elated to say the least. We then called one of the other group members and got them to call everyone else. Lastly, we called Ollie. I could hear her screaming over the phone as we told her what happened. We then went back to the "Y," checked out and caught the next bus back to D.C. The first stop we made was at Ollie's apartment. When she opened the door, she turned around and ran back in the apartment and began her little praise dance. All three of us hopped up and down and ran around the apartment. She had made a little banner that she hung up saying "CONGRATULATIONS CELESTIALS."

The rest of the group came over and we had our own little celebration, thanking God that He had opened this door for us. For several days, I was on cloud nine. The first of the week came, and we heard nothing from Mr. Tucker. We waited until the end of the week and Wesley gave him a call. Mr. Tucker explained that he had not forgotten us but had been swamped by work, but the memo to his secretary was on her desk to draw up the contract. We waited another week or so and after not hearing anything, Wesley called him again. There had been a fire at Mr. Tucker's house and he was trying to deal with that, but he assured us that we should have the contract in about two-to-three days. Again, there was no contract and no call within that week. Wesley continued to call and get busy signals or no answer at all, until finally it began to dawn on us that this man was giving us the run around. I was crushed. I just knew that we had secured a contract with Brunswick. Time went on and we heard nothing. Finally we moved on, not knowing what had happened. About a year passed and a show came to D.C. featuring the Chi-Lites and other Brunswick artists. A group of us went to the show. While there, Wesley spotted a former Howard music student who had since graduated and ironically was now working for Brunswick Records. He greeted us warmly and we told him how we had enjoyed the show. We then began to tell him of our experience in New York at Brunswick. He asked us to give him more info about the person we had talked to. We described what he looked like, what he had on and gave him the man's full name as he had given it to us. He paused and began to chuckle. We stood there wondering what in the world was funny. His chuckle turned into laughter, I mean hilarious laughter from the diaphragm. I remember looking at him while he laughed thinking, "*I really want to hit him,*" because there was nothing funny that I could see. I had put all my little hopes and faith in what this man had told us and he had promised us a contract. Finally, he stopped laughing and said, "Are you sure that was his name?" "Yes!" we said. He looked away smiling and then back at us and said, "Man, THAT WAS THE JANITOR!!" Although it's funny now, it wasn't then. We were young and if someone promised us something, we certainly believed it. I have always wondered, why would the custodian take advantage of us kids like that? Why would he lie and promise something that he had no way of delivering? However, in this business of music, you will get lied to, lied on, promised things that people won't deliver, and taken advantage of. It's part of what we call paying dues. We were innocent, and were ignorant to so much. We really didn't know anything. However, it was part of my growing experience in this business. It taught me to put my trust in God; and I'm a firm believer that if God has preordained something for you, it will happen in God's time. There is a period of grooming that God takes us through so that we'll be ready for what He has for us in the future. Little did I know, this was the beginning of my season of preparation. However, when I look back on it now, it's one of the funniest things I ever experienced. No doubt, I had a lot to learn.

CHAPTER 17

DAD TAKES A TURN
FOR THE WORST

After a while, we felt the name the Celestial Singers was a little too old-fashioned. After all, Edwin Hawkins had ushered in a new age of contemporary gospel music. Since we were considered contemporary, we didn't want our name to sound too traditional. So, we decided to change our name to the Celestial Sound. Soon after, we recorded a song I wrote called "Come Together." The "B" side of the 45 was an arrangement of an old hymn, "At the Altar." We released it independently. "Come Together" was written to be more inspirational than "straight gospel," so that it would appeal to multiple listeners. It was all about people loving each other and trying to solve the ills of this world, while "At the Altar" was traditional gospel. Local gospel radio stations began playing them both. The most exciting thing was to hear something that you created on the radio for the first time. I remember the first time it was played. I called everyone I could think of to tell them to turn on the radio!

Probably around my second year at Howard, I began to let my hair grow. Afros were the hairstyle of the day at Howard. Mine grew longer and longer. I remember my father pulling me to the side to tell me that he didn't want me to wear leather jackets, because they made me look like a hoodlum. He also instructed me to cut my hair. I guess Howard had made me more vocal about what I believed, so I looked him in the eye and told him, "I appreciate all of the sacrifices you have made for me but I won't be cutting my hair." I was waiting for some kind of slap or hit upside the head, but he just looked at me and said, "I'm sorry you feel that way son," and walked away. I was shocked. He was mellowing. Other than getting it trimmed, I don't think I cut it until a number of years after he passed. When I look back, I think so much of it had to do with my rebellion towards him. I had been beat up too many times, for no reason! At some level, I felt I was only valued because of my musical ability. I don't think I could actually articulate what I was feeling. However, as I look back, I know it had so much to do with the many mixed feelings that I had about him. I think I purposely let my "fro" grow as big as I could. At its longest, it was a "super-fro."

My mom had always loved kids, and an opportunity presented itself for my parents to become foster parents. In 1970, they were part of a foster care program sponsored by the Rehoboth Baptist Church in SE, DC. We moved from our two-bedroom apartment on Dean Ave. NE to a newly renovated four-bedroom townhouse at 132 12th Street NE in Lincoln Park. Although I was 21, the thought of children coming into the home and calling my mother "mom" took some getting used to. After all, I was an only child. Even if I was grown, I had been the only one to have that luxury all of my life. Right after we moved, over a very short period of time, four children entered the home. The first one was Gloria who was 7. The next two were a brother and sister, Anthony and Stephanie, ages 5 and 8. Last but not least was Joy who was 11 years old. This would be the beginning of the next phase of Mom's life as a foster parent and mine as a foster brother. I got accustomed to it eventually and came to love all of the kids. Mom raised all four to adulthood and then started on another family. She was doing what she loved and that made her happy. Most of the kids came from an orphanage called Junior Village. Some came with problems that Mom had to address. But because of her love and her determination, she worked with them and worked through their problems. Many times, it was a challenge and I looked at Mom in amazement at her tenacity, her patience and her seemingly never-ending love. Sometimes there were kids sent to her home on a temporary basis. She loved them just as much as she did the ones who were permanent residents. Some had been abused sexually as well as physically. But Mom was always up for the challenge and her love and direction helped many children through hard and difficult challenges. Her calling was to "spread love and sunshine"— that's what she did all of her life. To this day, people still come up to me to tell me how Mom impacted their lives. I couldn't be prouder.

In '69, my father started a new church called Union Temple Baptist Church in a house at 16th and U St SE. It's interesting that in the years that he founded churches all over the country, some had the same or similar names. When we lived in Elmwood, Pa., (a suburb of Philly when I was about five years old), he pastored a Greater Union Temple Baptist Church on South 84th Street. When he started the new Union Temple in DC, I was busy with school and never attended the 16th and U location. Soon he found a new location up the street, which was an old Masonic Hall at 14th and U St SE. After they moved there at times I would stop by and help out on the piano. I never will forget, they had an old blue and gold upright piano. I had never seen such a colorful piano in my life. It was never completely in tune, however I made the best of it when I'd go by on Sunday mornings to help out.

On his 50th preaching anniversary, I decided to get a choir together for the celebration. By now, two of the former "baby Smallwood Singers" and part of the old "Whitestone crew," Brenda Jenkins Wanzer and Valerie Wright Williams, had joined over there. I got them and several other people who were members around our age, and also invited some people from the Howard Gospel Choir to be a part. Of course, I got Ollie, Wesley and Sully to be a part as well. The program was a success and the sound of the choir was awesome. Mom and Dad were very happy and pleased. I was proud of the choir and most thankful to all of those who helped out. By now Mom was known to many of my friends at Howard, because she would cook Sunday dinner and our table would be full along with all the foster kids. Everyone knew about Mom's famous fried chicken. I've had a lot of really good fried chicken in my lifetime, but never have I tasted the likes of what Mom used to cook. It undoubtedly was the best I'd ever eaten. Most of my classmates seemed to think so as well, and Mom was always cooking for a host of my friends and classmates. She was not only mother to our new family of kids, but she would become like a second mother to my classmates as well, many of whom were away from home. They would confide in Mom about their problems and issues. Mom would pray for them, advise them and walk with them through many of their problems, and cook for them. I can recall so vividly the feasts that would take place, especially at Thanksgiving and Christmas. About three or four days before the approaching holiday, Mom would drag me to the Florida Ave. Market, which some called the farmer's market, where local farmers would bring their fresh produce to sell. She'd get her fresh greens, string beans, her twenty-something pound fresh turkey (never frozen), cheese, fresh eggs and butter for the macaroni and cheese, her smoked cooking meat, sweet potatoes, onions and all of the ingredients for an amazing holiday meal. Everyone would be in anticipation of sitting around the long table and knowing you were going to have some of the best food ever. When we had the apple tree, she'd pick choice apples and either make pies or cobbler. Other times she'd make her amazing sweet potato pies or her famous lemon Jello cake. I'd be directed to "sneak" into the liquor store and get her some brandy for her brandied sweet potatoes. She'd make freshly brewed ice tea (never instant), fill the punch bowl with ice and mix it all together with pineapple juice and ginger ale. She fussed over every item and it had to be perfect in her eyes. She loved the holidays and put her heart into it. As she got older, sometimes she'd be so exhausted that she'd have to lie down on the couch in the living room after the food was done. These memories give me life and I can still smell that kitchen in my mind. She planted the importance of family, love and celebration of the holidays into me. Even today, although cooking is definitely not my "calling," I still celebrate with friends and family the way she taught me.

One day my father came into my room and told me he needed to talk to me. My first thought was "What is it now?" Is it my hair, my clothes? Is he going to insist that I start playing for his church again?" But it was none of that. He said to me, "Son, I know you want to do music for a livelihood. I know that sometimes in order to make ends meet, you may have to play in nightclubs or places like that. I just want you to know that your mother and I have raised you right, and I believe that you can withstand any kind of temptations that may be there. So what I'm saying is that you have my blessings to play wherever you may need to play as you go forward in your career." I was shocked, but I was really touched. This was so not like him. In fact, it seemed like he was mellowing into someone that I didn't recognize. There was a love and a support that I felt from him during those years. He'd show up unannounced sometimes by himself at concerts that the Celestials were a part of. Somewhere I think he knew that he was coming to the end of his life. I think in a way he may have been trying to make amends for a lot of things that had gone on between him and me. It was just so hard for me to reciprocate. By now, it seemed that I would snap at him in response to the littlest thing he said. Somehow it seemed that I couldn't love him the way that I wanted to. The guilt continued to consume me.

One Sunday afternoon, after coming from Mt. Sinai Baptist Church where Wesley, Sully and I had been helping out, I found Mom sitting on the couch distraught. When I saw her face, I knew something was wrong. Dad had gotten sick after he had preached that Sunday morning and had to be rushed to the hospital. Dad was from the Deep South and loved dishes like buttermilk and hot water cornbread, pig feet, brains and eggs, souse meat, Johnnie cakes, crackling bread dipped in cabbage "pot liquor," blackberry dumplings and anything fried. When I was young, I remember he had a gall bladder attack and was told by his doctor to stay away from fried foods. I'm not sure how long that lasted, but as far back as I could remember he was eating all of the things he wasn't supposed to eat. The day before, he told Mom he wanted some crackling bread. Cracklings are pork fat deep-fried in grease, similar to the rind on thickly sliced bacon. But the cracklings are then put into corn bread. I haven't had crackling bread in years, but I used to love it as a kid. At any rate, that's what he had the night before. That added to the cabbage, more than likely seasoned with pork, did the trick. Not to mention that he would soak up the pot liquor (the juice from the cabbage) with the cornbread. He had a gall bladder attack. But this time his gall bladder literally exploded. Wherever the pieces landed in his body they caused infection and it began to spread. I had seen Mom in the hospital many times, in fact Mom was always sickly it seemed. Even when I was really small, I remember her going in for different procedures, some of which I didn't know what they were. However, as far as I can remember this was the first time I'd seen my father in the hospital, so it was surreal. I was scheduled to graduate from Howard in three months from the time he entered the hospital. It seemed he was deteriorating more and more. He was 73 and seemed much weaker than I had realized.

I stopped working with the gospel choir during my senior year. Although I loved it, I had to reconsider my goals. I had not been sent to Howard to major in gospel choir. I didn't want a repeat of what happened during my sophomore year. I remember a number of students began to either "major" in gospel choir or in student lounge, where non-stop bid whist games were played all day long. Some of those same students who took part in those "majors" never graduated. I certainly was not going to let that happen to me. However, during this time, the Celestials were still singing and I was still diligently working with them. In April of '71, we were asked to do a concert in Andrew Rankin Chapel for one of the sororities on campus. I remember that we got new outfits made and the chapel was packed. The audience included sorority members, and sitting on the back row were some of the music faculty (who were also sorority members). I especially remember Carolyn Grant, who was the head of the voice department, being a part of that contingency. By now I had begun to write more frequently and had written some new songs especially for the concert, with a couple of Edwin Hawkins songs thrown in for good measure. I even did an arrangement of one of the songs that Donny Hathaway and Gwen Hines taught me when I was a freshman, "Heavenly Sunlight." We opened with a song I wrote called "We Must Love One Another," a song stressing the importance of loving all people, all nationalities, all cultures, all colors and all backgrounds. It opened up with a funky bass line and I came in with the piano along with the drums. By the time the voices came in, everyone was on their feet in the chapel jamming along with us. I noticed in the back row Mrs. Grant, the head of the voice department, as well as some of her sorority sisters sitting, arms folded, looking at us in disdain. Then as if someone gave a signal, all of them rose at the same time and walked out the door. By that time, we were used to not being accepted. We were giving praise to God in our own unique way and nothing else mattered. The year that the gospel choir sang for Howard's graduation, some professors walked out while we were singing. We were all numb to it by that point. I just know that night in the chapel was wonderful. Mom was sitting in the back with my tape recorder faithfully recording the whole thing. Thank God I still have it and from time to time, I go back and revisit it. The Celestials could really sing. We shouted and praised God for a while that night.

By now, I was in the last stages of preparing for my recital. Many times, I would rush home from school to go with Mom to see Dad in the hospital. I remember him telling me one day, "Son, you don't always have to come with your Mom to see me. Sometimes you can just come see me by yourself, when you aren't busy." But I didn't want to. I never knew what to say to him. I felt uncomfortable if we had to do any kind of one-on-one, and looked for the first moment I could escape. I cannot express how guilty that would make me feel. I loved him and I cared about his well-being. But there had never been a bond built between us, the kind of bond that kids really need with both parents. In a lot of ways, he was like a stranger to me who just happened to live in our house. I remember sometimes when I'd visit the church, he'd get up and brag about my accomplishments at Howard in the beginning of his sermon. I remember that Dr. Kerr, my piano teacher, had told him something that he would repeat every Sunday I attended. He said there were only two students who had come through his classroom, in his history of teaching, who were so gifted that he could only guide them and pray that it was in the right direction. That was Donny Hathaway and me. Although I was extremely flattered and honored to hear that, I would be so embarrassed when Dad would say stuff like that as everyone turned around in the church and looked at me, smiling and applauding. I would try to go under the seat. There was a running joke in the D.C. Baptist Ministers conference that the only reason he attended was to brag on me. I knew he was proud of me, and I believe he really loved me the only way he knew how. But it was almost like there was too much water under the bridge. There was too much irreparable damage for that father-son connection to ever happen. I loved him on one hand, but on the other hand, I didn't like him. Guilt and shame ate at me because I couldn't control the way I felt. Ours was such a complicated relationship.

I've had the opportunity to perform all over the world and for many different situations, but I don't think I've ever been as nervous as I was the night of my graduating piano recital. When I look back on it, it seems like a dream. Even when I was sitting there playing, it was like an out-of-body experience. It seemed my fingers were on automatic, my brain was on lock, and I was somewhere hovering above my body, looking down on my big Afro. Of course, we were required as piano majors to play a composition from each period. So, I played Bach from the Baroque period, Beethoven from the Classical period (although he was considered sort of a bridge into the Romantic period), and Chopin and Debussy from the Romantic period. For the contemporary period I played a piece by Professor Kerr, an arrangement based on the old Negro Spiritual "Walk Together Children," called "Easter Monday Swagger." It was not an easy piece to play, but when I finally got it under my fingers, it was a brilliant-sounding piece with great harmonic structure. To close the recital, I played the first movement of the Gershwin Piano Concerto in F. Whenever a piano concerto was done in the chapel, the orchestral part was always played on the pipe organ. Accompanist Ronald Tymus, who assisted on many student performances, served as the organist. When that last note was played at the end of the Concerto recital, the audience erupted into clapping, cheering and stomping. I have never been so glad for something to be over in my life. The lessons that I learned from playing classical music are something that can never be replaced. It has everything to do with who I am musically today.

Mr. Kerr and Mrs. Burwell were so proud of me, which made me happy. However, the most important thing to me was that Mom was so proud. After all, I was the first one to graduate from college in her family. She and I took a picture at my graduation reception, and I look at it often. The love and the pride on her face was so evident by her smile. That meant more to me than anything in the world. She had a beautiful piano cake made for me and surprised me with it at my reception after the recital. It was so beautiful that I didn't want to eat it! But my love for sweets got the best of me. It was just as good as it was beautiful. The hostesses for my reception were my Smallwood Singers crew, Valerie and Brenda. We had gone through a lot together since the days of our childhood and they were there to share this milestone with me. Also added were dear friends who were students and gospel choir members: Jackie Cadlett, Gail Murray, Mona Jones and of course, my play sister Ollie. Dad was still in the hospital and was too sick to attend my recital, but we took the recording to the hospital and played it for him. He laid there listening and smiling with his eyes closed. He was also too sick to attend my graduation, which happened not long after my senior recital. I remember the weather was perfect on graduation day and there was hardly a cloud in the sky. I graduated Cum Laude, despite my second year goof off. Thank God that the one semester I messed up, was the semester that most professors decided to use the Pass or Fail grading system because so many classes had been interrupted by the sit-ins. Thankfully I passed everything, and of course I turned my Incomplete F into a permanent A, so the grading system for that semester didn't affect my overall GPA. To be there with all my friends graduating together, as well as those who had returned to see me graduate, was incredible. As long as Mom was there though, nothing else mattered. She was the one who started me out on this road, the one who encouraged me and convinced me that whatever I set my mind to I could do with hard work and perseverance. It was not only a day to celebrate the fruits of my hard labor, but hers as well. We took my Bachelor of Music degree to the hospital for Dad to see right after we left graduation. He read it over and over again, smiling. He looked at me and said, "Boy, you did it. You graduated from college. You got your diploma!" Even with all he and I had been through, I knew without a doubt that he was proud of me. Mom believed that he was holding on until he could see that piece of paper. After he saw it, I think he slowly started letting go.

By now, I started attending Union Temple a little more often; especially helping out with the music. Ollie, Wesley and Sully would go as well, to help support Mom. They had all become "her children" since my freshman days at Howard. Rev. Simon Beamon, an associate minister, was carrying on in Dad's absence. I still hadn't been led to become a part of the church at that point. I had played for all of my dad's churches and I just wanted to do something else. I had graduated and my dream was to go to the Julliard School of Music in NY for my Masters. However, with Dad sick I couldn't leave Mom with the four kids by herself. So, I resigned myself to stay as long as she needed me. Plus, the foster care association had a rule at that time that there had to be two parents in the home wherever foster children stayed. Dad being in the hospital, I had to assume the male role in the household if Mom was to continue in the program that she loved so dearly.

Dad continued to get worse. One day while Mom was sitting at his bedside, he looked at her and his eyes began to get larger and larger. They shifted from looking at her to looking upward towards the ceiling. She began to call his name. By this time all the machines' sounds began to go off. His heart had stopped. Within minutes, doctors and nurses were running toward him and getting Mom out of the room. They administered the paddles and got his heart beating again. After that he was never the same. He told Mom and I later that he had left the hospital and had gone over to the church to make sure that everything was OK over there. He had walked in the basement and down in the kitchen and inspected everything. After he saw that everything was fine, he came back to the hospital. I still believe that when his heart stopped, his spirit made that trip. Not long after, his heart stopped again. Again they got it restarted, but this time he was put into intensive care. It was a daily vigil with Mom and me sitting in the waiting area most of the day. He was slowly deteriorating. I remember walking into the intensive care unit. By this time, he was unconscious. His eyes were half-open and I remember trying to walk in front of him to see if he would focus on me. But he seemed to look right through me. I called his name, "Daddy," but there was no response.

I believe that he heard me. It's widely believed that people in a coma can hear what's going on around them. They just can't respond. I was at home when Mom got the call from the hospital saying that Dad had passed. His body had succumbed to the overwhelming infection that was continually spreading throughout his internal organs. It was August 1971. I'm not sure how I felt. I cried because I didn't want him to die, but at the same time there was this uncomfortable feeling of relief. I couldn't process what I was feeling, nor could I understand it. At the funeral, right before they closed the casket and the family viewed the body for the last time, I finally broke down to the extent that I lost my balance. I remember I had to put my hand out to brace myself from falling. My hand ended up breaking my fall, landing on his chest. It felt cold, hard and strange. With my life-long fear of dead people, I think that brought me back to my senses quickly. The eulogy was delivered by Rev. Edgar Williams, pastor of the Second New St. Paul Baptist Church, a great friend of Dad's, and a preaching machine. Again, I had asked my friends from Howard to form the choir for the funeral. Wesley played for them and I remember thinking, this makeshift choir has a lot of possibilities. At the cemetery, as they began to lower the casket into the grave, Mom cried out, "Rev. I tried, I

REALLY tried, I tried so hard!!!" Today I'm still not entirely sure what that meant. Although it did hurt to lose him, I don't remember going through a grieving period like I had with so many others. After I got over the initial shock, which didn't last long, I just went on with life as normal. I felt guilty about that as well, and for a time I struggled with it constantly. A couple of years later my father came to me in a dream and said, "Richard, don't feel guilty. Stop worrying! It's all right. Everything is fine." Something about that dream changed everything. The guilt left as if it had never been there.

CHAPTER 18

RICHARD SMALLWOOD...
YOU'RE FIRED!

N ot long after Dad passed, the Gospel Choir called all the original members back to record a complete album called "Beginning." It was an incredible day as everyone who started with us in 1969 came together. We re-recorded Henry's "I Found God," as well as other songs he had written. We recorded my arrangement of "The Lord's Prayer" in spite of what had happened a few years before. We also did songs that Leon Roberts and others had written and arranged. That album became a classic, and I'm fortunate to still have a copy of it.

Mom and several others worked hard to keep the church running with Rev. Beamon. I felt that I needed to be there to help and support Mom. Word began to spread about a vacant church in the Baptist ministers' community and ministers were lined up to be guest speakers, or "to audition" as I called it. The Baptist ministers' conference tried to assist in sending over prospective ministers. However, no one seemed sufficient to fill the vacancy and Rev. Beamon continued to lead and carry the church forward. Not long after, another minister came on board and joined us, Rev. John Moss. He began to assist Rev.

Beamon in the running of the church. His wife Ruth Moss was a powerhouse of an alto, and Wesley, who had started to play for the senior choir, would assign solos to her as a part of the choir. Mrs. Moss could tear up a church and she did just that many Sundays. Soon Rev. Beamon left and Rev. Moss was left alone to lead the church. Rev. Moss was a very kind and wonderful person. He still didn't seem to be the one to lead us to the next level. But the music department began to grow with Brenda taking over the children's choir that Mom had initiated.

In 1972, I started a permanent Young Adult Choir made up of my friends. Like me, some of them weren't members of the church yet, but sang with the choir. I had baby Smallwood Singers alumnae, Valerie and Brenda, and I also asked Ollie, Wesley and Sully to join. They agreed. So I began to work on a sound similar to the Celestials, but larger and more choral. I remember especially working on the soprano section. Before Edwin Hawkins, most choir soprano sections sang in more of a head voice placement or *mezzo voce*. It was similar to the European classical way of soprano production and placement. Edwin's sopranos sang in more of a natural tone. It brought about a whole new kind of sound to gospel, one that inspired and intrigued me. I set about to try to produce a similar sound with the Young Adult Choir. I found out that even if there were some sopranos whose natural ranges didn't extend as far as I wanted, if they changed the quality of the tones they were singing even in their head voices, it would closely match the natural sound that I was looking for. I began to be more and more fascinated by the human voice and what it was capable of. Again, with Wesley's powerful voice in the tenor section, the rest of the choir had to come up to that kind of sound. The choir began to grow as word began to spread about it, and more people were drawn to visit the church and join. I never stood in front of them and directed them but sat at the piano. With head movements and the wave of a hand, and sometimes signals for chords or dynamics, they started to become accustomed to singing without anyone standing in front of them directing.

At Dad's funeral, there had been many friends of his and Mom from years past. Among them were members of Greater New Hope Baptist Church, the church that Dad had founded in 1933, the year before he married Mom. One of these people was Rev. William Roundtree who had been a small child under Dad's pastorate. He had reestablished contact with Mom at the funeral and soon came over to Union Temple with his wife and family. Along with him also came members of Greater New Hope who had known Mom since the beginning of her marriage to Dad. They all, in turn, joined and the church continued to grow. It was an influx of great church workers. They all began to concentrate on burning the mortgage. Rev. Roundtree, an educational leader, showed great potential for leading the church to the next phase. It was the consensus of the church that he should be our next pastor. I remember Mom telling Ollie, Wesley, Sully and I that in order to help make Rev. Roundtree pastor, we would have to become members of the church in order to vote. By now all of us had fallen in love with the church, with our church family and of course everyone loved Mom and admired her tenacity, strength and determination in carrying on the last work that Dad had started. The Sunday of the vote, Ollie, Wesley, Sully and I joined and Rev. William Roundtree was unanimously voted in to become the second pastor of the Union Temple Baptist Church. Under him the church really began to thrive. The choir continued to grow. My other two friends, Jackie Cadlett and Gail Murray, officially joined. They were two dynamite sopranos, with the natural kind of quality I was looking for.

I still would go up to Howard to practice and write, and the Celestials still rehearsed there. By now all of us had graduated except for Mary (or "Lou Lou" as we called her). She was now a senior at Howard and a member of Star of Bethlehem Church of God in Christ where the late Harvey Lewis Jr. directed one of the baddest choirs in the area. Also, another young lady who was a member of Star had come to Howard who was a phenomenal gift by the name of Tawatha Agee. Tawatha used to help the Celestials out from time to time as well. She went on to do great things in secular music singing with Mtume and doing backgrounds for everyone from Aretha to Luther. One day while walking through the practice area, I heard an amazing voice coming from one of the piano rooms. It was one that I had not heard before and I began to follow the sound until I came to a room. I looked in the window and there seated at the piano playing for herself was a beautiful young girl killing me with her vocals. Her range was from rich tenor to first soprano. I stood there transfixed for a while, listening. I think she must have sensed me staring and she turned around and smiled at me in the window and waved. I took the opportunity to open the door and go in. I introduced myself and told her I was a graduate of the School of Music. "My God," I said. "You can sing AND play like crazy! Who ARE you?" She smiled shyly and told me that her name was Ángela Winbush. She was a 17-year-old freshman and an Architectural Major. "ARCHITECT?" I exclaimed. "With the kind of talent you have, why in the world are you in Architecture and not in Music?" She explained that she loved architecture and financially it was more stable than music. I remember saying to myself that she had about as much business in architecture as I did. I made a mental note to persuade her after I got to know her better, and I was determined to get over to the music department as fast as I could. What an awesome gift! I knew I had to get her in the choir. What an asset she would be. We became friends fast and I adored hearing her sing. She joined Howard's gospel choir, but before long she was a part of the Young Adult Choir at Union Temple and a member of the church. Not only that, but by the next year she was a student in the School of Music where she belonged! Another young lady by the name of Elett Ricks who was a phenomenal pianist and a Music major became a part of the church and choir as well. This woman could PLAY a piano! Like Wesley was a tenor section, Elett was an alto section all by herself with a similar Wesleyesque-type vocal quality. I used to jokingly call her "God's trombone" because she had so much vocal power. When I think back, there was so much talent in that one place.

By now, two more influences had taken my attention. Sly Stone had to be one of my biggest influences. Most of the time people cite the classical influence, which there certainly is. However, Sly inspired the "funky" part of me. I am and always will be a huge fan. He's one of the few people I've never had the opportunity to meet, but he inspired me greatly. I probably would be speechless if I did meet him! Later, Earth Wind and Fire became another great inspiration. I think I have every recording that Sly and Earth Wind and Fire ever recorded. I would write a song years later called "He Won't Leave You" for the Smallwood Singers. This was my version of an Earth Wind and Fire groove and was directly inspired by them. Another composer began to influence me by the name of Jimmy Webb. A lot of people remember his song from the 70's, "Up Up and Away in My Beautiful Balloon" made famous by the 5th Dimension, as well as another song he penned called "Didn't We" and also "By The Time I Get To Phoenix." I still love the music this man wrote. There is an old adage that says, "You are what you eat." I never sat down to write a particular style of music, or any kind of particular genre-influenced music. It was just all of the different genres of music that I loved that were inside of me. When I began to write, it all just began to spill out. It was all of the styles, composers, and artists that I have ever loved and consumed. On the gospel side, another person was becoming an influence and that was Andraé Crouch. I remember knowing his music, especially songs like "The Blood," but not really knowing the artist in the early 70's. He was mostly CCM (Contemporary Christian Music) in those earlier days, so the general black audience didn't know a lot of him. I think I only had one recording by him at the time. Tramaine had sung with him while a teen and recorded a song called "Lord, I'm Coming Home" with him and The Disciples when she was around 16. Being a complete Hawkins fanatic since the late 60's, I purchased that album to hear her sing. But in 1975 "Take Me Back" hit the gospel scene like a tornado, featuring Danniebelle Hall. I was mesmerized by the sound, the album cover, the instrumentation...everything! It was not your normal gospel presentation, but it was a sound and style that would attract people from all walks of life. I immediately became a fan of Andraé and his music began to color mine. I loved his contemporary stylings and the way he would combine styles and genres. The Live in London 2-album set came out several years later and literally changed my musical life. The MUSIC, the arrangements, the vocals, the harmonic progressions, the sound, the TECHNICAL expertise. Many early gospel LIVE albums around that time and before sounded like someone sat in the back of a church with a cassette recorder and pushed "record." This was clean perfection at its highest. I remember thinking "... *if ever I get the chance to record...whether it's studio or live...I want my album to sound like THIS!*" I remember going to see him in the 80's at Constitution Hall. He had a hit out called "It's Gonna Rain" and it was a JAM!!! I recall him strolling across the stage with a huge red and white umbrella raised while singing, "It's raining ohhh. It's raining," accompanied by a LIVE horn section. Never had I seen live horns in gospel nor such a slick and unique professional performance. I remember thinking, "I want to do THAT kind of gospel presentation if ever I get the chance!" I remember going to his house and there we were able to write a song called "You're the Light of the World" together for my album "Testimony." I remember touring his studio, but all the time thinking, "*this is one of the nicest people I've ever met.*" He was one of the most down to earth people I've known. I remember our last conversation in person, sitting in the lobby of the hotel in Nashville sharing for almost an hour during Stellar Award weekend. The encouragement he gave me in that conversation I will never, ever forget. We had promised to get together again to write for my next project. Sadly, that never happened. What a blessing he was to humankind, not only musically, but his spirit and his heart. Andraé, the world will never be the same because you're gone, it is forever changed because of what you deposited while you were here. You not only changed the face of gospel music, but you made a difference in people's LIVES!

In the mid to late sixties, Shirley Caesar did the first of two solo recordings after leaving the Caravans. One was entitled "I'll Go" and the other was "My Testimony." I was always a fan and made sure that they were in my collection. Immediately I noticed an amazing sounding choir backing her up. I found out that it was the Institutional Church of God in Christ Radio Choir. The director of the choir was an amazingly gifted writer by the name of J.C. White. Not only did they have great music, but they also had some of the greatest soloists around. I immediately began to collect their projects and became a major fan of J.C. White's music. That was another musical influence. I taught my Young Adult Choir at church all their songs, as well as the J.C. White Singers material. It also inspired my writing as well. I once heard Shirley Caesar say that we all stand on the shoulders of someone else. I stand on the shoulders of many.

After first graduating from Howard, I got a job teaching at the Washington Community School of Music. The director of the school was my second Mom, Mrs. Burwell, and she welcomed me with open arms. I taught piano and music theory to everyone from elementary school students to senior citizens. I thought I'd be perfectly happy doing it, but honestly I didn't like it at all. I think if I had some uniquely gifted students, it would have excited me and challenged me. But it was nothing of the sort. Honestly, there wasn't a lot of talent there. A lot of the school students were taking piano simply because their parents had instructed them to do so. They couldn't have cared less about piano or theory and brought me the same unprepared lessons every week. The senior citizens were sweet, but most of them were just learning to play so that wasn't challenging me either. I began to dread going. I guess it showed in my face because Mrs. Burwell called me in the office one day in her motherly way and fired me. She said to me, "Richard Smallwood, you have no interest in teaching. I know exactly what you want to do. You want to perform. You're wasting my time and yours. I'm going to do you a favor and let you go."

I remember being a bit upset—after all it was some good money— but honestly she was exactly correct. I had no interest in this. The several talented students that I had didn't make up for the non-talented ones and I was bored to tears. I wanted to perform. That's all I ever wanted to do as far back as I could remember. The Celestials and Howard Gospel Choir whet my appetite for what I really wanted to do. I loved to travel. I loved writing songs and I loved performing them. The only time I was completely happy was when I was doing that. But God wasn't ready for me to do that yet. Already, classmates of mine had started to work in the business. Phylicia Allen (Rashad) was in New York playing in the Broadway Show "The Wiz." Debbie Allen was in NY dancing professionally. Donny Hathaway was putting out some of the most incredible albums and becoming known world-wide. My old teacher Roberta Flack was huge in the music business. I was teaching and didn't want to. The Celestials couldn't seem to get a record deal. Although my love for music was great, one thing I hadn't a clue about was ministry. I didn't realize that ministry had to do with so much more than just the music. Ministry was about making a difference in people's lives. I grew up believing that ministry could only happen behind the pulpit. Ministry was reserved for preachers only and I certainly had no desire to be one of those! No one had ever taught me about music being a ministry. However, my season of preparation was still taking place. I just didn't know it. When I left teaching at Washington Community School of Music, I ended up substitute teaching in the DC Public School System, which I probably hated more. I was working at an elementary school in NE Washington and was substituting for a teacher who was out on maternity leave. I thought elementary would be easy but honestly, those kids were so bad. Many times, I felt more like a disciplinarian than a teacher. One day, after the bell rang, a little girl ran outside in the hallway paying the bell no mind. I went out and called her into the room. She ignored me. I called her again. She ignored me again. I went up to her, pointed my finger to the door of the classroom and told her in a firm voice, "the bell has rung and it's time to go into the classroom. Get in there NOW!" She looked at me and screamed, cursing, "You ain't my father, #$%!" Before I knew it, I had grabbed her by the neck of her dress and lifted her up off the ground. Of course, it scared her to death and she began to cry. It scared me as well in that I had no intention of doing that. I didn't want to have to fight anybody's family. It was a combination of my temper, her disrespect and my frustration. I knew this was not for me, especially not this school. That day I left and I never went back. A little later I started subbing on the Jr. High level, specifically at Rabaut Jr. High in NW Washington. Surprisingly I enjoyed that better. This time again I ended up subbing for an English teacher who was on maternity leave. My room was right across the hall from the principal's office. I had a homeroom class and five English classes during the day. I've always loved English. In fact, I always thought that if I hadn't gone into music, I would do something with English whether it was becoming a novelist or maybe teaching on the college level. However, the first week of my new job my homeroom class decided to get there before school and before I arrived. My room was on the first floor and they found a way to climb in the window, smoke weed in the room and climb back out the window before I got there. Of course, when I unlocked my door, the room was saturated by the smell of weed. I'm surprised I didn't get a contact high. That day, of all days, the principal decided to pay me a visit to see how things were going. Imagine his surprise when the smell of weed greeted him as he came into my room. I explained what had happened and was praying he didn't think it was me. I guess he knew how the students could be and didn't say much about it. However, after that day, it got easier and I never had that particular problem again. It was nonetheless hard for me, because I was shy even with the kids. There was a part of me that remembered the fear I used to have going to Jr High School; the anxiety, the fear of speaking in front of the class and all of the things that happened at Browne Jr. High. But eventually I learned some key lessons. Firstly, don't let a kid see your weakness if you are in a leadership position, because they will hop on it in a minute (forget the fact that I looked like I was about 18). Secondly, assert yourself no matter what. For me, it took a minute to really assert myself so that they would respect me. But after I figured out my approach, it got much better. At one point, I even subbed for one of the music teachers who was on sick leave. I did enjoy that more. I needed the money, but I still wasn't entirely happy.

CHAPTER 19
TO SWITZERLAND WE GO!

After Donald Byrd became the head of the jazz department at Howard, he took personal interest in much of the talent in the School Of Music. He put together a group of very talented musicians who were students and called them the Blackbyrds. They began to record and started to get quite popular. These brothers were bad! He also took interest in the Celestials. He loved to hear us sing. He loved the music that I wrote and of course this was quite encouraging to me. However, he was always trying to convince us to sing secular music. His argument was to sing secular and once you get famous, then you can sing whatever you want. We weren't hearing it. Gospel is what we did and it was what we were going to continue to do. I was never a person who thought that secular music was wrong, like so many of my church peers thought. However, I knew that the Celestials were supposed to be doing what we did and that was that. Donald still loved what we did and he began to take us around with the Jazz Band and would give us twenty minutes to perform our gospel tunes. I'll always be grateful to him for not only the exposure, but also the experience he gave us. By this time, Howard's Jazz Band had gotten pretty popular. They were constantly being called to perform at Universities and other venues throughout the country. Donald always saved a spot for us. These invitations opened up some very special doors in the future. We also continued to sing all over the city at churches and traveling on our own as well. One of the churches we frequented was down in Eastern Shore MD, where Rev. William Revely was the pastor and Rev. Willie Wilson was the assistant pastor. Both of them were graduates of Howard's School of Religion and Rev. Wilson was the same minister who preached the sermon on the night of the Gospel Choir's debut at Howard. Both of them were great preachers and everyone always enjoyed hearing them speak. Rev. Wilson was interested in Mary "Lou Lou" Lewis, who of course was a member of the Celestials and asked us to introduce her to him. As I look back, that may be why we ended up singing down there so much. At some point, they began to date. The Young Adult Choir sang there as well on a couple of occasions.

Rev. Roundtree served as our pastor for about a year and then he left for other obligations. Again we were without a pastor. I remember Wesley saying to Mom, "What about Willie Wilson?" Mom remembered him from not only the night at Rankin Chapel, but also accompanied us down to Eastern Shore a couple of times. We had a church meeting about it and invited Willie to come and preach for those who had not heard him. Willie was always a dynamic speaker and did not disappoint. He came to preach on several occasions and not long after was voted in as the third pastor of Union Temple Baptist Church. It was 1973.

In my opinion, the Young Adult Choir was a major catalyst for my second phase of maturity in songwriting. In addition to teaching them the standard songs of the day, I began to write even more for them. They became my second set of "guinea pigs" after the Celestials. I learned more about creating a choral sound, and the Smallwood Sound continued to grow. People would come from all over to hear the choir. They would leave their churches on days they didn't have to sing and come to Union Temple. Students from Howard, and people from out of state, would travel to hear them. Another friend from the early seventies and a member of the choir was Sandra Fagans, an attorney and a true character. She became a member of the choir and the church. Sandy was known to have quick wit, a quick tongue and an incredible sense of humor, even when she didn't mean to. She talked quite properly and enunciated her words distinctly and clearly. Sandy could be irreverent just as quickly as she could be reverent. We never knew where she would be coming from. Sandy was a bit older than we were and her Mom had been deceased for quite some time. One day, we were all piled in my car and I was taking the Howard crew home from church. It was the beginning of the Christmas season and most of the students were going home for the holiday. As everyone got out of the car we all hugged and said to those going home for Christmas, "Be sure you tell your mother hello for me." Ángela hugged Sandy, and not knowing her Mom was deceased said, "Tell your mother hello for me too Sandy." All of the other Howard students chimed in with Ángela. "Oh yes Sandy, tell Mom hello!" Sandy replied in her husky tenor, proper and distinguished tone, "That would be very difficult to do unless of course we had a séance." Everyone went into shock mode for a minute and then we laid out in the car and laughed for at least ten minutes. Everyone had their "Sandy stories." She was a great person and definitely a character. Sandy, along with Wesley, were two of the ones that really pushed me in terms of my music. Honestly, I didn't have much faith in what I did, although I wanted to do it more than anything else in the world. I just didn't think I had what it took. Sandy used to look at me with her hazel eyes and say "Richard sweetheart, YOU are going to be famous! The WORLD will know of the wonderful music that you write." I would say to myself, "Sure Sandy, what do you know? You're just saying that because you're my friend and you love me." Later she would become my attorney, and with Wesley as my manager they would push all the harder.

That same year, Willie Wilson and Lou Lou were married and she became a part of the Union Temple family and choir. I was scheduled to play for the wedding. I was driving on the day of the wedding and a pain hit me like nothing that I had ever felt before. It started in my side and then moved around to the pit of my stomach. Linda Gravatt, a dear friend and Howard graduate, had a house on 16th Street NW known as the "gold coast," and she rented out rooms to friends, mostly students and former students. Wesley was staying there with a bassist from Howard, Tommie McKenzie. Linda was also a member of Union Temple and the Young Adult Choir. I was on my way to pick Linda and Wesley up for the wedding. I tried to turn back around and go back home as the pain intensified, but I realized I wouldn't be able to make it. I remember making it to Linda's house and staggering up to the door, knowing that I was getting ready to pass out. I rang the doorbell and collapsed. The next thing I knew, Wesley and Linda had put me in the backseat of my car and were speeding towards the emergency room. I gripped Linda's hand as hard as I could and I screamed in pain. I just knew I was dying. The pain was indescribable. They had called my Mother who met us at the emergency room. Mom was so worried because no one knew what was going on with me. Someone called Lou Lou to let her know what was going on. Thank God for Elett who filled in for me. It seemed like an eternity before the pain meds finally kicked in and the pain subsided. I was diagnosed with having a huge kidney stone, something that ran rampant in my family. To make it even worse, I had to end up passing it. It ran in my family. Mom and many of my family members had been plagued by them. But this was my first time having one and unfortunately, it wouldn't be my last. I would have twenty or more kidney stone attacks up through the mid-nineties before they stopped just as suddenly as they started.

The choir steadily grew in size and sound. I remember being at a concert at Temple Church of God in Christ. The MC called on a group by the name of the Jackie Ruffin Singers. We sat there waiting for the group to come up and minister. All of a sudden, there was a voice coming from the back of the church that sang in a loud and powerful voice, "Come on Annnnddd" and then a couple of other voices joined in singing, "Ease on down, ease on down the road." We all turned around to see what in the world was going on. It was the Jackie Ruffin Singers, Jackie whom we had never seen before and two other young ladies marching down the aisle towards the front singing the song "Ease on Down the Road" from "The Wiz." The way we laughed that day and kidded her about that for years after. That's how I met Jackie and the rest is history. She would later join Union Temple and the choir and become one of the Smallwood Singers. Regardless of our first meeting, there was one thing about Jackie that nobody could deny: she could sing!

Even though the choir took up a lot of my time, the Celestial Sound as we were now known, was still prospering, maturing and traveling. "He was the head of the Montreux Jazz Festival in Montreux Switzerland" after the sentence, one day after performing at the University of Pittsburgh with Donald Byrd,

Claude Nobbs approached us. It was a huge weeklong jazz festival where the cream of the crop of jazz artists performed yearly. He had been in the audience and was impressed by our performance, and asked if we would be interested in performing at the festival. If we agreed, it would be the first time that gospel music was featured in the festival. Elated was not the word. We were beside ourselves with excitement. There was only one catch. He asked what record label were we with. Of course, we weren't with a label. We had put out our little independent 45 single and that's the only recording we had ever done. He went on to explain to us that different record labels funded their artist's trip to the festival. Since we had no label he told us, "If you guys can get to Switzerland, then I'll reserve a spot for you and let you perform on the main stage." What an incredible opportunity this would be, but how in the world could we raise enough money to go overseas for a week? There were five of us. Just the concept of going to Europe was something we couldn't even fathom. We finally came up with a couple of ideas. One idea was to go to parents, professors, ex-professors and whatever loved ones we could find and get donations. Wesley came up with the other idea to approach the National Urban League and see if they could come up with some ideas. The National Urban League is a civil rights organization that advocates on behalf of African-Americans in the United States. It's the oldest and largest community type organization of its kind in the United States. This wasn't a civil rights issue, but we were African-Americans. We also were current and former Howard students and we sure were poor. So, we thought maybe they could help in some kind of way. We met with the Urban League who came up with the idea of sponsoring us in a concert at the All Souls Unitarian Church on 16th Street N.W. We sold tickets to everyone we knew for ten dollars. The National Urban League advertised and we got our friends and supporters who were DJ's to mention it on their shows. The night that the concert took place, there were family, friends, teachers, curiosity seekers, fellow gospel artists and people from all over the DMV area. We raised quite a bit of money from the concert and private donations. Wesley, as our manager, then went to price plane tickets to see what was available. He found out that we could definitely get five round trip tickets to Switzerland. The only catch was that to get the special rate that we could afford, we would have to stay for three weeks. Sully could only stay for two week because of his job. We did have enough money to get him the ticket for those two weeks. Staying in Switzerland for three weeks however, was a dream. The festival was only one week. We had only arranged for our hotel stay for one week. Where would we stay the second and third week? We were all young, in our twenties, and we just decided we'd cross that bridge when we got to it, toss caution to the wind and just go! Donald Byrd would be going. Maybe he had some ideas. We couldn't pass up an opportunity like that! I've always had a sensitive stomach and when I would have major things going on in school, like exams or if I had to speak in front of the class, that morning before I left the house my stomach would hurt so bad. I think it was anxiety more than anything else. The night before we were to leave for Switzerland, my stomach was hurting so bad I had to lie down. "Lord" I was praying, "please let my stomach clear up. I can't let anything keep me from this trip of a lifetime." Thankfully the next morning it had cleared up. I don't think I've ever been that excited. We flew to Kennedy Airport in NY, and left for Switzerland from there. We had never been on a trip of this length, much less overseas, so I don't think we probably knew how to pack. I packed almost every item of clothing I had and so did everyone else.

Rosalind showed up with multiple pieces of luggage, plus wig boxes. Sully, whom something crazy always happened to, came directly from the laundromat with an armful of unpacked clothes on hangers draped over his arm. As he boarded the plane, late and rushing down the aisle, one of the hooks on a hanger snagged a flight attendant's stocking and promptly ripped it and she cussed him out in French. If it were something hilarious, it would happen to Sully. I remember once when we were going on a trip and Sully again had gone to the laundromat before we left. Something happened with the dryer that contained his clothes and it went haywire and wouldn't stop. When he finally got the manager or whoever was in charge to stop it, all of his clothes had shrunk to tiny versions of their former selves. This time, although the clothes were on hangers, they were at least normal size. All five of us finally got settled in our seats: Lou Lou, Rosalind, Wesley, Sully and myself. We couldn't afford to take a drummer or a bass player, so we figured with all the musicians that would be at the festival, we'd find someone to play for us. It probably was an 8-hour flight, but I could hardly sleep because I was so excited. We landed in Zurich and got a car to Montreux. I remember when we first entered Montreux, my breath was literally taken away. I had never seen anything so beautiful in my life. Montreux was nestled in a little valley in between the Italian Alps on one side and the French Alps on the other side. It looked like something out of a storybook or a fairy tale. It was the first week in July and the weather was perfect. We could still see the snow far in the distance on top of the Alps. We stayed at the Grande Hotel, a huge beautiful hotel that seemed to be a couple of blocks in length. We got a great hotel rate through Donald Byrd and his band. If I recall, there were other jazz bands from other Universities there that week, and students got good rates. We did have the problem of eating which we had not taken into account (considering our tight budget). We didn't have money enough individually to last us a week. There was another University band staying at the hotel that had their meals included at the hotel restaurant with their lodging. Some kind of way, we found out and some of us snuck in with them for our meals. I know it was dishonest, but we were hungry AND broke. Nonetheless, we were in Montreux, Switzerland! Everyone was there from Miles Davis to Cannonball Adderly. The festival, the music, the sightseeing and the scenery were incredible. I remember the night that we went to see Miles Davis. By this time, Miles had changed his style to a sort of jazz/funk fusion. Gone were the melodies and he played strange bursts of sound over a funk feel. It was different from the old Miles Davis recordings I remembered, and seemed very atonal in nature. I remember that when he played that night, he played with his back to the entire audience much to their anger. So between the different style of music and him ignoring the audience, there were quite a few "boos" during his set. But still, it was Miles—the brilliant, temperamental, genius innovator. I remember we got the chance to go back to his dressing room after his set. We were definitely in the presence of music royalty. He greeted us while a young lady was rubbing his legs with some kind of lotion. I think we all were in awe. Me, being the shy one, just stood there and smiled and stared in awe. Lou Lou excitedly exclaimed, "Oh Mr. Davis, I really enjoyed you tonight." He looked at her from behind his dark shades and said in a husky, raspy half-whisper, "yeah, I know." Miles was a character, but it was an incredible and historical moment in all of our lives just to be in his presence.

CHAPTER 20

A CONVERSATION GONE WRONG
WITH SAMMY DAVIS JR.

C laude Nobbs put us up to perform late on Thursday, July 5. I remember sitting backstage as nervous as I could be. For musicians, we asked one of the bass players and one of the drummers from one of the university jazz bands in attendance to help us. The bass player couldn't keep up with my changes very well. However, the audience didn't seem to care, because when we took the stage, they showed us so much love. They didn't have a clue who we were, other than the fact that we were from Washington DC, but they got with us just like it was church on Sunday morning. We let Rosalind loose on the last song "Search Me Lord" by Edwin Hawkins, and she walked off the stage and into the aisles singing like she was at a revival meeting. They loved it. We had no idea we were making history as the first gospel group to perform in the festival. We were just some kids whom God had blessed to be overseas for the first time in our lives. We made so many new friends that night, and people were coming up to greet us from the festival and from Switzerland. I could tell by the way Donald Byrd was smiling that he was really proud. That made us feel good. After all, he was the reason we got there in the first place. Imagine our elation when we awoke the next morning to newspaper reviews that described our music as "swinging contemporary gospel, powerful arrangements, and supple and harmonious." Rosalind got a nod saying that they had discovered an "impressive African-American voice." I began to think, maybe someone would like my music after all. We were at one of the most prestigious festivals ever. If they thought it was good, why couldn't everybody else? The weekend was approaching fast and we were going to have to check out of the hotel pretty soon. We came up with the solution that we would sleep in the park. It wasn't dangerous back then, especially in Switzerland. The weather was perfect and the major park in the center of town was absolutely beautiful. But God does take care of fools and babies, and I think we were a combination of both. The last night of the festival a single Mom (who had a beautiful Swiss Chalet) and a doctor and his wife (who had a chalet in the mountains), heard of our plight and opened their doors for us to stay in their homes. They heard us on the night we sang and were some of the many people we befriended that evening. They housed us and fed us for that following week. Rosalind and Lou Lou stayed at the doctor and his wife's house. I remember his wife's name was Daisy and she was the most delightful person with the bubbliest personality. Wesley, Sully and I stayed at Monique's house, the single mom with two sons. Monique's home was like a small castle, the outside was made of stone and the inside had high ceilings and huge rooms. We stayed in the music room, which looked like something from out of "Tales of King Arthur." It was awesome. Monique talked very fast in French and was very dramatic and excitable, but nonetheless very sweet. Her home was probably hundreds of years old and beautiful. When I decided to plug in my electric razor one evening, it blew out all the lights in the whole house. I could hear Monique screaming in French a mile a minute in the distance. After a while, someone must have found the fuse because the lights returned. None of us ever dared tell her what happened for fear she would have gone off on us in French. We always said that she reminded us of a Jacqueline Kennedy type. She reminded me of a woman of "high station," who looked like she belonged at the most exclusive functions and gatherings of the day. We had a term we used for people like that: "very high and perched." However, she was down to earth, a lovely person and laughed and joked with us the entire time we were there. I remember one day we were having dinner and I was starving. I was about 24 years old and always hungry, and still weighed hardly anything. I remember Monique made some spaghetti with marinara sauce. Now I come from a home where if you're making spaghetti, then there is a huge pot of sauce to go along with it. There was a medium sized dish on the table that contained the sauce. I remember thinking, *the pot with the rest of it must be in the kitchen,* so I liberally poured the sauce on my spaghetti. Monique started talking fast in French in sort of hushed tones. By now we were used to it, so we didn't think much of it. But Sully who had a degree in foreign languages whispered to me, Monique is saying "HE'S TAKING IT ALL! HE'S TAKING IT ALL!" I was starved and I guess there wasn't any more spaghetti sauce in the kitchen in the pot.

God opened even more doors while we were there. One of the friends we had met at the festival was a manager at a coffee house in a nearby city called Basil. He offered us a job singing in the coffee house for the entire third week. Sully had to return to the U.S., but the rest of us gladly sang nightly at the Club Atlantis in Basil. Basil was in the German part of Switzerland

and that was the language they spoke in that region. They didn't drink anything but coffee at the Atlantis, but if I remember correctly they sure did smoke while drinking their coffee, so we had to get adjusted to the constant cloud hovering in the air above us. Overall, it was a wonderful week. The audiences were so receptive and it was packed each night. One night Lou Lou decided she would try a little German on the audience. She stepped up to the mic after our first song and greeted the audience by saying "Gute Nacht!" There were bewildered looks on the faces of the audience. The promoter later told us that the reason for the confusion was that Lou Lou had announced not exactly a greeting, but "good night, I'm going to bed." The way we laughed! I don't think any of us tried any languages on stage other than English the remainder of our stay there.

I remember on the way back home from Switzerland we stopped in Paris, France for a day of sightseeing. That trip was one of the most memorable ones of my life. When I returned home, I was so glad to see my Mom as well as the kids. The next thing I asked was where was Skippy, my dog. Skippy had been my constant little companion since I was 11 years old. He was now 13 years old. Mom opened her mouth to say something and broke into tears. Then all the kids began to cry, and although no one could get it together to tell me exactly what had happened, I began to cry because I knew it wasn't going to be good news. Skippy had gotten old, was crippled, and couldn't see well. He was clearly in a lot of pain. Mom had taken him to the vet to see what could be done but was told that the only humane thing to do was to put him to sleep. Anyone who has ever had a family pet knows what we went through with that loss. I was messed up for a while. Skippy had helped to see me through a lot in my life. We had many more pets down through the years, including a beautiful Siberian Husky named Misti, another dog named Puddin', two cats Tiger and Precious, and others. We loved them all, but no pet ever quite matched Skippy. He was in a class of his own. I still think of him often after all of these years.

It wasn't the only death I experienced in that season. In October of 1973 as soon as I got back from my trip, Lula Cain Banks, the matriarch of my Mom's family, passed. I can't recall if Mom went to the funeral or not. I can't remember why I wasn't at the funeral, but I wish that I had been. Her grandson, Robert, his wife Rosa and the kids, would still come and visit frequently as we would them.

Montreux was one of the most memorable happenings of my life. I think on some level, it encouraged me that maybe I really could write, and maybe I could do this thing called the music industry. When we returned I began to write even more. Although I was still substituting in the DC Public School system, I knew that I wanted to do music as a fulltime career. There was no doubt in my mind. Of course the insecurities were still there, but with my friends pushing me and constantly telling me that I had a gift, I began to believe in myself a little more. In 1974, I would write an entire album of songs for the Young Adult Choir. It would be the first time that I wrote that many songs in such a short period of time. Elett, who was not only a superb pianist but a writer/arranger as well, would also contribute a song to that project. We would go into the studio and would release what was our first independent album called "Look Up And Live," with Ángela on lead on the title cut. By now the choir was in their prime. Not only did we sing every Sunday at Union Temple, our home church, but we would travel all over the country. I was still terrified to sing, other than behind the piano. Other than singing "I Found God" when I was with the gospel choir at Howard, I still felt comfortable only at the piano. I will never forget that time the Young Adult Choir sang in Reidsville, NC one weekend. I can't remember what the song was, but I was doing the lead, and I was seated at the piano. It was one of those times when the Spirit just falls on a service and people were rejoicing all over the place. Before I knew it, I had jumped up from the piano and grabbed the mic and was going down the choir stand steps toward the audience while the choir continued to sing acapella. I remember in the back of my mind thinking, "What in the world am I doing?" But it seemed like it was something far beyond my control. The only way I can describe it is that the shy Richard had taken a back seat and something else, something more powerful was now in control. I was growing. God was still grooming me.

One night the choir was coming back from singing down in Eastern Shore, Maryland. There were a number of cars that had driven down. The concert had been great, but it was very late. Everyone was exhausted and Lou Lou was a couple of months pregnant and in the car with a bunch of us. Wesley was driving and speeding trying to get everyone home. All of a sudden, we saw police lights behind us and heard a siren. We were now nowhere near a major city and were out in the boonies. Wesley pulled over as a highway patrolman got out of his car and came to the driver's window. He asked for Wesley's driver's license and told him he had been going way past the speed limit. Wesley began to explain frantically that he was speeding because Lou Lou was pregnant, albeit two or three months, and he was trying to get her home. The policeman shined the light in the back of the car where Lou Lou was sitting, shined the light on her stomach which was barely showing and said, "Sir, follow me please." He took us through these woods and winding roadways. I think all of us were starting to get nervous because we didn't know what he had in mind. I remember thinking, "Lord will we ever be heard from again?" Finally, we got to a small little building, which I guess was the police department. Once we went in, he told us how much the ticket would be and informed us that we'd have to pay on the spot. I can't remember what the charge was, but it was a lot and we didn't have that kind of money between us. He then told Wesley that he'd have to lock him up until we could find the money. Wesley immediately began to cry saying, "Don't leave me y'all! DON'T Y'ALL LEAVE ME!!!!" It wasn't funny at the time, simply because of all the horror stories that one hears of the brutality that sometimes happens. But we had no choice but to leave him. There were no ATM machines then, and the only thing we could do was go to the bank the next morning once we got home, get the money out and drive back down and bail him out. Wesley cried like a baby though. I think I might have too if it had been me. Of course, after we got him out the next morning, our fear turned to laughter and we had yet another incident in which we could emulate Wesley crying and hollering "Don't leave me y'all!"

Later that year we (The Celestial Sound) got a call from the promoter in Switzerland who had been manager of the Atlantis Club in Basil. Although he was no longer managing that club he wanted to set up a tour for us throughout Switzerland setting up dates in venues, clubs and schools. Again, we were elated and couldn't wait to get back to Switzerland. By now Rosalind was not singing with us any longer so it was just Lou Lou, Wesley, Sully and myself. This time we figured that we would take a bass player and drummer, John Nichols and Sherman Blair. They had played for us around town from time to time. Lou Lou was actually pregnant with her first child, Anika. We weren't sure how her doctor or

Willie would feel about her traveling, especially such a distance. However, she got the OK from both and was excited about going as well. The promoter had been nothing but positive the last time we had gone. He had paid us and we got our money on time at the Atlantis Club. So we had no reason to doubt his validity. That first trip to Montreux had been nothing but a pleasurable experience. I must insert this though. Always make sure all of your details are in print, contracted and signed. Make sure that you have round trip tickets to wherever you are contracted to go. Of course, we were still young and naïve. When the promoter told us he could only send one-way tickets and would have the other part of the ticket waiting for us when we arrived, we saw nothing wrong with it. How wrong we were! When we arrived in Switzerland the promoter told us that some of the concerts had been cancelled. As time went along, we found out that actually the majority had been cancelled. Venues had not been paid for and very little promotion had been done. There was no radio time set up. Even more importantly, there were no return tickets home nor did he have the money for them. I remember us performing at three or four concerts at the most and that was all. One was a high school, where the kids really loved the music. We had a song that I wrote called "Who Have You Helped Today?" When we started singing, all the kids who had no idea what gospel music was got up and began to dance the slow drag. If someone had a picture of our faces as the kids grinded while we were singing! Nonetheless they were a great audience. I also remember all of us walking to the grocery store through some of the suburban neighborhoods and all of the kids running out of their houses pointing at us. I don't think they had ever seen black people before.

The promoter put us up in a nice three-bedroom apartment. One morning someone knocked on the door. It was a lady screaming something at us in German. She was walking back and forth, ranting and raving. We didn't have a clue what was going on. Even Sully couldn't make out exactly what she was saying other than it was something about money. We later found out that she was the landlady and the rent had not been paid and she was basically putting us out. Thank God again for friends who opened their homes and let us in. Not long after, we raised enough money and sent Lou Lou home and Sully followed soon after. Wesley, John the bass player and I stayed at an elderly friend's home in Basil. She fed and mothered us like we were her own children. Since we were stranded, we thought we'd try to obtain some contacts and set up some engagements while we were there for future use. However, that never happened, at least not for the Celestials. Little by little we stopped singing as the 70's progressed. With help from family at home we finally got enough money to get back to the United States. It was an eye-opening lesson for all of us. I don't even leave my house now unless the round-trip ticket is either in my hand or waiting for me at the airport.

My good friend and fellow graduate of Howard, actress Linda Gravatt, was the goddaughter of the late great Sammy Davis Jr. One day she approached several of us, including Sandy and Wesley, and informed us that he would be coming to perform at the John F. Kennedy Center in DC. She wanted to know if we were interested in going to the show. I had never seen Sammy Davis Jr. live in my life. I had only seen him on all of the biggest TV shows. What an opportunity it would be to see him in person. Linda got us tickets and several of us went to see the show. As expected, it was amazing. Sammy Davis was the ultimate performer, the Michael Jackson of the traditional pop era. He sang, danced, played instruments, did impressions and was a masterful entertainer. As someone who is a shoe fanatic, for some reason I remember these burgundy shoes he had on and thinking they were the most amazing shoes I had ever seen. I thought, one day when I get some money, I'm going to get me some burgundy shoes. We were most fortunate to go backstage to see him after the performance. I remember when he came into the reception room, I just knew that I was, indeed, in the presence of royalty. In his day, they just didn't come much bigger than Sammy. He hugged Linda and she introduced him to all of us. He was so gracious and so friendly and immediately made us feel at home. Of course, I was still in awe and didn't say much. My shyness was working big time. When Linda got to me in her introduction she said, "Uncle Sammy this is Richard Smallwood, an amazing pianist and musician. You really need to hear him." Sammy looked at me and smiled, shook my hand and said, "Great to meet you Richard. That's really cool! Fortunately, we have a piano right here in the room. Come on over here and play something for us." I immediately went into panic mode. I reverted to the 7-year old when my Mom introduced me to Clara Ward. This was Sammy Davis Jr., one of the biggest entertainers in the world! I couldn't play in front of him. Plus, the room was packed with other celebrities and people that I didn't know. Every song that I ever knew went out of my head. I managed to say weakly "No, that's alright." He looked at me strange and said "OK, man" and moved on to the other people waiting to greet him. Wesley and Sandy gave me a look that actually should have killed me on the spot. How could I have turned down the opportunity to play for someone like that? I wanted to kick myself if I possibly could have. When we all got into the car I can't even tell you how they all lit into me. I can't even repeat some of the names I was called. I think Wesley and

Sandy went at least a week without speaking to me. How do you say no to a request to play in front of someone of that stature? They just didn't understand how insecure I still was and how my anxiety at times would just paralyze me. I never lived that down. I was such a contradiction. There was one part of me that wanted to perform more than anything else. And there was another part that really thought that I wasn't good enough.

Tawatha Agee, Elett Ricks and Ángela Winbush had a group called Genesis I. Their accompanist was pianist and vocalist extraordinaire Shelton Becton. This group was so incredibly talented that they would demolish wherever they would sing. They just had a blend that was second to none. The arrangements that they would come up with were fresh, unique and musical. At some point in their career, they changed to secular and called themselves Hot Tea. The interest began to spread far and near about this talented group and they asked me to join them. I would definitely call it a "super group." Some of the most amazing musicians, singers, and writers anywhere were a part of this aggregation. Certainly my track record with trying to find a label to do a gospel record was not good, so I thought maybe I'll do secular. It was never anything that I considered wrong. Most classical music and opera is secular in nature. This was just secular with a beat. My record collection was comprised of just about every genre of music but rock and country and western. I told Mom about my decision. My mother was the most supportive person on the planet. I'm sure a part of her was disappointed, but she never let on. She simply smiled and said, "If that's what you want to do, I'm behind you one hundred percent. I know you'll be successful in whatever you choose to do." Immediately the late great Van McCoy, composer of the mega hit "The Hustle," took interest in us. He began to talk to RCA about us, and other labels. He was even thinking about me doing a solo project. It was around this time that I wrote my first secular song. I had fallen hard for a young lady and wrote it as a tribute to her. I may as well admit, I was smitten with Ángela from the very first time I saw her. The song had been for her. But our paths would take different directions. However, she will always have a special place in my heart, even today. The song was called "You are Love." Years later I would change the lyrics, retitle it "I Give You Praise," and record it with the Smallwood Singers. Hot Tea began to sing in clubs around the DC area. After Van McCoy, next it was producer, writer and ex-Miles Davis musician Mtume who began to work with us. I remember us being in the studio and I had a solo I had to sing on one of the songs. Mtume kept saying, "Richard, sing it like you sing those songs in church." I closed my eyes and asked them to turn the studio lights down to try to recapture what I did normally without even thinking about it. But I couldn't feel the music and I couldn't feel the song. It was a great song, but as hard as I tried I couldn't muster up the same emotion and spirit as when I sang gospel. I admired everyone's gifts so, but I just couldn't feel the music. After a while, I knew I had to leave the group. I had no idea why. As I stated before, I didn't see anything wrong with singing secular music. It was just that I couldn't feel it. It was a different feel than when I was singing gospel. I remember going to rehearsal one night and telling them that I was going to have to leave. No one really seemed surprised. I remember saying, "I love all of you! It has nothing to do with any of you or anything like that. It's me! I'm just not comfortable." I never will forget what Elett said to me: "Richard, maybe God has something else for you to do."

I don't know if that ever occurred to me before. The whole concept that God had some kind of pre-ordained plan for me hadn't entered my mind. I mean, I had loved music since I could remember being alive. I wanted to do it as a livelihood as far back as I could remember. But God having some kind of predestination lined up for me was mind-blowing. Her words hit me like a ton of bricks. God's revelation was taking form, little by little. He did have a plan for me. I have many Christian friends who are in secular music. I believe one of the reasons that they are put there is to witness to those in that industry. But that was not where God wanted me to be. He had a different plan, a plan much larger than I could have ever imagined. When I think of Hot Tea, I believe it was training ground and a launching pad for all of us. Elett would go on to teach music which was her passion. Shelton would become a major force on the Broadway scene in NY doing musical directing, composing and performing. Ángela would become an "all-in-one" at her craft in the industry, as a solo artist, producer, writer, musician and session musician, something that few females had ever done. Tawatha would go on to become the quintessential background and session singer in the business, as well as the go-to vocal contractor for all of the A-list artists in the industry. She would not only do sessions but tour with everyone from Luther Vandross to Aretha Franklin. Tawatha's biggest solo recording was with Mtume on a song called "Juicy". Hot Tea didn't last long, but it definitely added training and experience to the gifts that were a part of it.

CHAPTER 21

THE POWER OF HYMNS

In 1975, I decided to return to Howard to get my Master's degree in piano and ethnomusicology. By now there were courses in black music, the business of music, a jazz department and so many other areas that were needed by those who were going into the industry outside of classical music. I took some great courses that gave me the basic knowledge of publishing, royalties and other things that would serve me well in the future. I also took piano, but the love I had for playing classical musical just wasn't there anymore. My concentration and my focus seemed to be off. I remember playing a Chopin piece in a student recital, when my mind suddenly went blank (which had never happened to me in my life). So, I just began to improvise in a "Chopinesque" like manner until I could remember how to get to the end. No one seemed the wiser and the students stomped and screamed their approval. Mr. Kerr looked at me over his glasses at the end and said, "Richard, that was a very interesting interpretation of Chopin. But I'm glad you recovered and kept going." My interest seemed to be in a different place, and I ended up only doing one semester. Something wasn't the same, but I couldn't put my finger on it.

Also in 1975, the University of Maryland located in College Park, Maryland contacted me. They were interested in taking their already existing gospel choir and making it into an accredited course. They were interested in me heading the class. How ironic! The University of Maryland- College Park was not an HBCU but they wanted to make gospel choir a one-hour accredited course. Howard didn't even want us using their name. I agreed to take the position and the class became a part of the University's music program. My class was huge and we would give concerts on campus as well as travel. There was a gospel college choir festival that used to take place in Atlanta every Thanksgiving. I usually took the choir and we were always the biggest choir there. I continued with that class until 1980. It was a great experience. By now, I had also begun to teach privately. I had flyers made up and began to distribute them at church and other places, letting people know that I was taking private students in my home. I actually enjoyed that and had several students who stayed with me for years.

I remember we decided that the Young Adult Choir would do another project after the first one had been quite successful. I figured I had better start working on the music, as I knew I would have to write an album full of songs again. I was sitting in the practice area of the school at the piano. As stated before, I grew up on hymns as a child. I had no choice because my father insisted upon it. Among the regular hymns in the hymnbook, I would hear the common meter hymns. Those were the hymns that the deacons would "line out" a-cappella during devotional service when I was playing for Pleasant Grove. The audience would fall in with the most amazing harmony in an exercise in call and response between deacon and congregation. One of the common meter hymns that always stayed in my memory through the years was "I Love the Lord, He Heard My Cry." I would still go up to Howard's Fine Arts Building and write in the practice rooms in the basement. One day, as I sat at a baby grand piano down there, a melody entered my mind to go with those old lyrics. The harmony fell right in with the melody and before I knew it, the first original song for the next album was done. Little did I know the impact that song would have in the future and that a young girl growing up in Newark, New Jersey named Whitney Houston would introduce it to a worldwide audience many years later. That's how "I Love the Lord" came to be. I also wrote a song called "Give Us Peace" which became the title cut from that Union Temple Young Adult Choir project. My friend Edwin Hawkins would also record that song years later. When I listen to both of those Union Temple projects, so many of the songs that I wrote may be classified as "message songs" or songs that speak to the political ills of our nation and our world. Ironically, the many issues that we were facing in the 70's we are still struggling with today. That same year my old friends the Hawkins, this time with Edwin's brother Walter Hawkins at the helm, released an album called "Love Alive." It swept through the country like a tornado. Now pastoring the Love Center Church in Oakland, California, Walter featured his wife Tramaine, his baby sister Lynette on lead vocals, his older brother Edwin on piano, his brother Daniel on organ, his nephew Joel Smith on drums, and others all backed up by the church choir, the Love Center Choir.

It was definitely a family affair. "Changed" and "Going Up Yonder" entered the repertoire of almost every choir in America. I was in love with the Hawkins sound all over again. I was now beginning to see just how great a writer Walter was. I remember thinking, "how much talent can be in ONE family??" There was something about musical families that always fascinated me, especially since I was the only one in my family, other than Dad, who seemed to really gravitate towards it. I had always longed for a family full of brothers, sisters, cousins, uncles and aunts who could sing like angels and play anything they heard at the drop of a hat. I was always the lone odd ball in my family when it came to music though. "Love Alive" was a bit churchier in feel, but they delivered that familiar contemporary Hawkins sound that I loved so much. It made me want to write even more and I did.

CHAPTER 22

THE SMALLWOOD SINGERS

I n 1976, Union Temple's Young Adult Choir recorded the second album, "Give Us Peace." That same year the radio began to blast a scheduled appearance by Walter Hawkins at Constitution Hall. It had been a minute since we had talked to them and all of us were super excited that they would be coming to D.C. We weren't sure what the configuration would be. We imagined it would be members of the Love Center choir as well as some of the Hawkins brothers and sisters. This was also huge because "Love Alive" was still the hottest record in the country. Everyone wanted to hear those songs live. The laid-back Tramaine from the Hawkins Singers now had a new element to her vocals. She still had that beautiful crystal-like, pure soprano quality, but somewhere along the way she had learned how to squall with the best of the hard gospel singers. She would demolish a place as she would literally bend backwards while singing "Changed," and then go from that southern squall back into that crystal-clear tone. How did she do that? It was amazing. Everyone wanted to experience that firsthand, in person and in living color. Walter still had the most incredible vocal range that I'd ever heard in a male singer. It seemed even more powerful now. Lynette had come into her own after spending some time with the Hawkins Singers. Here was another incredible range, and powerful anointing reminiscent of Elaine Kelly from the Hawkins singers. When they walked out on stage at Constitution Hall, I realized immediately that it wasn't the choir. I saw along with Walter, Lynette and Tramaine, Ed at the piano and brother Daniel killing the organ. However, along with them was their cousin Shirley Miller from the original Hawkins Singers and lead singer of "Oh Happy Day." Also with them were their two older sisters, Feddie and Carol, with whom I was familiar from Walter's very first album "Selah," in which they did background vocals along with Lynette. When they opened their mouths, it was that same full, choral Hawkins sound that I remembered from the Hawkins Singers. There was nothing like it. We all sat there transfixed as they not only did the newer stuff, but also went back to some of the early Hawkins Singers standards. I was in heaven. Then something very strange happened. Tramaine stepped forward to do "Changed." Everyone knew the familiar introduction and people began to react even to the piano intro. I felt the strangest chill go from the top of my head to my feet. Before Tramaine could start to sing, I felt tears welling up in my eyes. By the time she got to the first line, I was basically uncontrollable. Yes, the song was and still is anointed. Yes, Tramaine is anointed and there is no one that can even attempt to do what she does with that song. But there was something different going on. As she began to minister, I had an epiphany. It was as if I could hear God speaking to me clearly and audibly in my head. Although I was looking at the stage where the Hawkins Family was standing, it was like I could almost see another curtain opening to reveal them yet again. I could hear God say, "Richard, this is what I want you to do." It's ironic how God has always seemed to use that family to inspire me to go to the next level of my pre-ordination. By now, I was crying uncontrollably, and I was patting my foot rapidly hoping that somehow that would control it. I didn't want to go hollering to the top of my lungs or running down the aisle as my Momma would have done! I'm sure everyone who was with me thought that I was just "caught up" by what I was hearing, which indeed was absolutely heavenly. The Hawkins family was ministering like I can't even explain. But God was using this moment to speak to me in a way that I can't ever remember Him speaking to me before. I was inspired, excited, encouraged, yet a little frightened at the same time. All I knew was that what I was seeing in front of me was what I was supposed to do. It was more than just loving this music and always wanting to do this from the time I could walk because I enjoyed it. This was a directive from God Himself and I knew it without a shadow of a doubt. Yet, with the urgency that I heard it, I knew it had to do with something more than just singing, writing or playing. That was definitely the foundation of it. Yet, still it was something much bigger and more important than just doing music because I loved it. I didn't have all of the information yet. I couldn't put it into words and certainly couldn't explain it to those who were around me. I couldn't stop the tears. The understanding of ministry was starting to take form in my mind and in my spirit.

By now, the Celestial Sound was no longer singing. I knew that I needed an ensemble to help me in the direction in which God wanted me to go. I struggled with the name that I would call them. I remember Sandy saying to me, "Richard, it needs to be something with your name in it. People need to know who you are and what it is that you do. There needs to be name recognition as soon as they hear the name. This will be tied in with your sound, your music and your brand." Years later, from that little kids' group of the same name, I would again form a group called *The Richard Smallwood Singers*. My biggest source of singers at this point was the Young Adult Choir. I pulled eleven members from the choir to form a smaller, more mobile group. Wesley, Sully and Lou Lou (former members of the Celestials) were automatically a part. In addition, there was the incredibly gifted Ángela Winbush, Wesley's cousins Betty Lea and Diane Price, Brenda Wanzer who ironically was an original baby Smallwood Singer from when we were kids, Jackie Ruffin, Gail Murray, Delores Linder and Wayne Powell. I added the former drummer of the Celestials, Robert Morton, and a new young multi-gifted musician on bass from North Carolina, Aaron Graves. On February 14, 1977, we had our first rehearsal. I immediately began writing music for the new ensemble and very shortly after we had our debut concert at Union Temple. The very first original song I wrote for the Smallwood Singers was called, "I've Got Something This World Can't Take Away." I remember Sully not being able to be there because of a family emergency at home in North Carolina. Everyone else was in place however, with the ladies in brand new peach outfits and the guys in black suits and brand-new matching peach shirts. Union Temple was packed and the concert was a success. I especially remember the outfits because I remember how hard it was to find a peach shirt that would exactly match the girls' dresses. That was not an easy task, and we were elated when we finally found a shirt that had a beautiful print on a peach background that matched perfectly. We wore those outfits for quite a while being that it was the only outfit that we had. One day, while donning our outfits before a concert, we were shocked to discover, upon very close examination of the guys' shirts, that the print was actually hundreds of naked ladies. The print was so small and so intricately done that no one ever noticed it before. That was the last time we wore those shirts!

In March of that same year, the Young Adult Choir celebrated yet another anniversary. This year we decided to get my friends the Hawkins Family for our celebration. We held it at Cramton Auditorium at Howard University. That anniversary is so special in my memory. Firstly, where it was held had such significance for me, and secondly the special guests were my friends and God had used them in so many ways to inspire me. God had used Edwin's writing style to inspire me to finally and seriously write my own music. God had used Walter and the family to show me exactly what it is that He wanted me to do in music ministry. Cramton was packed to the hilt that night. I had written a song for Ángela called "I Won't Be Troubled No More." I can only remember a few times in my life when I have seen that kind of outpouring of God's Spirit as she sang that song that night. When she finished, it was hard to restore order in the place. She sang with an anointing that night like I had never heard her sing before. I remember thinking, as I had known all along, "Ángela is destined for greatness."

That same year, Ángela told me that Stevie Wonder was looking for a new background singer. She was interested in auditioning for the job and needed to do a demo tape. Ángela was such an integral part of my music ministry and a dear friend. I hated to think of losing her. But at the same time, she was such a phenomenal gift and if she was afforded such a great opportunity as that, then I was elated for her. She and I went into a local studio and I helped her lay down several songs. A few weeks after she sent the tape, Stevie contacted her. He wanted her to come to LA immediately and become a part of his group, "Wonderlove." It's always hard to see family leave the nest. She was the baby of the clan. But I knew she had the training and the talent to accomplish whatever she set her mind to do. More importantly, she had God at the forefront. I knew that the sky was the limit. She left for LA in 1977 and the rest is history.

In the fall of that same year my mentor, Dr. Pearl Williams Jones, approached me. Someone had contacted her about a music festival called the Festival D'Automne à Paris, which was going to be taking place in Paris, France in October. The festival would feature different kinds of ethnic music and they were looking for a contemporary black gospel group. She had told them that she knew of just the group and wanted to know if I would be interested in taking the Smallwood Singers. God is amazing in the way that He opens doors on the way to our predestination. We had only been together for about nine months. We certainly were not a well-known name and already the opportunities were starting to happen. In October, with round trip tickets in hand, all fourteen of us boarded Air France to participate in the festival. The festival ran from the 18-23 of October and we performed every night. The venue was an old theater called Bouffes du Nord. It was an incredible experience. I recall that not many people spoke English fluently, but with multi-lingual Sully by our side we didn't have much problem in breaking the language barrier. I remember one night especially, when the Holy Spirit fell during the concert. The audience didn't particularly understand what was going on, but as I looked out at them they were weeping and did not know why. At the end of that concert, two French ladies came up to us still in tears and asked Sully why did they feel that way? Sully was able to witness to them in French. It was an amazing night. While singing on the final night, I noticed that my words were becoming slurred when I tried to sing. It was a strange feeling and at first, I didn't pay it much attention. When we went out to eat after the concert it was hard to contain the food in my mouth while chewing, and the slurring in my speech was getting worse. I also noticed that when I blinked my right eye it wouldn't close. By then I knew something was horribly wrong. My first thought was that I'd had a stroke. I didn't know what it was. Here I was thousands of miles from home and something major was going on with me. I was terrified. I knew we were leaving the next day for home. If only I could hold out until then. After finally arriving in the States, I immediately went to my doctor. She found out that it was a condition known as Bell's palsy that is caused by an infected nerve in the ear. I'm not sure if that came from the long flight to Paris or what the origin was. My face was paralyzed for several months. The frightening part was that my doctor wasn't entirely sure that it would clear up. Thank God, little by little, my face returned to normal. The kidney stones continued to plague me though. It seemed like my health was falling apart, but I was only in my twenties. There were undiagnosed stomach ailments that the doctors thought might be coming from my nerves and anxiety. So I was put on relaxers. By then I was carrying around a big bag with nothing but pills in it. I had the relaxers, the pain pills in case I had a kidney stone attack, the pills for the Bell's palsy, and the list went on.

Sigma Sound in Philly was a major studio during that time, and I decided to do a recording with the Smallwood Singers there. The day that we were to leave for Philly another major kidney stone attack happened. I just loaded up on Tylenol, prayed and we got in the cars and journeyed to Philly. I was in so much pain that I couldn't drive and Betty Lea, Wesley and Sully's cousin, drove my car. By the time we got to the studio and started recording, the pain began to subside. Thank God.

We made it through the session, but it just wasn't the best to me for a couple of reasons. I think the first thing was that I was in such pain off and on, it was hard to ignore that and concentrate on the recording. Secondly, as I look back, the kind of recording that I envisioned in my mind would have cost much more than the little pennies that we had, and certainly would have taken weeks in the studio as opposed to one day. But still, it was good experience.

Around this time, there seemed to be some underlying controversy around the church about why I had started the Smallwood Singers. There were questions as to who was selected to be a part, and why, and about if I was trying to be a "star." It just seemed to go on and on. It hurt like I can't explain. I started the Smallwood Singers because God instructed me to do it. That directive from God helped to ease my insecurity about my music and myself. The last thing I was trying to be was a "star." I just wanted to do what God wanted me to do. I picked the people whom I thought had the vocal expertise to give me the kind of sound that I wanted. It wasn't because I loved any one more than anyone else, or favored anyone above the other. I had friends who were closer to me than some of the members of the Smallwood Singers who were not asked to be a part. It was all about what I needed vocally. I had no idea that this would cause confusion. When I look back, I realize that probably most of those illnesses that I was experiencing came from me holding things inside. I've always been the kind of person who wouldn't talk about what was bothering me. I was a worrier, so I carried the weight of whatever it was around with me. That can easily manifest itself in illnesses of all kinds. By now, I knew this was what I was supposed to do and began to actively seek record labels that might be interested in signing the Smallwood Singers. One thing that seemed to get in the way was that the group was too large to be mobile. There were fourteen of us including musicians and we didn't have a known name. I began to think that maybe, if I cut the group down, not only would it be easier to move the group around, but maybe a record deal would be easier to obtain. Also, it might help cut down on some of the controversy swirling around me. It was one of the hardest things that I've ever had to do because I loved each member dearly.

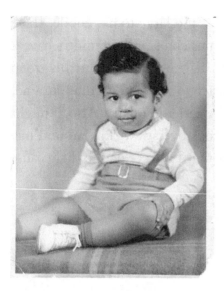

Richard Smallwood's first formal baby picture (1949)

Richard Smallwood with his first toy piano at age 2. (1950)

Richard's sister, Dorothy Jean holding him as an infant.

TOTAL PRAISE | 255

Richard Smallwood's 6th Grade Class at Stanton Elementary School (1960)

Richard Smallwood with Ángela Winbush back in the day (Los Angeles, CA 1978)

Richard Smallwood with friends Andrae Crouch, Walter Hawkins, & Sandra Crouch

Bishop Walter Hawkins
inducts Richard Smallwood
into the Gospel Music Hall of
Fame (2006).

Smallwood's most recent recording "Anthology" (2015)

Aretha Franklin & Richard
Smallwood at Madison
Square Garden (2015)

Richard Smallwood participating at one of the Hawkins Seminar with Walter Hawkins & Edwin Hawkins (piano) (1980's)

Smallwood's First Contract signing with Benson Records celebrating along with the Smallwood Singers (1981) Pictured left to right: Benson Executive Donald Watkins, Lisa Burroughs, Simme Neal, Head of Benson Records, Bob McKenzie, Dottie Jones, Wesley Boyd, Richard Smallwood, Carolene Adams, Jackie Ruffin

Clara Ward and the Famous Ward Singers (Philadelphia, PA)

Pictured here: Richard Smallwood's Stepfather,
Rev. C. L. Smallwood

The Celestials performing
in Basel, Switzerland at
Club Atlantis (1975)

Dr. Thomas Kerr, Howard
University Piano Professor

Richard Smallwood supporting Edwin Hawkins as he was being honored with the BMI Trailblazer Award

Richard Smallwood featured in the local newspaper (Philadelphia, 1958)

Richard Smallwood's influence during collegiate career. Pictured here: Edwin Hawkins Singers (1970)

Family at Anthology Recording: DeDe (brother), Rob (nephew), Michael (brother), Momma Rosa, Richard, and Robyn (niece)

Family: Marques (nephew), Robyn (niece), Richard Smallwood, Denise (Cousin), Michael (Brother) Michael Jr. (nephew), Marquis (nephew), Robert Jr. (Nephew) Momma Rosa, Dede (Brother) at a family wedding ceremony

Smallwood Singers' First recording session with Benson Records Lisa Burroughs, Carolene Evans, Wesley Boyd, Richard Smallwood, Dottie Jones, Jackie Ruffin (Nashville, TN, 1981)

From the Live in NY Journey Project: Bishop Walter Hawkins, Lynette Hawkins Stephens, Richard Smallwood, Tramaine Hawkins and Chaka Khan (2005)

High School Group: Gospel Stars circa 1966. Richard Smallwood, Valerie Wright, Sue Givens and Brenda Jenkins

Undergraduate Graduation Ceremony from Howard University School of Music (1971)

Senior Recital Reception
Left to right: Valerie
Wright, Mona Jones,
Brenda
Wanzer, Richard
Smallwood, Ollie
Milligan, Jackie Cadlett,
Gail Murray

Great Grandmother Lula,
Grandmother Bessie,
Aunt Olivia, Little DeDe
and Richard's father,
Robert

Richard Smallwood's Great Uncle, Ockie
Cain, one of the first African American
men to pursue entrepreneurship
(Durham, NC)

Hawkins Seminar, Vanessa Bell Armstrong with Daryl Coley, Walter Hawkins and Richard Smallwood doing background (1980's)

The Mark IV, high school secular musical group Pictured left to right: Clinton Derricks, Richard Smallwood, Cleavant Derricks, & friend.

High School Graduation, McKinley Tech (Washington, DC 1967)

Founding Howard Gospel Choir members at rehearsal (Richard Smallwood on the piano) (1969)

College secular musical group, Hot Tea. Pictured Left to right: Ángela Winbush, Richard Smallwood, Shelton Becton, Elett Ricks, Seated: Tawatha Agee (1970's)

Richard Smallwood Singers: Tim Linzy, Richard Smallwood, Jackie Ruffin, Wesley Boyd, Jeff Davis, Lisa Burroughs, Carolene Adams, Steven Ford, Dottie Jones

Richard Smallwood's maternal grandmother, Nellie Locklear

Richard and his mother, Mabel Smallwood at his graduating senior recital reception at Howard University. (1971)

Richard and mom during his early college days.

Richard and mom at his graduation ceremony with Masters of Divinity degree from Howard University (2004)

Richard's mom with siblings, Michael and DeDe.

Richard's mother & grandfather, Richard Locklear (Durham, NC 1930's)

Richard's mother as a baby (Durham, NC 1915)

Richard's mother, Mabel Smallwood

Mozart, Richard's ride or die pet Yorkie Terrier.

High School Music Teacher, Mrs. Gilkes, who helped Richard to obtain a full scholarship to Howard University.

Mrs. Beatrice Gilkes, Richard's high school music teacher at age 90

Richard with brothers, Michael and DeDe, back in the day.

Richard's father,
Robert Clements

Richard with his
parents and siblings.

Richard's first robe at 5 years old.

Richard's great, great, grandmother, Winnie Cain (1800's)

Richard's sister, Dorothy Jean

Richard Smallwood, Kurt Carr, Edwin Hawkins and Donald Lawrence

Grammy Award Nominee, Richard Smallwood, on the red carpet.

Patti Labelle and Richard Smallwood at music festival in Terni, Italy (1996)

Phylicia Rashad and Richard Smallwood, friends and former Howard University schoolmates (New York, 2016)

Richard Smallwood preaching at home church, Metropolitan Baptist Church (Largo, MD 2017)

Hillsborough, N. C., 22d April — 1867.
Received of 2d Leut. Isaac Porter, V. R. C., and Jn C. Turrentine, Agents for the distribution of corn for the destitute of Orange county, One — bushel corn.
A. C. Murdoch   Jack X Cage
                                         his mark

Receipt for a bushel of corn given to Richard's great great great great great grandfather when he was freed from slavery. Notice the "X" to mark his signature (Hillsborough, NC 1867)

Richard received the BMI Trailblazer Award; standing with his brother, DeDe (2014)

Richard, MC
Hammer and
Edwin Hawkins
(Washington, DC)

Roberta Flack, Richard's 8th Grade Music
Teacher at the Stellar Awards

Roberta Martin Singers (Chicago, IL 1960

Howard University students taking over the Administration Building (1968)

Richards's Great Uncle Clea and Great Aunt Viola (Durham, NC)

Legendary songwriter and musician, Valerie Simpson with Richard (New York)

Vision Chicago
Gospel Fest
(2015)

Vision praying before first recording, Adoration Live in Atlanta (Atlanta, GA 1996)

Vision in concert at First Baptist Church in Glenarden, MD

Richard Smallwood plays for the Roberta Martin Singers at the Smithsonian Institution. Pictured left to right: Eugene Smith, Lucy Collier, Richard Smallwood, and mentor, Dr. Pearl Williams Jones (1981)

Wesley Boyd, Richard Smallwood, and Edward Sully waiting backstage during a Howard Gospel Choir concert (1970)

The Celestials, first gospel group at Howard University, awaiting to go on stage at the Montreux Jazz Festival (Montreux Switzerland, 1973) L to R: Mary (Lewis) Wilson, Richard Smallwood, Wesley Boyd, Edward Sully, Rosalind (Thompkins) Lynch

Richard marching in the
Howard University Band (1968)

Original Smallwood Singers (DC, 1977) Left
to right: Jackie Ruffin, Mary Wilson, Edward
Sully, Brenda Wanzer, Wesley Boyd, Ángela
Winbush, Betty Lea, Wayne Powell, Richard
Smallwood, Gail Murray.

Union Temple Young Adult Choir (1975)

Richard's Howard University "Dad &
Mom," Dr. Thomas Kerr & Mrs. Anne
Burwell

Howard Gospel Choir members during sit-in demonstration in a hotel hallway (Dallas, TX 1970)

Famous Davis Sisters (Philadelphia, PA)

A major part of my family's history. Hardscrabble Plantation, built in 1776

CHAPTER 23
ONLY GOD CAN OPEN DOORS

When God is trying to get you to move to the next level, He has a way of lighting a fire under you to get you to move. I'm a person who loves my comfort zone and I've never liked change. Change is strange, unknown and frightening to me. But it is necessary for growth and necessary to get to the place where God wants us to be. Change is a part of life. Instead of letting God take control of the situation, I was busy trying to fix it myself. The group was cut to include: Delores Linder, Brenda Wanzer, Jackie Ruffin, Diane Price, Wesley Boyd and Edward Sully. A new bass player, Chris Suggs, came on board. Although it was easier to travel around in a small van, and cheaper in terms of airfare, it certainly didn't help the controversy. It actually got worse. Speculation about my motives continued. It was said that I didn't need a group. We didn't need to try to record. I already had the choir and that was enough. Then, other mean-spirited things started circulating about me. No question, many people supported me while all of this was going on. But it seems that we always hear the negative things louder than anything else. It got to the point that I couldn't sleep at night. The different illnesses that were popping up were getting worse. Union Temple had always been like a family church to me. There were so many close friends and love was one of the main things that everyone who was a part of it felt. Even visitors could feel it. Rev. Wilson, a student of the late great theologian Dr. Leon Wright, was a great teacher as well as a preacher. We were taught principles that would guide us throughout our lives. When I look back on it, it was like a nurturing place where you were prepared for whatever it was that you were to do in life. So many great people and gifts were launched from that place. For many it was not the place where you would be for the rest of your life, but a place that prepared you for who and what you were to become. But the family element that had been so prevalent there began to change for me. I felt unappreciated. But more than anything, I felt misunderstood. I remember Walter Hawkins saying once that the biggest hurts that he got were not from the world, but from the church. I talked to Mom about it and she instructed me to let God lead me in what I should do. The feeling that I had to leave had surfaced and was getting stronger and stronger, but I didn't want to. It was the last church my father founded before he passed. It was my comfort zone. It's what I knew and what was familiar. My Mom was there and there was no way that I wanted to leave her. Looking back, I now realize that God was trying to usher me into my next season. But in order to get there, change had to occur. I had been prepared adequately. I had learned what I needed to learn during my time there. My season of preparation had come to an end. It was now time to move. In the fall of 1978, I resigned as minister of music of Union Temple. Ironically my last Sunday there, the Smallwood Singers had a performance that afternoon at the Smithsonian Institution -- the largest museum in the world. It was an ethnic music day where all kinds of music were presented, from African to Native

American. We were asked to sing for a half hour, and to present black gospel music. I don't remember exactly what we sang. I'm sure we must have sung a couple of original tunes that I had written. Being a very mixed audience, I also remember singing "When the Saints Go Marching In" and "Amen," two songs that usually were recognizable to most cultural backgrounds. It gave the audience an opportunity to sing along with us in a call-and-response kind of way. After the concert, a friend who had come with us came up to me. She said a young Caucasian sister was sitting next to her during the performance. She continued that when we finished, the young lady turned to her and said, "You know, when I got up this morning I had contemplated suicide. After hearing this singing, something has changed inside of me. I'm encouraged and I know that my life is not mine to take. I also know that the God that they sung about is going to help me through my difficulties." When my friend told me that, it actually frightened me. That day it hit home to me how serious all of this was. You never knew who might be in the audience or how what you sang or played might make a difference in somebody's life. For the first time in my life, I realized the awesome responsibility we have as musicians. It's nothing that we can take lightly. There are people who are hurting and who are suffering. Our music ministries are to reach hurting people. We can't reach them if we are caught up in our own selfish egos, or glorifying whatever gifts we might have. Gifts are meant to be shared. We have to be continually yielded to God as vessels, so that He can use those gifts to help others. We have to be those conduits through which God's love flows. The responsibility frightened me because I also realized that it was something that God had called me to do. This was huge! This was serious. It was more than just loving music or enjoying performing it. This brought about an awareness of responsibility that I had not considered before. It was an "aha moment" for me. It was the first time that I can remember equating music with ministry. God was still teaching me.

Back in my Howard days, when we used to do the Sunday night broadcast circuit and go from church to church, one of the churches we used to frequent was Refreshing Springs Church of God in Christ. Gifted artist and the "Sweetheart of Gospel" Myrna Summers, composer of the mega hit "God Gave Me A Song" that swept the country in the late 60s, was in charge of the choirs there and they undoubtedly had some of the best singers in this area. Later I would even travel with Myrna as her pianist. One young lady who always stood out to me was Myrna Summers' cousin, Dottie Jones. First of all, she had one of the most awesome voices, and unlike anything in gospel that I'd heard before. It was silky, smooth and velvet-like in texture. Most importantly, it was anointed. I'd heard her on different recordings with Myrna as well and was in love with her voice. Somewhere between the Celestials and the Young Adult Choir, and from singing on musicals together, I got the opportunity to meet her. When the Smallwood Singers had a vacancy in the alto section after Wesley's cousin Diane stepped down, both Wesley and I thought of Dottie immediately. I knew she would be a tremendous asset to the group. It was not a matter of her auditioning. I knew what she could do. It was just a matter of her showing up for rehearsal. We reached out to her and she was elated to be a part. By now, the Smallwood Singers began to travel even more. I didn't have a church job on Sunday mornings so I was able to go wherever and whenever. We traveled everywhere from Texas and Louisiana, to Trinidad and Tobago. I remember driving in two cars from Washington, DC to Texas and one of the cars breaking down on the way. I remember showing up where pianos were so out of tune, or so many keys were missing, that the intro to a song you played was unrecognizable. I remember doing a glissando down the black keys on one piano and all of the keys came loose and ended up in a little pile of black keys at the bottom of the piano. It was dues-paying time, but we loved it and we enjoyed it. After a while we had a soprano vacancy and Wesley had heard of a phenomenal young 19-year-old soprano who was the baby sister of Dorothy Burroughs, one of our former classmates at Howard. She was a student at Howard, so I told him to go see if he could find her somewhere on campus because I would love to hear her. We were on the third floor of the Fine Arts building and within minutes Wesley had scoured the campus and found her and brought her into the classroom. Lisa Burroughs had an endless range, an incredible ear and the kind of quality that I loved. Within minutes of her singing, I knew we had found the right soprano. Sully, who was a great singer, really only liked to sing as a hobby. Although he had been with me since Howard, he really had no interest in trying to pursue this as a livelihood. He loved his job at the Library of Congress and although I hated to see him go, I definitely understood. Last but not least, there was a young lady whom we had known of for years singing around town with other groups. I remembered that whenever I would hear some of those groups that she sang with, I couldn't wait till they gave her a mic. This girl could really sing! Her name was Carolene Adams. We asked her to come to rehearsal and when we heard her, we knew she would fit right in. In addition to being a serious singer, Carolene's humor has always been one of the great parts of her wonderful personality. When she came to that first rehearsal we rehearsed a couple of tunes before we heard her sing and welcomed her into the family. While we were rehearsing and she was sitting on the front row listening, at some point she snatched off her hairpiece and threw it at us and hollered, "SING!!!" Yes, she would definitely fit in. I knew this was the group: Carolene Adams, Lisa Burroughs, Dottie Jones and the two originals, Wesley Boyd and Jackie Ruffin. This configuration would be the voices who would establish the "Smallwood Sound."

Of course, from the Smallwood Singers' inception, I was promised every kind of record deal known to man. Record execs would say they were interested and I'd never hear from them again. I'd even get contracts sent to me in the mail or handed to me, but for whatever reason nothing would become of them. But I knew I couldn't give up. Although I knew, there were many disappointments. I remembered what God had told me. I'd get knocked down, but I'd get up and keep going forward. By now, the late Rev. Donald Vails and the Choraleers had recorded "I Love The Lord" and a song called "He's Able" that had been featured on the Young Adults' second project. Donald was the first national artist that gave me a chance in terms of a national recording. He flew me in to Detroit to perform on that project as well. The late Rev. Isaac Douglas recorded "I Love the Lord" as well. My music had started to get around even though a record deal was nowhere in sight. I also began to travel with my friend Edwin Hawkins as his accompanist. At the time he was traveling with a well-known televangelist/healer, David Epley. When we came to D.C., the Smallwood Singers sang at the service down at Constitution Hall. During the service, the minister called an elderly crippled lady in the audience up, so that he could heal her. He prayed and rebuked every negative force he could think of and proclaimed that she was healed. He then instructed her to throw her cane away because she would not need it ever again.

She obediently did, and the cane landed at the back of the stage under a curtain. He then told her to walk around Constitution Hall. Now if you haven't been to Constitution Hall before, it seats almost 4,000 people. By no means is it a small venue. But mother obeyed and she made her way slowly around the hall. By the time she got back to the front we had dismissed and some of us were still standing on stage. As she approached the stage, she caught Jackie's eye and said, "Daughter, would you reach under that curtain and PLEASE give me my cane?" My heart went out to her, but at the same time I was a little tickled. Clearly, the "healing" didn't take. By now Edwin had started a workshop called the Edwin Hawkins Music and Arts Seminar in which I taught keyboard, and until this day I teach songwriting. Through the years, the Seminar Mass Choir would record some of my songs and I would usually be featured on keyboard on those particular tunes. They recorded "The Resurrection" before it was released on the Smallwood Singers' first project. They recorded "Give Us Peace" from the second Union Temple Young Adult Choir album. They would also record "I Won't Be Troubled No More," originally written for Ángela Winbush and the Union Temple Young Adult Choir. That song would later be recorded by the Smallwood Singers on the album, "Testimony." I would also play on some of the cuts that were written by Edwin such as "Give Us This Day" and a number of others. Wesley began to teach voice at the seminar as well.

Those early days at The Edwin Hawkins Music and Arts Seminar, in the late 70's and then starting annually in the early 80's, were like nothing I had experienced before. We were like a big family. We would have so much fun every year. There was no competition but you knew if you had to minister you had to put your best foot forward, because of the standard of excellence that the seminar carried. We all helped each other. I remember one of the many years that Vanessa Bell Armstrong was there and was scheduled to perform at the nightly musical. She told Walter that she needed some background vocals. Within minutes Walt had approached me and Daryl Coley, and after rehearsing all three of us backed her up on her set that night. Everyone supported everyone, regardless of what you had accomplished in your own ministry. Iron really does sharpen iron. I think we were all inspired by each other and the gifts that would come from all over the country to be a part. Here I was playing, writing and teaching at a conference alongside the very people who had inspired me to try to make this a career. I was in musical heaven. Edwin, the very person who inspired me to write in the late 60's while I was a student at Howard, was allowing me to teach songs I had written to the Mass Choir and record them. Amazing gifts like John P. Kee, Yolanda Adams, LaShun Pace, myself and others got some of their early national exposure through this organization. I remember that I never wanted the week to end. I used to wish that whatever city we were in at the time, whatever hotel in which we were staying, that we all could just stay there forever and do music. It was just that inspirational to me. It was there that I would not only experience Walter's musical gift, but his preaching gift as well. I would sit in amazement as he would exegete the Scriptures. He would extract messages from Biblical passages that I had read all my life but had never seen or thought of the amazing insight he had. Every year it seemed like his sermons were directed to me. Whatever I was going through at the time, whatever fears and uncertainties I was facing, it seemed like he always had a Word that would speak to the deepest parts of my spirit. It was definitely a time of musical and spiritual refreshing.

I was really starting to get my feet wet in the gospel music industry. Little by little, things were happening. We started appearing on stage with major artists such as the Hawkins Family, Rev. James Cleveland and other artists of that time, and we didn't even have a recording out! God was moving! By now, all of the then-current members of the Smallwood Singers were on board to make this thing work. Although we couldn't afford to pay much, we put everyone on payroll. We just had to make sure that whatever we charged would cover our expenses and our little payroll. In 1981, everyone basically quit their jobs in a HUGE leap of faith. Our first endeavor was a West Coast tour. Wesley began setting up engagements. We did a Bon Voyage concert at Lisner Auditorium on George Washington University's campus to help with our expenses for the tour. Our first stop was LA. We certainly couldn't afford hotels so a dear friend, musician extraordinaire Maestro Shelton Kilby and his wife Clara, opened their home to us and fed us! We got sleeping bags and slept on the floor. It was like a giant camping trip with your best friends. We had a ball and sang all around LA. A couple of months before we left home from the West Coast trip, I had been contacted by my friend Pearl Williams Jones and the Smithsonian Institution. The Smithsonian was honoring the legacy of Roberta Martin and her music. Miss Martin was now deceased. The plan was to gather all the existing Martin Singers and do a two-day symposium and concert at the Smithsonian. It would end with a huge concert at Bible Way as they did when I was a little boy. By now, my idol pianist Lucy Smith Collier had had a stroke and although through physical therapy she was now mobile, she was still paralyzed in her right hand and unable to play. Pearl, knowing what a fan I was of her playing and how I grew up on their music, recommended me to play for the singers. Elated is not even adequate to express what I felt. These were some of the people who were my inspiration from my childhood. I cannot count the times I sat in Bible Way as a kid when they would come through for their revivals, mesmerized by their music. I cannot count how many times I gazed at Lucy's amazing fingers and thought if only I could be that good one day. The only problem was that the California trip was right in the middle of the Smithsonian dates for the Martin Singers. Although I knew that the California trip was already planned, I devised a way to work around it. I would fly to LA and do the first several dates. I'd then fly back to DC to do the final Smithsonian rehearsals and concerts for about a week. Then I'd return to California and continue the tour with the Smallwoods. There was no way I could miss this opportunity. I will never forget the day that I flew to Chicago for the very first rehearsal. I walked into the church and I saw my inspirations. There was Lucy Smith, sort of looking at me over her glasses as if to say, "Can this boy really play?" In addition to Lucy, there was Eugene Smith, Gloria Griffin, Delois Barrett Campbell, Bessie Folk, Louise McCord, Romance Watson, Archie Dennis and Norsalus McKissick. I was in gospel music heaven, but you best believe I was nervous. Before I left home I had to pull out all of my old Roberta Martin recordings and not only review the songs, but also review the style. It had been years since I had played that style. This was now the era of contemporary music. I had to divorce my mind from the way I played currently and remember how Lucy played when I was a little boy and how I used to emulate her. It was still there. But I had to dig deep inside and bring it back to the forefront. As I began to practice, some of the nuances and riffs she would do in a live setting, that weren't even on the recordings, began to return to my memory.

That day in Chicago, when I sat down at the piano and began to play, Lucy paused for a minute and hit me on my shoulder and said with a big smile, "BOY, you play like ME!!" No one could have ever given me a greater compliment. She began to coach me in little pianistic things she used to do when she was able to play. I caught them and ran with them. I was like a three-year-old kid who wanted to please his Mother. Of course, when the Martin Singers opened their mouths and began to sing "Only a Look," I did all I could to keep from crying. I never thought in a million years I would get this opportunity. The sound was still full, anointed, immaculate and powerful. A very gifted musician by the name of Charles Pike was on the organ and with him and me together, it was like the old Martin Singers sound on the instruments. As I flew back from LA to DC where the final rehearsals and the concerts were held, I remember thinking how God had begun to create so many different opportunities. It seemed like the minute I formed the Smallwood Singers, even though I went through some difficult times, doors continued to open. I wondered what was next. I knew God was not finished.

CHAPTER 24

MY FIRST RECORD DEAL

The Martin Singers symposium and concerts were awesome. During the day they studied her music: the theory of it, the structure of it and what she contributed to gospel music as a pioneer. In the evenings, the Martin Singers sang until the power of the Lord came down. Mom sat in the audience each night, beaming proudly. She alone knew what this meant to me. She had lived this with me through my childhood and now God had brought a childhood dream into fruition. I couldn't believe that I was playing for my childhood idols. No one will ever know what that meant to me. After the Smithsonian engagement ended, we did one more concert at Bible Way, where my love for them began so many years ago.

When I returned to California, Shelton Kilby had secured a date for us in a small Seventh Day Adventist Church in San Diego. There was a new younger pastor recently installed there and he wanted to bring the church out of its staunch traditional stance. They didn't believe in singing gospel music per se. They didn't believe in drums in the church. Shelton's idea was to do a workshop for a couple of days and then the final evening, the Smallwood Singers would do a concert. The lady who was the minister of music was the new pastor's largest opponent. I remember Shelton conducting the workshop and telling about our African history and the relationship to the drum, for not only music but communication, what it represented and what an integral part of our culture it was. Her response was "I don't speak African, I'm not from there and I'm basically not interested in what they played there." She was one tough cookie. Even when Shelton started citing biblical passages on praising "with timbrel and dance and loud sounding cymbals" she was not moved. When he talked about David dancing before the Lord, she was unmoved even more. I myself was ready to go home. I figured this was a losing battle and God only knew what she was going to do when we started to sing. The night of the concert as we brought our drums in to set them up, I heard an audible gasp from the audience. One lady ran up to us and asked, "Does pastor know you are bringing THOSE in here?" I explained as well as I could that it was pastor's idea that we brought our drums with us. He really was trying to expose them to something different. As we began to sing that night, after the first several bars, surprisingly most of the people began to get with us. I guess some of them were starved for change as well and were open to it. However, the minister of music along with some of her friends sat on the back row and glared at us. It reminded me of some of the Howard professors who used to do the same thing whenever we'd sing gospel there. I tried not to look at her and just continued to pray in my mind while we ministered. I will never forget the third song we sang, "I've Got Something This World Can't Take Away." Around midway of that song the Spirit swept through that church like a mighty wind. Jackie walked down the aisle, convincing people that no matter what the world says, God has given each of us something special. People began crying and waving their hands. Way in the back of the church I saw a white handkerchief waving. It was the minister of music. I felt pretty sure that she might have been waving it to tell us to sit down. Then I realized that it was her way of giving her affirmation. Something had touched her. God is amazing the way He orchestrates things. He could reach her through His spirit in a way that logic and workshops could not. At the end of the concert I saw her heading toward me. I was definitely nervous and wasn't sure what she was going to say. She said, "Son, come here!" "Oh Lord," I thought to myself. She continued, "Do you have any albums?" "No ma'am," I replied. "We haven't recorded anything yet." She said to me, "The minute you do, I want you to send several boxes out here. We need to hear more of you," and she hugged me. "Yes ma'am," I replied half-way in shock. However, I shouldn't have been shocked because that's just the way God works.

We continued the tour in the LA area and then left for the Bay area. Our friend, Edwin Hawkins, had set up some engagements in Oakland. One was at the Ephesians Church of God in Christ, the church that the Hawkins family and many of the original Hawkins singers came out of. He also set up a performance at a gospel nightclub called "Noah's Ark." No one knew who we were, and he introduced us as if we were royalty. The audience accepted us with open arms. Edwin has always been such an incredible support. I remember telling him around that time that I wanted to do music ministry as a profession more than anything else in this world. He looked at me and in his matter of fact way he said, "Richard, you CAN and there is no reason why you can't." This coming from a mentor and someone who is considered the father of contemporary gospel music meant more to me than words could ever express. You never know how your words can impact a young person. Always be quick to encourage and give wise counsel. Wesley and I stayed with Edwin while the girls stayed with his sisters. This is how I found out about Edwin's cooking skills, which are second to none. He would make something new every night, from main courses to desserts all from scratch, right down to the whipped cream. We had so much fun that week with Walter, Tramaine, Lynette, Feddie, Carol, Shirley and the whole clan. They were all so incredibly hospitable to us. It was amazing that these friendships extended all the way back to when I was a teenager in college. The California tour was a great success in terms of promotion. We also traveled to Sacramento where my friend Ollie had relocated and did concerts there. The word began to spread about us and what we were about. People really seemed to like the music that I wrote. I was feeling even more encouraged.

Lisa was always the fashion plate of the group. She'd always have the latest clothes, the latest shoes, the latest hair and whatever else was cutting edge. While we were in California, someone approached her about braiding her hair with extensions. Not too many people were doing that then and Lisa jumped at the opportunity. It really was cutting edge for that time. The girl told her she'd even do it for free. She was just honored to do it. We had a sound check that evening and told Lisa what time she would have to be there. Lisa left for the hairdresser's before dawn. When it was time for sound check, Lisa was nowhere to be found. I remember being furious because I had told her exactly what time she'd have to be at sound check. I remember thinking that I was gonna really let Lisa "have it" when she got there for being late. Somewhere near the end of sound check the door opened and in walked Lisa. We were all on stage. The first things I saw were Lisa's eyes that always got large if she were laughing, being comical or was upset. I think it was more the upset look though. When I looked at her head, it was clear that the hairdresser didn't have a clue what she was doing and must have experimented on Lisa's head. Instead of braids cascading from her head, neatly arranged, as I imagined it should have been, all of the braids and extensions were sticking out from her head in different arrangements, more like twigs on a tree. Some were sticking straight out while others were curved but still sticking out from her scalp. The only thing I could think of was the mythological creature Medusa with the snakes on her head. Lisa's face said, "I am COMPLETELY done!" I couldn't even get angry with her after I saw what the girl had done. I'm not sure how she fixed it so it would work for the concert that evening, but somehow she worked her magic. After it was over we all laughed until our stomachs were hurting as Lisa, in her own inimitable way, explained how the girl had messed up her hair after working on it for the entire day. "I'll do it for free" should have been a hint!

Later that year, Wesley got a call from Donald Watkins who was a friend of ours. The Smallwood Singers had gone to Louisville, Kentucky for Donald in the past to perform. He was now working in some capacity at Benson Records in Nashville, Tennessee. Benson at the time was basically a Contemporary Christian Music label and other than the great Larnelle Harris, who was also CCM, they had no Black artists. He wanted to know if we were still singing and exactly what we were doing. Wesley informed him that we were singing all over the place, but still hadn't been able to secure a record deal. Not long after Donald mentioned us to Bob McKenzie the head of Benson and he expressed an interested in hearing us. We sent him a demo tape of about four songs. He in turn asked us to come to Nashville. We rented a station wagon and drove to Nashville. We had all kinds of food, fruit and drink in the car. Lisa fell asleep on some bananas and by the time we got to our destination she was wearing smashed banana from her neck to her feet. We arrived on a Friday. Bob McKenzie asked us to go into a studio after we got there, record as many songs as we could and report back to him on Monday. We spent Saturday and Sunday in the studio putting down every original song that I could think of. On Monday morning, bright and early, we reported back to the Benson building to Mr. McKenzie's office. He put the tape on, that we had worked on all weekend, and when it was finished he turned to me and said, "I want to sign you to Benson." It was just like that. It was like the room was spinning in front of me. My mind went all the way back to the janitor at the label in NY. Was he kidding me? Was he really serious? Was he secretly a janitor pulling my leg? He pulled out a contract and gave it to me to read. Clearly he had already planned this as it was already drawn up.

Now let me insert this: Never do what I did! Always get an entertainment attorney to look over any kind of contract to make sure that you are getting the best deal possible. Out of all of the contracts that I've signed since then, I've never done it again, but that first time I read it through and signed immediately on the dotted line. Thank God Mr. McKenzie had given me a great deal for a first time, which included me not having to give up all of my publishing rights. After over ten years of trying to get someone to appreciate what I did in the record industry, someone finally seemed to get it. Of course, it didn't hurt to have some of the "singingest" folk this side of heaven singing it! The Smallwood Singers could deliver! Don't ever give up on your dream if it doesn't happen immediately. If it's for you, it will come to pass. It was ten years from the time I graduated from Howard 'til the time that I signed my first record deal. I recalled Dr. George Butler saying to me "Richard, you are ten years ahead of your time." He certainly was prophetic. To me it seemed like it always took me the longest to accomplish anything. I was a "late bloomer" all my life. Everyone around me seemed to be moving forward and I was marking time. But here I was, at 33, finally getting what I had been working toward for so long. Looking back, I realize that it was my time. Friends and classmates of mine were recording straight out of college, performing on Broadway and writing for other great artists. But I realize now that we each have our own path, our own time and our own predestination. Don't ever compare or judge your progress or lack of it by anyone else's journey. We are all unique entities. Just keep learning, preparing, pressing forward, and striving towards your goal even if it seems like you are going at a snail's pace. I read the most wonderful quote once that said, "the soul doesn't know a thing about deadlines."

Most of the tunes that we did on the demo for Mr. McKenzie were songs that would end up on our first album. When Dottie first joined in 1979 I pulled out one of my favorites, "I Love the Lord," and gave it to her. Dottie would literally demolish wherever we were when we'd perform it. We used to call her the ad-lib queen because she could get on the vamp of that song and literally deliver a sermon about "hastening to God's throne." The amazing thing is that she would never repeat herself during those ad-libs. The words and the encouragement would just flow effortlessly. We also did "I've Got Something This World Can't Take Away" with Jackie on the lead. Jackie was as dramatic as one could be, and she wouldn't stop until she took the song all the way home. I remember one time we were singing it and Jackie got down on her knees to the delight of the audience. She began to moan and the more she moaned, the more the audience reacted. Somehow her heel got caught in the hem of her dress and she couldn't get up. Every time she attempted to get up, her dress would get caught on her shoe, and pull her back down. I'll never forget her turning around to Wesley who was singing behind her, still on her knees, and giving him the loudest moan with her hand outstretched toward him as if she were saying, "Help me get uuuupp!" Thankfully he reached down and helped her up while all of us were giggling on the stage.

I had written a song for Lisa called "All I Have Is Yours" which was inspired by the sound of the Doobie Brothers. I was still listening to everything around me. Carolene took us back to church whenever she sang "Sure Been Good to Me." The song "The Resurrection" was very special to me. For years while I was student at Howard I had played a piece by Rachmaninoff for many of the vocal students called "Vocalise." It had one of the most beautiful melodies I had ever heard. I always said that I wanted to do something with that melody one day. When I arranged "The Resurrection," I used the Vocalise melody, added an original bridge to it that stylistically was similar to the original and basically kept the original idea of the accompaniment. How ironic that Rachmaninoff was the composer of the first classical recording Mom introduced me to. In my opinion, that tape featured some of my strongest songs during that time.

CHAPTER 25

PRODUCING MY FIRST PROJECT

O n September 9th, 1981 my cousin Robert, cousin Lula's grandson, made his transition at the age of 53 after a four-year battle with cancer. He was always kind to me and it always was amazing to me how strong the genes were on Momma's side of the family. I remember standing at the wake with other family members and thinking whenever I would see Robert, I could almost see my own face. The resemblance in our family was always so striking to me. Mom nor almost anyone in her family could ever disown me. It was so obvious. As a kid when I'd go and visit my father's family in NY, I'd search for that same kind of resemblance in my aunts and uncles, and even my cousins. They were always so nice to me and I loved being around them. But that same familial resemblance that I saw on Mom's side, I could never seem to find. As I grew up, I remember thinking "These Weavers, Locklears, Bankses, Cains and Clements have the strongest genes I've ever seen."

Soon after, I was flown down to Nashville to meet with my producer and to start the recording process. The top studio musicians in Nashville, who were usually paid double scale, were hired for the process. I was the only musician outside of that circle. The producer was a gentleman who actually didn't know that much about black Gospel music. But he had surrounded himself with recordings of the greatest Gospel artists of that time to familiarize himself with the genre. He visited a number of black churches in order to prepare for us and to familiarize himself with the genre. He had produced for some of the top CCM artists of that time as well as produced music for film. He came with top-notch credentials, just not particularly in black Gospel. His name was Greg Nelson. He initially asked us to do background on a Larnelle Harris album called "Touch Me Lord." Imagine my shock when I went to lay down the keyboards and Greg put music up in front of me. I had never heard the music before and thank God for Mrs. Burwell teaching me how to read. If she hadn't, that would have been one job I would have lost.

It was our first time in a professional setting like that, and we loved it. Some of the background vocals were not written per se, and I had to come up with harmonies and background vocals on the spot. I really didn't want to mess that up, as I hadn't heard these songs before. But harmonizing was never a challenge for me. The Smallwood Singers always caught on very quickly and had great ears. I gave them the part, they sang it back to me, and then we laid it down. Greg was delighted. It was a great opportunity and a lot of fun. When I came back to Nashville to meet about the Smallwood Singers' record, I was stunned when Greg basically told me that we would have to find music to record on our first album because the music I had written was not good enough. I knew that my music was different and a bit alien to what was out there, but it's what God had given me. His words hit me like a ton of bricks and did little for my already low self-esteem. I had come all this way and finally got a record deal, and now they didn't want to use my music. Honestly, I don't think that Bob McKenzie was aware of the producer's feelings about my music. After all, he signed me not only on the strength of our singing, but also because of the music we sang. Greg continued by informing me that we would spend several days in the song vault, where they kept tapes of original songs by different composers, until we found an album's worth of material that we could record. For several days we listened to different tunes. Some of the tunes were great and some were not. However, none of them fit my style and what I did. Even then I knew what my sound was, and this wasn't it. I was so crushed that this man didn't want to use my songs. By now I had been writing consistently for over ten years. The Smallwood Singers had been together for four years and we were known for singing my music wherever we traveled, especially at home in D.C. Other national artists had even started recording my music. This was not what I had in mind at all in terms of recording. God had given me these songs for a specific reason and purpose. Yet he didn't want me to record them? Again, I got the feeling that the producer just didn't "get" me. I began to doubt myself again, thinking maybe I couldn't write. Maybe I wasn't commercial enough. Maybe no one would understand my music. I could tell at one point that Greg was getting frustrated with me, because the more music he played the more I said it wasn't for me. At one point he exclaimed, "Well what *do* you like?" He found a room that had a piano and said, "Now play something that *you* like." I played "I Love The Lord." After I finished, he said, "Now that's a great song. Who wrote that?" "I did," I replied. He seemed surprised and asked me to play something else that I liked. I remember playing "Don't Give Up." He again stated that it was a good song and inquired who wrote it. I again replied, "I did." This went on until I had played four or five songs. By then it was getting late and we broke for the day and I went back to the hotel. My phone rang later

302 | TOTAL PRAISE

that evening and it was Greg. He said excitedly, "Richard! I have an idea." I wondered what in the world could be next. By now, I felt beaten down and that maybe I had made the biggest mistake of my life by signing the record deal. He continued, "Let's record *your* music!" After all the changes he took me through, I couldn't believe he was finally saying this. I was definitely relieved, but at the same time annoyed that I had gone through a week of being told that I wasn't a good writer and then all of a sudden, out of the clear blue sky, he decided that my music was good enough to record. Maybe he had spoken with Bob McKenzie after going through this seemingly non-stop listening session with me that week. I was never sure. Mr. McKenzie never mentioned it. In hindsight, I realize that the music on that demo tape certainly was nothing like what was popular in mainstream gospel at that time. He, like most people, probably didn't understand what I had written simply because no one was doing that style of music. I guess he was listening for what he had heard on the recordings he had listened to, or heard in the black churches he had visited. I knew that a good relationship between producer and artist was of prime importance in order to make a great quality album. I prayed that it would be smooth sailing from there on out.

Things started out great. The musicians were great, the charts of the songs were on point and everything seemed to be going well. Things changed when I started laying down the piano track to "I Love the Lord." I guess I've always had a different approach to harmonic progression. But it's always been about what I felt in my heart and what I heard in my head. At one point, Greg stopped me and told me I had played a wrong chord. Thinking my finger had slipped and I had made a "clunker" that I wasn't aware of, we started that section again. Again, at the same place I was stopped again and told that I had made the same mistake. I asked to hear it back and as I listened to what I had done, I heard no mistake at all. I had meant to play that particular chord. So, in the most respectful manner I could, I told him that I had made no mistake. At this point he stopped the recording and brought all of the musicians and myself into the control room. The Smallwood Singers were already in the room, wide-eyed as to what was going to happen now. Greg began to explain to us how he had been picked to produce this project because of his track record, and his expertise in his craft. What he said was the only thing that mattered, and if he said something was wrong, then it was wrong. Honestly, I respected him greatly and his ability. He had accomplished some great things and I realized that I was just a little newcomer. But after what I had gone through with him about my music, as hard as it was for me to do, I knew I had to stand behind my convictions and what I believed. He was a very gifted individual, but my chord still wasn't wrong. I began to explain to him exactly why it wasn't wrong, but using music theory and a short explanation on borrowed chords or secondary dominants. I think he was shocked because he had no idea that I had studied, much less had a degree in my craft. After I finished, he abruptly told everyone to break for lunch. After coming back, we continued laying down the "I Love the Lord" track and I played my chord and he never said anything else about it. I remember him having an idea he wanted to try on the song "All I Have is Yours." However, instead of approaching me about his idea, he approached Wesley and asked him if he thought I would be open to trying it. Wesley told him, "Sure, just ask him. I'm sure Richard would be open to any kind of suggestion that's going to help the album, but it's all in your approach." He seemed to get the hint and told me about his idea for the song. It sounded great to me, so I said, "Sounds good, let's try it and see how it works." The idea worked fine. It was something that didn't take away from the arrangement and actually added to the clarity of the song. I understood that he was the producer and I respected him to the highest. But don't talk down to me like I'm some little ignorant kid who knows nothing about music other than how to play a gospel song. I may have never recorded on that kind of professional level in my life, but that didn't override the musical knowledge I had as it pertains to my craft. We got along famously after that and the rest of the recording was an incredibly positive experience. I love the sound on that first recording. For 1982, it was cutting edge for black gospel. Greg did an incredible job of bringing the orchestrations, band and finally the mixes together to make what I think was a top-notch project. Honestly, I don't know if anyone could have done a better job producing when it was all said and done. After we got over that first hump, everything went great. I ended up learning a lot about the studio by observing him. It ended up being everything that I had ever wanted in a debut album. I remember all of The Smallwood Singers trying to scrape our little funds together to buy outfits for the album cover. That is still probably one of my favorite album covers that I've done. It was taken in the living room of Bob McKenzie's home. I remember finding a white silk sweater, lavender wing tipped shirt, with a purple bowtie (my favorite color) and finally a pair of navy blue pleated wool pants from a second hand high end store called Classic Clothing in Georgetown. I remember Wesley and me going to a shoe store to find some shoes. I found a pair of gray boots that I knew would top the outfit off. I had a Master Card, which I had basically maxed out. However, I thought that I might be able to squeeze enough out to pay for the shoes. When I got to the teller, she ran my credit card. She never said anything to me, but reached in her drawer and pulled out the biggest pair of scissors you have ever seen, held up my credit card in the air for all to see and cut it in half. The line was incredibly long behind me and I'm sure almost everyone saw it. I was done! She turned to me and said, "That's what your credit card company instructed me to do." I knew she was just following instructions, but the way she said it made me want to strangle her. Fortunately, I had my checkbook and my check went through. Those were some poor times. Every time I look at that album cover and see those shoes, I think about my credit card in little shreds.

CHAPTER 26
PERFORMING AT THE WHITE HOUSE

In 1979, Tramaine released her first solo project called "Tramaine." Songs like "Look at Me," "Highway," and "Holy One" became major hits across the nation. Still busily touring with the Hawkins Family, the biggest group in gospel music at that time, it was around 1982 before she did her first major solo tour on the east coast, south and in the midwest. Her album still was super-hot and of course "Changed" and "Going Up Yonder" had become gospel classics. The Smallwood Singers had already recorded our first album but it wouldn't be released until later that year. So, when she came to DC on her tour, Wesley suggested that I go on tour with her as her pianist. It would be my first real tour experience and I was elated. Tramaine was excited to welcome me on board. She had an amazing group of singers: Shirlene Hall, the late Dennis Sanders, and the amazing gift of the late great Daryl Coley. I met Daryl in the late 70s through Edwin and Walter Hawkins while in Oakland, CA. Of course, I immediately recognized that he had one of the most amazing voices I had ever heard. When Tramaine's tour came to DC, Daryl was doing double duty as pianist as well as singing backup. Stepping in as pianist gave him the freedom to stand up with the other vocalists and sing while I played. The Winans' song "The Question Is" was also huge and this exciting new group of brothers had blown up overnight. Ironically, Fred Hammond and other members of a group yet to be formed called "Commissioned" served as the Winans' band. They opened for Tramaine and it was an absolutely amazing tour. It was the first time I had ever ridden on a tour bus and I was like a kid in a candy factory. Daryl and I were roommates during the tour. I'm surprised that Daryl had a voice each night, because all we did during the day was shop and laugh. Whenever we'd get together we'd laugh at any and everything. I remember in one city we were in the hotel room watching Redd Foxx's "Sanford and Son." In this episode, one of the characters played by Grady Wilson had to go undercover as a woman and was in full drag. He looked just like a church mother, complete with blue dress and church hat. Grady in no way, shape or form made a pretty woman. In fact, he had to be the ugliest woman we had ever seen. When he walked on camera with that outfit on, both Daryl and I both fell on the floor at the same time in tears. I think we laughed all day after the show was over whenever we would think about it. The next night when Tramaine got up to sing, I sat at the piano and Daryl walked in front of his mic, and dead center in front of us in the audience was a lady with the exact same hat that Grady had been wearing. We giggled through the entire concert. Daryl would look at me, and I at him, and then we both would look at the hat and fall out. If Tramaine had seen what was going on, I'm sure we would have gotten in big trouble. I had always been a fan of Tramaine since the Hawkins Singers, but there was one thing that endeared her even more to me during that trip. At one point she became sick with the flu, however she persevered even not feeling well and gave her all. Of course, her voice never faltered and was as strong and beautiful as ever. No one would have ever known she was ill. Instead of going back to the hotel as soon as the concert was over and just saying she wasn't feeling up to par, she sat out at a table and signed autographs on a little pad for hundreds of people while the sweat was pouring down her forehead and face. As someone who was just starting in the industry on the professional level, it made a great impression on me about going beyond the call of duty not only for ministry but for the people who support you. Every night when she would introduce me, she'd always announce that my first album was on the way out and remind the audience to be sure to go out and get it the minute that it hit the stores. I never forgot that tour and what an amazing opportunity it was. I thought about that tour years later when the Smallwood Singers were in LA and I got food poisoning. It hit me right before we went on stage, and when they called my name, my head was literally in the toilet. But I got myself together and walked on stage like nothing was going on. I wasn't sick while we were on stage, but as soon as I hit that bottom step coming off of the stage, that nausea hit me and I was knocking things out the way to get back to the bathroom. Over time, you learn how to press through whatever is going on and give God your absolute best.

Right before the album was released, we did our debut at GMA's Dove Awards in Nashville. We were scared to death. Everyone was there from country western singer Barbara Mandrell to Al Green. We were positioned behind this beautiful red velvet curtain trimmed in gold waiting to be introduced. The place was packed. We all had individual mics and were going to sing along with the freshly made "TV tracks" from our soon-to-be-released debut album. As we were introduced and the curtain slowly began to ascend and the applause began to sweep over us, Dottie's mic somehow got tangled in the folds of the curtain. It then began to rise with the curtain pulling it off of the mic stand and continued to head skyward still tangled in the curtain. By now the audience could see us and we all were frozen looking at the mic slowly moving heavenward leaving Dottie's and our sight. All of a sudden Dottie began to leap trying to catch the cord to get it untangled and to pull it back down. By now the curtain and the mic were way above her head and she had turned into a cross between Michael Jordan and Lebron James leaping for a jump shot. We were too scared for it to be funny at the time and I'm sure the audience wasn't sure what was going on, when the first full view they got of us was all of us standing watching Dottie leap. Each leap got subsequently higher as the mic started to leave our sight. I'm not sure why Wesley or I who were taller didn't help, especially with Dottie being the shortest member of the group, but I think our minds froze along with our bodies in front of the packed crowd. So we just stood there paralyzed staring at her jumping up and down while reaching for the mic. She took one final giant leap and got a hold of the cord, got it untangled and the mic fell down into her hands to her relief. However, the audience welcomed us with open arms and seemed to really enjoy our presentation. I think after hearing her minister "I Love the Lord," everybody forgot about what happened with the mic. She ministered so that night. Of course after it was over we were in tears laughing and we never let Dottie forget it. That first album was a resounding success with "I Love the Lord," "I've Got Something," and "Call The Lord" sweeping the country. The song "Call the Lord" by the way, was directly influenced by Andraé Crouch's "Jesus is Lord." By now, Benson had created a subsidiary label specifically for black gospel called Onyx International. They called in record exec Gentry McCreary to head it. Gentry had been instrumental in helping promote the Hawkins Family, Andraé Crouch and so many others. Soon, the late great Thomas Whitfield as well as Vanessa Bell Armstrong would join the label as well. That first album called "The Richard Smallwood Singers" dropped in 1982 and would stay on the billboard charts for 87 weeks. God was definitely up to something. That was unheard of, for someone's very first time out. The bookings increased and we traveled constantly all over the country. One thing I can say is that no matter where we went, the DMV area, our home was the most supportive. It's always a blessing to be loved and received in your own home.

I'm not sure when the depression actually started. However, I know the anxiety went back as far as I could remember. I had no name for what I felt, just being terrified, anxious in certain situations, like school, or being in public places that I was not familiar with. Being painfully shy, but also imagining that in some way everyone was looking disapprovingly at what I had on or what I looked like. My words would get stuck if I was trying to talk in those kinds of situations. There is a phenomenon that can sometimes be a major part of anxiety where it seems like nothing is real. It's called depersonalization. It's as if you are a part of a dream. I remember vividly the first time that happened to me, I couldn't have been more than about 7 and it was around Christmas. We were living in Philly and Mom had taken me downtown to see the Christmas decorations in the department store windows and to look at the toys. I remember we were walking down the aisle in the toy department and all of a sudden it felt like something snapped and everything around me became as if it were a dream. I didn't know how to explain it and I remember saying "MOM!! NOTHING IS REAL!" She had no idea what I was talking about. Of course, I couldn't explain it. I'd never felt that way before. I just kept saying, "I don't know! It feels like nothing is real." It didn't last long and after a while everything felt normal again. I definitely believe that may have been when the problem began. I remember my Mom used to tell me when I was pretty young that I would grind my teeth at night and she could hear me doing it all the way in her bedroom. She didn't know what was going on during that time, and neither did I. I didn't have a name for it. It was just all I knew as far back as I could remember. In terms of depression, I believe it wasn't until somewhere around 1983 when I actually became aware that something was wrong. I didn't know that much about depression. In fact, I didn't even know that was my problem. Back then I had never thought about what the catalyst could be for my grandfather's death by his own hand. Nor had I wondered if depression had anything to do with that. People just didn't know much about depression in the black community and certainly didn't talk about it. I had always been plagued with what my family thought was mood swings, and Mom used to tell me I was the moodiest child she had ever seen. Most creative people deal with that from time to time and I thought maybe it was just that. But at some point, I realized that I was unhappy and very sad, and I couldn't shake it. To add to my confusion, I had no idea why I felt the way I felt. It would go away for a time and then it would unexplainably return. I remember the exact year because Sandra Crouch, twin sister of Andraé, had just released her debut album "We Sing Praises." It was that album that I would put on and it would bring me out of that deep sad feeling. It inspired me for a little while, and then in time that dark feeling would return. At times, it was very hard to come out of my room and join my Mom and the rest of the family. I didn't worry about it much. I attributed it to the frustration of having not really attained the level of success by a certain time. I figured that if and when I did reach that goal which I had dreamed about for so long, I would be fine. But that would not be the case. As time went on it would get worse, much worse.

That same year we were contacted to be a part of "In Performance at the White House," a Christmas television special that was televised during that season every year. It would be performed in front of then President Ronald Regan and First Lady Nancy Regan. In the audience would be political figures as well as dignitaries, such as Vice President Bush and his wife and the late gospel great Willie Mae Ford Smith and her family. I was not only asked to perform but to also provide most of the piano accompaniment throughout the program. That year, Diva Leontyne Price whom I idolized, would host the special. I had so many of her recordings and had been exposed to her like never before, while a student at Howard. I was in heaven as well. There was just no one greater than she. She was so gracious and so friendly. I remember at rehearsal when we met her, she looked at Dottie's spiked hair do and exclaimed "Aren't you gorgeous?!!" The theme of the program would be black music and it would be traced from the Negro Spiritual to Contemporary Gospel. The Contemporary Gospel segment would feature the Smallwood Singers. It's so ironic that when I first started out, I was considered the most contemporary around and now I'm considered traditional. It's funny how time changes things. I have no problem with it. I'm just glad to still be doing what I love to do! Also featured were the Howard University Concert Choir, DC's Shiloh Baptist Church's Choir where the program would actually be recorded, child singer Kevette

Cartlidge, David Weatherspoon and Lilias White. The late Howard Roberts who pulled the whole thing together, asked that we sing, "Come By Here" and "Sure Been Good To Me" from our then only album, "The Richard Smallwood Singers." Both of those songs were based on old traditional songs and the arrangement would show the contemporary take on them. We taped the show on December 1, 1983 not at the White House but one of the oldest historical black churches in DC, Shiloh Baptist Church. I remember being nervous, but the audience received us warmly and Miss Price along with the Reagans clapped, smiled and nodded in approval as we sang. Miss Price not only did the narrative and traced the history of this great music but did a couple of Negro Spirituals including "I Just Come From the Fountain." We were mesmerized. One of the most incredible moments of my life was that I got to accompany her on the hymn Amazing Grace. Gospel pioneer Willie Mae Ford Smith was in the audience as well as her family so it was a very exciting night. A humorous moment was at the finale as all took to the stage singing "Down By The Riverside" when Mrs. Regan was so caught up by the rhythm and the music that she went forth in a little dance. It was an incredible experience. Of course in the audience was Mom beaming proudly along with my Aunt Netha. It was not the first time, or the last that I would be honored to perform for a President and First lady. Not long after graduating from Howard I performed with my former professor, Evelyn Davidson White's Collegiate Chorale for President and Mrs. Nixon at the White House. During the Clinton administration, the Smallwood Singers would perform for President and Mrs. Clinton also at the White House. Ironically, during the George Bush Administration and right before the election of President Obama; to help celebrate Gospel Music Month, I was asked to perform for President Bush along with the Hawkins and other gospel artists. When a background check was done on me and it was found out that I had ministered a number of times at President Obama's former Chicago pastor's church, Pastor Jeremiah Wright who was also a friend, I was called back and uninvited. It was said that because of all the controversy that was surrounding Pastor Wright it probably would be better if I didn't come. Pastor Wright did as most black preachers have always done, preached against the ills of racism and talked about the plight of being black and in America. To some that was controversial. I had grown up hearing that kind of preaching all of my life. I think it has to be one of the biggest slaps in the face of my career. I was hurt as well as angry and insulted by this kind of political ignorance.

CHAPTER 27

PAYING DUES AND TRAVELING

In 1984, we recorded our second album entitled "Psalms" again in Nashville. It was decided by the label that I should produce this project. That terrified me because although I was getting some great experience I wasn't sure that I was ready to do it on my own yet. I kept saying that I couldn't produce it by myself and needed some help and direction. Thomas Whitfield was asked to sit in from time to time during the recording to help guide me through the process and to help with the production. Not only was Thomas a great musician, but he was also a really great person. He played organ on "I Won't Forget." Just his presence and suggestions helped me through the process. It's funny that although I was six years older than Tommy, I always called him Uncle Tommy and he called me Nephew. I think it was because I respected his genius so much, he always seemed older and wiser. The engineer on the "Psalms" project was Roger Holmes. We hit it off immediately. Before the advent of editing with computers, you would have to edit the tape with razor blades. Roger was the king of doing an edit with a razor blade – perfectly. He really understood what I was trying to convey musically and was one of the nicest people I had ever met. Roger had other hidden talents. When I wanted an acoustic guitar to play on "I Wish You Love" and we couldn't find anyone to do it at the last minute, he played the guitar on that track. Little did I know, our relationship would turn into a lifelong friendship and business partnership. He became instrumental in furthering my ministry. By now DC's amazing bassist, Tim Linzy had come on board as a part of the group, as well as drummer Spike McCrae from Philly. They both were a part of that session as well. Lisa was pregnant with her first child, Bianca. She had to be eight months going on nine it seemed, and I was terrified that she was going to have the baby in the recording studio. We did all the background vocals first. By now she had started to have some kind of pre- labor pains and held her stomach and grimaced through the entire session. I kept saying, "Lisa! I ain't playing! Don't you have that baby yet!" We finished all the background vocals, first did her solo on "I Wish You Love," and put her on the next flight to DC. She gave birth to Bianca not long after she got back home. "He Won't Leave You," "Psalm 8," and "So Glad I'm Here" would be the most popular songs from that project. The feel on "He Won't Leave You," still one of my favorite songs, was inspired by my favorite band at that time, Earth Wind and Fire. Another song, "When Jesus Came Into My Life," was originally written for one of my favorite singers, Elaine Kelly from the Edwin Hawkins Singers. She had come to Union Temple years ago to do a solo concert and I wrote the song especially for her to do on that occasion. The album soon zoomed up to number one on the billboard charts—another first for me. That album was also my first Grammy nomination, the first one of many that would follow. I don't think I've ever been that excited in my life. I remember scraping my funds together so I could attend the Grammy Awards. But I wanted my mother to attend so badly. A dear friend, Dr. Wilbert Jordan, a former member of Union Temple, and one of the leading doctors in the country in AIDS research, volunteered to pay for her airfare. He had recently relocated to LA and had bought a beautiful home in a section called Mount Olympus. He also invited Mom to stay with him and his mom in his home. So, I didn't have to worry about trying to come up with money for another hotel room. That stands out as one of the most memorable moments as Mom sat next to me at the Grammy's in her formal sequined gown. I knew she was proud. But she couldn't have been prouder than I was to have her by my side.

By now I had started to do workshops not only in the U.S. but overseas as well. I get amused sometimes when I see young people first starting out traveling, having assistants and entourages. No one had any money to bring anybody except me. Roger would always travel with us when the group went overseas, however for workshops, I traveled overseas for years by myself, being choir director, pianist and sometimes soloist all in one. The first time I went to Norway, I was strip searched by security as I entered the country. Of course, I couldn't speak the language. They spoke little to no English and I was scared to death. I'm not sure if they thought I was a drug dealer or what, but finally they allowed me to dress and enter the country. Traveling by myself was sometimes scary, especially in foreign countries. The only foreign language I spoke was a little bit of Spanish, which I learned in Jr. High and High School. But bringing me alone was all anyone could afford. Again, it was called paying dues, but a great opportunity to spread the ministry I had been given, and for people to become familiar with the music I had written. I would travel all over the world doing workshops, from Holland to Finland. Although it was the U. S., one of the most beautiful places where I conducted a workshop had to be Hawaii. I went for the military base over there. I will never forget how beautiful it was, but I also won't forget how big some of the bugs were. I have always had an aversion to bugs. I have serious arachnophobia. However, they had the hugest flying cockroaches over there. I remember being in the middle of the workshop with the choir that I was working with. The church door was open and I remember seeing one flying into the auditorium where we were. I called myself keeping an eye on it while I was teaching and the choir was singing. However, at some point I lost sight of it and could only pray that it had flown back outside. I was sitting at the piano teaching parts with the mic positioned between my legs. I had on some linen pants and I remember the mic cord kept brushing up against my leg as I was playing the piano. After a while, I realized that the "mic cord" seemed like it had changed positions and was brushing further up against my leg than previously. To my horror, I realized after a minute that it wasn't the mic cord, but the bug was on its way up my pants leg. Needless to say, I turned that workshop out!

Many times, the Smallwood Singers would travel by van all over the country. I remember once performing in a small southern town with a program full of quartets. At that time, we were considered one of the most contemporary groups around, so imagine us in the middle of a completely traditional concert featuring quartets. The audience loved each quartet that performed and shouted for half the night. But when we began to sing, they sat and looked at us like we were from another planet. When we'd encounter audiences like that, Carolene would always call them a "painting." They sat frozen and still like a Rembrandt. I imagine they were trying to figure out what in the world we were singing. After all, we were a hybrid of gospel, classical, jazz, Motown, and God only knows what else. To me it was the most normal sound in the world, but to many it was very different and something I guess they hadn't heard in gospel before. For a while Dottie's former husband, Donell Jones, served as our road manager, while Wesley sang, did the booking and handled the main business. After the quartet concert was over, Donell went in to collect the rest of the little money that we charged. The promoter told him he didn't have the money. Donell insisted that the man give us our money. We had a van to pay for, singers and musicians to pay, not to mention gas to get back home. The promoter's response was "I SAID I don't have your money" and proceeded to pull a gun out of the desk drawer and placed it on the table. We were all waiting in the van. The next thing we saw was Donell running towards the van hollering "LET'S GO, LET'S GO!" "Did you get the rest of our money from the promoter?" I demanded. Donell's response was, "HE HAD A GUN!" and began to explain what happened. We took off down the road in that van as fast as it could go. None of us were trying to get shot that night. Dues paying time again!

Later that year, I got a call from choreographer/producer George Faison whom Hot Tea had worked with briefly in the 70's. He was getting ready to mount a musical production on the life of the late great Mahalia Jackson called "Sing, Mahalia Sing", and had gotten Aretha Franklin to agree to come on board in the role as Mahalia. He wanted to know if I would be interested in being musical director, vocal arranger, help write original music for the show and be the principle keyboard player. I was bouncing off the wall. First of all, working with Aretha was like an unobtainable dream to me, and then of course working with George and the sheer opportunity of what he had asked me to do was mind-boggling. Of course, I knew it would take me off the road for a while, so I told him I would do it if the Smallwood

Singers could be involved. George was ecstatic about including them. I moved to New York for a while before rehearsals started and worked on the show and the music along with George and others. When the rehearsals started, the Smallwood Singers moved as well. George was looking for the finest singers, dancers, and actors that we could find. We auditioned prospective cast members for weeks. I reached out to a former Howard music student, Felicia Coleman who undoubtedly has one of the most incredible soprano voices ever. I also reached out to Edwin and Walter's baby sister, Lynette Hawkins-Stephens. Within days they were in New York and a part of the cast. Aretha's background singers, Sandra Feva, Aretha's cousin Brenda Corbett and Margaret Branch, were added to the cast. Actors like the great Epatha Merkeson, KiKi Shepard, and singer Glen Jones also came on board as cast members along with some of the finest dancers on Broadway. Mahalia's godson, Brother John, also came on board as well as my friend and one of DC's great musicians, the late Wayne Davis. I remember that a lot of us stayed at the Beacon Hotel. It was close to ABC Studios. Most of the Smallwood Singers and I were fanatics of the soap opera "All My Children" at the time. At lunchtime, we would stand outside the hotel and watch the actors break for lunch. We'd see the characters Adam, Erica Kane, Brooke, Angie, Jessie, Greg, Jenny and the whole crew almost every day. To me that was as exciting as working with the show. In addition to creating new songs and arrangements, and of course the songs Mahalia was known for, George and I added songs from the Smallwood Singers to the show, "Call The Lord", "You Sure Been Good To Me", "I Love The Lord", "He Won't Leave You," and "So Glad I'm Here." The song "Be Faithful" which was on The Smallwood Singer's album entitled, "Vision" was actually written for that show. We rehearsed for probably two months or so until we found out that Aretha wasn't going to be able to do the show. It was really disappointing. The show was one of the best I had seen with unbelievable talent. We stopped rehearsal and moved back home until the show could regroup and find another lead. By now we had added organist Steven Ford and drummer Jeff Davis to the Smallwood Singers.

CHAPTER 28

COLLABORATING WITH THE GREATS

The Smallwood Singers were doing a concert somewhere in Ohio. It was an outdoor concert in a park and people were everywhere. Lisa had a way of reacting when she saw something funny. Her eyes would get as huge as saucers and this one tear would come out of her eye and run down her face. We were singing "Call the Lord" and there was a bit of choreography with the song. I was out front singing, and the group was busy doing their steps. All of a sudden, I noticed that voices were dropping out in the background. When I turned to see why everyone wasn't singing, Lisa's eyes met mine. Sure enough, they had grown twice their size and the one tell-tale tear was rolling down her cheek. From the corner of my eye I could also see something lying on the stage. It was white and sort of shimmering. I couldn't figure out what it was. Our road manager at the time, Jerome Bell was standing on the side of the stage pointing at the floor of the stage with his hand over his mouth. I finally realized that it was a white slip. At some point during the choreography, Carolene had lost her slip. She basically stepped out of it, kicked it to the side and kept on with the choreography. The group was laughing so hard, that they couldn't sing. Fortunately, it was the last song on the concert and I ended it quickly before I laughed in the mic. I was really trying to keep some sense of dignity since everyone else on stage had lost it. But by the time I got backstage we were all on the floor in stitches.

Another embarrassing situation happened while I was at the Grammy's. That particular year, it was held in NY at Radio City Music Hall. Being the lover of clothes that I am, I had bought an awesome new outfit including shoes. I had not bothered to scuff up the bottom of the shoes and the soles were very slippery. Right before the pre- Grammy's began, I was sitting with my manager Roger. I looked behind me and saw Edwin Hawkins enter the building. I tried to get his attention to tell him to come and sit where we were, but he didn't see me. I knew I had about a minute before the ceremony started, so I decided to get up and run back and get him. When my slippery soles hit the marble floor of Radio City Music Hall, and as I turned to venture out of my row to go up the aisle, I literally went up in the air and came down somewhere between the rows with a resounding "Ka-Blam!" The acoustics were very good and the sound echoed so that those who didn't see me fall heard me fall, including Edwin. Instead of helping me up, Roger, my manager, collapsed in his seat in tears. When I finally did get up, Edwin was coming down the aisle towards the noise, hollering laughing. From that incident, I learned how to scuff the soles of all new shoes before wearing them.

That same year, George Faison called me again to inform me that Tony Award winner Jennifer Holiday, fresh from her Emmy winning role in the play "Dreamgirls," had consented to do the lead role of Mahalia in "Sing Mahalia Sing." We all assembled in New York again, to start rehearsals once more. The majority of the original cast returned without Aretha's background singers who were replaced by Jennifer's background singers. The late Michael Powell from New York City conducted the band. Jennifer's understudy was singer/actor Queen Esther Marrow whose voice sounded remarkably like Mahalia. I added a choral arrangement of Malotte's "The Lord's Prayer" for Jennifer and the cast. Years later, I would start using that same arrangement as a piano solo, and I still play it today. We opened in Washington, D. C. on March 26, 1985. Every night Jennifer would stop the show with "I've Got Something This World Can't Take Away." I remember at one of the shows in D.C., she sang with such intensity while this one tear ran down her face. The shout broke out in the audience when she finished like an 11am Sunday morning service and spread to the stage. I remember I could hear George running around back stage screaming at the cast to go on with the show, but it was hard for him to restore order. I also remember one night in particular, the piano bench leg on which I was sitting had somehow worked its way off of the platform in the orchestra pit. Right at a very poignant and quiet time in the play, I felt the piano bench slipping off the stand and I knew I was getting ready to plunge down several feet below onto the floor of the orchestra pit. The only way I could save myself was to grab onto the keyboard. All of a sudden, the cast and audience was startled by a loud cacophony of dissonant notes in the sound system as I grabbed onto the keyboard hanging on for dear life. Thank God the cast was professional and kept going, although the band was in tears from laughing. Although financial issues plagued the production, it had to be one of the best plays ever mounted. The dancing, the acting and the vocals as well as the band were first rate. Jennifer was an incredible Mahalia and nailed the part every night. Our second stop was Cleveland, Ohio. I awoke one morning to find that my right hand was painfully swollen up to twice its size. I was terrified and was rushed to the emergency room in Cleveland. It was diagnosed that I had arthritis in that hand. I imagine that the months of working as rehearsal pianist in mounting the show and as principle keyboard player of the show had taken a toll. I had never had any issues with my hand before, as I was only in my mid-thirties. I was put on ibuprofen and prohibited from using my hand for two to three weeks. I had no idea what I was going to do. I had to play shows every day except Monday, plus two shows on Saturday and Sunday. Thank God for the keyboard artistry of Steven Ford and Willard Meeks who were a part of the band. I played only with my left hand for the next couple of weeks while they took up the slack for my missing right hand. There was a scene in the show that showed the disdain a lot of churches had for gospel music during Mahalia's time. It was a scene that Carolene was a part of that took place in a church between members of the Eastern Star, a Masonic organization based on the teachings of the Bible. They were discussing Mahalia and her "bluesy" stylings and how they didn't ever want that kind of music in their church. One of the members began relaying how she heard about Mahalia, "shaking and carrying on like she was in a club" at a local church. Carolene's character was appalled and horrified and gasped in disbelief. However, the more we did the show, the more Carolene improvised and at one point she began passing out on the floor, from the sheer horror of what she had heard. It would always stop the show and the audience would scream in laughter. However one night, when she collapsed, somehow the masonic hat fell off, along with the wig that was under it and rolled dramatically across the stage. The audience was in tears, as well as the cast, and no one could go on. George was running around backstage hollering "line, line, NEXT line," but no one could speak because everyone on stage had collapsed in tears of laughter. Even the band was in tears. There are so many fond memories of that show. It ran for six months and traveled to places like Philadelphia, New Orleans, Chicago, Atlanta, and other major cities all over the country. It closed in Oakland, California on September 1, 1985. If the show had been funded properly, I believe it could have gone straight to Broadway. It was such a great show and traced Mahalia's journey from a little girl in New Orleans to her rise throughout her life in Chicago as the greatest gospel singer. It ended with her singing on the steps of the Capitol in Washington DC, right before Dr. Martin Luther King did his "I Have a Dream Speech. Ironically I had watched her do that performance on TV when I was a kid. It was one of the greatest musical experiences of my life. During the run of the show, Roger Holmes informed me that he and his business partner had gone into management and that he was no longer working as a studio engineer. Wesley, who had basically held the business managerial position from the Celestials in the 1960's up until the Smallwood Singers was ready for someone else to take over that position. By now he had become known as a great vocal coach and had coached voices like Tramaine Hawkins, Lynette Hawkins Stephens, and others. I had learned almost everything I knew about vocal techniques from him. His vocal student roster had begun to grow as well. He continued singing with us, but gave up the management position to Roger.

Right after the show closed in Oakland, I stayed out there a couple of weeks to work on a Christmas album with Edwin Hawkins. This was the first time other than some of the seminar albums that I ever recorded with the Hawkins. I was so excited.

Walter, Tramaine, Lynette and their cousin Lawrence Matthews along with the Love Center Choir member Brenda Roy were a part of the recording. Edwin, Walter, and I played most of the keyboards and put our heads together on some of the arrangements. We also recorded one of my Christmas songs on that album, "Follow The Star." That was a great moment for me.

I had met songwriter Bill Gaither not too long after we released our first album. He had invited us to sing at his Praise Gathering, which was a huge conference that took place every year in Indianapolis, Indiana. After he heard the Smallwood Singers and the music that I had written, he shared with me that he would love for us to write together one day. I had never written with anyone in my life and was unsure of the process, or if it was something I'd be able to do. However, I was elated at the prospect of writing with such a great composer, who had written such standards as "The King is Coming" and "He Touched Me." Soon after, Benson Records announced that it was no longer interested in doing black gospel music. At the same time, they were trying to secure secular distribution with one of the secular labels. This would ensure wider distribution for their artists. Imagine their surprise when the secular label informed them that the only way they would be interested in taking Benson under their wing is if they had African American artists, because black gospel was selling. After realizing that we were needed to secure the secular distribution they wanted, Benson came back to us stating that they had changed their mind and wanted to keep their artists. I was insulted, and angry about the whole situation. Fortunately, because Benson had not lived up to some elements in my contract and they were found to be in breach of contract, I was able to leave and I walked. It was not long before I signed with Word Records.

I'm always asked under what circumstances certain songs are written. Certainly, there are times when life situations whether good or bad will inspire a song. There are times when songs are given to you in very mystical, spiritual ways. I've always been of the mindset that many times the songs are already written in the spiritual realm. I believe there is something about those who have the gift of songwriting and a sensitivity to that realm. Every now and then, songwriters have a way of plugging in to the heart of God. They become a conduit, if you will, to receive whatever music He wants us to give to the world. I read somewhere that Michelangelo believed that God had already created the sculptures that he did. When he would begin to work on each one, he was simply removing the excess marble or whatever materials that he was using. Once the excess material was removed, the statue was already created inside.

I was in Nashville at Word records on business when I happened to run into Bill Gaither at the offices. We began talking and he asked me did I have any time since we both were there to maybe find a piano and see if we could come up with a song. We found a piano somewhere in the building and Bill pulled out a notebook. I always tell my songwriting classes to keep a journal with you of songwriting themes, possible titles, or musical concepts. It always works best to have some way of writing them down when you get an idea. Usually, if you wait to get home, or if you wait for a more opportune time, you'll forget them. Of course, this was before the advent of cell phones where you could actually record your ideas. I sat at the piano as Bill went through some of his ideas that he had listed in his book. At some point he said, "Richard I have an idea about Jesus being the center of our life, or of our existence, or the reason for our joy or happiness. What do you hear musically when you hear that concept?" Immediately, in my mind I could visualize a model of an atom that I remembered from biology class in junior high school. There was a nucleus while other parts of the atom traveled around the nucleus. In my mind, Jesus became the nucleus or the core—and our joy, our contentment and most of all, our peace were the parts of the atom that traveled around Him. Immediately, I heard a very clear melody in my head and I began to play what I heard. It was the chorus to "Center of my Joy" basically the way it sounds now. Bill and I began to work on the lyrics of it until the chorus was finished. We had to break for meetings but we came up with a plan for me to come to his home in Alexandria, Indiana at a later date and complete the song. Not long after, I flew to Alexandria. This time Bill's wife, Gloria, joined us. I believe Gloria Gaither is one of the greatest lyricists ever. She has a gift of putting words and concepts together that are second to none. She is a true wordsmith like no other. She began to work with us on the lyrics of the verse. Again, the basic musical structure of the verse came to me quite easily without much thought. Bill and I polished up the musical part of the verse and after that was finished, Gloria began to expound lyrically on what Jesus meant to the Christian faith and who He was personally to those who love and trust Him. The rest is history. That's how that song was born. It was one of a very few times that I would collaborate with other writers to create a song. It's never been an easy thing for me to do. I tend to write at my own pace and have gotten used to going through my own odd process. However, the times I have written with others, I believe that there was something about the nature of the chemistry between us that worked. We understood each other musically and there has been a musical admiration going on between us – especially with me. The other examples of that kind of chemistry had to be when I was blessed to write with Andraé Crouch, Edwin Hawkins and Walter Hawkins. Andraé and I did a song called "The Light" on the Smallwood Singer's "Testimony" recording and Walter and I collaborated on two songs for the Vision album "Journey."" "I Won't Give Up" and a song that we did for the Hawkins family appearance on that project "We've Come Too Far." Bill, Gloria and I would collaborate on one more song called "The Glory of The Lord," which would be featured on the next album entitled "Vision."

CHAPTER 29

THE NEXT RECORDINGS

With the acquisition of the new Smallwood/Gaither song "Center of My Joy," I began to work on the other music for the new album that we would record for Word Records. I had already arranged "Calvary" many years before but never had the chance to record it. I pulled out another song that I had written in the late 70's that I had never done anything with. It was called "Your Love Divine." I began to work on a little song called "Holy, Holy" as well. At some point, I had an interesting dream. We had not too long finished the run of the show "Sing Mahalia, Sing." After doing it for six days a week with a matinee on Saturdays and Sundays, I guess it was still somewhat embedded in my brain. I dreamed that we were doing the show and all of a sudden, the curtains on the stage parted and Jennifer stepped out. She looked at me and said, "Richard, we're going to do that song." I had no idea what she was talking about and I remember the theater being filled to capacity. "What song, Jennifer????" I asked as I began to feel the first signs of panic and anxiety. She looked at me and smiled and said, "You'll know it." Suddenly there was a full orchestra in the pit around me and they began to play. Jennifer began to sing the words "I have come too far, I have come too far." It was like

I knew the song as if I had heard it before. It was as familiar to me as some of the hymns that I had played all my life. I began to play it while she sang. I woke from my dream with the song still ringing in my head and jumped up and ran to the piano while it was fresh. As I developed the rest of the song I laid it down on my cassette player so I wouldn't forget it. "I've Come Too Far" was the first time I had ever gotten a song in that way. It remains one of my favorites.

After I had completed all of the songs, we laid down everything on a demo and I flew to Nashville so that Word could hear what I was proposing to do on the new project. They had obtained producer Norbert Putnam to co-produce the project with me. I had brought my own musicians on board, Steven Ford on keyboards, Jeff Davis on drums and my right-hand man, Tim Linzy on bass. Norbert was a great producer and had worked as a musician back in the days of Muscle Shoals with great artists like Aretha and Otis Redding. He owned a beautiful state of the art digital studio in Nashville with the newest of everything. I remember sitting in the office in front of some of the Word execs as they listened to the songs that I wanted to do on the album. This would be my third album, but I was a new artist at Word and still was at the level of having to prove myself. I remember after each song they would stop the tape and discuss it. To my horror, they began to grade each song as if I were taking a test. They told me "Calvary" was a "C" and made no sense because of that classical "thing" at the end. I was asked why I decided to mix those two genres together. I had no answer. The way I wrote was nothing I ever did on purpose or by design. It was the sum of everything I loved and every genre I had ever embraced. It was my influences that I had heard since Mom brought me my first recording when I was just a tiny kid. I had done a reggae-influenced song called, "We Can't Go On This Way." The style of it was critiqued, as well as the meaning of it. I think they may have given "Center of My Joy" a B-" which was probably the highest grade I earned that day. I was devastated. All of my insecurities about my abilities came rolling back. Was this something that I was going to have to endure for the rest of my musical life? I was so excited about the music for this project, but here was the same old response once more from the "powers that be." I left the office feeling dejected. I wondered if it was even worth staying in the music industry. I wanted to give up. Talk began among the execs about finding suitable music for me to record on this album. I couldn't go through this again. They started to complain to my co-producer Norbert about the songs I had written. At some point, Norbert listened to the demo tape that I had done. After hearing the songs, he called the Word offices and basically told them that I had some great material, to back off, leave me alone and let us produce a great album. They backed right down and said nothing else. Thank God for Norbert! I remember Norbert asking me what I was going to call the album. I had no idea. By now, I wanted to stay with a one-word title, since the last one was called "Psalms". He said when he listened to the music I had written, it was like he heard so many different musical textures. He said Carole King's huge album "Tapestry" kept coming to his mind. He said instead of naming it after a title tune, what about a thematic more avant-garde concept like Textures? That title immediately resonated within me. We began working on the new project "Textures." That was the first time I had ever worked with a Midi piano. This was where a Boosendorfer acoustic piano (my favorite) was hooked up electronically to other sounds so that when you played it, not only did you hear the natural sound of the piano, but strings, electric piano or whatever other kind of sounds you were hooked into. I was amazed as the technology changed through the years. It seems every time I record, more technology has evolved to make it an easier process. Long gone are the big analog tapes that weighed a ton a piece. Long gone is the tedious editing process that would take place after the recording. It sometimes would take a whole day to edit one song with that razor blade until you got it just the way that you wanted it. Now it was little more than a push of a button. I think for me, the recording of "Textures" was the beginning stages of a whole new evolution of technology that we hadn't witnessed before. "Textures" became the Smallwood Singers biggest selling album to date with "Center of my Joy" being the biggest song that I had ever done at that point in my life. The traveling began to escalate even more. By now, we were traveling on a tour bus many times if we weren't flying. We were traveling all over the world to places like Paris, London, Norway, Italy, Germany, Amsterdam and the list went on. Finally, it seemed like things were beginning to break. Although it was grueling sometimes in terms of the touring, we enjoyed it. We were like a family and genuinely loved each other. Like all families, we had arguments and disagreements, but the love, the connection that we had between each other superseded any disagreements. That bond and love between the Smallwood Singers members has never been and cannot ever be erased. Another thing that got us through some of the rough times was humor. Lisa, Jackie, Wesley and Carolene had to be some of the most hilarious characters you'd ever want to meet. Most of the time, Dottie and I would just sit back and laugh until we were breathless. I'd have to write a complete separate book just on them and the crazy things they used to say and do. Sometimes we would laugh so much on the tour bus that when we got wherever we were going we'd all be hoarse.

Traveling all over the World was fun and we loved it. However, we did have some close calls that could have easily gone the wrong way. Three frightening situations come to mind. While flying from one country to the other in Europe, I looked out my window as we were coming in to land and noticed that the engine closest to me was on fire. Flames were shooting out everywhere. I remember Roger sitting next to me calmly saying as if he was observing a beautiful sunset, "oh wow, the plane is on fire." I was panicking and wanted to hit him for not panicking like me. As I looked towards the approaching runway, I could see fire trucks, ambulances and flashing lights. I immediately started praying, however my brain was frozen, and all I could think of was "help Lord, Help Lord." Thank God He knows our hearts. We landed safely and were ushered quickly off the plane without anyone further incident.

We were in Atlanta, GA for a huge gospel concert at the Atlanta Civic Center with gospel artists from all over the US. Recently there had been a lot of unusual racial unrest and the Ku Klux Klan had marched in Atlanta. This particular day they were marching nearby in one of the counties outside of Atlanta. We took the stage and did our opening number. As we started on the second number, Roger came over to the piano where I was playing and said, "stop this song now and exit the stage." I immediately responded, "Rog we just got on stage and we have twenty more minutes." He said Richard leave now, there is a bomb threat. I moved quick and in a hurry as Roger began to usher the singers and band off stage. By now, I saw the police and bomb sniffing dogs coming down all of the aisles. Someone had called in a bomb threat, because I'm sure this was the largest assembly of black people in one location in Atlanta that day. We literally ran from the venue. Thank God no bomb was found, but the concert was canceled for that day.

The most frightening thing that I can remember happened in Chicago, Illinois. It was a huge outdoor concert in one of the large parks in Chicago. There must have been at least twenty different stages of different sizes all over the park with artists performing different genres of music. The gospel stage was huge and it towered above the sound board and other equipment below. It was summer and the weather was very hot, great for an outdoor performance. By the time we were called to sing on the "gospel stage" it had begun to get darker and the lights began to come on in the park. There were huge light trees that illuminated the stages and giant speakers that went up both sides of the stages and crossed over top, above the performers. Above the lights all of the stages were covered with huge canopies. Directly behind our stage was a small trailer where we could wait in the air conditioning with food and drink before it was time for us to go on. The last step on the trailer led right to the first step on the stage. With the band already in place as they were calling our names, we began to climb the stage to take our places. I remember being excited because instead of having some kind of electronic keyboard for the main keys, they had an acoustic grand piano which has always been my first love. Roger who would always help with the sound was on the monitor board across from where I was seated at the piano on stage. The park was packed with people as far as I could see and they were swaying and clapping to the intro by the band. The singers stepped to the mics with our first song "Holy, Holy" and everyone was jamming and singing along in the audience. It felt like this was going to be a good concert. As we began the second song, all of a sudden the temperature changed and cooler winds began to blow towards the stage. It began to drizzle, but the audience wasn't leaving. They were still singing and clapping and some began to raise their umbrellas. Roger looked at me sitting at the piano and motioned me to cut, to stop playing. I had no reason to stop playing so I continued. At that point Roger cut off the sound so we couldn't hear ourselves in our monitors. People had begun to move back away from the stage and were scattering in different directions. When I asked Roger later what had happened he said, "Rich all I know is I heard a voice in my head just as loud as if they were on a mic say to me, "GET THEM OFF STAGE NOW." Little did he or I know at that time that a twister of sorts had entered the park. Rog ran over to me screaming "LET'S GO, LET'S GO NOW! Hearing the urgency in his voice I knew something was terribly wrong. I made sure that all the females were off the stage, I remembered I was the last one as they were all in front of me running into the trailer. As my foot hit the last step of the stage and first step of the trailer, I heard someone scream "OH MY GOD!" As I looked up towards the stage a huge whirling wind had risen to the top of the canopy and had lifted it up off the top of the stage toward the sky. The light trees in turn had started to teeter and totter like a huge hand was trying to push them over. Before I could even respond they began falling, crushing the mics and the sound equipment. By this time Roger was screaming "get out the trailer." We could hear stages crashing in the distance and people screaming above the roaring wind and rain. With debris falling they had dispatched a little mini bus to get us out of the park as quickly as possible. All I remember is that we boarded that little bus as quick as possible. Immediately I heard another huge crash coming from the stage, and watched as the entire stage collapsed as a light tree hit the grand piano and smashed it to bits. I had been sitting at that piano and the Smallwood Singers had been performing standing at those mics with the band behind them literally minutes before. The bus began to try to make its way towards the exit of the park, dodging people running and debris falling. It certainly wasn't funny at the time, but later as true to form we laughed about it. I heard a voice hollering "wait, wait, WAIT!" Somehow Wesley had gotten lost in the confusion and missed the mini bus. When I looked out the back, Wesley was running behind the bus like Usain Bolt, his knees literally under his chin hollering "wait y'all, WAIT!!!" I had never seen Wesley move that fast. The bus slowed enough for him to jump on board. We continued to move forward as we were watching stages fall all around us until we reached the exit. By now the wind had calmed and the rain had slowed to a drizzle. When we got back to the hotel, I don't think I slept that night. I found out later there were some serious injuries, one especially by a stage hand who was on one of the light trees on our stage when it fell. It was definitely the most frightening thing that had happened to us. It would be years before I wrote that song, but there is no doubt, that there were angels watching over us. In all of our traveling all over the planet God always built a hedge of protection around us. Thank God for Roger who definitely heard his voice that night in Chicago.

Not too long after the release of "Textures", we were contacted by ABC's "Ryan's Hope," a popular soap opera that was interested in us appearing on their show after seeing us in "Sing Mahalia, Sing." The story line centered on a young girl who was missing. The detectives in search for the young lady stopped by the church where she attended to ask questions of the pastor and members of her whereabouts. We were supposedly rehearsing at the church when the detective arrived. We did two songs from the "Textures" album, "Get on Board" with Carolene out front and "Shine Your Light" with Jackie on the lead. Around 1987, after the huge success of "Center of My Joy," Wesley told me, "Rich you've finally made it. From the days of Howard University when you came in as a freshman in 1967, look where God has brought us from. I think it's time for me to branch out and work on some of the things that I want to do." I definitely understood his desires and his goals. He was undoubtedly one of the best friends I've ever had and although it was hard to see him go and not hear that incredible tenor voice that I had heard for the last twenty years, I knew he had to do what he had to do. That by no means affected our friendship. Years later he was still that encouraging, supportive Wesley that I always knew. Raymond Reeder a talented musician/composer whom I had known since he was a little boy at Union Temple would step in as tenor and sometimes additional keyboard player, as Steven Ford had left to pursue other opportunities. Little did I know down the road Steve and I would forge a co-producer relationship that would take me to another level and another season. Also, not long after another great classically trained tenor voice and dear friend, Rikki LaFontaine would become a part of the group for a while. Members would move on to pursue other things. Lisa to raise a family although she would come back to work with us from time to time down through the years, and Dottie to do a solo project. Darlene Simmons would replace Lisa and continue with us through my next years with Vision. We had heard Darlene initially as a part of the famous Eastern High School Gospel Choir directed by the gifted Joyce Garrett. However, she was still a teenager and when Wesley asked her mother could she sing with us, her mother said no. She didn't want it to interfere with her schoolwork. By now Darlene was 19, finished with school and came on board. She's definitely one of the most awesome singers around and vocally she fit right into the Smallwood Singers. Later other members would come such as Dennis Sawyers and Patti Teagle. They were both awesome singers who joined and sang for a while. When I was in need of a new alto for the Smallwood Singers, one of my best friends of over thirty years, Toby Palmer, mentioned a young lady he knew who might fit the bill. He set up a meeting at his dad's church who was a pastor so that I could hear her sing. As she sang for me, I knew she could handle whatever part or vocal assignment that I would need. Whatever Smallwood Singers song I threw at her, she knew each part, perfectly. Her name was Vanessa Renee Williams. Little did I know what an integral part of my music ministry she would become. Another person who would become my right hand around 1987 started working with me; Bryant Pugh, fresh out of high school would come on board to become my pianist and musical director where he still is today. He approached me at a concert where he was playing for gospel artist Keith Pringle. I remembered listening to him as he was playing for Keith, marveling at how great he was. After the concert, he came up to me and gave me his card and told me if ever I needed a keyboard player to please give him a call. When that slot opened, that's exactly what I did and the rest is history. Bryant is not only an awesome musician but also, he is one of the greatest people to work with. He has worked closely by my side with just about everything that I've done since then. The Smallwood Singers would continue to record. The next album for Word Records in 1987 would be called "Vision," ironically the name of my next group. Raymond Reeder was a great asset in helping me put that project together and assisted me with the string arrangements. "Portrait" would be next in 1990, which was recorded in Nassau, Bahamas at the world-famous Compass Point Studio which was an incredible experience. The scenery alone on the island was enough to cause every creative juice that one could ever have to flow. After that, I joined Sparrow Records and the next two projects would be "Testimony" in 1992 and "Live at Howard University" in 1993, where I came back home to where it all started. However, there was never another Smallwood Singers album that would eclipse "Textures" or another Smallwood Singers song that would eclipse "Center of My Joy." But God was by no means finished. He had even larger plans, that I had no idea about.

CHAPTER 30
FINDING HOME AND
A NEW CALLING

In 1991, we were singing at Morgan State University for the anniversary of their incredible choir under the direction of the late, great Nathan Carter. After the concert, Dr. Carter approached me about hearing a student of his. He took me back to the choir room and there I met a young man named Darin Atwater whom Dr. Carter asked to play for me. I was blown away as he began to play. Little did I know at the time that he had grown up on the Smallwood Singers from the very first album. It was like listening to a younger version of myself on the piano. I knew I was hearing something great but had no idea just how great he would become. I think immediately on the spot I asked him to start playing for me. We were leaving to go out on the road in a matter of days. I remember him coming by the house to learn the material. Mom was in the kitchen cooking and I walked in to talk to her while Darin was in the living room practicing. She looked at me with a look of confusion on her face and said, "I thought for sure that was you playing!!!" I told her that was one of my new keyboard players and she was astonished at the gift of this young brother. Even then I could hear nuances of him taking my influence on him and taking it to the next level. We all stand on the shoulders of others. That's what life is all about. Don't ever selfishly keep your gift to yourself. Always freely share what God has given you with others. You never know the impact that it will have on them and where it will take them. Darin would travel with the Smallwood Singers for the next several years. He is now rapidly becoming one of the premiere orchestral arrangers and conductors in the country. His "Soulful Symphony" is bringing orchestral music to a whole new community. I don't use the word genius lightly, but Darin definitely fits in that category.

Most people don't know, but after leaving Union Temple I was without a church home for eight years. My relationship with the Lord never wavered, in fact if anything my love and dependence on Him increased. But if I can be perfectly honest, I was still so hurt and afraid to be involved in a church setting. For a long time, I had been praying for God to direct my path as it pertained to the next season of my life. Not too long after I left the church, my mother left as well. She joined a new church called Randall Memorial Baptist Church. She and the kids began to work diligently in that church. I visited her church, but was never led to become a part. In 1986, a religious announcer named Don Edwards Miller contacted me from our gospel radio station WYCB. He was a member of the historic Metropolitan Baptist Church pastored by one of the greatest preachers around—Dr. H. Beecher Hicks Jr. They had recently moved into their new church and he wanted me to come and work with one of the choirs for a special service they were planning. He wanted me to come teach "Psalm 8" to their Young Adult Choir. I remember the choir not being very good and was very small. It certainly wasn't what I was used to in terms of singers. However,

I was more than happy to help out. I brought Jackie from the Smallwood Singers over to do the lead. When I heard Pastor Hicks, his preaching blew me away. I needed to hear that kind of Word, that kind of power, and that kind of anointing. I needed that kind of spiritual food. I found myself sneaking back on Sunday mornings hiding in the balcony. Whenever Pastor Hicks found out I was there, he would always call me up to minister in some kind of way. But I didn't want to do that. I was starving. I needed *Word*. I needed food. I just wanted to sit there and take it all in. I would always sit where I thought he wouldn't see me. An incredibly talented young brother, David Warr, directed the Young Adult Fellowship Ensemble. As time went on, he invited me to become a part of their annual Spring Concert. "Textures" was still hot and he wanted to teach the choir several of the songs for the concert. I began attending rehearsals. The choir by now had begun to grow. They started to take on a sound of their own. Metropolitan was in a transition period. The Metropolitan that I knew of as a kid growing up, didn't sing gospel music. You didn't say Amen and certainly there was no shouting. It was what we would call "high church." After Pastor Hicks was called to pastor there, he brought about a new element. There was a new style of preaching and a new style of worship that he had envisioned. However, old habits die hard. Older members from the old days didn't want drums in the church, and no instruments other than the Pipe Organ and piano. They couldn't get with the livelier services. But as the Young Adult Fellowship Ensemble began to grow, they wanted to be free in their worship. They wanted to praise, they wanted to be vocal about what God had done for them in a new way. The Spring Concert went great. Honestly, I think that some people didn't know how to react. There was shouting in the choir during the musical worship service. Some in the audience just stared as if they were trying to figure out what was going on. After the concert, I continued coming on Sunday mornings. One thing I loved, other than the incredible preaching of Dr. Hicks, was the diversity of music. As one who came up listening to all kinds of music it was so refreshing to me. It reminded me of the days at Pleasant Grove where all forms of Christian music were represented on Sunday morning. Metropolitan had one of the premier senior choirs in the country, directed by the gifted Thomas Dixon Tyler. The anthems were top notch. They had the kind of power that would make you want to shout just as hard on an anthem as you would on a gospel song. I remember the hymn one morning being "Oh God Our Help in Ages Past." By the time they finished singing it, I wanted to come out of the balcony and run around that church until I passed out. The tears just flowed down my cheeks as that old hymn of the church blessed me in ways that I hadn't been blessed in years. The sound of the powerful pipe organ washed over me. Little by little, I started seeing the congregation loosen up in terms of their worship. On Sunday, October 25, 1987, I had come down for prayer at altar call after a powerful sermon by Pastor Hicks. When I went to return to my seat, it was like my legs were paralyzed and I couldn't go back to my seat. By then Pastor Hicks had started the invitation to discipleship. People were coming forward to join the church and sitting on the front row. I knew this was where I was supposed to be for this season. But I didn't want to join. I was still afraid. Before I knew it, I had sat down with the rest of the people who had come forward to join the church. It was like the weight of the world was lifted off my shoulder. I knew that I was home. When I got home, Mom said to me, "You joined Metropolitan didn't you?" I remember thinking that someone must have called her.

"Why do you say that, Mom?" I asked, not really answering her question. She said, "Because I was sitting in the pew at my church and all of a sudden, I had a vision of you walking down Metropolitan's aisle and giving your hand to the Pastor." I was grown and still couldn't get away with anything without Mom knowing it. As a kid, she instinctively knew everything. We had such a connection, it was unexplainable.

I began working officially along with David and the Young Adult Fellowship Ensemble. He would usually do the directing and I would do the playing. It felt good playing for church service again. It's all I had known all my life. The choir grew by leaps and bounds. Many of the older church members began to transition and a new configuration began to become a part of the church. There was a young to middle age crew that began to grow in the congregation. Little by little, the style of worship began to change. This was definitely a new Metropolitan, one that was like day and night from the one I remembered as a child. For years, wherever I was traveling on the road I would always try to make it back for Sunday morning service. At the same time, I kept getting prophecies from different preachers that I was going to preach. I remember doing a workshop in Miami and conducting a class as a part of it. I think the class might have been in Gospel Music History. At any rate, there was an elderly man sitting on the back row of the church, though not a part of the class. When it was over, he came up to me and shook my hand and said, "Son, are you a preacher?" "No sir, I'm just a musician," I replied. He responded, "Well, son, just remember when you do your trial sermon that an old deacon in Florida prophesied that you're going to preach." I didn't want to hear it. Music was fine and that was enough.

I had a vivid dream one night that I was standing backstage at Andrew Rankin Chapel on Howard's campus. My father was praying for me and I was about to go on stage to preach my first sermon. I woke up in a cold sweat, and pushed the dream in the back of my mind. I didn't want to think about it and I certainly had no desire to preach.

The frightening visions of my childhood had passed. However, I still wouldn't sleep with the door open. Until this day I still can't. Something new and strange was happening. I would find myself in a state somewhere between being asleep and awake. I was aware of what was around me because I could see and I could hear. At the same time, my body was paralyzed and I couldn't move. It used to frighten me so. I remember I used to pray when it would happen, that God would take it away. But it would take its time in leaving. Sometimes I would even sense something in the room when it would happen, but I would never see anything per se. The feeling of being paralyzed as if something were pinning me down was terrifying to say the least. I dreaded it.

CHAPTER 31

SIGNED TO VERITY RECORDS

A s I look back, there have been so many "firsts." The Celestials were the first gospel group on Howard's campus. The Celestials were the first gospel group to perform at the Montreux Jazz Festival in Switzerland. However, in 1989 the Smallwood Singers became the first gospel group to tour the then Soviet Union. One of the promoters who brought us to Sweden and other European countries reached out to Roger, my manager, and wanted to know if he thought we would be interested in performing in Russia. The promoter had taken rock groups over there in the past but gospel was unheard of. Roger approached me and although there probably was a small bit of apprehension on my part, I said yes. Little did I know, this would be an opportunity to minister in a way that I had never ministered before. Then Soviet President, Mikhail Gorbachev, had decided to try a more open policy for the country. To show you how God works and how He uses whom he chooses, the tour was sponsored by two organizations in the Soviet Union, The Young Communists and the Red Guard. These are not the kind of organizations by which one would expect the Word of God to be brought through song to Russia. However, God is God and you never know which way He will decide to work.

We did a European tour and then left for Russia. When we landed in Russia, the first thing that frightened us a bit was all of the armed guards that were all over the airport. When we went through customs, we were ordered to surrender our passports and were told by security they would not be given back until we left the country. When going overseas, one of the most important things is to keep your passport with you at all times, however we now had no passports. An entourage of six people, who were very friendly, greeted us. One young lady was an interpreter and I was never sure who everyone else was. I found out later that one was a KGB agent. I guess they were there to make sure we did nothing wrong and said nothing wrong. Before the tour ended, we all became friends. On several of the dates a heavy metal rock band opened up for us. I remember the first night they blew the sound system out before we could do our set. It had to be repaired before we went out. I had no idea what we were going to do. While the rock band performed, the audience was going wild. The Rock band was breaking instruments on stage, jumping out in the audience, and the whole place had gone bananas. At one point, the sound board actually caught on fire! I remember saying to God, "I know You know what You are doing, but I think we might be in the wrong place." When we went out to sing, the interpreter talked a little bit about us, our music and said we were singing about our faith. We entered the stage and began to sing. Everything was very quiet at first. I'm sure the difference between the decibels of the band and what we were doing was like day and night, much less the style of music. Somewhere in the concert, people began to come down to the foot of the stage though. I noticed tears in some of their eyes on some of the ballads that we did. When we left the stage, they gave us a rousing ovation. God had proven once again that He didn't need language to get his message across.

One night on the bus from one city to the next, the leader of the rock band came to me and spoke in broken English. He said, "Richard, why is it that when we sing, I feel bound, but when I hear all of you sing, I sense freedom?" The tears began to roll down my face as I explained the Good News of Jesus Christ to him, and the principles of what we believed. It was another opportunity to witness in another country. I knew I was there for a reason. We fell in love with the people. One thing I learned is that people are the same everywhere, no matter what kind of propaganda you may read. Everyone wants love, peace and a family unit. Everyone is searching for a higher power outside of themselves. The poverty was overwhelming. There was no middle class. You were either rich or poor. The food was the worst. One hotel was infested with roaches. It was considered a four or five-star hotel over there, but it would have barely made a two-star rating in the States. There were so many roaches that the girls would light incense and kill the roaches by burning them as they would run up the walls. When you turned on the water in the bathroom, it would run out a kind of orange rusty color. I tried to wash a white t-shirt in the sink and it permanently turned orange. There was a black and white TV in the room, but it only had a few channels and, of course, everything was in Russian. I remember one particular day, my bass player Tim Linzy knocked on my door and said he had something to show me. We had been told not to drink the water unless it was bottled water. Tim showed me a sealed, unopened bottle of water. As he held it up to the light at the bottom, I saw a dead spider floating along with parts of a spider web. When we would eat at the restaurant in the hotel, and ask for grape juice, they would put grapes basically in a big pot of water, boil it, and pour off the juice from it. However, these were some of the happiest and kindest people I had met anywhere. One of the cities where we stayed had no movie theaters. Someone in the city had a VCR that he had saved all year to purchase. There was a small auditorium that he would rent out and show videos on a television and people would come from all around and pack it out. I had traveled all over Europe but had never experienced anything like that. It made me appreciate the United States like never before. We take so many things for granted that people in other parts of the world are not blessed to have. Although most of the churches had been closed and turned into museums, there was a part of the older population that still would go to the few churches that were left. We were asked to sing at a Russian Orthodox Church one Sunday morning. As we were riding and getting closer to the church we saw elderly people, some walking with canes, coming from everywhere, going in the direction of the church. We were told that they would walk for miles on Sunday just to get to worship service. As we entered the church, we noticed that there were no seats. The services were several hours long and the people would stand for hours. There were no instruments and I remember we sang "I Love the Lord" a capella. It was one of the most moving experiences that I've ever had. As we sang, I saw weather beaten faces with scarves covering their heads and tears in their eyes. I must say, there were tears in mine as well. As our voices echoed through that church, it was another example of how God didn't have physical limitations of speech or language to get his message across. There was one concert we did in a stadium one evening. There were no lights in the stadium, so they pulled up buses in front of the stage and turned on the headlights to light it. We were way out in the middle of a field and the audience seemed miles away in the stands. Jackie was leading one of the songs and decided she would get closer to the audience in order to interact. She left the stage in the direction of the audience. Of course, since there were no lights, she soon disappeared in the darkness where we could neither see nor hear her. We had no idea where she was or what part of the song she was singing. So, we just repeated whatever phrase we were on until she finally appeared back on the stage much later. Knowing Jackie, she was probably up in the stands with the audience. It was definitely a humorous moment. We made a number of friends there. One gentleman was in a Russian band. One of the national instruments of Russia is the livenka, which is a type of an accordion. The instrument is beautifully crafted and is so expensive that we were told it would take a whole year of savings to purchase one over there. No one made very much money. The Russian band that our friend played in was made up of these instruments and they were brilliantly and skillfully played. At the end of our stay, he presented me with his livenka as a gift. The generosity and the kindness of the Russian people overwhelmed me. Even though the living conditions were very difficult, the appreciation from the people and the love that they showed all of us made up for it. I remember learning how to play "Nobody Knows the Trouble I've Seen" on the livenka and the Smallwood Singers laughing at my song and singing along with me in our hotel rooms. Although the people were great, we were ready to go HOME! When we got back home, I literally kissed the ground at the airport. It was a tremendous opportunity to minister, but it was also a teaching moment about how fortunate we were in the United States.

A lot of people don't know that I originally wrote a number of songs especially for my church choir, The Young Adult Fellowship

Ensemble at Metropolitan. Songs like "What He's Done For Me," "Holy Spirit," "It's Working," "My Everything (Praise Waiteth)," "I'll Trust You" and "His Mercy Endureth Forever" were all originally written for concerts and special occasions for my church choir and later recorded by the Smallwood Singers and my current group, Vision. In fact, YAFE as we call the choir, is featured on the recording along with the Smallwood Singers on "Holy Spirit." YAFE began to grow by leaps and bounds in size and sound and traveled all over the country representing our church and pastor. My pastor (now emeritus) Dr. H. Beecher Hicks Jr. is featured on the narration on the song "T'will Be Sweet" on the Smallwood Singers CD, "Testimony." Ironically that song was written by my father C. L. Smallwood and originally recorded by the Union Temple Young Adult Choir in the 70's on their album "Look Up and Live." As a child, I used to hear him play and sing it around the house. However, his version was an up-tempo kind of a swing tune. I decided to make it into a ballad and when the Smallwood Singers re-recorded it, I got the old Union Temple Young Adult Choir together once more to do it on the recording. What a wonderful reunion that was. There were so many great and wonderful old memories and there always will be from those Union Temple years.

In 1991 my friend Mervyn Warren, founding member of Take Six, an incredible musician, producer and arranger in his own right, reached out to me. He told me that he was helping Quincy Jones do a black version of "Handel's Messiah." He was assembling different groups and artists to arrange and produce tracks based on the original oratorio. He asked me would I consider doing something with "Rejoice, Greatly O Daughter of Zion," ironically one of my favorite arias in that piece. I was more than happy to be a part of it. Artists like Stevie Wonder, Patti Austin,

Take Six, Al Jareau, Fred Hammond, The Clark Sisters, Vanessa Bell Armstrong singing with Daryl Coley, Tramaine Hawkins and others helped to make this CD a classic. In addition, Mervyn and the late Michael O. Jackson arranged an awesome version of the Hallelujah Chorus and assembled artists and actors from every corner of the globe to form a massive choir to record that final piece. The choir was directed by the genius himself, Quincy Jones. I will never forget walking into that studio in LA and seeing the likes of Chaka Khan, Johnny Mathis, Clifton Davis, Joe Sample, Edwin Hawkins, Andraé Crouch, Sandra Crouch, Stephanie Mills, Kim Fields, Patti Austin, Gladys Knight, the late Thomas Whitfield, my former Howard classmate Phylicia Rashad and so many more amazing artists who made up the choir. We rehearsed and recorded as well as videotaped for two days. The LA riots after the Rodney King beating would begin in South Central that second day. I was staying at the Sofitel right across the street from the Beverly Center. Newscasters were saying that the riots could very well spread to that area. Thanking God that the recording was over, I made my way to the airport as fast as I could. I had no idea how far the rioting might spread. We won a Grammy for that project and it remains something of which I am extremely proud to be a part.

People always ask me the secret to my longevity. I have no idea other than, it was God. I haven't done anything musically other than stay true to who I am. I never set out to consciously combine genres or start a new trend. I just did music the only way I knew how and that was from all of the influences that God put in my path. Over the years, I've tried to follow His will to the best of my ability. I've definitely made mistakes and I'm not perfect. But because of God's unmerited favor and his mercy, He has kept me down through the years. I sometimes fail, but God hasn't! Around 1992 or so, God began to lay on my heart to start a new singing aggregation. By now you know that I don't like change. Even though it's necessary for growth it does not make it any easier. I kept pushing the concept of starting a new group to the back of my mind. In my heart of hearts, I felt that I had taken the Smallwood Singers as far as they could go and it even began to be a little more difficult to come up with fresh new music. However, that was my family, I loved them and wasn't trying to do anything to change any of that. Little by little, I felt I was just going through the motions when I was on stage. It had nothing to do with the members of the group. It was me. Something was changing. After the "Live at Howard" CD in 1993 I had no clue what direction I should go in next. In 1994, I signed with a new label, Verity Records. At that point, I had no interest in doing any recordings. Honestly, I didn't even want to sign a new record deal. I was experiencing burnout and didn't even know it. My manager Roger kept stressing the fact that Verity was interested and honestly there were not a lot of people knocking on my door in terms of labels. It was a better deal than any deal that I had ever been offered, including a signing bonus. I knew Roger was looking out for me and for my future but honestly, I was not that interested in signing. I was at a strange place. I flew to New York and met with Verity on a couple of occasions. Recording was all I had known for the last twelve years, so I decided to go on and sign. I kept hoping that the excitement about recording would come back. It seemed that I had lost my zeal. The first recording with Verity in which I was involved was a compilation CD in celebration of Rosa Parks. Different artists came together and did original songs that saluted the tenacity and courage of Mrs. Parks. I wrote a song called "Faith" and took the Smallwood Singers into the studio to record that. It would be our last recording together until a reunion years later on the CD "Journey."

That same year, I had an opportunity to be a part of one of the most awe-inspiring historical events of my life. Bill Gaither, with the help of the late Ed Smith, did a video session of several days with just about all of the gospel legends who were around at that time. The sales from these videos were to help African-American gospel artists who needed medical care and other types of help and who didn't have any insurance. When I got the call to be a part of it, I couldn't believe it. Walking in Bill's studio in Alexandria, Indiana I couldn't believe my eyes. So many of the people who I had come up on as a child and a teenager were all in this one place together. There was Billy Preston, The Ward Singers, The Roberta Martin Singers, The Original Gospel Harmonettes, The Barrett Sisters, Albertina Walker and the Caravans including Cassietta George, Inez Andrews, Delores Washington and Dorothy Norwood, members of Mattie Moss' South West Michigan State Choir, members of Detroit's Voices of Tabernacle including one of my favorite sopranos Hulah Gene Dunklin Hurley, members of the James Cleveland Singers, Ralph Goodpasteur, Robert Anderson, Jessy Dixon, The Angelic Singers, The Soul Stirrers, The Mighty Clouds of Joy and the list went on and on. I think Walter Hawkins, Darryl Coley, Donald Vails, Jeffrey LaValley, Patrick Henderson and I were the youngest ones there when it came to the artists. All of us had grown up on these pioneers and legends. I was dumbfounded when I saw my idol, Herbert "Pee Wee" Pickard and got the amazing opportunity to hear him play during those sessions. When I first met him and I went up to him, more or less speechless, he bowed to me. I told him to please get up, I was the one that should be bowing and I was so unworthy. This man taught me so much as a teenager. We all sang the songs that I had grown up on in the church as well as the songs for which each artist was known. I was honored to once again play for the Roberta Martin Singers and not only that, but the Ward Singers with Clara's sister, Willa Ward Moultrie, Kitty Parham and Esther Ford. Esther was the last member to join right before the infamous break up and was a part of the "post" Ward group, The Stars of Faith. She took the lead that day for the ailing Marion Williams and did "Surely God is Able." I couldn't believe, after being too shy to play in front of them all those many years before, I was actually playing *for them*. The late Donald Vails served as narrator. Two videos were done out of these sessions, "I'm On My Way To Heaven" and "Highway To Heaven." After years of legal issues surrounding its release, a partial version of those sessions called Gospel Pioneer Reunion was released on DVD in 2016. Awesome vocalist Sandy Patti even stopped by and I got the chance to play "We Shall Behold Him" for her. What an opportunity! "Center of My Joy" closed out one of the videos. It was such an honor. I never will forget those three days.

The nagging feeling of starting a new music ministry wouldn't leave me alone. By now, Mom was getting older and having more health problems. She was on a walker as she had fallen and broken her hip. Arthritis had ravaged her legs as well. Even with her health problems she had raised all of her foster kids to adults and had started raising a new set of children, a brother and sister named Danny and Lisa. Danny was about three when Mom first got him and his sister was five. She now had raised them through their teen years. By now he was in high school and having some emotional issues. One of my best friends Robert, my god-brother, was having health issues as well. It seemed like so much was going on all around me. About four years earlier we had lost my dear friend of so many years, Sully. That was hard to process for me. The depression had gotten a bit worse and was not as intermittent as it once was. It would stay longer now before it would let up. I still had never called it that, nor do I think I actually knew it was depression. However, I knew something was wrong. It would seem to leave for a time. However, each time it would return, it seemed like it was stronger and longer.

CHAPTER 32

THE SONG THAT CHANGED EVERYTHING

In order to appease this strong feeling of starting a new music ministry, I decided to form a choir. It was something in the back of my mind that I always wanted to do. I had never done a choir album, at least not on a professional level. I hadn't done anything like that since the Union Temple days. Of course, that had been an independent effort. I had just started out in a studio setting then and honestly, I didn't know what I was doing (technically speaking). Over the years Atlanta, my birthplace, had become one of my favorite cities. It was one of the cities where I would travel most doing concerts with the Smallwood Singers, doing workshops and personal appearances. Through the years, I had established some close ties and friendships down there. In fact, at one point, I had even considered moving there. There was so much talent in Atlanta, some I had used from time to time whenever I didn't take the Smallwoods with me. So, I decided to form a choir for the next recording just as a temporary thing. I planned to use some of the talent from Atlanta, combined with talent from home in the DMV area. The plan was to travel to Atlanta to have rehearsals with whomever I chose down there and have rehearsal weekly with the members in my area. I would write music that was more choir-oriented. I would do a live recording in Atlanta. The only live recording I had ever done was the "Live at Howard" CD with the Smallwoods. Maybe after that, I would go back to the Smallwood Singers or either I'd come up with some other concept. I'd cross that bridge when I got to it. I had even mentioned to a couple of Atlanta singers about it and they were interested. I figured if I did this, the nagging feeling of starting a new ministry would go away. By now I was doing workshops all over the world with choirs. I had played for and directed choirs since I was eight years old. *Why not do a choir album?* It made sense.

I definitely wanted the current members of the Smallwood Singers to be a part of the choir and I reached out to everyone about it. By now the anointed and gifted Vanessa R. Williams (not the secular singer/actress) had become a part of the Smallwood Singers. The majority of them were interested and wanted to know when rehearsal was going to take place. I told them I'd get back to them as soon as I put it together. I was sitting in my den thinking about who I wanted to be a part of the choir. All of a sudden, names just began to pop into my head as God began to lay on my heart who he wanted to be a part of it. I didn't just want people who sang; I wanted people who understood my ministry and would support it. I didn't want egos or prima donnas. I just wanted folk who were willing to work and who loved God. Of course, Vanessa Williams, Carolene Evans who had been with me since 1980 and Darlene Simmons (all a part of the Smallwood Singers) were on that list. Raymond Reeder who had worked with the Smallwoods on and off throughout the years and who I had known since he was a child, was also on that list. Then God began to give me people from my church choir YAFE at

Metropolitan Baptist church: Sharon Orr, Stephanie Winslow, Burl Binion, Vernon Love, Dayle Atterberry, Tara Fentress, Desi McClure and Joanna Johnson. An incredible tenor with an amazing range was laid on my heart whom I knew from hearing Howard's Gospel choir many years after I had graduated, Jeffrey Waddy. Two sisters had worked with Tramaine Hawkins from time to time, Angie Bell and Renee Adams. There were two others I had heard sing with my friend Nolan Williams, who is another incredibly talented musician in the area. They were Byron Nichols, an amazing vocalist whose tone and quality I loved, and Lorree Slye, who had an incredible jazz flavor to her singing. She could scat like Ella Fitzgerald! There was another young lady who I had known since the days of the Celestials with an amazing soprano voice, Debbie Steele Hayden along with her then-husband Sean Hayden. There was Maurette Brown Clark whose voice I had loved from years ago when I first heard her with a local group called the Keyth Lee Singers. Last but not least was an awesome vocalist whom I had watched grow up from a little girl in the DMV area, Charrisse Nelson. Charrisse was not only an awesome vocalist but had an incredible anointing upon her ministry. I reached out to the people on that list and their response was, "When is rehearsal? I'm there!" It's amazing how God orchestrates things. I had jotted down some names from Atlanta to reach out to, but for some reason I never did. Thinking I still needed more people as I was going for a more mass sound, there were several more that I added after God had given me the original list. They weren't available or just never showed up for rehearsal. I knew the original list contained the people whom God had chosen to be a part. By now I started getting excited about this new undertaking. I remember my god-brother, Robert Dace, being so positive in dealing with the issues he was having with his health. I had been complaining and nitpicking about things that weren't even important. He told me one day, "Richard, I am so thankful to God for the little things." Immediately I went to the piano and the song "Thank You" began to pour out. We take the little things in our lives for granted many times; our life, our health, food and shelter. With Robert, my Mom's health failing, and my little foster brother's emotional issues, I had become overwhelmed. I found myself going from hospital to hospital feeling helpless as I tried to be there for my loved ones. That dark feeling began to overtake me again. It was overwhelmingly oppressing and one day I sat at the piano and just burst into tears. I felt abandoned, alone and it seemed like I couldn't feel God's presence. I felt helpless as I watched my loved ones suffering. I wanted to write a "pity party" song, a song that would ask God to hold me, dry my tears and make the pain go away. Immediately the scripture, Psalm 121 came to my mind while sitting at the piano, "I will lift mine eyes to the hills. From whence cometh my help? My help cometh from the Lord, who made heaven and earth." It was comforting to me and I wanted to develop it musically into a song that asked for God's help. However, the more I worked on it, the more it kept going in the direction of a praise song. Praise was the last thing I felt like doing. I kept tugging in the opposite direction, but it was like the song was already written and I was just receiving it. The words came so quickly, "Your peace you give me, in time of the storm. You are the source of my strength; You are the strength of my life. I lift my hands in total praise to you." I had never thought of the concept of "Total Praise" before that day; a praise that is complete and implemented with mind, body, soul and spirit. Praise using the total person, with every fiber of your being. It was like the song had a life of its own and was writing itself. It was written so fast that before I knew it, it was done. I sat there, knowing something very special had happened. As I listened back to it on my cassette player, I began to cry. It was not a cry of despair this time. But it was a cry of hope, a cry of victory, a cry that I was witnessing something that was not of me. When I listened to it, I realized that it was part-prayer and part-praise. In other words, it started out as a cry for help, but in the middle of it there was a metamorphosis as it transformed into a song of appreciation, a song of acknowledgement of who God is and of His power. There was a statement of remembering: "Your peace you give me in time of the storm," then transferring to a statement of praise and affirmation after realizing every storm I've had, "You've been in the midst of it." You have been the one who has brought me through it. So, what am I despairing about? "*You are* the source of my strength." The more I listened to it over and over again, I realized that it needed an "Amen," an "it is so," a "so be it" to seal it. The "Amen" I was hearing in my head sounded a bit involved. I had a TEAC four track recorder on which I could record parts separately. I pulled it out and began to put down separately what I was hearing. I could feel the classical musical influences take a hold of my spirit as the parts began to flow out easily and quickly. When I laid down the three parts I listened to it all together. I began to cry again. I can't explain what I felt. One thing I knew was that God was saying something especially to me. He was saying, "Richard, I know it's hard, I know what you're feeling. I see your tears, but even in the midst of your valley, I want your praise. I'm the One who is still in control. I'm the One who is going to bring you through. Trust me because I've got this! In the meantime, praise Me for what I'm getting ready to do in your life, even if you can't see it or visualize it and even though you don't physically feel like

it. Use your faith because I've already given you a measure of it."
I began to do just that. Although I knew immediately that this
song was something very special, I had no idea what God was
going to do with it.

There was an excitement in the air that night in October
1995 when I had the first Vision rehearsal at my home church,
Metropolitan. Certainly, there were people whom I knew well,
some I knew barely and some I didn't know at all. But it was
like something clicked that night. It's hard to explain but it was
like a feeling of familiarity, a feeling of home. It was like we all
had sung together before with everyone coming together like a
family. It felt right. I knew without a shadow of a doubt, that
everyone there was supposed to be there. God had ordained
this. As I began to teach the very first song that night, "Thank
You," the sound began to fill the church auditorium from their
voices. It had that same familiar ring as the Celestials and
the Smallwood Singers. The voices assembled that night had
instinctively duplicated it. I imagine it was some who had grown
up on the music, as well as those who I had worked with in YAFE
for years and of course the Smallwood Singers. The rest sort of
fell into place vocally and followed suit. The sound was rich, full
and satisfying. I knew I could work with it and even bring it to
another level and I was excited about the possibilities. Creating
a sound is more than the tone or the quality, which of course is
of prime importance. But it's also phrasing, diction, breathing,
approach to vocal placement, blending, approach to vowel
sounds and so much more. The possibilities were limitless and I
had so much to work with. However, in my mind this was still a
temporary group and I hadn't thought much further than that. I
did however need a name and I couldn't come up with anything.
I asked for suggestions from the group members. Lorree Slye

raised her hand and said, "Richard since this whole concept is a vision of yours and it's something new and fresh, why not call us "Vision?" Immediately it clicked. It was simple, straightforward and it encapsulated who we were and the concept of what we were. However, when I look back, it probably was more of God's vision for me, than mine. Again, here was something that had been predestined long before I was born.

I remember the night I taught "Total Praise" and how the Holy Spirit entered our rehearsal. It was just something about that particular song. My god brother passed in December of 1995. I think other than Sully, his was the closest death I had experienced at that point. It hit me hard. Close deaths always seemed to happen around the Vision recordings. Many times, I'd feel that my god brother was close by, checking on me, making sure I was ok. That feeling caused me to write "Angels." The whole concept of me having an Atlanta contingent of Vision just faded away. What I had was enough and I knew it would work. I remember the night I taught "Angels" to Vision. I had this huge boom box that I would carry to each rehearsal and would record the songs after I taught them to Vision that night. I'd come back home and listen to the rehearsal to see how I felt about the song, if I liked it or wanted to change anything about it. I got back to the house, set the boom box on the little glass dinette table right outside my kitchen and pushed the play button. I walked into the kitchen, opened the refrigerator to get me an after rehearsal snack. The rehearsal tape began to play of Vision singing the song that I had taught that night. Their voices rang out "Angels watching over me. Angels watching over me!" All of a sudden I heard the loud distinct sound of someone whistling along with the melody of the song. I stopped in my tracks thinking back to rehearsal. The boom box had been on the piano while Vision was in the choir stand when I taught it. There was no one other than me by the piano, no one in the rest of the auditorium, except for Vision in the choir stand. The whistling was just as loud as the piano as if someone were either standing next to the piano whistling or either someone was standing next to the dinette table whistling along with the play back. It was a happy whistle as if someone liked the song. Honestly, I thought maybe something was going on with my mind. But it was clear, concise and pitch perfect while whistling along in unison with the melody of the song. It lasted maybe for twenty seconds and stopped as suddenly as it had started. I went into the little dining area and listened as the tape continued to play. I heard nothing but the original voices and music. I pressed stop, and then rewound to the beginning where it had begun playing originally. There was no whistle, but just the sound of the voices and the piano. I rewound and started again and again and again with no hint of the whistle. To this today I have no clue who or what it was. First I thought maybe it was my godbrother, Robert, letting me know he had heard the song that was inspired by him. Then I said well "maybe it is an Angel." One thing I do know without a shadow of a doubt: there have been protecting and ministering angels hovering around me all of my life. Maybe they were just reminding me. It in no way was a frightening experience, but it was definitely one of the most fascinating things I've experienced.

We recorded our first CD, "Adoration" in Atlanta, Ga. at the Cathedral of the Holy Spirit where Bishop Earl Paulk was pastor. How ironic that Visions' first CD and the beginning of this new phase in my ministry would be done in my birthplace, Atlanta. Cathedral of the Holy Spirit was a huge and beautiful church. It poured down raining that whole day and I was afraid that no one would show up, but the place was packed. My home church Metropolitan brought an entire bus of members from D.C. People did not only come from Atlanta but from other places as well. My dear friend of many years, Tramaine Hawkins, had a concert in North Carolina and she and Jerome Bell (who was both her road manager and mine at the time) drove all the way down to Atlanta in the driving rain. I remember thinking that maybe the people wouldn't accept a new group. All of my life in the music industry had been with the Smallwood Singers. Would people accept a brand new group, an ensemble at that, one they weren't familiar with? I had gotten Mervyn Warren to create a string ensemble arrangement for the beginning of Total Praise, which was the first song of the night. We took our places in the dark: Vision on risers, me at the piano. I had brought back my good friend Steven Ford to serve as co-producer, MD and organist for the recording. I had brought on an incredible new keyboard player, Tony Walker. Of course, there was also my right hand for many years with the Smallwood Singers, Bryant Pugh. On drums was Garfield Williams, who had also been the Smallwood Singers' drummer, Mark Walker on bass and on guitar Jonathan Dubose who had been on just about every Smallwood Singers album. The string ensemble began to play a classically flavored overture. I began to play the two-bar quarter note figure and Vision sang "Lord I will lift." The sound went through me and continued to the rafters of the Cathedral. It was like I could feel my hair stand on end. By the time they got to "You Are" people had begun to raise their hands in praise. When we got to the "Amen" people were on their feet. On the reprise, everyone was up. I remember it being the hardest thing to move on from that song. I was thinking, "This is only the first song and we've got a long way to go." But I could feel the anointing thick in that place. All I really wanted to do was praise and forget the rest of the concert. But it set the tone for that concert, and it set the tone for that recording. Little did I know, it was setting the tone for the next chapter of my ministry. Later on, Charrisse stepped to the mic and did "Thank You" as God's Spirit filled the place. Carolene who had been with me since 1981 in true Smallwood Singers fashion walked the aisles, singing "Great Day." Maurette and Vanessa delivered the song "Angels" in an incredible duet while the band did an incredible instrumental reprise. I had written a song in honor of my god brother, "I'll See You Again." Tramaine Hawkins who was in the audience and who had just lost her dear mother, joined me on stage for an impromptu duet. She sang it with conviction and fervor like she had known the song all her life. Tramaine's voice has always been phenomenal to me, and one of my favorites. It has such clarity and purity. We ended it with a favorite hymn of mine, "Till We Meet." The recording could not have gone any better and I could not have been more pleased. It was released in 1996 while the Smallwood Singers were in Paris, France performing. "Total Praise" began to take on a life of its own. Even today, it seems like it's still growing and spreading. There are generations that weren't born who are singing it. I am still totally amazed as I travel all over the world. I've heard it done in French, Japanese, Norwegian, Portuguese, Swedish, Samoan as well as other languages. It has to be the most popular song I've done to date. I've heard it done by HBCU bands during halftime and even saw someone do a tap dance to it, which was definitely interesting. I'm honored, humbled and blessed that God used me as the conduit to write it. He was ushering me into yet another new season.

CHAPTER 33

MY GIFT MADE ROOM FOR ME

S oon after, Vision began traveling extensively. People began to request Vision and I more and more as "Adoration"began to gain popularity. In a similar situation as the Celestials going to Montreux, Vision was in Chicago ministering. A man by the name of Carlo Pagnotta was in the audience. He was the head of a festival in Terni, Italy which took place every Easter weekend. My friend, Pam Morris, was assisting him to secure talent for the festival and had invited him to come and hear us. He came backstage after it was over and invited us to be a part of his festival. We were invited, along with Patti Labelle, The Staple Singers and the Mississippi Mass Choir. The festival took care of all expenses for the entire aggregation. It was an incredible experience and it bonded the new group even closer. Maurette was pregnant with her first child, Jaylen. After my scare with Lisa during the Smallwood Singers recording, I was a little nervous about her going, but she insisted. Early on during the tour, we decided to walk from our hotel down to the little village to shop and Maurette went along with us. I'm not sure if it was the walk or what, but immediately upon our return to the hotel Maurette got sick. I really thought she was going to have the baby there in Italy. Thank God there was a doctor who was a part of the Mississippi Mass Choir. He looked out for her until we got back home. He put her on bed rest and I think she only sang once that whole tour. As she says, "Jaylen was almost an Italian citizen." Vision and I would return once again, Easter of the following year; this time with Bobby Jones and the Super Choir, Erykah Badu, and the Thompson Community Singers. On that particular trip, Vision traveled all over Italy doing concerts. The men overseas were always attracted to Carolene and she'd get some of the funniest proposals. While Vision was in Italy and as we exited one of the churches where we performed an excited gentleman who had been in the audience grabbed her and lifted her up in the air. He told her in broken English that he had a farm. I think he was looking for a wife to take care of him and his farm. Her infectious smile, singing gift, and the wonderful way she related to the audience was always an attention getter. It was an awesome time. It was my first time visiting Rome.

In 1996, I received another call from my friend Mervyn Warren in LA. Producer/actor Penny Marshall was doing a remake of the 1947 movie, "The Bishop's Wife." It would be called "The Preacher's Wife," starring Denzel Washington and Whitney Houston. Merv was musical supervisor for the film and it was filled with gospel music, a genre to which Whitney certainly was no stranger. He told me "I Love the Lord" was one of Whitney's favorite songs and one that she had grown up singing in church. It also was a song that she wanted to do in the movie. When I found out… excited is an understatement! One of my songs in a major motion picture sung by one of the greatest singers ever, was a dream I never thought was possible. I love the arrangement that Mervyn did. It stayed true to the original, yet gave room for Whitney to make it her own. Merv kept me up with the process as it was recorded by sending me cassettes and playing sessions over the phone, from scratch vocals to the final mix. It's still one of the highlights of my life. My then road manager Jerome Bell helped put together a DC premiere and sent invites out to all of the major preachers and their wives in the area. The theater was packed. Vision and I performed "I Love the Lord" live, right before the movie began. It was a wonderful and memorable night. As I watched my name roll with the credits at the end of the movie, I began to thank God. He still was doing unexpected and great things. I met Whitney briefly backstage one year when the Stellar Awards were at the Apollo in NY. I am still trying to deal with the loss of such a gift to the world of music. What an incredible loss.

As years went on, I would write for others: "That Name" for Yolanda Adams, who I had known since she was a teenager singing with Southeast Inspirational Choir in Houston, Texas and "Secret Place" for one of my favorite singers, Karen Clark-Sheard. Destiny's Child would record part of "Total Praise" in an Inspirational Medley; Boys to Men would record "I Love the Lord" and Ruben Studdard, "Center of my Joy." I'd work with Jennifer Holiday once again on her CD, "On and On," helping out with keyboards and she'd record one of my tunes on it, "I'll Praise His Name." I'd work with awesome vocalist, Ledisi on her Christmas CD "It's Christmas," writing a tune for it called, "I'll Go." Singer Chrisette Michelle would do a mix tape that contained "Total Praise" and she, Fantasia and Patti Labelle would all add it to their live concerts. I'd do piano accompaniment on Kirk Franklin's song "Don't Cry," a song which he told me had been inspired by me. I would co-write several songs with Earth Wind and Fire legend Philip Bailey as well as help with keyboards for his gospel CD, Family Affair. Last but certainly not least, my friend Valerie Simpson would include "Angels" in her set. I'm just saying how amazing God is and how He will create opportunities for you.

By now, Mom's health had begun to fail even more. Her mind was as sharp as a whip, but her body had started to get weaker. She had raised two sets of foster children to adulthood. Gloria, the very first child, was now grown and married with twin boys and recently separated. We all knew that Mom was not able to continue on in the foster care system that she loved so dearly because of her health. Because I was on the road most of the time and Mom would need someone around to help, it was decided that she would move in with my sister Gloria and her twins. A caregiver would come in while Gloria was at work to assist Mom. It was great because Gloria's apartment was about ten minutes from my house. Around that same time, I began to work on Vision's Christmas project, "Rejoice" which was released during the Christmas season of 1997.

In 1998, I got my first computer. It was a black and white Mac with a small screen. I was fascinated by it and I guess it was my introduction into the world of new technology. Of course, this was before wireless technology and it was hooked up to my phone line. I hadn't gotten a second line yet, so when I was on the Internet, all calls would go directly to voicemail. Not many people had cell phones even though they were in existence. I certainly didn't. Sometimes it would take forever to get online on those early computers and I could go in the kitchen and almost fix a meal while the computer made those strange dial tone sounds struggling to get online. One particular morning I had been online for several hours. When I got off, I discovered that I had several messages from Mom's caregiver. I called the house and found out that when the caregiver had arrived she had found Mom on the floor and she couldn't get up. She called the paramedics, they came and checked Mom out and said she was ok and left. I told her to put Mom on the phone. As soon as I heard her voice, I knew something was wrong. Her speech was slurred very noticeably. She told me she had gotten out of bed that morning to go to the restroom, and had fallen and couldn't get her bearings together. I immediately rushed over to the house. When I saw her, I noticed that her mouth was a bit twisted as well. I called the paramedics immediately. I remember her protesting that she was fine and there was nothing wrong, but when we got to the hospital my worst fear was realized. Mom had suffered a stroke. It was determined that it took place in her brain stem and had affected her left side. I was terrified. This was the most debilitating thing I had ever seen happen to Mom. I wasn't sure what the outcome would be. I remember praying like never before. I would stay at the hospital all day, afraid to leave. I often think even now that if I hadn't been on the computer and if I had been able to respond sooner, maybe it would have affected her less than it did. The stroke never took all of her speech and little by little, with therapy, it began to return to normal. Right in the middle of all of this, Vision had a contracted obligation to do a tour in the UK and France. I didn't want to go and I was afraid to leave her side. One day Mom called me to her side at the hospital. She said, "Richard, you go on overseas. I'm not going anywhere. I'll be here when you get back." I never talked to Mom about her dying. The only thing we used to do was joke when I was younger and I would tell her, "If you go before I do, don't be coming back checking on me, I'll be fine!" I never wanted to seriously think about her dying. I knew that more than likely I'd have to face it one day. But it was almost like if I didn't talk about it, it didn't exist. I know that's living in denial, but honestly it was the only way I could deal with that probability. She sensed my fear. Mom and I were so close, sometimes we knew what the other was thinking or feeling. It was her way of letting me know she wasn't planning on leaving anytime soon. I reluctantly left to do the tour. It ended up being a great one and I was glad that we did it. Even today whenever Vision and I go anywhere, whether it's the States, overseas or up the street, it's the most wonderful time. We are such a close-knit family and we always have a great time when we are together. Honestly, those people are some of the kindest and most loving people anyone could meet. They look after and protect me fiercely. I knew they were all praying for me on that trip and I tried not to show my worry. I remember Vision member, Debbie Steele, coming up to me while we were over there and saying, "Richard, you're worried about Momma aren't you?" Clearly, she could see it in my demeanor. "Yeah, I really am," I replied. She said, "Momma is going to be fine, and she's going to be waiting for you when you get back." I don't know if Debbie even remembers that, but she will never know how much that meant to me nor how it encouraged me while we were over there. I tried to call Mom every day. As long as I have been going overseas, whenever I would call Mom from wherever I was, she would say "Hey baby, how are you? I'm fine, take care" and basically hang up. I'd want to talk to her, let her know what was happening over there and have a conversation. After all, I was paying for it. But she knew that overseas was long distance and she was not trying to stay on the phone. Sometimes I would get the nurse's station and Mom would be going through tests or doing rehab and they would give me an update. Other times, if I did get Mom, you can believe it was a few seconds to reassure me she was fine and then she would abruptly hang up. When we returned to the United States it was decided that Mom would go to a rehab center for a little while. She still couldn't walk, although she had regained some small movement in her left arm and her left leg. Her left hand was still paralyzed. By now she had regained all of her normal speech. I would go up to the rehab center and sometimes go to her sessions with her. Their main goal was to get her to walk. However, Mom seemed to have a fear of falling and seemed to think that any attempt at walking would lead to that. Between the fall that happened a number of years back when she broke her hip, and the fall when she first had the stroke, she froze whenever the therapist would try to get her to take any kind of steps. She was already walking with a walker before the stroke. She would never walk again. The rehab center released her after a while and she went back to live with my sister. By then she needed a hospital bed with bars on the side. Not long after, Gloria and her husband reconciled and they got a big four bedroom house even closer to me. I got an elevator chair installed in Gloria's home where Mom could ride up and down the stairs. Honestly, the stroke seemed to be the beginning of her deterioration little by little.

This same year, I got news that my longtime bass player, Tim Linzy, was in the hospital. I remember talking with him on the phone and I had planned to go visit him. Before I could get to the hospital, he passed. I was stunned. It was so quick and so sudden. Tim was one of the most gifted musicians around. So much of the drum programming and all of the bass arrangements you hear on the majority of the Smallwood Singers projects was Tim. He's even singing on the song "Today" from that same album. He was young and in his prime. I remember rushing back from the road so that I could get to the funeral. I sat there in disbelief. It seemed that so many of my friends were leaving and it hurt badly.

In 1998, we began to prepare for the next Vision project. By now I understood that Vision was definitely going to be a permanent ministry and that God was taking me in a different direction. I remember the Smallwood Singers performing in Venezuela in the mid-nineties. After that, little by little, we stopped performing as Vision's first project "Adoration" got larger and "Total Praise" took on a life of its own. We had begun to minister quite a bit in Detroit at the Straight Gate church pastored by Bishop Andrew Merritt, and where Steven Ford who had co-produced "Adoration" was music director at the time. I decided that's where I wanted to do the next CD. While writing the music for the CD, I received a call from a good friend, Derrick Anderson. He knew that I was writing and asked if I was writing anything on the subject of healing. His mother and father both had transitioned within a period of weeks and his family was devastated. I told him I wasn't working on anything with that theme in mind at the time. He asked would I consider it because they were hurting in a way that they had never experienced before. I remember hanging up the phone and going to the piano to see what I could come up with. As hard as I tried, nothing would come. I got frustrated and went back to working on something else. Again, I would try to come up with something later and still nothing clicked. That same week while asleep, I heard the first part of the song "Healing" in a dream. I can't quite recall what went on in the dream other than the music I heard. I awoke and ran to the piano with tape recorder in hand and put down what I had heard and began to develop it into what became the title song of that next CD, "Healing". Although Darin Atwater and I always kept in touch, I had no idea that he was now orchestrating. When he informed me, I immediately asked him to come on board for that project and not only orchestrate some of the material but compose an overture. Musically he thinks so much like me that

I very seldom had to tell him what I wanted. He always sort of instinctively knew. Since I was going to be doing the lead on "Healing", I asked him to play piano on it. I knew his approach pianistically would be the way that I would have played it. Of course, I brought Steve Ford on again. By now that was a given. He just knew my musical insanity so well, knew how to capture it and was such a joy to work with. With my right hand Bryant Pugh, the amazing keyboard artistry of Tony Walker, the solid bass playing of Mark Walker and Garfield Williams on drums, I knew I wouldn't go wrong. "Healing, Live in Detroit" was released in 1998 with the title song being most people's favorite. "You're Not Alone," "Holy Thou Art God" with Vanessa out front and "Come Before His Presence" with Debbie out front are three that are close to my heart.

By now, Vision was traveling extensively. Sometimes we would fly, other times we would do tour buses. We were on our way to South Carolina on two tour buses and we stopped at a rest stop. We were there for a while, so that people could get food and do whatever they needed to do. Someone came up with the bright idea to have a race while we were waiting. I think it was Darlene. Although I never went out for track in high school, I ran pretty good. So I was down with it. Darlene, Dayle and I decided to be the ones who raced while others looked on. Vanessa was the starter. We assumed our finest starter position as if we were at the Olympics. Vanessa hollered, "On your mark, get set, GO!" I think I must have started off too fast or either my head was heavier than I had originally thought. However, I took about three steps, toppled over and slid about four feet on my knees on the asphalt. As Dayle took off, somehow his shoelaces came loose and the last thing I remember was him tripping and flying through the air next to me. Darlene got tickled, stopped running

384 | TOTAL PRAISE

and ran over to the side of our "track," bent over laughing. I'll never forget while lying there, Garfield my drummer was coming back from the store and just stood over me shaking his head like a disappointed parent. My pant knee was torn out and both of Dayle's knees were scraped as well. I think his shoe was lying over in the grass somewhere. My dear Vision family helped the injured back on the bus. Fortunately, Charrisse found a first aid kit on the bus and tried to doctor up my knee as well as she could. Dayle's toe had begun to swell and he couldn't get his shoe back on. What a sad sight we were that night at the concert. I came hobbling out with a huge knee and Dayle came hobbling out in the tenor section with a bedroom shoe, and a toe twice its normal size. At some point as we were getting ready to sing, "I Will Sing Praises," I quoted the scripture that talks about "the angels lifting us up less we dash our foot against a stone." When I said that, the whole group got so tickled that they could hardly come in when it was time to sing. I officially retired from racing that day!

CHAPTER 34

HOWARD DIVINITY SCHOOL

O pera diva, Kathleen Battle was one of my favorite singers. I had fallen in love with her voice after hearing her along with the incredible voice of Howard graduate Jessye Norman on their CD of Negro Spirituals. I immediately went back and found everything I could that Kathleen had recorded. I was still doing workshops all over the country when I wasn't doing concerts with Vision. I was called to do a workshop in a little town called Portsmouth, Ohio. I would always take Bryant with me to play and take charge of the band. Portsmouth had to be one of the smallest places that I'd been. I remember some of the people who lived there telling me that they didn't have a movie theater and would have to go to the nearest city to go to the movies. But everyone was so friendly and welcoming. I vividly remember the choir I worked with. It was a mixed age group: some teens, some young adults and all the way up to senior citizens. Halfway through the first night of rehearsal, an attractive young lady entered and took a seat in the soprano section. She immediately began to sing the songs, seemingly very familiar with everything we sang. She had a "Healing" songbook with her and something about her drew my attention. She was a dead ringer for Kathleen Battle. I had watched Kathleen on TV shows but had never seen her in person. But this young lady even held her mouth like her when she sang. I couldn't stop staring and remember thinking, *well everyone has a twin*. After the rehearsal, several ladies from the choir approached me saying they wanted me to meet their sister "Kathy." As the young lady began to approach me smiling, I think I went into shock. It was Kathleen Battle, at MY workshop in Portsmouth, Ohio. I found out as they began to explain that this was Kathleen's hometown where she had grown up. Some of her sisters and other family members were a part of the choir. As I shook Kathleen's hand still in shock, she began to explain to me that she was an admirer of my music and had been for a long time. She said when she found out that I was doing a workshop in her hometown, she decided to fly from New York and be a part of it. She then asked if I minded if she sang in the choir and in the concert as well. Did I mind?! I can't tell you how honored and still in shock I was. That evening she told Bryant and I that we needed a home-cooked meal and she took us to her family home. As I sat in the living room still in disbelief, she called Bryant and I in the kitchen. "Come talk to me while I cook," she said. We talked and laughed like old friends as she prepared a wonderful meal. I remember she cooked some amazing salmon that night. That final night she sang in the workshop choir soprano section at the concert. After that workshop in Portsmouth, there were a number of times when Vision and I were in concert in different cities and we'd walk on the stage and Kathleen would be sitting on the front row in the audience smiling. You never know where your music is going or whom it is going to reach.

I remember one of my closest friends was severely depressed. I was so worried about it and wanted to try to get him help. I remember I went on the Internet to find out what direction I could point him in, and they had the list of symptoms or signs of depression. I had a weird sensation in the pit of my stomach as I read them. I had ninety percent of the symptoms. Again, I pushed it to the back of my head. By now, there were times I didn't want to get out of bed, and didn't want to come out of the house. But to me it was just the idiosyncrasies of a creative person. Whatever it was, it seemed to be getting worse.

Because I had two keyboard players with Vision other than myself, it gave me more of a chance to be away from the piano. It seemed like more and more when I would talk on stage, it would launch into a mini sermon. People including my Vision family kept asking, "When are you going to preach?" My pastor knew it as well and he would joke about it to me. I kept saying, "Oh I'm not called to do that." But something in the pit of my stomach was telling me differently, I just didn't want to hear it. I kept saying to myself, "Music is enough." I remember being a part of a symposium at Howard's School of Divinity on the subject of the Minister of Music and the Pastor. At the end of the symposium, Yolanda Adams and Vision did a joint concert at my home church Metropolitan. At the end of the concert, the then-Dean of the School of Divinity, Dr. Clarence Newsome came up to me, shook my hand and asked, "So Richard, when are you coming to Divinity School?" I laughed it off. What in the world was he talking about? But the feeling got stronger even to the point that I would wake up at night and that was all that was on my mind. Finally, at some point I considered going to school. However, I hadn't been to school since 1975 and that had been for music, with which I had no problem. This would be different. I had been out of school for so long. Suppose I didn't do well in my studies? I didn't want people to say, "Richard

Smallwood is in my class but he sure is dumb!" All kinds of crazy
thoughts ran through my mind. I still hated talking in front of
people unless it was an audience during a concert. I'd have to
talk in class! Maybe I'd have to give reports! How was I going
to get through that? I finally decided that I would go and try
a couple of classes and maybe the feeling would go away. If I
went in order to strengthen the lyrics in my music that would
be a great reason. I had to get several letters of recommendation
from preachers to gain admission. One of the letters had to come
from my pastor, Pastor Hicks. I remember thinking, *how am
I going to get this letter from him without hearing him talking
about me preaching?* I approached him at breakfast between
services one Sunday morning. I told him I needed a letter from
him to go back to school. His answer was "Sure Richard, where
are you going to go? What are you going to major in?" I weakly
replied, "Howard's School of Divinity". He laughed at me and
said "Oh really????" I began to explain about how I was going
to learn more about the Word so it would strengthen my lyrics.
He just looked at me laughing. He said, "I want you to come
back and tell me the same thing again after about two years in
Divinity School." I made a mental note to be sure that I did. It
was my story and I was sticking to it. In the winter of 1999, I
entered Howard Divinity School starting with two classes, New
Testament from Dr. Cain Hope Felder and Christian Ethics
from Dr. Cheryl Sanders. When I sat down in Dr. Sander's class
it felt like the world had been lifted from my shoulders. It was
like I was finally home, a place where I was supposed to be, and
a place where I belonged. One of my first assignments in Dr.
Felder's New Testament class was to do an exegetical paper. It
was undoubtedly the hardest thing I had ever encountered in
my life. Imagine my terror after I turned it in. I was one of the

students he called up in front of class to substantiate and explain what I had written. No one but God got me through that. Imagine my surprise when Dr. Felder complimented me on my paper and my presentation. God never sends you to do anything without first equipping you to accomplish the task; that includes taking your insecurities and your fears and working through you in spite of them.

In 2000, I began rehearsals for the next Vision CD, which I wanted to record live in our hometown, DC. On the third rehearsal, one of my altos Joanna Johnson was conspicuously absent. This was strange, because Joanna never missed a rehearsal or a performance unless it was something catastrophic. If something did happen, she would always call. No one had heard from her. I called the next day but didn't get an answer. Joanna was a ten-year cancer survivor and from time-to-time she would testify about it. Joanna was probably six feet tall, a former model and was dressed impeccably to the hilt all the time, complete with stilettos. Even when she had on jeans Jo had on the highest heels she could find. She was a "diva," no questions asked. Other members began to call. She hadn't been to work that week, and neither was she answering her home phone or cell phone. We had a concert not too far from her house that following Saturday and we all were pretty sure she'd be there. However, she didn't show up for that either. This was not like her. Several members got concerned and the next day went out to her house, but didn't get an answer. Finally, while standing outside of her door, and ringing the doorbell, someone called her home number on their cellphone. She finally picked up, but said she was upstairs in the bed. She was too weak to get down the steps. The paramedics were called and they had to knock down the front door to gain entrance. They called me as she was being rushed to the hospital and I got in my car and headed to where she was. The last thing she said to me in ER was, "Did you have enough altos last night?" She was speaking of the concert. I replied "Jo, we were fine, I just need you to get well." She looked at me and said, "Pray for me." The cancer had returned but she hadn't told anyone. After her chemo treatment ten years before, she always said that if the cancer ever came back she wouldn't go through that again. So, she refused treatment and suffered in silence. She never missed a concert except that one the night before she was found sick and unable to function. I remember the doctor saying that sometimes she'd come in and her lungs would be full of fluid. She'd tell him to do whatever he needed to do and get rid of the fluid because she had a plane to catch and had to go and sing with Vision. For how long this had gone on, I'm not sure. Several of us gathered around her bedside after she had been admitted. By the next day, she made her transition. I stood there when the nurse said they were going to remove the life support because she was gone. My mind couldn't comprehend what was happening. I think we were all in shock. Joanna was so full of life and fun. She was a character from her heart. We all loved her dearly. How could she be gone? It didn't make sense. We funeralized her at our home church, Metropolitan, and then again in Dallas, Texas where she was from. It was such a rough time for Vision and we held on to each other tightly trying to deal with the feelings of grief and unanswered questions. I hate the word "replace." I don't think anyone can ever be replaced who was originally meant to be a part of. It took a long time to get over Joanna's death. But years later, I would add another alto to Vision to stand in her stead, an incredible vocalist named Andrea Dumas.

After a while, rehearsals continued. By now I had added an awesome singer and good friend, Ted Winn to the tenor section whom I met through my friend and director extraordinaire, the late Olanda Draper. Ted was also known for amazing recordings with his childhood friend, the incredible Sherri Jones under the name Ted and Sherri. God laid it on my heart to do so, and I knew he would be a tremendous asset. I was in the airport in Washington DC and a little melody began to ring in my head based on the 150th Psalm. I put it down on my phone. It was different, very different. Every other day I'd change a part or rewrite a section. When I finally started teaching it, Vision basically thought I had lost my mind. In fact, one of them jokingly asked me what I was growing in my backyard. It was definitely different. It made no sense to them, and they clearly didn't know where I was going with this. I wasn't sure that I knew either. All I knew is that I couldn't rest until I finished it. Sometimes I would change a whole part that I had written by the next rehearsal and re-teach something entirely different than the previous week. I told them, "Just bear with me y'all, I'm going somewhere." I thought I would name it Anthem of Praise. When I finally finished it, it fit together perfectly. I was bringing Darin Atwater in again to work on the orchestration for the CD and told him I wanted a special kind of introduction to set this song up. Darin came up with the brilliant Procession of the Levites, which fit it to a "T." Of course, Steve Ford was on board as usual. I had planned to redo some of the old standards as well that the Smallwood Singers were known for like "Calvary," "Your Love Divine," and "Psalm 8" as a walk down memory lane. Two of my good friends, Freddye Jackson (not the singer) and Nolan Williams, got with me to write the title song for the project "Persuaded." I wanted to include them in this effort. I was so excited about this upcoming CD. I really felt it was going to be something special. One thing special about it was that, God willing, Mom would be there. She hadn't been able to attend any of the out of town recordings simply because she wasn't strong enough. I prayed that God would give her the strength to make this one in our own city. I don't think I really understood at the time, but by now, dementia had begun to set in, little by little. Sometimes she would tell me things that were so convincing but I knew they weren't true, and it would confuse me. I was in denial. She was getting weaker.

I loved Divinity School. It was challenging but so incredibly interesting. It opened up a whole new world of knowledge and information for me. It had to be one of the best things I have ever done in my life. Certainly, it wasn't easy. I had never read so much or written so many papers. But at the same time, it was all very fascinating. It was harder in that I was still traveling full time, but would try to get home mid-week to attend my classes. I did homework and papers on planes, buses and in hotel rooms. Sometimes, I would have to email my work to my instructors while I was out on the road. Almost every moment of my life during that time, was spent reading and writing. Sometimes we had three or four textbooks for one class. But God allowed it to work out. I started out part-time, but as time went on, I went full-time. I felt like I'd be there forever if I kept taking two classes at a time. I ended up earning A's in every class except for one in which I received a "B". I never expected that. That was nothing BUT God! But when you are in the will of God, He causes things to work for your good. By my second year, I knew that I had to profess my calling. I couldn't run any longer and made an announcement at my church one Sunday morning. No one was surprised. Although everyone was excited and congratulated me, most of my church family's response was "What took you so long?" My pastor, Dr. Hicks, never said I told you so, but he sure was delighted.

My cousins Mike and DeDe, Robert's sons, were grown now. I always wanted to be close to my cousins. I didn't have a large family and they were the only ones I had in DC. Although we would visit each other when Robert was alive and they were small, I never really hung out with my younger cousins. I found out later that Bessie, their grandmother and Robert's mom, didn't want us to be close and told them not to hang around Mom and I. I didn't get it. Why would she say that? She and Mom would talk on the phone monthly for hours. So, I never had a hint that she didn't want them to hang around us. However somewhere around the late 90's we started to get closer. Mike and DeDe looked so much like me that we could pass for brothers. I still didn't get it, because to hear Mom tell it, we were very distant cousins. I loved getting close to my family and would go over for holidays and Rosa would cook. They began to come to my concerts. Their support meant the world to me. Sometimes Mom was even too sick to come to some of the local things as time progressed. To have my family in the audience encouraging me and supporting me was one of the best things in the world. I remember doing a workshop in Durham at North Carolina Central. I got a chance to spend the whole day with Bessie, not long before she passed in 2000. We had the best time together that day.

CHAPTER 35

THE SECRET

I adored my Mom. I loved her and still do more than words could ever express. Because of that, I think it has always been hard to see and accept her humanity. She made mistakes like all of us but she was larger than life to me. I put her on a pedestal of sorts. She did so much good and helped so many people that I never thought much about her having flaws (like each of us). It was 2001 and in several weeks we were scheduled to do the next CD, "Persuaded Live in DC." On this particular day, I was to meet Vision in Indianapolis to do a concert. I stopped by the pharmacy to get a prescription filled before I left for the airport. As I entered the store, I called Mom to let her know I wasn't going to be able to come by and see her before I left, but would come and check on her as soon as I returned. She understood but she seemed to be rambling a bit. All of a sudden, she said to me, "Richard when a woman gets to be around 19 years old, she has certain needs." I didn't know how to respond. My first reaction was, "*man that dementia must have really set in.*" But then I thought, "is she trying to tell me about the facts of life at *my* age?" She continued, "But he never touched me." I had no idea what she was talking about. "Mom, what are you talking about?" I asked. "He never touched me," she repeated. "Who never touched you Mom??" She replied, "Rev. Smallwood." I was entirely clueless and was trying to piece together what in the world she was saying. Little by little, I surmised that she was trying to say that she was never intimate with my father. Clearly, Mom's mind was confused. So, I sort of jokingly said, "Well Mom, he had to touch you at least *one* time, or I wouldn't be here." "He's not your father," was her reply. By now, I was standing at the pharmacy counter and the pharmacist was saying something to me. I could see his mouth moving, but I couldn't hear anything he was saying. I turned and walked out of the store; it seemed like everything was spinning around me.

"What are you talking about Momma?????" I asked, when I was finally able to speak.

"He's not your father, Richard."

By now I was sitting in my car in the parking lot. I know I must have been in shock, because it seemed like I was in a dream. Even now as I look back, there are parts I can't recall. "What do you mean he's not my father, Momma?" She just kept repeating, "He's not your father. I'm so sorry Richard." I remember asking, "Well WHO is my father, then?" I honestly don't remember her answer. She was being really vague by then and it seemed like she was rambling. I can't remember how she responded. The next thing I remember was telling her I'd see her when I got back. I don't remember the ride home. I don't remember the ride to the airport. I just remember that when I got on the plane, I broke down. I remember I had on sunshades fortunately, but I couldn't stop crying. It's like everything I thought I was, I was not. It was like someone had pulled the very foundation out from under me and I was falling headlong into some kind of chasm. Who was I? My life had been a lie. Why was she just telling me now? Maybe she was just having a dementia episode. But there was a sick feeling in the pit of my stomach, a part of me knew she was telling the truth. All of my childhood I felt like something was wrong; something that I just couldn't put my finger on when it came to Rev. Smallwood. I remember thinking when I was a kid, *I wonder if I'm adopted.* But when I looked at Mom and looked at all her relatives, I knew there was no way that was true. We all looked like carbon copies of each other. At the same time, when I looked at my father and all of his relatives, I didn't resemble anyone. None of his family ever made me feel like I wasn't a part, and they always treated me like family. I never got anything but love from them, but something was not quite right. It was like I was in a dream. I had to talk to someone. Once I arrived in Indianapolis and got to sound check, I pulled one of my members, Sharon, aside. I can't remember how I told her, but I basically told her the whole story as much as I knew. Sharon has one of the most compassionate spirits ever. She immediately said I needed to talk to a counselor/therapist. She said she would reach out to a mutual friend of ours who was an assistant minister at my home church. Dr. Carolyn Francis was a grief counselor and conducted a class called "Good Grief" which was probably the largest class at our church at the time. She had counseled us as a group when Joanna passed and had been such a help to us. She was also a licensed therapist and a psychiatric nurse. I respected her greatly. That night when it was time to go on stage, I kept praying, "Lord, help me get through this concert." I didn't want to do it, but I had to pull myself together and minister. I can't remember the concert. I do remember the beautiful young ladies of the group Virtue opened up for us. I remember coming off the stage. It was a very high stage, with steep wooden steps going down the back. I remember coming down the steps and feeling the tears coming back. If I could only get backstage to the green room. By the time I got to the green room door, the tears were uncontrollable. By that time, I didn't much care who saw it. I remember there was some man with a camera who kept snapping pictures while I was walking. I remember my road manager Jerome telling him not to take another picture. The man could see that I was upset about something. Why would he invade my privacy like that? By the time I got to my seat, Sharon had Carolyn on the phone. I think Sharon had given her a sort of heads up as to what was going on with me. I tried explaining on the phone as much as I could, but I just couldn't keep it together. She told me to come see her the minute I got back home and we would talk. That whole day or so is a blur in my mind and my memory only holds bits and pieces. I was in a very dark place. It was like being in a well and not being able to climb out of it.

The first thing I did when I returned home was to go see Mom. She reiterated what she had told me previously, that Rev. Smallwood was not my father. "Mom," I asked, "Who is my father?" She again got very vague and said that it had been many years ago, it was something that she was very ashamed of and that she couldn't remember many of the details. I remember not understanding how one could forget who fathered your child. She began to tell me the story of Smallwood; that he was a pedophile when she married him. She told me the horror of sometimes having to leave town to get away from the authorities or the parents of whatever little girl he had molested. She told me of a loveless marriage where she was little more than a trophy wife, never touched. She said sometimes she just wanted to be held. That never happened. She said all of the many years they were married he was never intimate with her. There was no affection in their 35 years of marriage. She told me she never was in love with him. She cared for his wellbeing but that's where it ended. She told me how relieved she was when he passed. She told me of him being in the newspaper more than once for molesting little girls and how ashamed she was.

"Why didn't you leave?" I asked. She said she had nowhere to go. She was embarrassed to return home. Everyone in the family knew about him. It had even been in the papers down there. She had no money. She said even my Uncle Joe, Smallwood's brother, told her he would pay her bus fare back to Durham, because he knew that his brother wasn't right. I definitely believe there was emotional abuse although I never saw physical abuse. She said that he never hit her, but I would see him lash out at her the same way he did with me. Only with me, it would go further and end in beatings. But abuse is abuse. I think of the women in physically abusive marriages who won't leave, but stay to be subjected to the abuse over and over again. I think it was the same situation with Mom. I don't think she could leave. How did she live that unhappily all of her life and I never saw a sign of it? She always had a smile. She was always helping, loving and caring for others. I never saw her depressed and I lived with her. As a child, I was probably with my Mom more than I was with anyone else on the planet. I never saw a clue. She had become an expert in hiding it. How many lives had he ruined? I knew he was a very sick man. However, I was furious with him. She asked me did I remember one particular incident when we were visiting Durham when I was very small. We were sitting in my Uncle Clea's backyard. I ran over to Smallwood to climb up in his lap and he pushed me away and said, "Get on away from me. You're not my child." I think I had buried it in my mind. But as she began to tell me, the memory started to resurface. It was as if I was reliving something that I had buried so long ago.

I believe it was the beginning of him planting the seeds in my psyche of not being good enough, not being wanted, not feeling accepted, anxiety and every insecurity that I've ever dealt with. I also believe that that hurt caused me to want to write songs for people who are hurting years later. I knew the pain of rejection firsthand. I remembered running to Mom telling her what he had said about not being his. She told me not to pay him any mind, and not to listen to anything he said. The pain hit me just as it had when I was a small child on the day it happened. I still feel it at times today. I knew so many of the beatings had to do with his resentment of me, which in some way I always felt. I just thought he resented me at times because she and I were so close and he and I had no similar bond or connection. But it went much deeper than that. I wasn't his. I'm not even sure if he knew whose I was. Mom never said, and the strange thing is that his name is on my birth certificate as my father. I was never adopted by him. What did he know? What didn't he know? If they were never intimate, he had to know that I wasn't his. At any rate, he was angry about me being someone else's and he took it out on me. I was an innocent kid who had no control over how I got here. I started to become furious all over again as I thought about the way he would beat me for no reason. I was furious about what he subjected her to those many years and the humiliation she felt. I now had all this anger and nowhere to put it. He had been dead for thirty years. Where could I even take it? Where could I put it? I couldn't go to him and "have it out." He was dead. Now all the moving around that they did began to make sense. Some of it, I believe, was him running away from the sexual abuse he had done in those different cities and dragging Mom and me with him. Mom even told me that she believed that his daughter Dorothy Jean's alcohol addiction came from him sexually abusing her as a child. I'm not sure if she was surmising or if she had some factual information. If she did, she never told me. Later I would find out that he married one of his wives, Mable Harvey, when she was 15 years old in 1920. Certainly people married much younger back in the day, but with his problem, it made me wonder. I wasn't sure how old the other wives were. Mom told me that when they went into foster care, she took Smallwood to the side and told him this was something that she had always wanted to do, but if he ever touched any of those kids, she would kill him. Thank God that he didn't. I think she meant it. I tried steering her back to the question of who my father was. She kept being evasive and honestly it seemed like she couldn't remember much about it and that she had put it out of her mind many years ago. I still didn't understand how someone could forget something that important. After I continued to badger her about who he was, she finally said it was a pastor in Detroit. I asked his name, but she couldn't remember. When she and Smallwood moved to Detroit, she became so love-starved that she had an affair with a pastor who lived in the same complex as them. As a result, she became pregnant with me. Finally, after really pressing her to try to remember, she said that his last name may have been Colvin. She wasn't sure. At least that would give me something to go on. I asked her did anyone else know this. She said her family didn't and neither did his family. Everyone thought that Smallwood was my natural father. I wasn't entirely sure of that. There had always been questions on the minds of even my friends when I was growing up about him. I was determined to find my real father or at least his relatives. I left that day feeling like the wind had been knocked out of me. Soon after, I would begin seeing Carolyn my therapist weekly and she began to help me through this incredible situation. But the darkness got heavier. The only thing that kept me going was that in a couple of weeks I had a recording scheduled to do. Vision was ready and had the songs down. The band would be coming in the following week to rehearse. Darin had put together an orchestra that would be playing throughout the whole recording. People were coming from everywhere. I had friends who were coming from all over the United States as well Paris, France, Guadeloupe and other countries. I remember calling several close friends and telling them what was going on. I called my manager Roger and his wife who have been so dear to me down through the years and told them. But the majority of the people I knew didn't have a clue. Most didn't know what I was going through. I began searching Ancestry.com looking for Colvins in Detroit who lived there around the time I was born or at least conceived. But I kept running into a brick wall. Things were not adding up. I had well-meaning friends who told me not to worry about it and that God was my father. I knew that, but I wanted to know where I came from. I became frustrated and I didn't want to be around anyone. I'd stay in the house unless I had rehearsals or had to check on Mom. My feelings about her fluctuated from *why did she wait this long to tell me*, to *maybe I wasn't ready to know before now*. She kept apologizing to me, sometimes on the verge of tears. Honestly it didn't bother me that Smallwood was not my father. Somewhere inside there was a bit of relief. My issue was the shock of not knowing the truth and the mystery of who my father really was. I remember telling her, "Mom, however I got here, I was meant to be here. You've seen me grow up. You've seen what God has done with my life. You've seen my calling come into fruition. There is no question that I'm supposed to be doing what I'm doing. I had to come through somebody. It had to be God's permissive will that I came the way that I did." I believe this to be true, but it didn't seem to console her and some days she would be so upset. She told me she kept praying for God's forgiveness as if it had just happened. My response was that she was going to have to work hard on forgiving herself. I don't think she ever did.

Rehearsals began for the band. The recording would take place at Jericho City of Praise, where the late Dr. Betty Peebles was the pastor. We rehearsed the band there as well. Halfway through the rehearsals I began to think about canceling the recording. I didn't think I could go through with it. I had very little energy. It was a struggle to even come out of the house to rehearse. Steven Ford took charge of everything. I was going through the motions. By now, my old drummer from the Smallwood Singers, Jeff Davis had come on board as drummer for Vision. The other musicians, Mark Walker our bass player, Bryant Pugh of course on keyboards and Tony Walker on keyboards had all assembled. Jonathan Dubose, one of the "baddest" guitarists anywhere and who had been on most of my projects, was on board as well. Also, two other major gifts were added: Mike Pugh who played guitar with us on the road as well as drummer Warren Jones who played for Vision from time to time. The band was kicking! Steve's arrangements were brilliant and Darin had outdone himself on the orchestration. Still I just couldn't seem to get into it and continued to go through the motions daily. On the day of sound check, I remember telling God, "I can't do this. How can I get out of it?" It was too late. Everything was in motion. The record execs from my label were arriving. My manager was there. The new outfits had been made. Everyone was excited... except me. Jericho City of Praise holds 10,000 people. The overflow holds about 5,000. The night of the recording, people had to be turned away. I hadn't done a live recording at home since the Smallwood Singers did the live session at Howard in '92. I certainly hadn't done anything like that here since "Total Praise" had hit. The place was packed, including overflow. I remember standing backstage for prayer with everyone and thinking this was all too much. I was afraid that I would break down in the middle of some song and ruin everything. My emotions were like a roller coaster. I was hurt, I was still in shock. I was furious with Smallwood and some days I was even angry with Mom. I never knew how I was going to feel from one moment to the next. How could I even concentrate? I remember hearing the first bars of "Procession of the Levites" as Vision began to file out on stage. I had a musical cue for when I was supposed to walk out. Honestly, I was so out of it, I missed the cue and came out too late and the band had to repeat a bar as opposed to going directly into "Anthem of Praise" while I got into place. However, when I finally walked out on that stage, the love in that room hit me in the face. Mom and some of my foster brothers and sisters were on the front row. My cousins, Rosa, Mike and Dede and Dede's children (my little cousins Rob and Robyn) were directly behind Mom. My church family was all over the place. There were friends and loved ones everywhere and of course supporters who had been there for me down through the years. It was like the love and the energy swept me up and I forgot all about what was going on with me personally. I had one desire that night, and that was to minister like I had never ministered before. God showed up in that place. Vision sang like I had never heard them sing before. There was a spirit of worship and a sense of freedom in that church. It seemed like each song went higher and higher in terms of God's presence. The shout from that night after "Calvary" is probably one of the most popular shout videos on

YouTube. That's an edited abbreviated version. We shouted and praised for a while that night. I knew it was God who was taking me through it. I couldn't have done it myself. He just took over and did what He does so well.

The hardest thing that night for me was to play the piano solo. One of Mom's favorite hymns is "It Is Well." I did a little medley of "It is Well" and "Come Ye Disconsolate." When I got to the chorus of "It is Well," I heard Mom holler "Thank you!" I knew that sound too well. When she was younger and I was a kid she would holler like that and run all around the church, laughing and clapping her hands praising God. All the kids would laugh at me and point and say, "Your Momma is shouting" and I'd be so embarrassed. But I didn't understand when I was little. I didn't know what my Mother was going through. I hadn't a clue as to what she was dealing with. I didn't understand how God was sustaining her through it all. Now she couldn't run anymore as she was in a wheel chair. But her voice was still loud, strong and clear: "THANK YOU." It's like when she began to shout, something connected between she and I. The words "It is Well" had a new meaning. I believed she finally was releasing what she had been holding all those years and it was all right. It was well with her soul. It was like she was thanking God for bringing her through every heartache, every burden and every hard time that she had ever experienced. I had my eyes tight shut through the whole solo and I could feel the tears starting to well up under my eyelids. The more she shouted, the more the tears began to burn. I knew that if one tear escaped my tightly shut eyes and rolled down my cheek, it would be over. I wasn't crying because of what I'd been going through, but because I felt a release in my Mom and I was rejoicing in my spirit for HER. I started to pray, "Lord hold back the tears and please let me finish this solo." I knew if I lost it then, there wouldn't be any coming back. Thank God I did make it through and I think my absolute favorite part of that recording happened. The whole church erupted into that old hymn, "It is Well" like it was Sunday morning. I remember not only seeing the tears in Mom's eyes through the tears in my eyes, but in dear Dr. Peebles' eyes as well, as she lifted her hands in praise. There is something about that hymn that touches me like no other. It was a long night, but it was a blessed night and I know that it was God that brought me through it.

CHAPTER 36
THE DARK CLOUD RETURNS

On September 11, 2001 I was lying in bed and watching the "Today Show." Matt Lauer's interview with an author was suddenly interrupted as America watched a plane slam into one of the towers of the World Trade Center in New York City, soon followed by another which slammed into the other tower. At one point, I remember feeling my house shake, like from an explosion. I panicked thinking that we were being bombed. Moments later I realized from the news that the Pentagon had just been hit. Our country was never the same. Our world was never the same. Not long after, I stood in a room in NY singing with artists like Diana Ross, Roberta Flack, Chaka Khan and many other legendary artists and actors. Spike Lee and Nile Rogers directed a video called "We Are Family." The lyrics of the old Sister Sledge tune were changed into a cry of solidarity, unity and standing together fearlessly as we faced the worst case of terrorism that the US had ever experienced. Later I stood at the ruins of the Trade Center, a mass of twisted metal still smoldering and smoking. A strange smell of smoke and death hovered in the air. Photos of missing loved ones and signs of "Have you seen this person?" hung all over the city. People were walking around Penn Station with big posters around their necks with photos of loved ones and numbers to call if they were spotted. It was such a devastating time.

I continued my search to find information on my father, but to no avail. Sometimes when I'd go see Mom, she'd ask me was I still doing research to try to find him. I told her I was. She didn't say much else about him. I noticed that her mind had started to deteriorate even more as time went on. Sometimes she would be just as lucid and clear as when she was younger. Other times she would seem confused and would imagine things that weren't happening. Once she told me that my sister and her family came and took her whole bed with her in it, carried it down to the basement and she slept down there and she hated it. She said before I got there they hurriedly brought it back up to her bedroom. I started to learn how to humor her and go along with the things that she was imagining. The deterioration was hard for me to deal with. I got to the point that I didn't want to talk about my father situation anymore. I guess I buried it in the back of my mind and I stopped going to therapy. Vision continued to tour extensively and "Anthem of Praise" blew up. After the haphazard way in which I wrote it, I never thought it would. School got even harder and sometimes I wondered was I going to make it all the way through while balancing my travel schedule. However, God has a way of bringing things to pass that He has preordained. In 2002, I delivered my initial sermon at my home church, Metropolitan. It was called "There Is Something About A Song" or "How To Survive A Babylon Experience." I remember being incredibly nervous. I was not used to speaking in front of an audience without a band and singers behind me. I had no idea how I would do it alone, and on top of that, I had to exegete a text in front of a crowd of people! However, God never sends you without equipping you, and honestly it felt as natural as doing a concert. My mom was on the front row beaming proudly along with my family, my church family and my Vision family and friends from as far back as my childhood. I relaxed and it all began to feel so natural, like it was something that I'd done forever. That night I received my license to preach. My pastor seemed very proud and that meant a lot to me. I had received so much from him down through the years. Even though I was taught in Divinity school, I really learned how to structure a good sermon by listening to Pastor Hicks. He influenced me greatly.

In the summer of 2002, my dear friend Freddye Jackson with whom Nolan and I had written "Persuaded," had an aneurism while at rehearsal preparing for his upcoming live project with his group, Agape. He only lived for about a week after he was stricken. I went to the hospital and talked to him every day. I encouraged him to fight although he couldn't respond. I prayed that he would pull through. He was young and only in his thirties. When he made his transition, I was devastated. To have Joanna pass before the recording and then Freddye to pass not long after its release was too much to bear. I needed to deal with Freddye's death and still process my father's situation, so I got back into therapy. I began to get frightened. The depression had gotten worse and by now I had been officially diagnosed with clinical depression. I had suffered with it for so long that I don't think I ever admitted it to anyone. Some days, I didn't want to live any longer, but I was too afraid to end my life. I became preoccupied with death and that's all I thought about for days at a time. I'm really not sure how I did so well in school. But it seemed that school took my mind off of everything. I was happiest when I was on stage. The moment I walked off stage, my world would come crashing in around me. As it got progressively worse, my therapist recommended medication. I didn't want to because I had heard so many horror stories about it, so initially I refused to. I was ashamed about it and I didn't want anyone to know. I remember telling my psychiatrist (whom I saw once a month in addition to my therapist) if I could sing about healing, then how could I be depressed like this? I felt like a hypocrite. How could I tell others about God's healing power and be so messed up myself? My psychiatrist who also was a minister answered, "Richard, as God told Paul about the thorn in his side, my grace is sufficient. That didn't stop God from using him nor did it keep Paul from encouraging and ministering to others." Depression is a sickness just like any other kind of disease. Mine was genetic and environmental. I was told that depression was nothing more than anger turned inward. I remembered times when I would get so angry with Smallwood for beating me as a child, but I couldn't say anything; so I would retreat to music, to my room, to my own little fantasy world. That's how I learned to cope. But it didn't take away the anger. Therapy helped me to learn who I was and why I reacted certain ways, and why I coped in certain ways. However, the depression still got worse. I never let Mom know, because I didn't want to upset her. She was still having issues with forgiving herself and I didn't want her to think that she had anything to do with what I was dealing with. It would only add to her problems. Holidays had always been very special to Mom. But now she seemed to be just a shell of herself. Her excitement over Thanksgiving and Christmas seemed to fade. Whenever we opened gifts for Christmas she would smile, but it seemed her eyes were far away…almost as if she was only partly there. For many years, Mom was the cook, of course, and all would gather at the old house for Thanksgiving dinner. After she moved in with Gloria, we would all pitch in together. I'd usually do the vegetables. My foster sister Joy would sometimes do the turkey or ham. I'm sure my family remembers the year that I got bold and decided to do the turkey. When we cut into it, it was partially raw. That was my last attempt at cooking a turkey. Another foster sister, Bernice, made the best mac & cheese and potato salad. We'd all pull together and try to make it the best one we could. But it just wasn't the same anymore. Although Mom was there, she almost seemed to be another person. Two of my best friends, Mark Hubbard and his brother Reggie Staggers, would have huge Thanksgiving dinners in Chicago. Reggie is one of the best cooks around and people came from far and near for his home cooking. I'd have dinner with Mom and the family. We'd put her to bed and then I'd catch the last flight out to Chicago to have dinner with them, just to get away from all of the pressure. On Christmas and New Year's, I'd end up at dinner at my cousin Rosa's, which I still do as well. A couple of times, I took Mom over there for dinner. She kept saying, "Richard I'm so glad you're close to your family now." I think she knew she wouldn't be here much longer and wanted to make sure I had my family around me after she was gone.

It was 2003 and by now, other than school and ministering, the depression was affecting every other part of my life. When I didn't have to travel, many times I would just stay in bed. It was even a struggle to go see Mom as much as I loved her. It was a struggle to get to the airport. But it was something about seeing my Vision family that always lifted my spirits. Once I was out on the road, I was fine. But the minute I walked in my front door it all would come back. I knew I had a depression issue, but there was something about that house that added to the depression. It was something spiritual, something that pushed me even further down in that black hole. By now, my record company started pushing me to think about the next recording. But I just couldn't do it. I didn't have the energy. I didn't seem to have the creativity. I just wanted to be left alone. My good friend, Joseph Burney who was the head of A and R at Verity, flew in to see about me. I think he sensed something was wrong from our conversations on the phone. I remember we met at the Cheesecake Factory. I was still embarrassed to tell anyone I had a depression problem so without calling it by name, I began to tell him a little about what I was going through. Joseph seemed to understand and sense what was going on without me actually coming out and saying it. He immediately came up with a suggestion. Instead of me recording something new, we would do a Praise and Worship compilation CD. They assembled all of the praise and worship songs I had done since the Smallwood Singers' second album up until the last Vision project and put out the CD that year along with a video/DVD and called it "The Praise and Worship Songs of Richard Smallwood." As time went on, I started to become concerned about my random thoughts to do something drastic to myself. I actually felt like one day, I might do something. The feeling of wanting to end it all began to increase. The more time passed, the more tired I became. Not long after, I finally consented to the antidepressants. For several months, I went through side effects from them. After several weeks of being on the medication, they started to kick in. I must say that it made a world of difference in my life. It made life easier to live. It never made me "high" or anything like that, nor did it make me sluggish or unaware of what was going on around me. It never affected my creativity. After the initial side effects wore off, it was as if I wasn't taking anything. The only thing was that I didn't go into those deep, dark seemingly never-ending periods. There were times when the depression would hit, but it would be very brief and didn't last for long periods of time. But I could manage it. I continued with my therapy as well as with my psychiatrist.

So many people suffer with this. But it's something the church doesn't talk about. They'll tell you "let Jesus fix it" and pray for you. Don't get me wrong, God CAN fix it, and prayer is absolutely essential. But also, sometimes we need people that God has given the ministry of counseling and therapy to help us just like we need doctors for other ailments. Sometimes we even may need medication just like we need meds for hypertension, high cholesterol or acid reflux. Because it has such a stigma attached to it, that one is possessed or somehow crazy, people don't want to talk about it or own up to it. But it's a sickness. Mental illness is real! There can be physical causes in the brain that can trigger it. We are finding out so much more about it now than years ago. That's one of the reasons why I wanted to talk about it in this book. It can happen to anyone, from any walk of life, from any background, as well as from the church door to the pulpit.

CHAPTER 37

REVELATION

It was 2004 on New Year's Day. I celebrated with my cousins. By now we were all so close that I decided it was time to tell them about my father situation. I was sure that they were under the impression that Smallwood was my natural father. But they were family and they needed to know the truth. Rosa cooked and we all had a ball eating, talking and laughing. I remember that Mike, DeDe and I were sitting in Rosa's living room. I told them I needed to talk to them about something. I took a deep breath and began to tell them the story that Mom had shared with me. I told them about my father being someone whose last name was possibly Colvin, but I couldn't figure out who he was exactly. When I finished the story, the room was deathly quiet. For a minute, no one said anything. Rosa's head was bowed. When she looked up, it seemed like she had tears in her eyes. I went on to explain that I didn't mean to upset her. She looked at me and I'll never forget these words. She said, "Richard, do you want to know who your father really is?" I didn't know how to respond. I had gotten up the nerve to tell them the whole story so I had just told her who my father was! I don't think I responded one way or the other. Rosa simply said, "They say that your cousin Rivers is your father."

As I look back, I knew there was something I wasn't being told. There was always something unfinished hanging in the air. However, I was again in a state of shock and at the same time trying to process everything. Rivers was Bessie's brother. He was not one of the relatives I remember seeing a lot growing up. But I do remember seeing him every now and then, but at a very young age. I don't even remember him having any kind of interactions with me as a child from the few times I saw him. All I kept saying as Rosa relayed the story was, "*What?!*" She said when she married my cousin Robert (who is Bessie's son), Lula took her to the side and began to explain about all the family secrets. According to Lula, Mom and Rivers had fallen in love when they were teenagers. They were the same age but Rivers was two months older. Because of the shame connected to Lula's father and my mother's father being the same white man, James Cain (the former slaver and plantation owner), nobody knew they were half-sisters. The Cains had owned our family at least from the middle 1700's. How many slaves and former slaves he had fathered, I'm sure no one knows. Lula and the family were all supposedly very distant cousins, almost not cousins at all.

I was tired of speculation. It was Rivers and that was settled.

I wonder did my grandfather know the real truth, or did he think Mom just ran off and got married? Did he know about Mom and Rivers? I had also heard a rumor later that it may be one of the reasons why he committed suicide. His only child and the light of his life had been sent off to marry a pedophile. One thing that bothers me up until this very day is this question: *why didn't Mom tell me the whole story?* I knew she didn't want to go to her grave having me think Smallwood was my real father. Why not tell me the rest of it? Had dementia sat in so bad, that part of her memory had been affected, or was she just too embarrassed to tell me? I found out recently that Mom had shared the complete story a number of years before with my play sister Ollie, complete with telling her that her cousin was my father. It seemed like she was trying to get up the nerve to tell me, because she had shared it with a couple of my foster sisters as well. But she only told Ollie who my father really was: her cousin. Now my dilemma was, should I mention what I found out about Rivers to my Mom? I didn't know what to do now. My cousin DeDe and little Rob his son and I even drove to Durham to try to press my cousin Olivia for more info. The only thing she would say is that Rivers and your Mom loved each other very much. On the drive back DeDe kept saying, "Olivia isn't telling you everything, I think there is more to this story." I had no idea just how correct he was. There was never a feeling of relief for me after hearing this story. It just led to more questions and it led to me feeling more confused than ever about the whole thing. Something was missing. It reminded me of the way I felt about Smallwood when I was growing up. I couldn't put my finger on it, but it just didn't seem like everything was being told.

That same year I realized that the responsibility of taking care of Mom was just too much for Gloria who was raising three boys as well. Although we had help coming in, they left after Gloria got home from work. Mom had to be bathed and changed and it was hard. I never wanted to put her in a nursing home. That was something I'd said I would never do. I began to pray to ask God to make a way where Mom could be completely cared for, and that her every need would be met. I prayed for somewhere where she would have around the clock care, all day and all night; where there would be doctors and nurses standing by, should she need them. I wanted her to have the best of care. I had to do a paper for one of my classes in Divinity School on how the African American church could better support institutions like senior citizen homes, hospitals, nursing homes, prisons and places of that nature. I had a dear friend Rev. Annie Lanier who was an assistant minister at my church and also served as chaplain at the Washington Home (a nursing home in upper northwest Washington DC). I called and asked her if I could interview her for my paper. When I walked into the home it was like walking into a hotel. It was beautiful and spotless. Annie took me around to some of the different rooms where the residents lived. Everything was immaculate. There were no urine smells. The staff seemed alert and on top of everything. There was a beauty parlor, a physical therapy center, all kinds of recreation and the food in the cafeteria was great. Several weeks later I approached Annie about the possibilities of getting Mom in. She referred me to the person in charge of admissions. When they told me the cost to secure a spot for Mom there, I almost choked. Surely, I would have to dip into my savings to make this work. However, nothing was too expensive for Mom. I didn't care what it cost me. I was also informed that there was a waiting list probably about a year out. That certainly didn't sound good. I had looked at other places and honestly, I would have been nervous about my dog staying at those other places. They were run down, dirty and it pained me to see that people were living there in those conditions. I began to pray harder. Within a week, I got a call out of the clear blue sky that they had a spot for Mom. I was elated. I knew God was moving. While going over Mom's insurance information with admissions we found out that Mom's insurance and social security would cover everything and we didn't have to pay a dime. I knew this was from God. I immediately remembered the verse of scripture that says, "I've never seen the righteous forsaken nor his seed begging bread." Mom moved in within several days. We took her favorite recliner, her TV, her radio, her VCR and CD player and she was set. I blew up pictures of her mother, her father, of me and of all the children she had raised including all of my friends that she considered her children and put them on her wall. I must say that they really took care of my Mom well. She was comfortable and she loved it. I was there almost every day when I was in town. Of course, the dementia would affect her mind at times, but that same loving spirit that everyone knew never left, and the staff loved her.

Mom loved the Easter season. Every year she would ask me to bring her an Easter basket. I would go get a basket, get the artificial grass and fill it with all kinds of chocolates and those marshmallow peeps that she loved so well. When I gave it to her she became just like a child, tearing into the basket seeing what she could find. Not too long after Easter I went up to the home to see her. As I entered the room, I could see fear in her eyes and she was talking to something or someone in the chair across from her bed. When she saw me, she looked at me and said, "Do you see that?" pointing to the vacant chair. "What Mom??" I asked. She said, "In that chair," pointing frantically. I saw nothing. I began to think it was the dementia kicking in. However, I didn't feel like playing along with Mom that particular day and I said, "Mom there is nothing there." She looked at me and I could sense anger in her, because I didn't see it. She said, "Richard I'm not crazy! I know what I see!" I looked in her eyes. They were clear and she seemed as rational as if she had been years younger. But I saw the fear on her face. I continued to insist there was nothing there. I asked her to describe what she saw to me. What she said terrified me. She said it was a snake, but it had the huge head of a cat, it had little cat's teeth but the tongue was extremely long. It was looking at her and the tongue was darting in and out. I went out into the hall and called the nurses to see if they had given her any kind of new medications. Mom couldn't take certain medications or else she would hallucinate. They assured me that all of her medications were the same and nothing had been altered. I went back in the room and now Mom's eyes were filled with terror as she fixed her eyes on the chair. To prove to her that there was nothing there, I thought I'd sit in the chair. As I approached the chair, she screamed, "Don't sit there Richard, Don't sit there!!!!" Trying to prove that I was right, I sat down in the chair. The Easter basket now mostly empty was sitting on the floor next to me. "It just jumped down into that Easter basket," she exclaimed. "Can't you hear the grass making noise? It's moving around in the grass!" Something immediately spoke to my heart and said, "PRAY!" I got up and went over to her bedside and I began to pray. I rebuked every spirit that was not of God in that place and covered her and her room with the blood of Jesus. When I finished and opened my eyes, her eyes were calm. She looked at me and smiled, "Thank you baby," she said. "It's gone!" For a while I thought it might have been dementia, but something deeper was telling me that it was not.

The spring of that year, I graduated with honors from Howard's School of Divinity with a 3.8 GPA. It was nothing but the grace of God. We got Mom there for the ceremonies. It was a beautiful sunny and warm spring day and she had a front row seat on the Divinity School campus. She had seen me through a countless number of graduations, concerts, recitals, and award ceremonies and was still there to support me through yet another milestone. The picture that she and I took after graduation is my favorite of all times. In June, I was officially ordained as a minister at my home church, Metropolitan. Mom was there as well. There were many times when I'd go up to Washington Home to see her, and I tried to find a way to bring the Rivers story up. But I'd always lose my nerve. I didn't want to upset her. She seemed so frail and I knew she was wrestling with forgiving herself. I didn't want her to get upset with Rosa for telling me, so I remained silent about it. I even went as far as asking her more about Rivers one day. We had a lot of family pictures, but there were never any pictures of him. I'd never seen any. I never saw any in Durham of him as well. I asked her why. She wouldn't say more than she didn't know and that they were close and great playmates when they were kids. Her eyes seemed to search mine to figure out what I was thinking or driving at. I let it go.

On January 12, 2005, Mom turned 90 years old. I planned an elaborate birthday celebration at the Bea Smith restaurant. I gathered as many of the children that she had raised as I could find, rented out a room and invited many of her friends. She went to the beauty parlor at the home and got her hair done in this elaborate up-do. She put on one of her favorite dresses and she was dressed to the hilt! She wasn't strong enough to blow out the candles on her birthday cake, but my sister Gloria did it for her. We had an incredible time that night. It's a memory I'll always cherish.

I had been playing with a concept for the next project where I would bring some of my favorite artists together along with Vision for a big live concert in NY. I wanted to call it "Journey" because everyone there would have something to do with my musical journey up until that point. I had considered Kathleen Battle, Roberta Flack (my 8th grade music teacher), Aretha Franklin, The Clark Sisters, the Hawkins Family, The Smallwood Singers reunion, and Kelly Price. Of course, I had been a follower of Aretha since I was about 18 years old. I own everything she's ever thought about recording and I am the biggest fan ever. I don't think I've ever admired anyone as much.

Let me stop here and say this. Sometimes I don't think people get what it's like when you've been in this music business a long while. They don't understand how your influences continue to be your treasures. You still feel the same way about them, just like you're still that teenaged, star-struck kid that you were when you first heard their record, or saw them on TV. That's my Aretha experience. I was an 18-year-old freshman at Howard when Wesley Boyd let me hear Aretha's "Chain of Fools." He and Sully turned me on to her. "Respect" had blown up that year and was huge. I loved it. There was something about when I heard "Chain of Fools" with the Pops Staples-styled guitar intro that blew my mind. I was aware of her dad, Rev. C.L. Franklin, because I listened to his 78s, which my father owned, as a small kid. I wasn't too aware of her though, because Motown was my secular stable. But I do remember a few gospel recordings from the radio from when she was a kid, especially "Never Grow Old." However, this was the first time I ever really remember *hearing* her. I was immediately absolutely blown away by her voice, her vocal power, the immense feeling and soul of this incredible instrument. It was soulful, it was blues, it was R&B, it was gospel, it was EVERYTHING. I fell in love with her voice and was instantly a super fan. I remember I bought the *Lady Soul* album that "Chain of Fools" was on and went back and bought the previous ones I had missed on Atlantic Records also. Never had I heard a vocalist who had the soul, the range, the depth of feeling and the vocal skills that she had. I had no idea at the time that she was influenced by some of the very same people I had been influenced by, such as Clara Ward, Marion Williams and the Davis Sisters. Maybe that's what I heard in her voice, but whatever it was, I was a fan for life. I couldn't get enough of her singing.

Every time she came to DC, MD or VA we Howard students - and even years after graduation - were there with the nearest seats to the front that we could afford. It was always a multi-faceted experience, usually ending with a Black church experience. She'd sing hit after hit after hit, with all of us singing along with her in the audience. We knew each song backwards and forward: her riffs, her runs, and the background vocals (although her improvisational skills were phenomenal and she never sang the song the same way twice). It didn't matter what situation or man Aretha was singing about, she always brought it home to the man called Jesus. I had never, ever experienced anything like it live in my entire life at a secular concert. It was so true what her dad said about her: "Aretha never left the church."

People would weep and they'd even break forth in a Sunday morning-like dance sometimes when she started calling the name of Jesus and talking about what He had done. She was never ashamed of who she was or where she came from. I remember thinking, "If I could ever meet her," not "If I could ever play for her and work with her." That was too much to even hope for. If I could just meet her I knew I'd probably be a "babbling idiot." Yeah I was just that star-struck. It was something about her voice that connected somewhere deep, where no one vocally had touched before. I had my favorite gospel singers and even secular ones that I grew up with. I had my favorite composers, pianists, choirs and groups. However, no solo voice had ever connected to my soul like Aretha! Her live concerts put me in some kind of trance. I'll never forget when she came to the Capitol Center in DC. Of course, a bunch of us went to see her. I can't remember what the song was, but what I was hearing was so powerful that when I came to my senses I was standing in my chair and hitting this poor lady who was standing in front of me on top of the head with my fist. I was so embarrassed when I came to my senses and apologized profusely. I honestly didn't realize that I was hitting her. I'm sure she thought I was crazy. I remember in an early interview in the 80's, someone asked me who was it that I wanted to work with at some point in my career more than anyone else. My answer was "I just want to carry Aretha Franklin's luggage." I was obsessed with this voice. Even in teaching songs I'd written, if the leader had that kind of range, I'd say "sing it like Aretha."

Needless to say, I just had to have Aretha on this project. I put it out in the air/industry about what I wanted her to do. I certainly didn't have a number for her or wasn't sure how to go about getting it. One afternoon I was on my way to see my Mom, and the land line phone rang. There was no number on the caller ID. In fact, the number was blocked. Now, please know that the best way for me *not* to answer someone's call is to block their number when calling me. I almost didn't pick it up. But on my way to the door, something prompted me to stop and answer. I picked it up quickly and said "hello." There was a pause and someone on the other end said. "Richard? Richard Smallwood??" I responded, "Yes, this is he." The voice on the other end said "This is Aretha Franklin." Honestly the room began to spin. I kid you not. I can't remember all I said. I was praying that it made sense while I was talking. She said, "Richard I heard you wanted to do some work with me and I would love to!" The room began to spin faster. She began to tell me how she loved my music. I'm thinking, is she kidding??? MY music????? OMG! She then told me how my song "Healing" helped her through the death of her sister Erma who had not long ago passed. In the middle of her telling me what the song meant to her, her voice broke, and I could tell she was crying. I didn't know what to say. I was trying to think of some words of comfort, but my mind was a jumbled frozen mess. At some point she recovered and began talking. I do remember saying that talking to her was a dream come true, and her considering to work with me was an even bigger dream. I remember saying jokingly to her, "My lifework is done, I can go home and see the Lord." She said, "No sir, you have a lot more songs to write" and just began to encourage me. She gave me her number and moments later, I remember bursting into Mom's door hollering "MOM, ARETHA FRANKLIN CALLED ME." Mom smiled proudly and said, "I'm not surprised." It began our journey.

Months later when Vision went to Detroit to do a concert, she called me and let me know she'd be in the audience. I don't remember seeing her, although other members of Vision spotted her. But when we got on the bus I had a message on my phone from Aretha singing "Healing," and saying "Richard, didn't our hearts burn within on tonight????We had church!!" I was walking on a cloud. She wanted to re-do "You're Not Alone" from the Healing project on the recording I was preparing for, "Journey." Aretha hadn't flown in years because of a bad experience she had on a plane. The night of the Journey recording she'd be on her tour bus on the way to California to do some dates on the West Coast. So the plan was to go in the studio and do it there. She wanted to do it at her house and bring in her engineer. Our conversations escalated on the phone. She was comical. One evening she called and said, "Let's see what key works for me for 'You're Not Alone.'" She sat at her piano in Detroit and I sat at mine in DC and we started fiddling around with the song. Finally she said "Richard, I think the key of C will be fine. We talked a little bit more and hung up. About a half hour later my phone rang again. When I picked it up she said, "Richard... I was on my way to the kitchen to get a small ham hock, and I had to pass the piano." Immediately I tried to suppress my laughter, but she laughed loud and heartily and then we both did. Aretha was known for her soul food cooking skills. When we finally stopped laughing she said, "I sat at the piano again, and tried the key of C, but I decided B would be more comfortable and THEN proceeded to get my small ham hock!" The Queen said it was B, so B it was! She was so wise. She talked of her influences who were some of mine as well: the Davis Sisters, Jackie Verdell and Clara Ward and the Ward Singers, who I also grew up on as a young kid in Philly. She talked about how all these people would come to her house when she was a little girl and sing around their piano. James Cleveland was instrumental in helping her with her already immense gift on the keyboard. After a while her Dad was calling her downstairs when superstars, both secular and gospel, would come to hang out at the house. Aretha would sit, play, sing and blow everybody away at her young age. Not long afterward she told me she was going to do several nights at Madison Square Garden in NY for the McDonald's Gospel Fest, and wanted to know would I come with Vision and sing with her. Those nights I will never, ever forget. During rehearsal she asked me, "What's that song about 'my everything?'" It was a song I had written for the "Persuaded, Live in DC" project. She continued, "I love that song." I thought she wanted to sing it on one of the nights. She asked to hear it so we sang it for her. Imagine my surprise when she announced during the concert, "We've got Richard Smallwood and the Smallwood Singers (she always called Vision the Smallwood Singers). He's gonna come and sing one of my favorite songs, 'My Everything.'" My mouth was as dry as cotton. As I sat down at the piano and Vision and I began to sing she stood next to me and began to adlib behind me as only she could. I was an 18-year-old all over again, living a dream I'd never thought was possible. A couple of years later she called me and asked me to bring Vision to her annual revival in Detroit. Yearly she'd have revivals and bring in singers from all over the country as well as preachers. I was totally honored. Aretha opened up the revival with "Mary, Don't You Weep" and destroyed the place. My Vision family made me so proud that night. The way they sang in that church was amazing. In the audience was my dear friend and musical genius Twinkie Clark. But imagine my surprise when at the end of the service a lady who I immediately recognized as Martha Reeves of Motown fame came up to me with a beautiful smile. Her sister Lois, who was a part of Martha's famous group the Vandellas, was with her. My God!! I grew up on these people! In fact, Martha and the Vandellas' "Dancing In the Street" was one of the first R and B records I bought when I was a teen and snuck it into the house and started playing it along with my gospel records. She came up and embraced me and thanked me for my music! She said it had not only helped her family through the tragic death of her brother, but inspired him during his illness. She and her family presented me with a beautiful key chain with her brother's name on it, my name and words of gratitude for my music. We became friends and Lois, her sister took me on a tour of the Motown Museum several years ago when I was performing in Detroit. I began to realize you never know where God is going to take your music and who it's going to help. It goes places and reaches ears that you cannot even imagine.

Because we did the "Journey" project in NY, the budget skyrocketed. The venue which was the wonderful Hammerstein

Ballroom was not cheap; we had to bring in all the guests, singers, including Vision, musicians, hotel and of course everything was double the price it would have cost anywhere else on the East Coast. Even the stage hands charged double. I definitely understand budget. But when it came time to go with Aretha in the studio I was told I had gone over budget and it would be impossible to do her song. I remember being so hurt about it. I knew I had gone over budget, but this was Aretha!! It was the Queen of Soul!!!

By the time we got to adding Aretha's song and I was told no, I wanted to scrap the whole thing and just forget it. To make it worse I had to call her and tell her that the label said I couldn't do it. I was embarrassed to do so and was afraid of what she would think of me. I procrastinated until finally I said, I've got to let her know what happened. When I called her apologizing she said, "Richard we can work something out. Don't feel bad." But by that time we were way past the release date. I remember her asking, "when is the next time you're going to record?" I told her I wasn't sure. She said, "Don't worry about it, we'll work something out." I still was so embarrassed and then she said, "I don't believe your label is aware of the caliber of gift they have in you. They should be bending over backwards helping you reach what it is that you have in mind for your recording." That statement lifted my spirits like she'll never know. I wish I had added her on the Promises or the Anthology projects, but I just didn't think about it. I think I was still embarrassed about the Journey fiasco. But we still talked on the phone.

Aretha, like Edwin, was old school when it came to technology. I remember trying to explain the whole internet thing to her. Aretha was still faxing. She also would change her number constantly. At some point she'd always call me and give me the new number. I called her one time and an irate lady on the other end hollered at me, "NOBODY NAMED ARETHA LIVES HERE"!! I guess people had been trying to reach her on that old number. Even later she called and said "Richard, I need a song for my next project." I wrote a song for her called "Faithful" that she and my friend Karen Clark-Sheard recorded as a duet on her recording called "A Woman Falling Out of Love." She wanted me to come to play for her when the Pope came to Philadelphia, but unfortunately I couldn't because of a previous commitment, but the conversations would continue. Each time she'd call I was just as nervous for at least a second as I was the first time, but after a few moments I would relax and we would laugh and talk. I just loved and respected her so much. I would save some of her voice messages that she'd leave. I never got used to her calling. There were many times when I'd get discouraged in this business called music and would just want to quit and to move to an island somewhere. I had called and left a message telling how she literally destroyed the Kennedy Center with "Natural Woman" on the night they honored writer Carole King. Within several days Aretha called back and left a message that I'll never erase. It said "Thank you so much Richard for your kind words, but remember you are the Master, *you* are the Maestro. *You* set the standard and everyone else has to come up to where you are!" That's the last message she left me that I saved. Coming from Aretha, I can't tell you how encouraging it was. Ironically one of the last things Edwin told me when I hinted to him about being tired of the music industry was "Richard we *need* your music, you can't go anywhere." How amazing that two of the people who inspired me the most would say such amazing things that I needed to hear, to encourage me through times of depression and a crazy business. I had heard Aretha was ill and we hadn't talked in a while. I was terrified because I just felt it was something very serious. When the news of her death came, it hit me like a ton of bricks. I know it doesn't make sense, but there are some people you just think will live forever. I knew I'd have to go to the funeral. I immediately called Aretha's cousin, my friend Brenda Corbett, and told her I was coming and to put me on the list. Once I got there, everyone kept asking me "What are you going to do?" I hadn't planned to do anything. I just wanted to say goodbye to my friend. But when music directors Fred Nelson, the amazing Pastor Rudy Stanfield and Aretha's MD of many years H.B. Barnum saw I was there, they immediately came to me and said, we want to open the funeral with "I Love The Lord" and "Total Praise" and escorted me to the piano. The choirs and the singers were amazing. I ended up playing "Total Praise" for at least twenty minutes or more while the family came in the church. Of all the honors that God has blessed me with, I have to say that being able to play "Total Praise" for Aretha while her family came into the sanctuary has to be the greatest honor of my life. Hopefully I said through my music and the piano what I could never articulate in words to her in terms of what an inspiration and amazing effect she had on my life from the time I was a teenager. I miss her terribly but what an amazing legacy and body of work she's left with us. There will never be another voice like that.

***

As I was preparing for the Journey recording, I got a call from my manager saying that someone for Chaka Khan had called the office. Chaka was going to be singing a song on TBN that I had written for Karen Clark-Sheard, "A Secret Place," and wanted to know if I would fly to LA to play it for her. I would have walked to LA! Chaka Khan was one of my absolute favorites and I started collecting her Rufus CD's as well as her solo projects when I was first out of college. What an incredible voice! Chaka did an awesome job with the song on the TV show. She told me that she had heard about the upcoming recording in NY and said that she would love to come. Then it hit me! What if I could get her to actually be a part of the project and sing on it? I asked her would she be interested in singing on it. She told me that she would love to. I was elated! I ended up writing a song for her called "Precious is Your Name." She was amazing on it, plus she was such a sweetheart and so easy to work with. I had written a song called "I Can Make This Journey." I had not a clue as to whom I could get to do it. I wracked my brain trying to come up with the perfect vocalist for it. Vision had to do a concert in London and I didn't know who else would be on the concert. However, when I walked into the hotel in London there was my friend and one of my favorite vocalists, Kim Burrell. She was scheduled to be on the concert with us. Immediately it clicked and I knew immediately that was the person who was supposed to sing that song. I think God gave it to me especially for her. It fit like a glove. She happily consented to be a part of it and came on board. We also reached out to another favorite vocalist of mine, Kelly Price, who also was glad to come on board. What an amazing voice Kelly has! Although logistically Kathleen Battle and Roberta Flack didn't work out, at the very last minute an incredibly gifted singer Janice Chandler Eteme stepped in for Kathleen Battle. I had written a song called "We Worship You." Her performance was awesome. Probably the two most special performances personally for me that night were the Hawkins Family and The Smallwood Singers. Edwin and Walter being two of the most influential and impactful musicians in my lifetime were the icing on the cake for me. Even more exciting, I had flown out to Walter's home several months before and we had spent two days writing together. I think there were times we laughed and joked more than wrote, but it was an awesome time of collaboration. We wrote two songs, "We've Come Too Far" which the Hawkins Family would perform and, "I Won't Give Up" which I along with Vision performed. Tramaine, Edwin, Lynette and Walter were on the stage again. It was magic. I had no idea that my friend Walter would make his transition five years later. It was an honor and I was like a kid in a candy shop hearing that incredible Hawkins sound that had influenced me so many years ago. There was a blend and a power that they had when they all sang together that couldn't be duplicated. Having the Smallwood Singers again on stage had to be the greatest feeling in the world. They sang like it was only yesterday that we all had been together. It probably had been about fifteen years since the originals had been together. But it was more than that. It was the love, the connection, the experience and all that we had been through together as a unit. To see, Dottie, Wesley, Lisa, Carolene and Darlene all on that stage together, brought up emotions in me that made it almost too hard to sing because of the tears. Dottie stepped out and did "He Won't Leave You," most definitely one of my favorite songs that God has given to me. We then did our old standard "Holy Holy." The power of everyone's voice together was still there. That sound was STILL there. Little did I know, Wesley and Lisa would soon be making their transitions. Ironically, after a Smallwood Singers rehearsal one night while preparing for the project, Wesley called me after he had left to tell me his father had just passed. I was so saddened to hear. I knew his family so well from the days that we were at Howard and we'd all go down to Reidsville during the summer. His mom was one of the greatest cooks ever and his dad was always the life of the party. Wesley said he was going home to take care of the arrangements, but he'd be there in NY for the recording, because there was no way he was going to miss it. He was so excited about that reunion. That reunion is one of my most treasured memories. Of course, Kim opened the whole recording up with "I Can Make This Journey" and demolished the place to say the least. What an amazing instrument! Kelly sent chills through the entire building with "Morning's Breaking." The audience ate Chaka up that night and it still seems like a dream to me that Chaka Khan was standing on stage singing something that I had written for her. All this was done at the Hammerstein Ballroom in Manhattan. It was sold out. People from everywhere were there. They came from overseas, from home in DC, Chicago, and every place imaginable. My dear friend Sandy Fagans from back in the day, who was one of the ones who encouraged me the most, was there. She would always tell me how successful I was going to be one day and I never believed her. By now she was very ill and on an oxygen tank. I remember her telling me she was coming and I tried to persuade her to stay at home because of her health. But she said she wanted to come and see more of her prediction coming true from many years ago. Sandy caught a bus dragging her oxygen tank with her from Richmond to NY. I will never forget seeing her big smile at the end of the concert as we hugged. I was so happy to see her. She would transition soon after. I was honored to have incredible artists like Ashford and Simpson, Melba Moore, Cissy Houston and singer Freddy Jackson in the audience. Ironically, most of these were people who I had either grown up on or who had some kind of musical impact on my life. In fact, later after the album was released and

I was doing radio interviews, Valerie Simpson called in while I was at a station in NY to encourage me. She'll never know how much that meant to me, and how I treasure her support! At the same time that night, my manager Roger was critically ill in Nashville and was unable to be there with me. I remember praying the entire night in the back of my mind that he would be ok. Thank God, within a few months he was doing fine. My assistant Kelvin Leach stepped right in for Roger and ran the whole recording like clockwork. I stayed in NY for several days shopping and relaxing after the recording was over. I went to see a Broadway musical "Wicked," and had a great time. It was the same week that Hurricane Katrina would hit New Orleans and create such devastation.

From time to time, I would still have these weird experiences where I would be half asleep, yet half awake. Other than my toes, I couldn't move no matter how hard I tried. I was completely paralyzed. Sometimes when it would happen, I could sense a presence behind me standing on the other side of the bed. I also felt something grab me, holding on to me tightly. It was terrifying. I would pray, I'd call on Jesus. I'd recite the 23rd Psalm and sometimes the Lord's Prayer. However, it would always take its time leaving. I hated it and it frightened me.

Mom's hospital trips became more frequent. Many times, they'd call me from the Washington Home to tell me that Mom had to be rushed to the emergency room. I would jump in the car and race to Georgetown Hospital where they would usually take her. Most times, they would release her quickly and sometimes she'd stay a day or so. But they would always send her home eventually and for a while, she'd seem to be doing OK. By now, she had started to lose her appetite. In the past mom, no matter how sick she was, would always have a healthy appetite. But now, even the things she loved she seemed to have no desire for. I would buy her favorite things, such as ice cream, crab cakes, all of the stuff that I knew she loved. I usually ended up putting it in her refrigerator and eventually throwing it out. I just couldn't understand it. She was still Mom, but she was becoming different. I thought I'd wait a minute before Steve and I started doing post-production work on the project because of Mom. It was hard to concentrate with all that was going on with her. She began telling me that she wanted me to meet a friend of hers, but he would never come around when I was there. When I asked more about him she said his name was Michael and that he worked there on the staff. He always wore white from head to toe as most of the nurses did there. He was young and probably in his thirties. She said the first day he came in the room, he asked, "Are you Mabel Locklear?" I remember thinking why in the world would he call Mom by her maiden name? Not many people even knew her by that name. At first I didn't pay it much mind, but she kept talking about him and how much she liked him. Then one day I came to see her and she said, "Oh Richard! You just missed Michael!" I remember going out into the hallway but saw no one. Then she began to tell me that today he had brought her a picture to see. She said he pulled it out of his pocket and it was an old black and white photograph worn around the edges. When she looked at it, it was a picture of her father Richard. She asked him how in the world did he get a picture of her father. He told her that when he was a little boy in Durham, they were very poor. His mother was single and raising a house full of kids with very little to eat and almost nothing to wear. He said that Mom's father Richard would come by the house periodically and bring them food and clothing. Michael said that he never forgot that and when he got grown he was going to try to do something to pay back the good deeds that my grandfather Richard had done. So, he had come to look after Mom and no one else in the home but her. I started to analyze what she was saying. Mom was 90 years old. If someone had been a little boy, when she was a little girl, or even before she was born for that matter, he wouldn't have been in his thirties. I began to tell Mom my thoughts. Her eyes widened and she said, "Richard, do you think it's an angel?" That's exactly what I thought. I know Mom suffered from dementia from time to time, but this story was different. It was too detailed and certainly had a ring of truth to it. I began to think then that Mom was being prepared for her transition. I didn't want to accept it, so I pushed it to the back of my mind. As time went on, she said he stopped coming completely in the room. But he would sometimes just peep in the door, smile and wave.

CHAPTER 38
THE LAST VOICE SHE'LL HEAR

On September 9, 2005 I was asked to do a benefit concert for my alma mater, Howard's School of Divinity. Vision and I returned to Jericho City of Praise where we had recorded "Persuaded" to another packed house including all of my former professors. It was a great night and thank God, a lot of money and pledges came in to help my alma mater. On the next morning, I received a call from Washington Home saying that they couldn't wake Mom and had rushed her to the hospital. When I arrived at the hospital, she was in the ER and was ranting out of her head. The doctors said it was an infection and her fever was high which was the cause of the things she was saying. When I look back, it was the beginning of the end. She was slowly declining. She remained in the hospital for about a week. When she returned to the home, they moved her to the third floor where the sicker residents were so she could be monitored 24 hours a day. Sometimes she'd look at me and say, "Richard I want to go home." I was in denial and thinking that she wanted to either go back to her original room or either our old house on Monroe Street. Once she looked at me and smiled and said, "Richard, God has taken care of me all of these many years and that same God is going to do the same for you." I still hold on to her saying that even now when I go through rough times. Over the next couple of months, there were more hospital stays. One particular visit, I arrived in her room and she was crying uncontrollably. I tried to calm her but she was inconsolable. "What's wrong, Mom?" I kept asking. She kept telling me, "I want my momma, I want my momma." To try to calm her down, I told her, "Grandmom couldn't come, but she sent me to take care of you. Is that alright?" She calmed down and told me yes, it was fine. Then she said, "She was just here before you came. She told me not to worry because she'd be back for me." I didn't want to break down in front of her. I knew in the pit of my stomach what that meant. I remember telling her I would be right back, the tears welling up in my eyes. I ran outside the hospital and found a place where I could sit by myself. I knew what Grandmom coming back to get her meant. I remember calling one of my best friends in Chicago, Mark Hubbard. I was hysterical on the phone. I knew it wouldn't be long. There was no way I could imagine being on the earth and my Mom not being here. It was all I knew. She was my life. She was my heart. Everything I was, was because of God and her. Mark had lost his Mom awhile back, so I knew he understood what I was going through. He had been a Momma's boy, too. After he calmed me down on the phone, I will never forget the call I later received from Mark's then-pastor, Bishop Larry Trotter. He will never know what his words of comfort meant to me at that time in my life. I thank God for Mark, my buddy Lo Ballard from Biloxi, Mississippi and my friends Rob Harper, Mike Freeman and Bamm Washington, who would call me every day during this period and encourage me. My emotions would go from calm, to denial, to hysterical. But they helped me walk through it. Before Mom was released from the hospital, I was called into the office at Washington Home where there was a hospice care worker. They wanted to place Mom into hospice. The doctor told me that her body was slowly shutting down. But they wanted her to be comfortable and not move her to a strange place. So, they wanted to put her in her old room on the first floor where all of her family pictures were, her favorite chair and everything that she loved. The hospice worker saw my face and said, "Mr. Smallwood, there are times that hospice care patients will actually improve and they can come out of hospice care, so don't despair." I guess I tried to hold on to every shred of hope I could, but my heart told me different. She was released into hospice care. All of my time was spent at her side. I did little else. Some of my friends and family had reached out to me and told me that I needed to get away for a break. They suggested I go to Chicago for a few days on Thanksgiving like I had done for so many years. They assured me that they would take turns to be at Mom's side and would keep in contact with me so I knew how things were going. I didn't want to go, but at the same time I was so tired mentally, physically and emotionally. I decided to go for three days. I told her I was going and she said she was glad that I was. She said I needed to get away. When Thanksgiving came, Mom was too weak to go to the dining room and celebrate with the other residents so they brought her Thanksgiving dinner to her room. I remember it was the first time I had seen her eat well in a minute. When she finished eating I flew to Chicago. I worried while I was away, but the change of atmosphere did me good. My friends and family watched her like a hawk for those several days. When I returned, I definitely noticed a change. Mom wouldn't open her eyes or talk. Although she was fully conscious the doctor explained that she was too weak to open them. Mom loved to watch any DVD that I had ever done. So,

I'd play those on the TV although she couldn't open her eyes to see them. I'd also played CDs softly of her favorite music. On November 29, the day before my birthday, the doctor told me that it was just a matter of time and he gave her about 24 hours. That meant, more than likely, she would transition on my birthday. I called all my family, all of my foster brothers and sisters, my close friends and let them know what the prognosis was. On my birthday the next day, I sat beside her bed all day. I remember my dear friend Cookye Rowe (who had been cutting my hair for years) telling me, "Richard, you have to let her go. She'll hold on until you let her go." I didn't think I could. I prayed for strength to do what seemed impossible. I remember standing by her bedside and taking a deep breath, grabbing Mom's hand and saying, "Mom it's alright to go. I know you are so tired. I'm going to be fine." As I spoke the words, I knew that I meant it. It ceased being something that I did because it was the right thing to do. She had been a part of my journey for all of my life, but I knew it was now time to part ways. Her eyes were still shut. She didn't respond but I know she heard me. It's one of the hardest things I ever had to do. The selfish part of me wanted to hold on forever. I didn't want to lose her. But I knew she was tired, she was hurting and she wanted to be at rest. By that evening as everyone started to get off work, the room began to fill with family. I must say my cousin Dede was my rock during that time. There were times when I would sit there and I would hear her struggling to breathe and I'd have to leave the room. I just couldn't deal. But Dede was right there by my side. We talked about fun times while we sat there. My sister Joy would tell of how Mom threw a hair brush and hit her in the back of her head for "sassing" back at her and we all laughed knowing how Mom WOULD get you if you acted up. As much as she loved you, she didn't play. I had gotten this addiction for Mountain Dew sodas and chili cheese Fritos while I was a student in Divinity School. One of my evening classes was two and a half hours long, and at break time, I'd go downstairs to the vending machine and get my caffeine kick of Mountain Dew and the accompanying Fritos so I could make it through the rest of the class. I had an urge for a Mountain Dew while we were sitting in Mom's room so I went around to the canteen to get me one. One of the custodians greeted me as I went in and asked how Mom was doing. I told him that she didn't have long and he said, "Oh Mr. Smallwood, I'm so sorry. She is such a loving person." He left and I noticed a nurse sitting at one of the tables. As I was leaving with my Mountain Dew, she said, "Excuse me." I paused and she got up from the table. She said, "Mr. Smallwood? This is really odd, because I never come down here. I work on the third floor and I took care of your Mom when she was up there a while back. For some reason, I just decided to come down here and sit for a while and you showed up. When your Mom was on the third floor she called me in her room one morning. She told me whenever it was time for her to make her transition to please find you and hug you for her. She told me to tell you not to worry; she was going to be fine and how proud she is of you." She then looked at me and said "May I hug you for her?" I cannot explain the emotions that ran through me. As she embraced me I thought, *what were the chances of this nurse coming to a section of the home where she never goes at the exact same time that I came in here? What are the chances that at the same time, Mom is preparing to make her transition?* I still marvel at how that worked out. I guess Mom was still thinking about me 'til the end, and made up her mind that she would not leave on my birthday, so she hung in there. After a while, everyone got tired and we all went home around two that morning. I couldn't sleep. I kept watching the phone knowing that it was going to ring, but it didn't.

It was December 1. I arrived at Washington Home around ten that morning. There was no change in Mom. My sister Gloria arrived and stayed for most of the day. Around four after she left, my godson Tre' arrived and asked if I had eaten that day. I hadn't. I really didn't want to leave the room. He said, "You really need to eat something. Let's go grab something and come right back." I said I would and walked over to Mom's bed. Her lips were chapped and she, as I do, LOVED Carmex. I said, "Mom your lips are chapped...let me put this on it." She poked out her lips, with her eyes still closed as I applied the lip balm. I said, "Mom, I haven't eaten. I'm going to run right across the street and get me something and come right back." She didn't respond. My godson and I walked across the street. Honestly, I can't remember what I ordered. I wasn't hungry. All I remember is that I had a strawberry lemonade. As we left the restaurant, my godson told me he was going to the gym. As I was going in the door of the home, my sister Joy was coming out. She said she saw my keys in Mom's room and knew I must have been somewhere nearby. She was going to get something to eat and she'd be right back. "But guess what?" She asked. "Mom's eyes are halfway open." My heart leapt in excitement. It had been weeks since she had opened her eyes. As I ran down the hall towards Mom's room, I saw Annie exiting the room. She stopped me. She said, "Richard, if there is anything you need to say to Mom that you haven't, now is the time. She's beginning her transition. I ran down the hall towards the room. When I entered the first thing I noticed was that her eyes were a little open and her breathing had become labored. I ran to the foot of the bed in the direction that her eyes were focused, so she would focus on me. I called her name, but she didn't respond.

There was this strange wheezing sound that accompanied her breathing. Her breaths were short and each one seemed spaced further than the one before. With tears streaming down, I ran out into the hall to get the nurse. When he saw my face his eyes widened and asked what was wrong. All I could say is, "She's going, oh my God she's going." He ran into the room behind me. He examined her and he looked at me and said, "Mr. Smallwood, she's transitioning." My legs got weak and I could feel myself going towards the floor. But the nurse's firm voice brought me back. He said, "Mr. Smallwood, pull yourself together. This is a time when you can be your mother's biggest supporter. This will be one of the most intimate times you'll ever experience with her. Help her cross over to the other side. Hold her hand. Talk to her and just think, your voice will be the last one she hears on this side, as she makes that final journey."

By now my sister Joy had come back in the room. She was taking in everything that was going on. Her eyes widened and I could see tears in them. I didn't know what to say to Mom. By now the nurse had exited the room to leave us alone in privacy. It all seemed like some horrible nightmare. Honestly, I really can't remember what I said to Mom. I could feel my heart pounding in my head. I wanted to let her know it was all right to go and that I was there with her. But I'm not sure what I said. I do remember telling her to forgive herself and let the whole mystery around my birth go. "I'm ok, Mom. I just need you to let it go." I could feel myself getting ready to break again when something just spoke to me and said, "Sing to her Richard." I began to sing ever so softly...

Jesus You're the Center of My Joy
All that's good and perfect comes from you

You're the heart of my contentment, hope for all I do
Jesus you're the center of my joy.

It was one of her favorite songs. My sister says she doesn't know how I did it. She said the tears were pouring down my face but my voice never wavered or broke as I sang to her. I don't know how I did it either. All I remember is that her breaths kept getting shorter and shorter. It was like she wasn't breathing from her lungs any longer. It was more like these breaths were just coming from her throat in short gasps. Maybe it was from movies I had seen, or stories I had read. I just expected a peaceful kind of scene where the loved one just smiles, closes their eyes and exhales for the last time. This was not that. It seemed as if she was struggling. Each time she'd exhale, I'd hold my breath wondering was that the last one, and then she'd take another sort of gasp. I was so out of it that I could not remember one word of any of the verses to "Center of My Joy," so I just kept singing the chorus over and over. I knew it was no one but God who gave me the strength. I kept singing. It seemed like forever. Finally, she did another short gasp and exhaled. Somewhere in my mind, I was praying "please take another one." As long as she was breathing, that meant she was still here. But there was not another breath, just silence. Somewhere on the inside, I remember thinking that the last voice she heard on this side was mine singing to her. She ushered me into this world years ago in Atlanta, Georgia and now I had ushered her out. That gave me some peace, and even though it's the hardest thing I've ever done, today I'm grateful for that opportunity. It was so quiet in that room. I remember looking at her face and all of a sudden, she seemed to look so young, so at peace, with a slight smile on her face. By now, one of my other sisters Bernice had arrived.

All I remember saying was that I didn't want to be there when the coroner arrived to take Mom. I had witnessed that scene so many times sitting with her when residents would transition and she and I would watch the coroner wheeling them on the gurney in zipped up body bags towards the exit. I didn't want to see it. There's no way I could handle it. I didn't want to deal with gathering her clothes together. My sisters said they'd handle it. She had a brand new motorized wheel chair only a couple of weeks old. I told Annie to just give it to someone in the home who might need it. I just needed to get out of there. I left the nursing home in shock but at the same time, there was a peace about the whole thing. I knew Mom was alright and she was happy now. I just had no idea how it was going to affect me. I think I was in shock. For a long time, that horrific scene of those last moments would play constantly over and over in my mind like they were on a never-ending loop. It was something that I wanted to forget. Whenever I closed my eyes I'd see her gasping for breath. The scene wouldn't go away. It wouldn't let me rest. It probably took a couple of years but little-by-little it began to turn into a treasurable moment. I got the chance to be there and take the first part of that journey with her holding onto her hand and singing all the way. She was the first person to ever hear me sing and that's the last thing she heard as she transitioned. My manager Roger had advised me to make the funeral arrangements before she passed, as it would be incredibly hard to do after the fact. I'm so glad I listened to him. When it was time for me to go view the body at the funeral home, my cousin Dede and my friend Darin Atwater were right by my side to go with me. If it weren't for them, I don't think I would have gotten through it. With them being there, it seemed to make it easier. Mom looked beautiful and it wasn't at all as hard as I envisioned it would be. It ended up being like a small reunion of sorts as some of my sisters joined me and we all ended up talking about their childhood and the good times.

The day before the funeral, I got a call from my cousin Olivia. At the time, Olivia was in her early eighties, was ill and unable to travel. She said, "Buddy, I'm so sorry I can't be there for Mabel's funeral because of my health. She was such a loving and wonderful person." She told me that she was sending her daughter who is also my cousin, Denise. Denise and I used to play together as kids when I'd go to Durham for the summer. Olivia told me that she was going to send some pictures she had for me as well. She said, "I've got some baby pictures from when you were down here in Durham." Then she dropped a bombshell on me. She said, "And I have a picture of Rivers that I'm going to send you as well. He and Mabel loved each other very much." That's all she said. I didn't even know how to respond. That was the first time I had an acknowledgement about any of that from any of my relatives from that era.

The funeral is sort of a blur. There were friends and loved ones from everywhere, from college, from old Union Temple and from childhood. Some of my closest friends were pallbearers. My friend Edwin Hawkins was there as well as my buddy George Faison whom I had worked with many years before. We held the funeral at Metropolitan Baptist Church where, although she wasn't a member, she would visit whenever she could. She had often told me that she wanted to join but she never did. I knew that the auditorium would be able to accommodate the number of people that I expected. My pastor and church family opened up their doors just as if she were a member. At the beginning of the service just as they were closing the lid of the casket, they began to sing "Total Praise." I think that was the hardest part to get through. My pastor, Dr. H. Beecher Hicks Jr. preached a wonderful eulogy. The choirs did an awesome job directed by Rev. Nolan Williams featuring Janice Chandler Eteme singing Nathan Carter's arrangement of Mom's favorite hymn, "It Is Well." Vision did "Anthem of Praise" and some kind of way and by the grace of God, I got through "Center of My Joy." I remember choking up in the verse, but thinking, "this is for Mom, Richard. Get it together NOW!!" After that I was fine. I had friends who came and stayed with me. Everyone seemed a bit reluctant to leave me by myself. My assistant, who had been with me for several years then and is still my right-hand man today, Kelvin Leach, was right there with me through it all. Two of my dearest friends Cornell Allen and Bill Clements were there during that time 24/7. People like Ángela Winbush, my sister Ollie, Jackie and Gail from the Howard/Union Temple days, and of course Wesley, were all there. My manager Roger and his wife Betty were also there by my side. There were so many people there for me and I'm just so grateful to everyone who supported me through that time. After the funeral, my cousin Denise handed me a manila envelope. When I got in the car on the way to the cemetery, I opened it. There were a number of pictures from when I was an infant, all taken while I was in Durham. Last but not least, there was the only picture that I've ever seen of Rivers Banks. Even seeing the picture, he still was a very vague memory to me. Several days after Mom had been buried, I began thinking, "Is this all there is? I think I can do this. Yes, I've definitely cried, and her death really hurt, but I think I'm ok now." I didn't realize that I was still in shock and little by little the shock would wear off.

I'm not sure how long it was; maybe it was a week after the funeral, maybe two. I know everyone had left and gone home.

I was sitting in my den and it was like, all of a sudden, the numbness wore off. Whatever shield that was around my heart shattered in a million pieces and the reality hit me. There was an actual pain, a physical ache that began in my stomach and traveled up to my heart. I have never hurt like that in my life. The cry started from the pit of my stomach and slowly rose to my throat. It came from a place I didn't know existed, a place that I had never known before. It was a wrenching pain that I was completely unfamiliar with. I couldn't stop crying. The more I cried, the more it hurt. The more it hurt, the more I cried. The sobs were uncontrollable and gut wrenching. It must have gone on for hours. The pain would come in waves. It was as if my body had never had any knowledge of sleep or what it was. I'd lie in bed staring at the ceiling between bouts of uncontrollable crying. My doctor prescribed sleeping pills and although the sleep was not the same as a natural one, at least I could sleep and forget for a brief time. Then the familiar darkness began to return that I hadn't felt since before the beginning of the antidepressants, slowly creeping over my body, my soul, like a moonless night. It had been awhile since I had felt it like that. In some crazy way, I had missed it. It was like a welcoming friend. It was all I had known for so many years, even before it had a name. It was familiar and dangerous at the same time. It was like going back home. It was like I belonged there. On top of that, every day the crying episodes would come, non-stop. I stopped answering the phone, I stopped singing, I stopped playing, I stopped writing, I stopped going to church, I stopped traveling and I shut completely down. I wanted only one thing in life, to be left alone. I had never hurt like that before in my life. The enemy began to convince me that I had lost the gifts I had and would never play, write or sing again. Because I was at a weak moment in my life, I embraced it, I accepted it and I believed it. It sounds crazy that I would entertain such an insane concept, but it was where I was at that point in my mind and in my spirit. I had resigned myself to the fact that I was done in terms of ministry and career.

In January, my dear friend Walter Hawkins called from Nashville at the Stellar Awards. He wanted to check on me and try to get me to come to Nashville. The Hawkins Family was being honored at the BMI Trailblazers Luncheon. All of the members were there. As much as I loved them, I just couldn't go. In February of 2006, my manager finally got me out of the house long enough to go to LA to receive the prestigious Recording Academy President's Merit Award. It was an extreme honor and they tried to get me to stay for the Grammy's which were starting the day after I received the award. I couldn't. It was too many people and I just wanted to go home. When I got home, I shut myself in again. I tried to go to church a couple of times. I didn't want to play. I just wanted to sit there and be ministered to. It was like I was there physically and I could hear the music, hear the Word, but it all seemed to bounce off my head and fall to the floor. My brain was on shutdown and my comprehension level was close to none. I didn't want people to feel sorry for me, or say they were praying for me, or hug me. I just wanted to be left alone and by myself.

CHAPTER 39

THE GOSPEL MUSIC HALL OF FAME

I t was Good Friday, 2006. I decided I was going to celebrate Easter weekend and try to pull myself out. I wanted to participate and I wanted to play. The Seven Last Words was always an amazing and inspirational service at our church with seven ministers each doing mini-sermons on the last words of Christ. Of all times, the choir decided to do "It Is Well," the same arrangement that was done at Mom's funeral. It was downhill from there. I remember heading out to my car before the benediction was given. It was raining. I got in the car and started in the direction of my house and the tears began so heavily that I had to pull over at one point. By now I had slowly weaned myself off of the sleeping pills for fear of becoming addicted and was taking Melatonin, a natural sleep aid. I had used that for many years when I would go overseas to help me get adjusted to the time difference. My sleep was just about back to normal. On Saturday, my assistant Kelvin called me to see how I was. Then he asked me a question that surprised me and took me aback. He asked, "Richard, are you angry at God?" I really don't remember what my response was. I had never thought about it before. But the more I thought about it, the more I realized that there was a part of me that was angry. It wasn't the kind of anger that would cause me to turn my back on Him. But it was the kind of anger that you have when a good friend does something that really annoys you, and you just think it better if you don't communicate with them for a while until you cool down. That's what I had been doing. I wouldn't watch religious programming on TV. I wouldn't even watch Bobby Jones. I hadn't picked up a Bible or read a Bible verse. I hadn't even realized it, but when I thought about it, I was angry for Him taking my Mom. I understand she lived a full life and that was a major blessing. God had allowed her to be there and experience almost every major occurrence in my life. But still, if she had lived to be 300, it still wasn't long enough. That was my Mom. She always knew what to say and what to do to make things better. I remember when we were putting "Journey, Live in NY" together. At one point, it seemed like everything was falling apart. I went up to Washington Home so frustrated one day and just felt like calling off the whole project. She saw my face and asked, "What's wrong baby?" I replied, "Mom, everything! Nothing is going right." She looked at me and smiled and said, "EVERYTHING is going to work out fine." Just to hear her say that lifted every concern that I had. She was right. It worked out fine. I missed her encouragement; her always telling me "You can do it," when I didn't think I could. But more than anything, I missed her presence in my life. I went to bed that night angry, frustrated, depressed and miserable. However, my plan was to get up and get to Resurrection Sunday Service.

I woke up early and fixed me some breakfast. I had a couple of hours before I needed to start getting ready for church, so I thought I'd lie back down. I remember having the television on and a "What's Happening" marathon was running (with Rog, Rerun, Dee and the whole gang). Within moments of lying back down I went back to sleep. It was a very strange sleep though. Immediately I started dreaming. I thought instead of the one bed in my bedroom, there were two. I was sitting on one facing the other and Mom was sitting on the other facing me. I was so happy to see her. But I couldn't help feeling that something was not right. I remember exclaiming, "MOM, I miss you SO much!" Her eyes seemed cold and distant and she seemed to be angry. She glared at me and without responding to what I had said, she said in a very vindictive kind of tone, "Your Grandmother hated you." There was something about her voice that sounded different. It was very similar to her actual voice, but there was something different about it. I remember saying, "Mom, why in the world would you say that?" She leaned forward and she seemed to get joy out of seeing her words sting me. "I SAID your grandmother hated you." I remember saying to myself that something is wrong here and I need to wake up. It hit me all of a sudden that whatever that was, that was not my Mother. It was as if something was trying to fool me into thinking it was. I started waking up as the dream faded. I could hear the TV blaring the "What's Happening" theme. I remember wondering what time it was because I didn't want to be late for church. I was lying on my left side, with my back to the TV. Behind me there was a sliding door that led to an outdoor patio. I went to move to put my foot out of the bed so I could get up. But I couldn't move. "Here we go again," I thought. I hate whatever this is. I tried to fight it. I tried to move, but I was absolutely paralyzed and other than my toes nothing would move. By now the dialogue had started on the TV and I could hear what the characters were saying, but I couldn't turn that way to look at the screen. All of a sudden I heard the floor creak behind me as if someone was standing there. I could feel something, a presence staring at me from behind. My first reaction was that someone had broken in and come through the patio door behind me. But I couldn't move. My heart began to pound and I started to pray. Just as I began to pray, something hit my bed so hard that the entire bed shook. Honestly, I can't ever remember being that afraid in my life. It was like someone dropped a huge safe in the middle of my bed. It didn't hit me, but I felt it when it hit the bed. The minute it hit and I gasped, something grabbed me from behind. It was like it had an arm or something around my neck, but I couldn't see it because it was behind me. I felt like I was being smothered and I couldn't breathe. I began to fight to try to move, praying all the while. The more I would try to move it seemed like the tighter it would hold me and pin me down. To my horror, I could feel someone's breath on the back of my neck. By now I was calling on Jesus to come and help me. Its mouth seemed to move near my ear, and I heard a strange sound as if it was mimicking my Mom's voice at first. But it sounded like several voices speaking together at the same time. It got really close to my ear and the voices said in unison, "So you miss yo Momma, huh?" Then it laughed, or I should say they laughed. By now it wasn't mimicking Mom's voice but it was a mocking tone of a group of voices speaking simultaneously. When it began to mock me all of a sudden my fear turned to rage. I thought, "How dare you (whatever you are) come in my house? Second of all, how dare you try to mimic my Mother's voice and last but not least, how dare you laugh at my hurt and my pain?" All of a sudden I realized I could move my left hand. I reached behind me and started hitting as hard as I could. My hand hit something; I couldn't tell what it was. But whatever it was started to fight me. The whole time, I was hitting and screaming "GET OUT OF MY HOUSE!" At some point, it seemed like I was getting the best of it with my one arm flailing away and I felt something like cat's teeth bite me on the back of my neck. I've had enough pet cats in my life to know what that feels like. They felt tiny but very sharp. When it bit me, it bit me hard. I think I went a little crazy. By now, other parts of my body seemed to be breaking free of the paralysis. I still couldn't turn over to face it, but I was swinging with everything I had within me. With one last scream while I was hitting as hard as I could, I yelled "GET OUT! Just as suddenly as it happened, it left. I bounded up out of bed, out of breath. Although I saw nothing, I began to scream at the ceiling. "DON'T YOU EVER COME IN THIS HOUSE AGAIN! I WILL BEAT YOU TO A PULP! YOU HAVE NO POWER IN HERE AND YOU HAVE NO BUSINESS IN HERE. THIS IS MY HOUSE!!!" I have to be absolutely honest here because I screamed at it "GET THE HELL OUT OF MY HOUSE!! My fear was gone and all I was left with…was anger. As I began to calm down some, I stood there trembling. It was as if God spoke to my heart and said, "All these many years, you've been calling me to help you when these things happen to you. I'm always with you, but I wanted you to see, that you always had the power to get rid of them. You can command demons to flee and they will because of the power I have given you. I have given you power to walk on serpents, yet you haven't used it. Use the weapons I gave you. You have everything that you need to get rid of whatever enemy comes your way. You haven't even begun to tap into the power that you already have. I have promised it and I stand by it. I want you to take this experience and write a sermon and let my followers know that they have the power. I want them to learn how to use the weapons that I've given them. You've read about it, but you don't act on it." I stood there in a pool of sweat by my bed while these words were entering my mind, just as clear as they could be. The scripture came to my mind, "Behold, I give you the authority to trample on serpents and scorpions, and over all the power of the enemy, and nothing shall by any means hurt you. (Luke 10:19 NKJV). I looked at the clock, which said it was around 1 pm. Well I had certainly missed church. I hadn't realized that much time had lapsed. I felt light, refreshed, almost happy. I jumped in the shower, got dressed and headed over to my cousins' for Easter dinner. When I got there, I began to tell them what happened. I was surprised to hear of similar stories from some of them. Things like that just seem to run in our family. I told my cousin Rosa about the sermon that I was instructed to preach. I was going to call it, "Get The Hell Out," but after thinking it might be a little much for some of the "saints," I changed it to "Use Your Weapons." Rosa told me, "Buddy, when you get home, as soon as you put your key in the door, I want you to start praying. I want you to go through that house, to every closet, to every cabinet, every room, every opening and rebuke anything in there that's not of God. Then I want you to pray that it's covered with the blood of Jesus and that you will be protected and safe from any future attacks. When I got home, I did just that. Not long after I got home, the phone rang and it was Rosa. She said, "God just spoke to me and told me to tell you something." She asked, "What Sunday is this?" "It's Resurrection Sunday," I replied. She said, "God is saying that today is the beginning of YOUR Resurrection!" I began to praise God for what I had experienced. I had put myself in a vulnerable position. I had not been spiritually fed, I wouldn't read the Bible nor would I study. Most important of all, I wouldn't pray. All of that time, my defense had worn down and the enemy was able to sneak in. The scripture came to my mind "Put on the whole armor of God that ye may be able to stand against the wiles of the devil." My mind often goes back to what Mom saw in the nursing home that day. It was a snake, but had a huge cat's head, cat's teeth and a snake-like forked tongue. I wonder if that was the same thing in my house that morning. I know whatever bit me on the back of my neck, felt like a cat. I also know that it never came back. The rest of the time I spent in that house, I never had another problem.

Sometime before that incident, my godson Tre was housesitting while I was on the road. When I got home, he told me of an experience that happened to him while he was lying on my bed. He said he fell asleep and he felt someone or something touch him as to awaken him. He paid it no mind and fell back asleep and something touched him again. He never saw anything, but I believe there was something in that house. I remember maybe about ten years earlier, being awakened one night by someone or something tapping in my room. It was if someone had their fingernails tapping on my dresser which was situated about eight feet from my bed. I remember lying there in the dark and listening to it. It wasn't a pipe, it wasn't the heat, but the unmistakable sound of fingernails tapping against a wooden surface. It wasn't a steady tap like a faucet dripping, but rhythmic in nature like there was an intelligence behind it. There was definitely a presence in that house. But whatever it was, after I finished yelling at it and pleading the blood, it never came back again. I remember being furious that something would have the unmitigated gall to come in my house uninvited where I paid a monthly mortgage and attack me or try to frighten me. Not only that, but I am a child of God. How dare whatever it was? I remember writing the sermon from that experience, "Use Your Weapons." When I finished, I decided that I didn't want to preach it. I thought that people would think I was crazy. But God kept laying it on my heart. The first Sunday that I preached it was at my home church, Metropolitan. The Holy Spirit really came in that morning. There were so many people who reached out to me, thanking me for obeying the leading of God's spirit. Some said they had experienced very similar things but they were afraid to say anything about it to anyone. I also preached it at the Hawkins Music and Arts Love Fellowship Conference one year. I will never forget when my friend Bishop Walter Hawkins came up to me afterwards and thanked me for preaching that sermon. He said he would have very similar experiences, especially on Saturday nights after he had prepared his sermon for the following Sunday morning but had never shared it with anyone. After a while, I got to the point that I didn't care what people thought when I preached it. I now understood that I went through that experience for more than my spiritual growth. I went through that because people needed to hear it. I was just obeying what God had put in my spirit.

I know that scientists have come up with a name for this phenomenon called, "sleep paralysis." I have researched it thoroughly having dealt with it so much. They have come up with explanations connecting it to REM sleep, the brain, sleep deprivation, sleep walking and other so-called causes. As someone who has experienced it for most of my adult life, it is my belief with every fiber of my being that it is a spiritual occurrence. I am not a scientist nor am I a doctor, but it is my belief that sometimes we get caught in a spiritual realm in which this phenomenon takes place. It's interesting to me that it is never a pleasant experience but one where an unmistakable evil presence is sensed. I think so many times the unexplainable is dissected over and over trying to find logical explanations. If anything is true, one thing is true: everything is spiritual. We are spirits first, housed in a temporary, physical body. We came from the spiritual realm, and one day that's where we will return.

Although the depression came and went, it wasn't as severe as it once was. However, I continued on the medication. Little by little, I began to play again and sing again, but for some reason the writing didn't seem to come back. Initially I didn't pay it much mind, because I've always been a sporadic writer. I remember the very first performance after Mom's death so vividly. Ironically it was for my former pastor Willie Wilson at my former church, Union Temple. It was an anniversary service in April of that year. I remember being so nervous as Vision and I took the stage. It felt like I hadn't done this in so many years. Even then, there still was a small part of me wondering if I could do this. As we began to minister, I could feel the power of the Holy Spirit moving Richard's fears and insecurities aside and taking control in that service. In addition, it was as if I could feel Mom standing right behind me saying, "You can do it!" and pushing me on. It was a wonderful night. In November of that year, the Gospel Music Association informed me that I was to be inducted into the Gospel Music Hall of Fame. It had to be the biggest honor of my entire life. I had just been, the year before, a part of the musical presentation as they inducted my friend Walter Hawkins. I had no idea that the very next year I would have the same honor. The only bittersweet part of it was that Mom wouldn't be there to celebrate with me. My cousin Dede went along with me because I wanted family with me, and of course my manager, Roger and his wife, Betty. As I sat there in Nashville reading the list of people who were members of that prestigious organization, my eyes began to well up with tears. I saw names like Clara Ward, Mahalia Jackson, James Cleveland, Albertina Walker, hymn writer Fanny Crosby, Thomas A. Dorsey, the father of gospel music, John Newton, composer of "Amazing Grace," my former pastor, Cleavant Derricks composer of "Just A Little Talk With Jesus," Elvis Presley and so many more. I remember thinking, "Mom, what an honor this is! So many of these people are people that I grew up on, or I've grown up on their music. Some you took me to see as a child, and some I've admired from afar. Wow, they are inducting ME? Into THIS"??" My friend Walter Hawkins surprised me by inducting me as he had been inducted the year before. My dear sweetheart, Vision member Maurette Brown Clark, my friend and Vision member Ted Winn, and my friend of many years Vanessa Bell Armstrong along with Walter saluted me with a medley of my songs, which I'll never forget. I did everything I could do to hold the tears back. In 2012, the Queen of Soul herself, Aretha Franklin also was inducted. In December of 2006, I got one of the best friends that I've ever had, a little Yorkshire terrier puppy about the size of my hand that I named Mozart. My therapist told me that I should get some kind of pet and I was glad I did. Even when I had bouts of missing my Mom, he seemed to sense it. He'd run up to me and would just begin to lick my leg and look up at me as if to say, "It's going to be alright." He would become such an integral part of my life. He helped see me through a lot.

CHAPTER 40

FULL CIRCLE MOMENTS

In 2007, Steven Ford and I finally began post-production work on "Journey." Steve is another talent that I would put in the genius category. I consider myself blessed to work with such gifts. We flew to LA to work with Chaka on overdubs, Oakland to work with the Hawkins Family on their song and New York to work with Kelly on hers. At the last minute, I decided to play a piano solo on it. It was the song that I used to hear Mom play when I was a little boy, "I'd Rather Have Jesus," and dedicated it to her memory. Journey was released in the summer of 2007 and debuted at #1 on the charts. It was the first time I had ever had a #1 debut. I bought a new home and moved to the suburbs of Maryland in October after being in the heart of the city of DC since I was ten years old. I loved it. I don't think I've ever lived in a place so peaceful. It's the perfect quiet retreat from when I come off the road and want to rejuvenate. Of course, Mozart is king and in his mind, he runs it. The same year that I moved, my assistant Kelvin and I would travel to Paris, France to do a workshop there. As I was getting out the car in front of the hotel where we were staying, I got the worst pain in my right hip. I'd never felt it before. It finally subsided but periodically would return. I dismissed it as probably from carrying my wallet on that side in my back pocket and decided to switch it to the other side.

In 2008 Vision and I were asked to perform at the Democratic National Convention, which was an extreme honor. For the first time, they were having an ecumenical "Interfaith Gathering" that would open the convention. People from all cultures, denominations and religions were coming together to pray for the success of that week as well as for our candidate, Barack Obama. What an incredible opportunity it was to stand before the delegates singing "Anthem of Praise" and "Total Praise" as a part of that great opening ceremony. We were also honored to do The People's Inaugural Concert as part of President Obama's inaugural celebration in January of 2009.

In the fall of 2008, after going to Japan with Edwin and the Music and Arts Love Fellowship conference, I returned to find out that Edwin's brother, my friend Walter, had been diagnosed with pancreatic cancer while we were away. He needed immediate surgery to remove it. The operation lasted 20+ hours. I prayed so hard. Walter was such a gift to the world. Many people didn't know, but he had a preaching/teaching ministry that was just as powerful as his music ministry. He had been such an inspiration to me since the days of the Hawkins singers, along with his brother Edwin. They had become such great friends and they both meant the world to me. I began to read up on how dangerous this particular cancer was and I remember being so worried. I called several close friends and just asked them to pray with me. Walter came out of the surgery successfully and I just believed that God was going to do a complete and total healing.

In 2009, Walter and the Hawkins family did a reunion concert in Richmond, Virginia. My sister Ollie and a couple of other friends and I drove down. When Walt walked out on the stage it was like he had never been sick a day in his life. Although he was a little smaller than usual, he looked great. He sang that night and hit notes that I had never heard before. Along with Edwin, Tramaine, Lynette, as well as Brenda Roy and Nona Brown - both members of Love Center - they brought the house down. It was an anointed service and they sounded amazing. It was so good to hear them again. But the thing that excited me the most was that Walter looked great and sounded wonderful. We hung out after and Walter gave us his testimony about what God had brought him through. He was so energized and positive. We all were mesmerized.

The same year I did my debut at Carnegie Hall as a part of a big musical celebration with other gospel and secular artists and actors put together by band leader Ray Chew. I sat at the piano playing a solo version of "I Love The Lord," wondering how many artists, classical and otherwise, had played this very piano down through the years. At the end, it segued into "Total Praise" with full orchestra conducted by Ray as former member of the Doobie Brothers Michael MacDonald took the lead, joined by the other artists in the background. I thought about "All I Have is Yours" on that very first Smallwood Singers album and how the Doobie Brothers were the influence for that song. Also, around that same time I had the opportunity to work with Howard classmate and opera diva Jessye Norman at the Apollo as well as a part of the Alvin Ailey Dance Company anniversary celebration along with Donny Hathaway's daughter, Lalah Hathaway. Things have a way of coming full circle.

I hadn't written a song in about four years. I actually thought that the gift was gone for good. I thought about how many songs I had written down through the years and thought maybe this was it for me. I had no inspiration to write and when I sat down at the piano nothing would come. During the presidential election I had become a CNN addict, and continued watching it religiously in 2009. When the recession hit, all I could hear was about how bad everything was. People were losing jobs, their homes and many had lost hope. After a while, I began to embrace the negativity that I was being bombarded with and had to stop watching the news channels. Out of what I was seeing around me, God laid it on my heart to write a project that had to do with his Promises. No matter what the media says or the naysayers say, or what's going on in politics, God is still in control. If He promised that He'd provide and take care of us, then that settles it. When the idea hit, the songs immediately began to come. Many of them would come in dreams, sometimes two at a time, and I would get up and run to the piano to try to put them down before I would forget. They continued to come.

The pain in my hip continued and my doctor recommended an orthopedic specialist. It was found that my right hip was degenerating and that a hip replacement at some point was eminent. It was recommended that I do physical therapy, which would hopefully help delay the process. I had never had surgery in my life other than having my tonsils removed when I was 19. The prospect of something that serious, terrified me. I was praying that some kind of way the physical therapy would take care of the problem and I wouldn't have to go that route.

Even though Wesley hadn't sung with me in many years, we always kept in touch. When he was teaching school, he'd always bring me to meet his kids and to do a little mini-workshop. We'd have the kids cracking up with stories like the one about the janitor at Brunswick Records. One day he called me to let me know he was in the hospital and it was suspected that he had had a heart attack. I called my play sister Ollie and we both rushed to the hospital. Of course, Wesley was as jovial as ever, cracking jokes and being the character that he always was. He said they found out that it wasn't a heart attack after all, but they weren't sure what exactly was going on. I looked at him and remember thinking that he didn't look good and that he needed to take better care of himself. He was released not long after.

On May 18, 2009 we celebrated Walter's 60th birthday in Oakland, California. Ironically it was also Wesley's 63rd birthday. It was a two-day celebration and a wonderful event that I'll always remember. We all went out to eat after Sunday morning service. While sitting at the table I got a call from home. Wesley was back in the hospital, paralyzed from a tumor that had been found on his spine. It had been diagnosed as cancer. I sat there in shock as the news was relayed to me, but I tried to put it in the back of my mind and continue on with the celebration.

By now, Vision had started rehearsals for the new project "Promises." Ever since our inception, my church home Metropolitan had been so supportive and had opened up its doors to us for rehearsals. Now with my new home, I had more than enough room to rehearse everyone there and could rehearse as long as I needed to. It was more of a homey and relaxed atmosphere and we'd eat after every rehearsal. The music continued to come, sometimes so fast that I couldn't keep up. I've never been able to multi-task well as I have a one-track mind. It was the first time that I had ever worked on more than one song at the same time. Wesley was in and out of the hospital. The tumor was removed from his spine but would return again. It was diagnosed that he had some kind of very rare cancer that's usually found more in Asia than in the United States. He and I joked about him having to find something exotic to have as opposed to something normal. He jokingly told me that he was going to be in all of the medical books. When I think of Wesley and the many years that I knew him, he was hardly ever serious. He rarely (if ever) talked about what was really going on with him. His sense of humor was what he was known for as well as being a great cook. He also had a wealth of knowledge when it came to music and vocal training. Because of that and his extroverted personality, he was never a stranger and people were always drawn to him. He was naturally outgoing and always the life of whatever gathering he found himself in. I remember years ago, Pastor Shirley Caesar saying to me that for years she thought Wesley was Richard Smallwood. She said I was always so quiet and didn't have much to say, while Wesley was all over the place, working whatever room the Smallwood Singers were in.

I remember going to see him in the hospital again. Honestly there were so many people in the room while he was holding court that I have no idea why the nurses didn't ask them to leave. It was like a party. It bothered me in that I knew he wasn't feeling well because I could tell when I looked at him, but people loved him so much they would just come, stay and wouldn't leave. I wanted to do like Jesus and "clear the temple." I knew he was very ill. At one point, I'd go up there and people were taking pictures with him. Of course, he loved every minute of it and the more attention, the better. But not long after trying ineffective treatment after treatment for Wesley's cancer, the doctors announced there was nothing more they could do. Wesley would be put into hospice.

I must say, it was a very nice and peaceful place. All of us really just wanted him to be comfortable. Of course, the waiting room at hospice was usually filled with friends and loved ones waiting to go up and spend a couple of minutes with him. He and I laughed about the crazy times at Howard, including the time that the man punched him in his chest. He looked at me with mock anger and said, "I'm still mad at you for driving off and leaving me on that ice." We laughed. He told all of the hospice care workers about his days singing with the Smallwood Singers and when I would go up to see them, they would relay stories that he had told them. I brought him all the Smallwood Singers and Vision CD's I could find to play on his CD player so he could listen. One day while one of the CD's was playing beside his bed, one of the hospice workers asked him to sing something. He looked at me with tears in his eyes and said, "I can't sing anymore." It was the hardest thing for me to see. We decided to do a big benefit concert for him at Union Temple to help raise money for his medical expenses. People came from everywhere! I tried to remember what transportation company I used for Mom, so we could get him transportation to the church. Wesley didn't want to come using any kind of "pedestrian" (as he would call it) transportation. He came in a white stretch limo thanks to our friend Becky Mays who looked after him in such a wonderful way during his entire illness. He arrived in grand style, sitting on the front row of the church, and directing how he wanted things from the audience. It was a great night, a grand celebration, with a great outpouring of love. It was in true "Wesley style." The last remaining members of the Celestials, Lou Lou Wilson and Rosalind Thompkins Lynch and I would hang out with him at the hospice house. That bond and love that we had established with each other so many years ago at Howard would never die.

People started coming from out of town to come see him, some whom we went to Howard with and some who sang in the Union Temple Choir. Wesley was so loved. Even when he got to the point where he couldn't talk and would drift in and out of consciousness, when I'd walk in the room and say "Hey Wes," he would immediately turn his head, try to focus where I was standing and try to smile. This just didn't seem right and was so hard to bear. On October 1st early in the morning, my phone rang. It frightened me, because I thought it was someone telling me Wesley had transitioned. But it wasn't. It was one of my Vision members telling me that our dear friend and Vision member Jeffrey Waddy had just passed suddenly. Jeffrey was one of the nicest and kindest people you would want to meet. He had an incredible tenor voice and most people knew him from singing on our song "At The Table" and "Hold On Don't Let Go" along with Ted Winn and myself. I was numb. He had gone in the hospital for a basic minor procedure and had unexpectedly and suddenly passed. It hit me like a house had fallen on me. There's no way I saw this coming. Whenever Vision would do a bus trip, Jeff would make the best homemade rolls, seven cheese macaroni and cheese and fried chicken. He had the biggest heart and the most generous spirit. He was just great to be around, not to mention the tremendous gift he had and the anointing on that gift. Three days after Jeffrey passed, on October 4th as Rosalind and I were preparing to go up to hospice to see Wesley, I got a call from Becky saying that there was no need to come. She had been with Wesley when he transitioned. The funerals were three days apart, Jeffrey's being on a Saturday and Wesley's being on Monday. That whole time seems like a dream to me. Vision sang at both funerals and the Celestials got together one last time to sing at Wesley's as he had requested. We did the B-side of the only recording we ever did, "Is Your All On The Altar?" It was the song that he wanted. He told Becky what he wanted down to the last detail for his funeral. He had never mentioned it to me. He knew how I was.

It was three of the hardest days I've ever experienced. Later I would add gifted vocalist Elder Steve Jones to the Vision family to stand in Jeffrey's stead. That same month, I went to Mississippi to do a concert with Walter Hawkins. I was so glad to see him and he looked well. As we were talking and riding in the van coming from the airport, I asked him how he was doing. He told me he was feeling pretty good but the doctors had found some lesions on his liver. My heart sank.

CHAPTER 41

MAKE YOUR LIFE COUNT

I t was 2010 and the rehearsals were going well for "Promises."
I decided that after many years of doing "live" projects I
wanted this one to be a studio project, like the old Smallwood
Singers days. I did plan to have a small, intimate live setting
at the recording studio for just friends and family to give the
singers that live energy that you can only get from an audience.
In the spring of that year, my friend Rev. Nolan Williams who
now was working with the Kennedy Center, contacted me. They
wanted to do an entire week of gospel music at the Center. This
had never been done before. Major artists like the Clark Sisters,
Kirk Franklin, Take 6, Walter Hawkins, Pastor Shirley Caesar,
myself and Vision would be featured that week. There would
also be seminars, singalongs, and classes on different aspects of
hymns, spirituals and gospel music. It was an incredible idea
and certainly groundbreaking for the Kennedy Center which
was usually only known for theatrical productions and classical
music performances. I applauded Nolan for coming up with
and implementing such an awesome concept. Opening night
(after an earlier concert by Vision) was to be an extravaganza
night, where the Kennedy Center would honor legends of gospel
music with the Kennedy Center Living Gospel Legend Award

including Edwin Hawkins, Walter Hawkins, Albertina Walker, and Andraé Crouch. I remember Walter not being able to be there that night because of treatment for the cancer. Andraé also was unable to be there that night and his sister Sandra accepted on his behalf. I was honored to be asked by my friend Nolan Williams who was the coordinator, to host that evening. It was an incredible night as different artists saluted the award recipients. I was shocked at the end of the evening as they surprised me, by saluting me with The Living Gospel Legend Award as well, along with the others. It's an honor that I will always cherish and never forget. Later that week Walter was scheduled to do a concert along with full choir and the National Symphony Orchestra honoring his music. I was so proud and excited for him. I had consented to help him out in any way that I could and was going to play for him as well as do backup in the trio "Marvelous", one of my favorite Walter songs. I hadn't seen Walt since October of the previous year and it was now April. When he walked into rehearsal, my heart stopped to see how small he was. He had just come from treatment and was still being affected in terms of his energy by the rigorous procedure. He told me he hadn't sang since the last time we were together in Mississippi in October. He sort of went through the motions at the rehearsal and saved himself. We went to eat and then he went back to the hotel to get some rest. The next evening before the show, my godson Tre', my assistant Kelvin and I sat in Walt's dressing room as he testified about his ordeal. The thing I remember so clearly was that I have never talked to anyone in a situation like that who was so incredibly positive. Talking to him encouraged me in ways I can't even express. It made me look at my own troubles as nothing. Here was someone who literally was fighting for his life, but still praising God and claiming healing for his body. Everything about him was an encouragement. I'll never forget that conversation that evening. When Walt took the stage, it was awesome. The Walter Hawkins voice that we all know and loved was fully there. Not only that, but the anointing was there. I remember standing behind Walt along with former Smallwood Singer Dennis Sawyers, as we backed him up with a feeling of elation as to how anointed and powerful he still was. He was very open with the audience and shared his testimony with them, which made it all the more powerful. The songs he had sung down through the years had a different meaning now. It was poignant yet intense. Although he would have to sit sometimes on a stool throughout the performance, the power and determination in his voice was so evident and so present. At the end of "Marvelous" I was so overcome by it all, that for a minute I forgot I had to run to the other side of the stage and play piano for the next song. My assistant had to call my name from the side of the stage to snap me out of it as the audience gave Walt a standing ovation. Shouts of "We Love you Walter" showered the stage. It would be the last time I would see him.

On July 11, I received a text from my friend Donald Lawrence stating "Walter is gone, Richard." He really had received his ultimate healing. He was free of pain and free of the disease that had ravaged his body. Donald had flown out to Oakland to see him and had arrived at the house right when Walt had passed. It was really strange. That morning when I had awakened, I had a strange feeling that he wouldn't be with us much longer. I went to my Facebook page and posted the statement "Life is full of unexpected twists and turns; some of which are incredibly painful. But in spite of how rough it may become, God is still the mender of broken hearts. Even though the pain may be devastating, it won't always be this way...."

Immediately after I posted it, people started asking was that a song. It wasn't, it was just how I was feeling at the time. I felt in my spirit what was coming, what was eminent, but still knew that God would take all who were affected through it. After I got the news about Walt, the whole concept about God being the "mender" began to take musical shape. The song "Mender" was born that day after hearing that terrible news. There was something about it that my mind couldn't accept. To me, it was impossible to comprehend. I traveled out to be with Edwin and the family. There was a musical the night before the funeral in which artists from all over the country came together to do a musical salute. The funeral was the next day and was completely packed to capacity as the late Bishop Kenneth Moales preached the eulogy. About a month later, Bishop Moales would make his transition as well. I have suffered so many losses of significant people in my life, many more than I had realized until I had to write about it. I know they are all with the Lord, and I know we'll see them again, but each time it happens it leaves a hole in your heart that can never be filled by anyone else. It's so important that we make our lives count and show love for each other while we are here to share it. For those who have gone, let's honor their memories by taking the positive things that they left with us and applying them to our lives, so they'll never be forgotten.

With this string of deaths, the depression seemed to worsen in spite of the medication. I started teaching Walt's "Is There Any Way?" to Vision because I wanted to honor him on the new CD in some way. That's always been my absolute favorite song by him. The words just speak to me in ways I can't even express. I had reached out to my good friend Donald Lawrence to do a song and to be a part of the CD. He had put together an incredible song called "Facts Are, Truth Is". Whenever we all were attending conventions or conferences I guess you could call us the four musketeers, Edwin, Walter, Donald and I. We always stuck together. They were my greatest friends in the industry. Talented musician Danny Weatherspoon had also contributed a song, "Promised Me Grace". I also reached out to Lalah Hathaway, daughter of my former classmate Donny to do a guest appearance. It was all coming together. It was during that time that I ran out of anti-depressant medication. I panicked because I didn't have any refills and for some reason I could not locate my psychiatrist who was in charge of writing the prescription for me. I had prayed often that I wouldn't be on those meds for the rest of my life, but at the same time, it helped me so much and I didn't want to chance the awful kinds of symptoms I was having before I started on them. I never caught up with my psychiatrist and by now I had become frightened as to what was going to happen without my medication. During the latter part of July, something happened. When I really think about it, I don't think it was a dream. It was too lifelike, too detailed. It was more like a vision.

It was night and Mom, Dad and I were living in a big house that seemed to be blocks long. I never saw Mom, but I heard her speaking from one of the other rooms to me. I can't remember what she said. The next thing I knew, I was walking down the street with my stepfather (Smallwood). This was strange because I don't dream of him often, hardly ever. He had on his hat, white shirt, dark pants, suspenders and black dress shoes as he always did. I never really remember him seen in anything else my whole life. It was a long street, and the lights were on. We weren't talking, just walking. When we got to the corner we crossed the street to the other side. On that corner was a huge building, which I remember thinking must be a church. However, I never looked up to see any windows or the top of it. All I saw was what was at eye level. It was a huge building made of grey stone. The front door to the building was right on the corner. From the doors, the building continued down both sides of the street, to the left of them and to the right and then the building met at the corner. When I looked down the street both ways, there seemed to be no ending to the building. It just went on and on. Right at the corner, there were four or five stone steps that led up to a stone archway. Going through the archway would lead you into an alcove and there were double cathedral front doors that were a reddish-brown color. As we got nearer to the stone archway, I heard the most beautiful music that I've ever heard in my life coming from the building. As I recall, it seemed like the music may have been coming from windows on an upper floor. However, I didn't look up. All I know is that the music was coming from above me. My stepfather and I sat down on one of the steps that led to the stone archway as the music washed over us. The music was indescribable in its beauty. Sometimes it was a vocal solo, sometimes, it was a small group, sometimes an ensemble, sometimes male, sometimes female. It varied. The musicians were incredible. The band that was playing had to be the "baddest" I've ever heard in my life. Sometimes I would hear orchestral accompaniment. The songs went from ballads, to mid tempos, to up tempos, to jams. They all seemed to be gospel in nature. I didn't hear any classical or any other genres. I had never heard any of the songs before and each one was exquisite in its composition. All of a sudden as we were sitting there marveling in the excellence of what we were hearing, people began to appear on the corner and while talking to one another, they went up the few steps into the front doors. They never seemed to see us or notice that we were there, instead they walked right past us into the building. After the last one had entered, I turned to my stepfather and said, "Daddy what place is this, what kind of church is this?"

"Son, I don't know," he replied. I said, "This church has to have the most awesome music department on the planet. What is the name of this church?" He said, "Let's see if we can find a sign or something that will tell us the name of it." He took one side of the building and I took the other. I went down one street as he went down the other. At eye level, there were still no windows, no openings except for the double doors on the corner. The building itself was not illuminated in any way and the only light was the light from the streetlights that lined both sides of the sidewalk. I never found any kind of sign, nor could I find where the building ended so I began walking back to the corner. I met my stepfather coming around the other side and he hadn't found a sign either. At the same time, we both saw something that looked like a cornerstone. As we both stooped down to look at the corner stone, we noticed that on it was a profile etching of a man. The man had long hair, a long beard and seemed to be a person of color. There was no date and no name. For some reason, I thought of Frederick Douglas as it reminded me a bit of photographs that I'd seen of him. "I wonder is it an AME Church?" I asked my stepfather. I knew we had a Douglas Memorial AME Church in our area and thought it might be a church that was named after him because of the resemblance on the cornerstone. But dad was just as puzzled as I was. We both walked to the other street to the right of the church. All of a sudden, a woman appeared. We asked her about the name of the church. She answered us, but for the life of me I couldn't hear what she said as the music by now seemed to be everywhere and drowned out her answer. I asked her to repeat what she said again. Still, I couldn't make out what she was saying. So I wouldn't appear dumb, I just went on like I understood what she was saying, but I still didn't have a clue. I remember her saying something about a musical being held here one Sunday out of the month. I imagined that this was what it must be. She disappeared as suddenly as she appeared and Dad and I both took our seats back on the steps. The sounds we heard seemed healing. They seemed to reach the inner most parts of my soul. The sheer beauty of what I was hearing made me want to cry. At that point, there was a phrase that a male group was singing that kept repeating over and over. I can't remember the words, only the melody and the harmony. For a second I thought about going upstairs, but I was afraid someone would recognize me and all I wanted to do was just to hear this music. I didn't want to take part, but just receive what I was getting. I'm not sure how long we sat there. At some point, we both got up to go back to our house up the street. When we stood, my stepfather looked at me and then reached down as if he was going to pick me up to carry me. It was a gesture of love, of carrying someone who was crippled or disabled. It confused me, and I said, "Dad, I'm good. I can make it." He said, "Are you sure?" "I'm fine, Daddy," I replied. We both smiled at each other and began to walk across the street towards the house. I sat up in bed literally and suddenly and began to cry uncontrollably. Immediately I knew that every bad feeling I had for him was gone, every hurt that I had experienced by him was gone, and all my anger was gone. As I cried it felt like all of the unresolved feelings I had about him, the part of me that did not want to forgive him, was being washed away. I knew at that moment that a healing had taken place within me. There was something about that music that did something that nothing else had been able to do. My emotions were healed, my hurt was healed, my spirit healed. I jumped out of bed and ran down the hall crying towards the music room. The only music I could remember hearing was that one phrase that the male group had still been singing as we walked down the street. I sat at the piano, put the music down on my phone as well as recited the whole dream/vision so I would never forget. However, what I experienced is just as fresh today in my mind as if it happened five minutes ago. Most dreams fade as time goes on. Every bit of that experience is still fresh in my mind to the tiniest detail. I believe that some kind of way, I was shown the place in the spiritual realm where music is born. I believe it's the place that at very special times, we tap into as composers and receive what God has already created in that realm. However, I do know that I am healed of the emotions that had me bound and troubled for so long. There was healing in that music that I experienced. My bitter feelings about my stepfather were gone. My anger was gone. My resentment was gone. I thank God for his faithfulness to me, His love for me, and how he continues to take care of and look after me. I have no idea how people make it without Him in their lives. I know that I couldn't. The little repetitious phrase that I was still hearing after I woke up, I used as an intro and an outro on the song "Sow In Tears", the second single on our CD "Promises". It was ironic that Steven and I couldn't come up with an intro for that song. We had a makeshift intro until we could come up with something better. When I ran to the piano after hearing it in my vision, it fit like that last piece that you've finally found in a jigsaw puzzle. I knew that it had been created just for that song before I had even written it.

I was so elated by the vision that I did something that I should have never done, I stopped my antidepressant medication. I had been on them for about seven years and I thought, *well I think*

I can manage without it. In the beginning, I would have little short bouts of melancholy that didn't last more than a few hours. I would have what I called "tune ups' with my therapist every now and then, but stopped our regular visits. In my mind, after stopping the meds and still feeling well in the beginning, I was under the false assumption that I didn't need them anymore. But little by little in increments so slight that I could barely notice, it was creeping back on me.

Promises, with the first single being "Trust Me" was released in the summer of 2011. It debuted at #1 on the charts and received a Dove award for best traditional gospel album. During Thanksgiving week that same year while I was in Chicago I received a call early one morning from Carolene. Our dear Lisa Burroughs Allen from the Smallwood Singers and the baby of the group passed after a lengthy battle with Lupus. We had just texted the week before as she entered the hospital. After texting her to let her know I was checking on her, she texted me back saying, "Thanks for checking on me" and in caps she texted "I LOVE YOU AND MISS YOU TOO"! I'll keep that text with me always. I miss my beautiful and crazy friend. It hit me hard and seemed to bring back all of the other significant losses I had experienced; Wesley, Walter, Jeffrey, Joanna, Freddye and most definitely Mom. It was a rough Christmas that year. Thank God for friends who rallied around me and helped me through it. Some of my friends from Howard and the old Union Temple days decided to come and have a weekend sleepover to encourage me through that holiday. It meant the world to me.

In January of 2012, while being in Nashville performing on the Stellar Awards, I was in so much pain that I could barely walk and knew I was going to have to have surgery because my hip was getting worse. I couldn't procrastinate about it any longer.

I returned home and was unable to travel until mid-summer. It was discovered that I had a birth defect, which miraculously had never bothered me until around 2007. The socket in which the hip fits was never completely developed. So instead of having a round space like I should have, for the hip joint to fit into, it was a sort of oblong space in which my hip had been trying to fit in all of my life. This caused wear, tear and degeneration until it was bone against bone. My surgeon said I should have had surgery long before and it was one of the worst cases he had seen. I had total hip replacement surgery on my right side in April and by late May, I was walking like I had never had surgery: limp free, pain free and cane free. God is still a healer, physically, mentally and emotionally. People like my Vision family Rhonda Chapman, my assistant Kelvin Leach, Baby Smallwood Singer and childhood friend Val Wright Matthews, sister Ollie, my godson Tre' and close friends Bill Clemmons, Cornell Allen as well as other friends and loved ones were there from the day I had surgery until I came home. They all helped nurse me back to health again. Some also made sure I got to my physical therapy appointments which were of prime importance. I believe God used that period of recuperation so I could write my story. Since 2007, I had been promising to do it. But because of schedules, recording and life in general, I could never seem to get around to it. I think I procrastinated because I knew it wouldn't be easy to tell and there were a lot of painful memories that I didn't want to relive. But everything happens for a reason and happens in God's own time. All things still work together for the good of them who love God and who are the called according to His purpose.

CHAPTER 42

HARD SCRABBLE

S ometime in 2012, my friend Jared Sawyers who had done so much of the incredible research on my family and had connected so many dots, reached out to me excitedly. He had found photos and information about the plantation where both sides of my family lived, and also where my great great grandfather and his family from "the other side" lived as well! The plantation home was built in 1775 by William and Elizabeth Clenny on a hillside adjacent to the old Indian Trading Path. In 1779, they sold the house and 227 acres to James Cain and his son John, who had immigrated to North Carolina from Maryland. Eventually the plantation was given to Dr. James Cain who was my great-great grandfather, in 1857. James Cain renamed the plantation 'Hardscrabble'. The name 'Hardscrabble' may have been derived from conditions at the plantation during the Civil War. James Cain served as Assistant Surgeon to the Medical Department in the Confederacy. They restored the house in the 1970s, and sold it in 1991. Jared first sent me an accompanying older photo of the house. I stared at the photo for hours wondering what must have gone on in that house and on the surrounding land. I remember a story that Mom told me once of Cousin Lula trying to get off the land as soon as she could, because of fear of "Old Doc Cain." From what she was told by Lula and by her mother Nellie, she intimated that he molested his black daughters. Mom said something to the effect that when he would return from his trips he would ride straight down to where my family lived on his white horse. When my grandmothers would see the white horse coming their way they were terrified. Did the reason that he was not mentioned by either one of my grandmothers have anything to do with something else that may have happened? Was their lack of acknowledgement of him as their father steeped in reasons that had to do with much more than just the shame of having a white father? Why didn't the family leave? Slavery was over. Were they sharecropping? Were they too poor to leave? Maybe that was their only way of survival. I remember reading how after Emancipation, many slaves wanted to stay in their situations because it was hard to survive on their own. At least where they were, they had a roof over their heads and a bit of food. I still was not sure what present state Hardscrabble may have been in or if it still existed. However not long after Jared found a current picture of it, I discovered that it was still standing. I cannot tell you how excited I was. We also found out that in 1995, the remaining land was developed into a subdivision by Chatham Development Corporation; the original dual-house was purchased by the then current owners in 2003 and was privately owned. I wanted to walk through and see it just once. But what would I do? I couldn't just go up to a private home and knock on the door and tell them my crazy story and request to see the house. Or could I?

More information kept coming in and not long after we found out that Hardscrabble was for sale! I certainly had no desire to purchase it. I didn't want to live there nor did I want to be a landlord. I just wanted to see where the beginnings of so much of my family happened. I wanted to know more about where I came from. I had seen so much written information. Now I wanted to see where they lived and where some of them died. I wanted to see the land that their eyes had seen long before I was born. I immediately reached out to my assistant Kelvin and told him what I had found out. His response was let me see what I can find out. God has an amazing way of moving in unexpected ways. Vision and I had been booked to do a concert in Durham at the Durham Theater in April of 2013. Kelvin called me back in a few days and asked if I could go down a day earlier before the concert. He had somehow found the realtor for the house and had told him a small portion of my story. He said, "I had to sort of hint that you may be interested in purchasing, just so I could get you in to see the place." Honestly, I didn't care what he had to say. I just wanted to see the house. I reached out to my cousin Robyn who was a senior at the time at Bennett College in Greensboro, NC. She was elated and we decided we'd go together.

As we drove out of Durham towards Hillsborough NC, while the GPS gave directions, my heart began to beat faster. At some point, I realized that I was pretty nervous. What would I see? How would I feel? How would I react? I had my cell phone and my iPad with me and I began to take video of the scenery, as we got closer to it. Large and beautiful old reconstructed homes were on one side while on the other there were rolling hills and beautiful green grass surrounded by white fences. My heartbeat picked up the pace as the GPS said, "Make a left on to Hardscrabble Drive." As we turned, the road narrowed and turned from pavement to a dirt road mixed with gravel. Huge trees loomed on our right, while the rolling hills, fields and the seemingly never-ending white fence continued on our left. Maybe 20 seconds after turning on to Hardscrabble drive, the GPS announced the address of the home. As I looked to my right, I could see the top of the house through the trees. All of a sudden, the trees were gone and there sat the house. My cousin and I were taken aback by what we were seeing as we turned into the graveled driveway beside the house. It was a beautiful white large two story colonial home in pristine condition. What used to be a screened in porch as seen in older photographs was now open and ran the entire length of the front of the house with old-fashioned high back rocking chairs on the porch. Black shutters framed each window matching the same color roof. By now my heart was pounding. Robyn pulled to the side door as the realtor came out to greet us with a big smile. I had stopped shooting video on my iPad and was trying to start it back up. However, my fingers were shaking so bad that I couldn't. It's like my mind went into freeze mode and the apps on my iPad made absolutely no sense to me. The realtor shook our hands as we got out of the car and was very welcoming. He said he had been hearing all about the concert the next day at the Durham Theater and was excited that I was there. As we entered the side door, there was a plaque to the right of the door that said "Historic Preservation Society of Durham, HARDSCRABBLE CA. 1775, 1790. Oldest continuously inhabited house in Durham Co. The Cain family lived here more than 120 years and once owned 1675 acres." When we entered the door, we were in the spacious kitchen. It was beautiful and contained a huge fireplace with a mantle. The realtor began to explain that all of the mantles in the house, the floors and some of the doors were original. I could tell that whatever was not original had been painstakingly recreated to give the feel of what it probably looked like in the

1800s. Even the paintings looked like something from that era. As he told us about the house, he said, "So I understand you have some history here." I answered, "Yes, my family lived here during slavery and for a time after." I asked, "Are you familiar with James Cain?" "Most definitely, Dr. Cain was the owner at one point," he answered.

"Well," I replied, "He was also my great-great-grandfather." I could see the look of astonishment on the realtor's face. I'm sure he was aware that this was once a plantation and, where there were southern plantations, there were slaves. But I don't think he was prepared for the fact that I was also related to the former owner. "That's amazing," he said and began to take us on a tour of the house. By now, I was so nervous, I don't think reasoning was foremost and I never thought to take photos. Thank God for the brochure which had pictures of most of the major rooms in the house. It was huge. A smell of history hung in the air. Honestly my mind was filled with mixed emotions, but the strongest one was that it felt like I was being welcomed home. I tried to shake the feeling and listen to him as he explained the different things that we saw. But honestly it was like I could only hear the words but they didn't make sense. I was sort of in a state of disbelief, where nothing felt real. It was like I was wafting through a dream. In one of the bathrooms the wall had a piece of glass in it about the size of a small window. Looking through the glass you could see the huge wooden beams, which were the structure of the house, all original as well. He explained that the house was owned by a married couple who were professors at Duke University. "Since you have so much history here" he said "you should consider buying it." I had no interest in selling my home in Maryland and moving to NC, nor did I have any desire to be a landlord, but this was one of the most fascinating journeys I had ever embarked upon. I also thought, knowing my background, I'd probably end up seeing relatives both black and white wandering around the house at night. I certainly did not want to experience that! At one point, the realtor told my cousin and I, "Take as long as you want, and look around until your heart is content."

We went from room to room and everything was beautiful. I think Robyn and I were not only blown away by what we were seeing but the significance of it all. Our conversation at this point consisted basically of "oh Wow!!" At one point, we ended back outside walking around the grounds. Across the way was a field of grass surrounded by a white fence but you could still see where the old road that led up to the house used to be, from the indentation in the ground. I imagined horses and carriages, soldiers on horses riding back and forth to and from the house. By now I had made a feeble attempt to take photos and video, but honestly my fingers were trembling and I couldn't seem to operate my camera phone in the correct way. My brain was definitely on hold, as it seemed that I even couldn't focus the camera right. As I looked around the grounds I began to wonder exactly where my family lived. On the old census reports they were listed as living on the land. I'm sure there were houses or shanties that had since been torn down. Maybe some even lived in the "big house." I wish I could have asked questions of my Cousin Lula, even my Uncle Clee who both had been born here on this land. But they were long gone, and at the same time, I'm wondering how much they would be willing to share if they were here. By now as I began to walk towards the barn, the feeling of sensing loving presences who were welcoming me, was overwhelming. The presence was so thick, it felt like I could touch it. I've never felt so wanted, so welcomed, so loved before.

It was hard to explain. It was a feeling of belonging, of me being a missing jigsaw puzzle piece finally fitting into and finishing the giant jigsaw puzzle picture. It was a sense of really being home. Actually, there was a part of me that didn't want to leave. This was the land; these were the trees, the view of the sky that my ancestors looked upon. For someone who never knew my history for many years, or how I was connected to anything or anyone other than my Mom, this was so needed. Again, as I did about my own step-father, I had mixed feelings about my great-great grandfather. But I did come from him and it's the same story of so many other African-Americans all over this country. Regardless of the circumstances, of which I'll probably never know, if it wasn't for him, I wouldn't be here.

My thoughts were interrupted as I heard the realtor excitedly calling my name. "Mr. Smallwood, as soon as you all finish I have something to show you!" As we headed back to the house and entered the kitchen, there was a big black book that hadn't been there before lying on the table. The realtor excitedly told me that he had called one of the owners while we had been walking around the land and told her my story. She in turn became excited and told him to find a book for me that she wanted me to see. As I looked closer at the cover of the book it read, "Information Relating to The Families of Hugh and James Caine, Orange County, North Carolina compiled by High Conway Browning." Here was the history of the Cains who by no stretch of the imagination I was directly related to. It contained family history starting at 1750: deeds, wills, personal letters by family members—even the deed of sale of the original land dated March 20, 1779 upon which the house was built. A slave narrative by Sarah Debro was included. I sought in vain to find anything written that included any of my ancestors that

I was aware of. Former Slave Miss Sarah who was kept in the big house and who was interviewed at the age of 85 stated that, "Marse (Master) Cain owned so many niggers dat he didn't know his own slaves when he met dem in de road." She went on to say that Doc Cain was good to his slaves and never beat them, but if they were insubordinate, he would sell them. I couldn't imagine what it must have been like to live in that time as a black man. Some were born into this and it's all they knew, so it was normal to them. They had no point of reference to any other way of living. An interesting document that we would discover later was a letter from President Andrew Johnson granting James Cain "full pardon and amnesty for all offences by him committed, arriving from participation, direct or implied by said rebellion." According to President Johnson, one of the conditions of this pardon would be contingent on the fact that "James Cain shall not hereafter, at any time acquire any property whatever in slaves, or make use of slave labor." The president signed this on August 21, 1865. But again, questions in my mind arose. In 1880, my family was still living there. What was that about? I was fascinated by what I was reading. The realtor asked me could he send me a copy of it. I told him I would love to have that as a part of my historical records and asked him to thank the owner for sharing it with me. Robyn and I finally left after spending several hours there. I felt I could have spent the night. I felt such a connection to that land. Several weeks later, I received the complete history that the realtor had painstakingly scanned page by page. I will always be grateful for him, taking the time out, listening to my story and the owner for sharing that part of my history with me.

CHAPTER 43

ANTHOLOGY

In the beginning of 2013, I decided to put together a medley of older Vision songs for our concerts. People were always asking, "Why don't you sing this song or that song?" So, a medley was a way of incorporating some of the songs that people wanted to hear. Raymond Reeder, Justin Savage (a brilliant musician who sometimes played for me) and I got together and started assembling the medley. While working on it, I realized there were songs from the Smallwood Singers era that people wanted to hear as well, so we began to work on a Smallwood Singers medley. Recording was the last thing on my mind during that time. However, one day while on the treadmill at the gym, a song called "Amazing Love" dropped into my mind while listening to music on my headset. A song waiting to be composed had never bombarded its way through other music that I was listening to, so I thought I'd better put it down when I came home. Putting that song down opened the floodgates, and songs just started pouring into my spirit. Some songs came to me in dreams but most were given to me when I was nowhere near a piano, and not particularly thinking about music. I began to put all the musical concepts on my iPhone as I always did. I remember thinking, "Maybe God is telling me it's time to record." At the same time, an album concept began to take form. I wanted to do a musical/historical perspective of my journey thus far, sort of a soundtrack of my life. The medleys would trace the recordings and the songs that many were familiar with, down through the years. Of course, the newer songs would represent where I was musically right now. I also had the idea of saluting two of my major gospel music inspirations. When I really thought about it, no one influenced me more than the Martin Singers in terms of my choral approach to gospel music and certainly Little Lucy Smith Collier was at the top of the list in terms of my pianistic approach. I worked hard with Vision trying to recreate that Martin Singers sound, which was an integral part of my life for so many years. My dear friend Edwin Hawkins was my biggest inspiration when it came to writing. After hearing his song arrangements from his debut album, I was never the same. I remembered his other group that many weren't aware of, "The Hebrew Boys" an all-male group consisting of he, his brother Walt and two male members from the Edwin Hawkins Singers. I pulled my Vision male section together to try to recreate that sound. Of course, I called my musical partner Steve Ford and we began to plan the whole record. The music continued to come and Steve came up with a brilliant song called "Anthology" that would open the project. I really wanted my musical history represented, some that most people knew nothing about. In 1989 I worked on Earth, Wind and Fire's Philip Bailey's Gospel solo project, Family Affair. Philip, Oliver Wells and myself composed "Lord You Reign" for the Family Affair project, which I also later revamped for "Anthology."

Hebrews 11 was one of my favorite passages of the Bible. I thought it was written brilliantly, poetically and really defined what faith was, how it worked and examples of it being put to work through history. Growing up on movies like *The Ten Commandments*, *Ben Hur* and *King of Kings*, I heard a kind of biblical movie score when I thought of the music that should accompany that great passage. Great composers such as Miklós Rózsa and Elmer Bernstein wrote some of the greatest music soundtracks for those epic films. These composers always inspired me. The music began to come, with the very last line "not seen" coming early on before the rest of the song was composed. I remember when I played back that last line on my recorder, without even having fitted all of the lyrics together yet, tears began to well up in my eyes. Harmonic progressions alone without lyrics have the capacity to move the listener at their deepest level. When you combine the right harmonic progressions with the right lyrics, something very powerful happens. It reaches the listening ear and affects the listener on two separate levels. That's why what you play under your lyrics is just as important. It should convey musically what you are trying to say in your message. In other words, it should be a total package, lyrics marrying music. When that song was completed, it immediately became one of the closest to my heart that I've done. We brought in Phil Lassiter, an absolutely amazing horn player who blew me away when I first heard him playing with Prince, and knew that I had to work with him on this new record. He assembled an awesome array of first class horn players and took on doing the horn arrangements for the project. Steven did the amazing string arrangements for the project which we added later in the studio. Of course, the Vision band along with Jonathan Dubose on guitar had to be on board. I contacted my dear friend Ángela Winbush who started out with me those many years ago as a teenager. I pulled out a song that I had written for her in 1975 while she was a Howard student called

"Look Up and Live." It had been the title cut of Union Temple's Young Adult Choir's very first album, and featured an 18-year-old Ángela singing her heart out. I brought back Smallwood Singer Dottie Jones to help out with the Smallwood Singers medley and recreate songs like "I Love the Lord," "He Won't Leave You" and "I've Come Too Far" which she was so known so well for. Both of these friends were so much a part of my anthology. I brought back Darin Atwater to play as only he can on "Hebrews 11" and parts of the Smallwood Singers medley. Vision rehearsed hard for over a year, weekly and sometimes twice a week as we approached the recording date. Warren Shadd (the first African American piano manufacturer in history) provided his amazing 9'3" grand piano that was absolute heaven to play. It has become my favorite piano, hands down. On August 24, 2014 almost 4,000 people gathered at Evangel Cathedral in Largo, Maryland for one of the most memorable nights of my life. My pastor emeritus Dr. H. Beecher Hicks Jr., opened up the night with a powerful prayer that set the tone for the rest of the night. It was definitely a night of anthology for me. So many important people from my life, past and present were there. My family of course and going all the way back to some of my White Stone Crew, some of whom were in that first little kids group of Smallwood Singers…they were there. People from High School were there, from Howard University School of music, members of the original HU gospel choir were there, members of the Celestials, the first group on Howard's campus were there, from Union Temple's Young Adult Choir, the original Smallwood Singers, my friend Edwin Hawkins, artists, musicians, pastors, friends from childhood up until now. So much of my history and my life were there. The energy and the love in that room was something like I had never experienced. There were people from all over the United States as well as Europe and from some of the Islands. It was an amazing night. It was like God put his stamp of approval on our efforts. My Vision family sang like never before. As long as I live, I'll never forget that night. When Steven and I started mixing, I knew then that this was a project closer to me than anything I had done. It was a definitive work showing where God had brought me from. It was the kind of project I had always wanted to do. I couldn't have been prouder of it and everyone that was involved. I was so glad that my dear friend Edwin was there and that I could salute him and thank him publicly for what he meant to me. I had no idea how important that would actually be.

It was the first recording of mine he had attended since Live at Howard in 1993. He hinted to me he wasn't feeling his best, and when we went to lunch together a couple of days after the recording I could tell something was going on. He seemed a bit disoriented as we were leaving the hotel and was walking slower than normal. It concerned me but not overly so. When we walked directly across from the hotel and sat down in the restaurant his old self seemed to return. We both love coffee and they had the best at the place down at the Washington Harbor. In no time we were laughing and talking with him telling how much he enjoyed the recording which meant the world to me of course. He left later that same day for home in California. Not long after he told me that he would have to have dialysis several times a week because of some kidney and blood issues. The next time I was on the West Coast several months later at his home, he was the old Edwin, with that bounce and pep in his step. He said he felt like a new man after treatment and I didn't think much more about it, other than I was elated he was back to the old Edwin that I knew and he felt fine. Since we are on opposite coasts we talked on the phone more than saw each other, but I noticed hospital stays and him not feeling up to par begin to follow him. When I would see him as I did at the Seminar, I just felt something was not quite right. However Edwin would always assure everyone he was fine and not to worry. The last time we would hang together would be September of 2016 in DC.

In 2008 Congresswoman Sheila Jackson Lee (D-TX) and Senator Blanche Lincoln (D-AR) led the passing of a resolution declaring September as "Gospel Music Heritage Month." Each year since its establishment, both local and global celebrations have been held to further educate audiences in Gospel Music's rich history and legacy. Each September at the John F. Kennedy Center in DC, legends in the genre and others are honored, among them being Walter Hawkins, Andraé Crouch, Civil Rights leader Rep. John Lewis and myself. That year Edwin was one of the honored recipients. I was excited for him and Congresswoman Sheila asked would I award him while the citation was being read and put the medal around Edwin's neck. Now Edwin was always, from day one, one of the best dressed people I knew. In fact he was the best dressed brother in gospel music. His style was impeccable and every hair was always in place. Everyone knew from the days back in the 60s, never touch Edwin's hair and it was a running joke between all of his friends who knew him well. As they read the citation Edwin looked at me holding the medallion in my hand, and under his breath he said to me, "don't mess up my hair", which caused us both to start laughing and when the official photo was snapped both of us were trying to keep from bursting out in laughter. In fact, I did. Its' one of my favorite photos. It was such a great celebration that night and after it was over he and some of my friends went out to eat and had the best time laughing until we were in stitches.

Edwin had a great sense of humor. The only difference was that he could hold his laughter in public and just grunt. I in turn, after hearing him grunt, would start giggling uncontrollably until my shoulders would start to shake. So sitting next to him in church was not always the best idea for me.

The day after him being honored at the Kennedy Center, we hung out in Georgetown for a day of shopping, ate at another one of his favorite restaurants and he left the next morning for home. More and more when I would talk to him on the phone he would sound weaker and weaker and I began to get extremely worried. He assured me that all the tests that they were giving him came back fine and all was great. There was a number of hospital stays and then reports of him losing his ability to walk. The following summer he was too ill to attend the seminar and I knew something had to be terribly wrong. We talked less on the phone because I didn't want to tire him out. Sometimes he'd be too tired to talk. Other times I'd leave a text just to let him know I was thinking about him and he'd text back later. But the more I heard his voice, the more I was so concerned. During the holiday season he did a concert in San Francisco with the orchestra there that was streamed live. I eagerly anticipated watching but noticed that he remained seated throughout the concert on stage. But his sense of humor still prevailed as he talked to the audience. He and his singers sounded great and it really gave me hope. I thought excitedly, "he's on his way back!" and I was so encouraged. However not long after I received a call from Edwin's assistant that Edwin was suffering from the same deadly pancreatic cancer that his brother Walter had suffered from. I couldn't believe it. I was in denial. People began to go see him including my friend Donald Lawrence who called me immediately and told me that Edwin was in a very weakened state and it was very upsetting to see. I called my assistant to book a flight for that Wednesday, January 18th. I had to go see my friend. I was traveling that previous weekend and had received a call from his sister, my dear friend Lynette, saying that Edwin wanted her to call me and tell me that he wanted me to write his obituary. He said I knew more about him than anybody else. I guess I had been following him since I was 19 years old and knew so much about all the amazing things he had accomplished during his career and ministry. I hung up and broke down. I could not accept this. This was my mentor, my friend, the big brother that I never had. Edwin had told a mutual friend a while back that I was the little brother he never had. He then laughed, went on to say," I do have brothers with the same name Hawkins, but they don't listen to me like Richard does!" I will always cherish that. I listened because I understood that he wasn't in my life by happenstance... but while he was there, I was to learn everything I could to be all that I could be. He was the one who inspired me to write. He was the one that had told me the sky was the limit for me, because he believed in me and he believed in my gift. I called my therapist. I just wanted her to sort of prepare me for the visit. I think on some level I was afraid to see him, but there's no way that I could not make that trip to see my good friend. But he left before I could get there. On January 15th 2018, I got that call that I had dreaded. He'd gone home to be with God. It hit me as if my house fell on me. It was harder than any transition I had dealt with in a long time and I couldn't remember hurting like that in a long time. Even now there are days, where it's still hard for me to wrap my mind around. The two memorial services in Oakland were wonderful. Everyone from everywhere was there, including an appearance by the original Hawkins Singers who had helped to inspire that

19-year-old young student at Howard University those many years ago. To have someone that important in my life gone is irreplaceable. But I'll always take the inspiration that he gave me, what he taught me by his example, the encouragement, the love and try to spread it to those who are coming on behind me. Whenever we would eat together or hang out, I would always revert to that 19-year-old skinny kid sitting with his mentor in awe. That never changed. I don't think he ever got that or how much he influenced me even when I tried to inadequately explain it. But most importantly, he was my friend. A true friend, one that I never had any questions about his allegiance or his love for me. He encouraged me through my own depression, prayed for me, told me I could get through it. He was never an acquaintance, or colleague, but my friend. He knew so much about me and I knew I could always go to him and he would give me his wisdom, his advice but more than anything his compassion and that same kind spirit that I first experienced as a sophomore at Howard University. I absolutely adore his family, because they have been in my life basically as long as he was. I will never, ever forget my friend and what he meant to me. I thank God for allowing him to be such an influential part of my journey. Edwin was meant to be a part of it and I am the better for it.

One of the hardest things I had to accept after having that vision in 2010, is that I actually loved my stepdad. I didn't know what to do with it. I felt guilty for loving someone who did despicable things to me. However, I know he was a very sick man. Recently we found a newspaper article from years ago, and I read in horror as it described how the police followed his car and caught him molesting a young girl. Unfortunately, when I was growing up they didn't have the kind of laws in place for people who did atrocious acts like that. I pray for all of the people down through the years who were affected by the things he did. I'm not sure what happened to him when he was a boy. He never talked about his childhood. But something must have happened to bring him to violate children. Even as messed up as he was, he still established some great churches around the country, many of which are still flourishing. He definitely had a gift for founding churches as well as preaching. He was the only father I knew and I think he loved me in the only way that he knew how. Yes, there were parts of him that resented me for what I represented. But then there was another part of him who was proud of me and encouraged me to be the best I could be in music. I believe he was put in my life to help me reach that goal. I've sat and pondered the idea of him never being in my life. Suppose my mother had not married him and she had raised me in Durham. Would I be who I am today? Would I have accomplished what I have? C.L. Smallwood had me working with live choirs at the age of 7 years old. He insisted I learn every major hymn in the old Baptist Hymnal. He insisted I play them in various keys. Before I was even good enough to play in public he had me standing in front of packed church congregations singing my heart out, while he played. I believe there is purpose in everything. If he had not insisted that this shy little kid hone his skills in the church, I don't know in which direction I might have gone. My foundation is in the church. I think my primary lessons on how to play songs I've never heard on the spot, picking up someone's key who starts singing acapella from the congregation, the rudiments of basic keyboard harmony (a class that I was exempt from in college because of what I already knew) and many of the elements of training my ear, I learned because of him. Certainly, I learned a lot from listening to recordings, going to concerts of my favorite artists and listening to the many sounds around me, but I was able to put them into practice because of him. Even though he was a very sick individual, God used him to push me into the very thing that I was put here for. Even though there was never a father/son parental bond, God used him for a purpose. I believe he was in my life for that specific purpose. It seemed like the minute he was sure that I had gotten my music degree, he transitioned. I also have to say that he was a very good preacher. I'm sure hearing him all my life influenced me as well. It also further proves the point that God has always used very flawed people; from David to Paul and the list goes on. We all have come short and because of God's grace and mercy, we are not consumed. I have to be honest. Even though it still troubles me about some of the awful things he did, I'm finally recognizing Smallwood's purpose as it pertains to me.

CHAPTER 44

DEPRESSION RETURNS

The year 2015 was a rough one for me. After stopping my medication in 2010 for no other reason than thinking I didn't need it any longer, the depression began to creep back in increments. It was so gradual that I didn't realize it was returning. By 2015 I knew that it was back, I just didn't want to admit it. I didn't want to talk to my therapist because I knew deep down inside I needed to get back on medication and that was what she was going to tell me. But each month, it seemed like it would get worse. Being consumed with death began to invade my mind again.

The depression was so thick it was almost physical. In fact it was so thick, it was almost visible. Day by day it got worse until it was hard for me to get out of bed. By the time that Thanksgiving, the anniversary of Mom's death, and Christmas all came around, it had gotten scary. I hid it from my family and everyone. I spent many days googling on the Internet how to end my life painlessly. I didn't want to suffer or be maimed in some type of permanent way and yet still be alive, I just wanted it to end. I watched video after video on Youtube of suicides, people shooting themselves in the head, people hanging themselves, and jumping from buildings, thinking I just needed to find a painless way to end it. I became morbidly fascinated by watching these suicides and couldn't stop watching them. Every time I would Google "painless suicides" a suicide hotline number would come up on the screen and say "call immediately." I didn't want help. I just wanted it to be over. It was nothing but God when one of my good friends Pastor Andre McCloud called me needing a temporary place to stay. I've known him since the 80's. I told him I have more than enough room, just move in over here. It really was a godsend because him being in the house really helped me. Being here alone was not good for me at all. In fact, if he hadn't been here I don't think I would either. By the time my Mom's birthday, Jan 12th arrived, I couldn't get out of bed. I had not slept in about two months. I knew every show that came on TV until 5:00 in the morning when my favorite "I Love Lucy" would come on. I watched the sunrise every morning, without having an ounce of sleep. I told Andre what was going on with me and he kept a watchful eye on me. There were days he wouldn't see me because I wouldn't come out the room or get out of bed. He immediately started calling my close friends letting them know something was very wrong and I needed help. Finally, I called my therapist and broke down on the phone. She instructed me to see my regular doctor immediately. When my doctor saw me he immediately knew something was wrong. I didn't even look like myself. When he checked my blood pressure it was so incredibly high. He said, "Richard, why is your pressure so high? Have you been taking your hypertension medication?"

"No," I replied.

"Why not??" he asked. I could feel the tears welling up in my eyes. Trying to get myself under control I said, "Because I don't care" and then I broke down in tears uncontrollably. He said, "Richard, don't worry, we are going to get a handle on this and get you some help." He immediately started me on an antidepressant and made an appointment for me with a psychiatrist that he highly recommended. The antidepressants had awful side effects so my new psychiatrist started me on a new medication. I started my weekly therapy sessions back with Carolyn after many years. She even had Andre join one of my therapy sessions to tell him what the danger signs were and make sure that he saw my face at least once a day. Little by little with the medications, with the prayers of many friends and family members, I began to heal. I had lost all interest in any kind of music other than just listening to classical which is always so soothing to me. It had never been this bad other than when Mom passed. I'm thankful that I'm on my way back, I'm healing and excited about what God is doing in my life.

Because I was saddled with depression for so many years, sometimes I would act out in abnormal ways. I shut myself off from so many people. It had nothing to do with them, but it was all about what I was feeling inside. Not everyone understood because most didn't have a clue what I was going through. I thank God for friends and loved ones who stuck by me regardless of what I was dealing with. I thank God for those who prayed for me and continue to do so. For those who are dealing with depression, please get help. So many suffer in silence because of shame and embarrassment. Talk to a friend, or maybe a pastor that you trust. Finding the right therapist is not easy, but it's necessary. Often you'll have to try more than one before the connection happens. But there is help available and there is hope. I was fortunate. My therapist was not only trained in that area, but she was also a licensed minister. Going to therapy was one of the best things I've ever done for myself. I'm forever changed because of it. I was not only treated for this issue physically but spiritually as well. We are spiritual beings housed in a physical body. The total person has to be treated. Don't be ashamed and afraid to reach out. Life can be better. It doesn't have to stay the way that it is. But you have to take that first step. God has not forgotten about you. He'll be with you through every step of the process. And don't let the stigma or how you feel in the moment cause you to make bad decisions. If you have to take medication because of depression, stay on it until you are instructed otherwise. Continue praying because conversation with God is important as well as therapy and meds if you need them. Don't be afraid to reach out for help. There is another side to depression and if you are doing the right things to help yourself, trust me, you can live a happy and fulfilling life.

During the time that I had started the new medication I got a phone call from Rosa checking on me. Actually the medication had not kicked all the way in yet and I was having extreme anxiety problems. I had issues being around a lot of people and if I was around a crowd, extreme panic would set in. I didn't want to go into detail with Rosa, so I just told her that I was doing okay. She asked me if I was sitting down. I answered "yes" as I was sitting at my dining room table. She said "I have something to tell you. I'm tired of carrying it around so I'm giving it to you. You can do whatever you want to do with it. You can ignore it if you want to, but I can't carry it around any longer." What in the world was she trying to tell me? She started by asking me, "Richard, who are Mike and DeDe?" I answered "they are my cousins," while wondering why in the world was she asking me that? She asked the question again "Richard, who are Mike and DeDe?" The side effects from the new meds had not worn completely off and I wasn't feeling that well. So I answered again a little impatiently "Rosa they are my cousins, double cousins to be exact because they are cousins on Momma's side starting from her grandmother Annie Weaver and on Annie's sister's side, Winnie Weaver. There was a pause and Rosa said, "Richard they are your half brothers." "WHAT????" I exclaimed. She said calmly "the truth is that Robert my late husband, Mike and DeDe's father, your Mom's second cousin, is your real father." As she told me I was definitely shocked at first, but all of a sudden a peace came over me, a truthful kind of peace, a peace like I was finally home. It was a familiarity, a welcoming kind of feeling as if all my ancestors were applauding and acknowledging me. I hadn't felt it before during this whole father quest. She began to explain the entire conversation that she had with Lula at the age of nineteen after first marrying Robert those many years ago while Lula was teaching her how to prepare cabbage. Lula told her that her grandson, Robert, was my actual father although Mom had been in love with Rivers. Rosa was now 81. For all of those years my family knew but no one talked about it. Rosa said to me that day, "Richard, I didn't know how you would accept it, that's why we just decided to leave it alone at first. Mike knows and DeDe knows and even some of your nephews and your niece know. You can do what you want with it. You can get a DNA test if you want to, you can accept it or choose not to. You can mention it to DeDe and Mike if you want to, or just leave it alone. I'm just dropping it in your lap so that I've gotten it off me. I believe you need to know the truth."

Seven years after I was born, Rosa married Robert and my half brothers were born. I'm twelve years older than my middle brother and thirteen years from my youngest. Rosa said after being told about my paternal truth by Lula, she approached Robert and asked "are you Richard's father?" He became infuriated with her and demanded to know who told her that. She responded that it was Lula. Robert stormed out of the room and called Durham and spoke to his sister Olivia. He began cursing and said, "She's asking questions, SHE'S ASKING QUESTIONS!! Who told her that??" When he realized that Rosa could hear the conversation his words turned into whispers. At some point Mom and Robert had clearly hooked up. I have no idea of what their relationship was or if it was more than one time. They both are gone and only they know. There was the story in our family of Rivers trying to kill Robert which I never understood. But now it made sense. When Rivers found out about Robert being my dad, my grandmother Bessie had to send him up north to save her son's life. Even though things quieted down and Robert came back home after about a year, Robert and Rivers never spoke again for the rest of their lives.

After I hung up with Rosa, I immediately called DeDe and asked him did he know anything different about my father situation. He immediately answered, "You mean the fact that we are brothers???" Ironically while I was talking to DeDe, Mike hit me up on Facebook and substantiated the same thing. They all knew. Everyone was afraid that I would pull away from the family or be upset if I knew. Rosa had said to my brothers at some point after they were questioning her about telling me the truth, "Would you rather Richard not know and we all stay as close as we are? Or would you rather take the chance that he may be angry and walk away from all of us?" Many have asked how I felt when I found out the truth. Was I angry? Was I upset? The only emotion after the shock was elation. After all I had been through, I had learned that things happen when they are supposed to. Mike and DeDe had been like brothers to me all along. It was the strangest feeling. When I was told it felt like something clicked into place. I knew in the pit of my stomach that it was right. So many things made sense. Things that were said in the past or things that I felt and couldn't explain all of a sudden made perfect sense. Now I know why I had the unexplainable urge to take my little brother to all of the big celebrations with me, like when I was inducted into the Gospel Music Hall Of Fame. I just knew he needed to be there with me. The same thing when I got the BMI Legend Award. Mom was gone, but on some level I just knew that DeDe or the closest family member I had needed to be there. Some friends have asked me "How could you not know? You guys almost look like triplets." Yes the resemblance was uncanny, but honestly the idea was so foreign to me, that it never crossed my mind. I remember we were all together at Olivia's funeral repast and a lady came up to DeDe and said "Oh Mr. Smallwood, I LOVE your music." He laughed and said "thank you" while all of us did the same. She didn't have a clue! But neither did I. People would always see one or the other of them downtown from a distance and think it was me. It was like something so completely obvious right in front of my face, but because of my blinders on, I just never saw it. Mike would relay to me how after DeDe, little Rob and I returned from North Carolina talking to Olivia about the Rivers story, how he called Olivia and told her he wanted the truth. "Olivia", he said "I want to know. Why won't you just go on and tell the truth? Isn't it true that Buddy is our brother?" Olivia's answer to him was "Leave it alone." When Rosa asked her the same question, her response to Rosa was "mind your damn business." No one wanted to talk about it. To think that now I wasn't an only child, and that I had nieces, nephews and great nieces and nephews—that was all so amazing to me! It would change my genealogy. Mike and DeDe were half-brothers on my Dad's side but still second cousins on my Mom's side. Bessie would be our grandmother with Lula being our great grandmother on the paternal side. I've always loved my "cousins," but the dynamics have changed. Loving my blood brothers is another level. A feeling much deeper, and feeling that you would do anything for them. I still look back to those days growing up and how Lula would spoil me when I'd go to Durham. I was her great grandson all along. It was absolutely mind-blowing. Not long after that Mike, DeDe and I had a "brother's celebration" at Rosa's house. We formed a circle while holding hands and spoke our feelings about the truth and how much it meant to us and then we prayed. We even had another celebration and Rosa cooked cabbage to celebrate that initial conversation when she was nineteen years old with Lula those many years ago.

On April 13, 2017 our Dad's birthday, DeDe, Rosa and I went to the grave and laid flowers. It's the first time I'd ever been to our father's gravesite although I had been to the wake. I can't even describe the feeling that I had. He loved Rosa and his sons. He worked hard to provide for them. I felt pride about the many sacrifices he must have made. Mike told me how in the early 70s when I had my first kidney stone, Robert dropped everything and came to Mom's house to see about me. I didn't recall it. I was in so much pain. But Mike and DeDe both remembered how they played with my little foster brother Anthony and his hot wheel's race track that I had gotten him for Christmas while Robert sat in my room and talked to me. He was always great to me. My brothers and Rosa believe that Robert more than likely helped my Mom from time to time financially after we moved to DC. But of course, I never knew of it. Mom was forever taking me over to their house and they came to ours. Ironically, Smallwood christened DeDe at the old White Stone Baptist Church when I was a little boy and he and Mom became his godparents. I just had no clue. Robert was just my big cousin whom I always admired. It's a blessing that I wasn't born with any birth defects other than one that caused me to have a hip replacement because of the relation between my parents as two cousins. It gave me joy to hear that my dad Robert was quite the singer which I never knew about and played piano as well.

In the end I understand that regardless of who I came through, that I was meant to be here. God's purpose and predestinations are perfect in nature and as my friend Sandy Fagans used to say, "There are no accidents in the universe." I finally felt the last missing piece of the jigsaw puzzle slide into place and I was finally home, home with my family who loved me unconditionally. Yes Mom, the light of my life was gone and couldn't be replaced. But I had great friends who supported me. I had a family. The feeling of having blood brothers was something I couldn't even explain. I wasn't by myself anymore, and that felt great. As Michael told me, "I don't love you because you're Richard Smallwood, I love you because you are my brother and I wouldn't care if you were a truck driver." I'll always be grateful to Momma Rosa, the last one living from that era (whom I call lovingly my "other mother") for being truthful about the dreaded family secrets and making it all happen.

CHAPTER 45

CAN YOU SEE ME NOW?

W riting this book allowed me to talk to my relatives in a very personal and real way. I got to know Mabel Ruth, the woman, the human being, the one with faults and the one who made mistakes. I got to know the total person. Honestly, when Mom was alive, all I knew was Mabel Ruth, the superwoman, the icon and the closest thing to perfection. This whole process made me appreciate her even more. It made me admire her even more because she persevered through so much without letting it affect the way she loved others. I have no idea how she continued to thrive and continued to smile and give no hint of anything being wrong. She carried a constant burden. She existed for over forty years in a loveless marriage with no intimacy. The only thing I can say is that the grace of God is real. Knowing her this way, proved how much of a superwoman she really was. I still have unanswered questions and probably always will. Looking back when I was a child, I can remember little things Mom used to say to throw me off track so I didn't find out the real truth. As close as we were, she had to know that I had questions. One particular thing I remember her telling me was that when I was born, I had gray eyes and my hair was jet black, straight and fitted my head like a little cap.

514 | TOTAL PRAISE

She told me that when Smallwood walked in and saw me for the first time, his question was "Where did that come from?" I guess he was referring to the fact that I looked like a little Caucasian baby. She said she hurriedly reminded him about everyone in her family who had straight hair, was light complexioned and had light eyes. It was like she was explaining to me why I didn't look like him or anyone else in his family without actually coming out and saying it. It also would lead me to the conclusion that he still was my father, but I just got the majority of my genetics from her side of the family. I don't know if he ever knew exactly who or where I came from. She never said. My gut feeling tells me that all of this was never discussed. In a lot of ways, it was the way things were done in my family. I'm not sure if Mom ever even discussed it with my stepfather either. However, he did know that I wasn't his. When I was small and Mom and I would go with him when he would go out to preach, he would always introduce us to whatever congregation that he was before. He would say things like, "That's my wife, Stand up honey...and that's Richard, HER son." He'd say it with a comical edge and the congregation would usually laugh along. It sounded on the surface like he was saying, I was a momma's boy which I certainly was. But in hindsight and under the surface, it was a sarcastic cut. Even though I wish I had found the truth out earlier before Smallwood passed, I'm glad on the other hand that I didn't find out when I was a child. I know that the resentment between us could have very possibly ended up in violence. When I got to be a teenager, the only thing that stopped me from lashing out physically was the fact that I respected him as my father. If I had known the truth, I'm not sure how that would have played out. God does all things well. I think I found out when I was supposed to. I was spiritually, mentally and emotionally ready to handle it. Before then, I'm not sure.

I remember Mom telling me after she had gotten ill that she wished she knew what it was like to be in love. I never saw affection between my mother and stepfather. I never recall seeing them kiss or even hold hands. Even the pictures that I have where they are together, my stepfather is always standing or sitting with his hands straight at his side. Mom is always the one who has her hand on his arm, or on his hand. He just looked very uncomfortable. I don't think it bothered me. I never saw anything different, so I didn't know anything different. I remember once when I was very small and the three of us were in the car going somewhere. Of course, this was before seat belts and car seats for kids. I was standing on the front seat between them, while he was driving. All I can remember is that he reached over to touch Mom in some kind of way. Maybe it was one of the few times he was trying to show her affection. I don't recall it being anything negative. Whatever the reason, I remember pushing his hand away from her and told him, "Don't touch my mommy. This my mommy and I'm gonna keep her." I hadn't even started talking well so I don't know how I can remember it so clearly. Mom used to laugh about it years later. For some reason, I didn't want him touching her. Maybe it was after the time that he pushed me away and told me I wasn't his. I have no clue. But children are sensitive. Don't think that they don't know when something is amiss because they are young. They may not be able to articulate it but you've got to remember we are spirits first, housed in a physical body. Their spirits can pick up things that are not quite right and it can stay with them for the rest of their lives.

I prayed long and hard and talked to loved ones, to relatives and to those who were close to Mom, about telling her story. I wasn't sure if I wanted to do it and I kept fluctuating back and forth about it. It's probably the main reason why I put off writing this book for so long. In no way did I want to hurt my mother's image or shed any kind of bad light on her. At some point during this battle within, I felt a release. I knew it was ok. I knew she was ok with it. I knew it was meant to be and planned before she or I were born. I was meant to find out the terrible "secret" exactly when I did. In the long run, I knew that it would help encourage someone to know that it doesn't matter who you came from, or where you came from, there is a reason that you are here. You're not illegitimate, you're not a bastard, you're not a mistake, but God planned for you to be here. You have a purpose. All of us had to come through someone in order to get here. Regardless of who it was or the circumstances surrounding it, it was the will of God that you were born. Don't let where you've come from, or the negative aspects of what you've been through, affect your present or your future. You can use your past or your beginnings, either to your benefit or to your detriment. God clearly purposed me to be here. I think from the time I was child, I've always known my purpose on some level, but as I grow spiritually the aspects of it continually become clearer. It's a constant revelation and I am trying my best to continue to walk in it.

It's ironic how God gives you songs. In your mind you are writing so others can be blessed. However, there are times when those lyrics that you wrote so long ago will come back and apply to situations that you are dealing with in your present. The song "Total Praise" was given to me in a time when I needed to understand the power of praise as I watched the declining health of some of those who were closest to me. It also taught me that praise was a weapon. As King Jehoshaphat defeated a mighty army with a song of praise (2 Chronicles 20:1-30), I could use it to defeat the spiritual enemies of my life. I needed to learn that praise was not conditional. It wasn't about how we felt at the time. It wasn't done from emotions, but it must be done from a grateful heart, regardless of the season in which we find ourselves. Even in our darkest valley situations, God still deserves our praise. He is still the same God that is getting ready to take us through our newest challenge even when our human eyes can't see it. If He's done it before, then He can do it again. I needed to learn how to praise God in advance for what He was going to do in the future. I needed to understand that if God never did another thing for me, He still deserved the praise just because He's God. Now as I look back over my life, those lyrics have an even greater meaning now. Writing has always seemed to take a lot out of me. It seems like when I write a song, part of me leaves, a part of the deepest most inner part of who Richard is. It's probably why I've never written frequently. It takes a while for me to rejuvenate and write from that place again. Many times, after I have given so much of me to birth a song, I have found myself frustrated when the industry doesn't seem to get it. Many times, I've felt unappreciated and misunderstood. But my prayer to God has always been to give me songs that encourage and heal, not necessarily the number one song on the Billboard charts. I look at songs like Amazing Grace, Precious Lord and other standards. I look at songs like that that are sung by different cultures, different nationalities and in different languages all over the world. I look at works like Handel's Messiah and works by Bach, Rachmaninoff and other classical greats. That's the kind of music that I've prayed for, not that my name would be great, but that the music itself will always make a positive difference in the lives of people. I give TOTAL praise to God for everything that He has brought me through, the good as well as the bad. He is still working miracles in my life. He is still showing himself strong. I am because of what I've experienced. I'm grateful for

His keeping power and even the difficulties that I've encountered that taught me something and made me stronger.

I heard Bishop TD Jakes say in a sermon once, "Don't ever ask for anyone else's anointing, because you don't know what it took to get it." He went on to say "you don't know how many sleepless nights I've cried nor the pain that I've gone through. It costs!" This is so true. Everything in my life that has happened to me has led me to the place where I am today. Every heartache, every death experienced, every bout of depression, every defeat, as well as every celebration has helped to write every song that I've ever written. I believe I had to go through what I went through for a purpose. Not only was it to strengthen me in order to make me a better person, but also it was to birth songs that would hopefully speak to the heart, the spirit and to the needs of people. My experiences caused me to write from a place from which I would have never written, if it had not been for some of the difficulties I encountered. I'm not saying that all good songs have to come through pain or hardship. Certainly, I've written songs that have come from a place of celebration. But at the same time, as for me and in my walk, the pain is what has birthed some of my strongest music. This may not be the testimony of all songwriters, but it's mine. Prayerfully what I've gone through in my lifetime will encourage and uplift those who are struggling with hurt. My prayer for the last twenty years or so has been that the music God has given me will minister to hurting people for centuries…long after I'm gone. As my Mom used to say, "It can either kill you or cure you." I pray that we will learn how to take those hurts and use them to make us stronger and more useful to the Kingdom. Don't give up. God has not forsaken you. Even during those times when you can't feel Him, He's still there. I don't necessarily believe in the old adage that "time heals all wounds." But I've discovered that God gives us the grace and the strength to live with them. The loss of my Mom will always be with me. It will never go away. There are still days when the loss hits home, but now, I have joy for who she was, and for what she left me. I give total praise to God for the way that He constantly reveals Himself to me, the revelations that He continually gives me about life, about getting over hurdles, about constantly learning how to trust Him in all things despite what my eyes may see. He is constantly teaching me. "Total Praise" has become more than a song to me, but a way of life because in all things I've learned to give praise, honor and thanks.

On the morning of September 23, 2015, I had just awakened and was lying in bed watching TV. The United States was ecstatic about the visit of Pope Francis that week and he had arrived in DC the day before. If I don't have to get up early I'm usually watching Antenna TV which has all of the shows that I grew up on, *Bewitched*, *Father Knows Best* and other sitcoms of my childhood. I was glued to the TV watching one of my favorites, when a friend texted me. He said, "Your social media is about to blow up." I had no idea what he was talking about and texted back a question mark. He replied, "Aren't you looking at the coverage of the Pope?" Honestly, I had forgotten about it. "Turn to it quickly" he texted. "They are singing Total Praise for the Pope." I quickly turned just as they had gotten to the second line of the song. There was St. Augustine's Church Choir standing before President Obama and Pope Francis in the White House garden singing a song that I had written twenty years ago that God had taken all over the world. St. Augustine was one of the oldest Catholic African American congregations in Washington DC. My Howard classmate, the late Leon Roberts, founded this choir many years ago when gospel music was not accepted as part of many Catholic services. He was also a founding member of Howard's Gospel Choir and was writing original songs for them long before I had become that confident in my own writing. He had written original gospel songs for St. Augustine's choir and the Mass, and had fought against traditionalism similar to what we had done at Howard's School of Fine Arts back in the day. How ironic and appropriate that his choir would sing many years later for the head of the church which had not readily accepted gospel music in the 60's. My heart beamed with pride at the many levels of history that was taking place in front of my eyes. I had heard "Total Praise" sung in almost every major language around the world. Videos of it sung in Russian, Hebrew, Korean, Samoan, Swedish and other languages had flooded my social media pages. I witnessed firsthand as it was sung in Norwegian, Japanese, Italian, French, German and Spanish during my travels overseas. I remember asking God years ago to give me music that would encourage, inspire and make a difference in lives all over the world. I remember asking Him to give me music that would last long after I was gone. He was allowing me to see this even while I was still here. "Total Praise" had been sung before Presidents, heads of states and now the Pope. Later that year, it would be sung for Queen Sofia of Spain, along with "Glorify The Lord" from that very first Smallwood Singers album, by members of Coro Gospel de Madrid. It would make history as being the first time gospel music was performed at the Vatican as a part of their Mass in Italian and English. Not long after that, I stood in the National Museum of African American History in front of a wall that displayed the names of musicians and artists who had made significant contributions from all genres. My eyes scanned the wall and saw names like Diana Ross, Rihanna, Nina Simone, Bessie Smith, opera star George Shirley and then my eyes fell upon one of my inspirations, Sly and the Family Stone. All of a sudden, my breath literally stopped. To the right of Sly's name was the name "Richard Smallwood." I can't explain how honored I felt as feelings of elation and shock ran through my body. I had no idea I was included in this display. To be a part of our history and to be mentioned in such a prestigious place with so many fellow African Americans from all walks of life was almost more than I could take in. This was a long way from that first song, "Shout For The Weary Alone." I smiled as I saw that little boy in my head who loved music so much and wanted to write so badly. I saw that little blue baby grand piano in my head that Mom got me for my second birthday. I banged on the keys so hard that the black and white paint eventually began to fade. I saw my Mom encouraging me, taking me to concerts, whatever was musical, buying me recordings and putting up with me playing records at the absolute highest volume level and singing to the top of my lungs. So many times, when blessings overtake me I feel like hollering as loud as I can to Mom "Can you see me now? Look what God has done. I can't believe how far He's brought me!"

Made in the USA
Middletown, DE
05 December 2023

44728281R00298